Final Fantasy VIII Basics

This chapter will provide some of the basics of playing Final Fantasy VIII. Topics include exploring in and out of towns and dungeons, using the Draw System, building up characters, collecting and refining items, and battling enemies.

Final Fantasy VIII has a wonderful built-in Tutorial in the Main Menu. I suggest you check it out to learn even more about the game.

Basics of Exploration

A large part of any Final Fantasy game is exploring towns, dungeons, mountains, and any other place important people or objects might be hiding. Why is this so important? Because talking to people will help you to better understand the events going on around you. As rich as the story line is, speaking with the people of a village under attack by a horde of misguided soldiers will help you better understand the who, what, why, and where of it all. It's one thing to know that a giant machine is damaging some buildings, but think about how much more moving the plot becomes when you find out what an impact the destruction has had on the townspeople.

Besides just building the plot and enriching the characters, talking also helps guide you through the game. Sometimes you may get stuck out in the open without any real guidance, but speaking with just a few people may help you realize what your next move should be.

People you meet will also sometimes try to assist you by giving you items or leading you to hidden objectives off the main plot. Usually, such items and sub quests offer players huge advantages over those who choose not to partake in them or completely overlook them. No matter how you look at it, exploration is a vital part of Final Fantasy VIII, and you should never be afraid to go looking for alternatives to what you're being told.

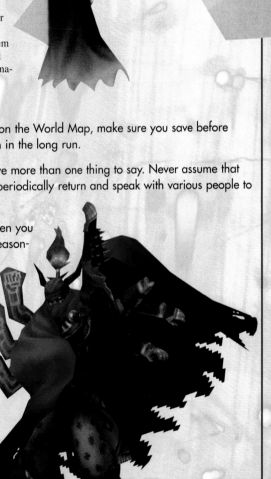

Here are some basic things you should keep in mind while exploring:

- Use Save Points often when inside dungeons and cities. When on the World Map, make sure you save before entering any new location. This will save you a lot of frustration in the long run.

- Talk to everyone, and then talk to them again. Most people have more than one thing to say. Never assume that someone has told you everything they have to tell. You should periodically return and speak with various people to see if their reactions have changed.

- Keep a close eye on your characters' stats. You never know when you might run into a nasty creature. Always try to keep everyone reasonably healthy, and keep a good supply of items that remove abnormal status effects just in case you need them.

- Consider keeping multiple saved games. There may be a time when you want to return to a part in the game to get something that you missed or to relive a particularly cool scene. You might even want to try a different approach to a Boss fight or something similar. Use an entire memory card just for Final Fantasy VIII, if you can swing it.

- The enemies in Final Fantasy VIII level up as your characters level up. If you spend a lot of time fighting in one area, you'll soon notice that your enemies are growing stronger and are learning new tricks and spells.

- Some save points are considered to be "Hidden," meaning they're invisible. You can see these Save Points by Junctioning an active character with the Move-Find ability.

Improving Your Characters

This aspect of the game works a bit differently from past Final Fantasy games. Characters still gain experience by defeating enemies, and then level up when they reach a predetermined amount of accumulated experience points. However, now all that is required to go up a level is 1000 experience points, regardless of the level you're trying to achieve. The flip side to this is that your characters' stats increase less from level to level than they have in past Final Fantasy games.

This being the case, you'll have to rely more on Junctioning with Guardian Forces (GFs), which is discussed later in this book. By Junctioning, you can quickly raise a character's stats, but what you raise and by how much is determined largely by the GFs you have and the magic you've stocked. This also means that you must decide which stats and characters you want to give priority to, and which ones you'll choose to ignore. Overall, this enables you to do a great deal of customization, but getting your characters to where you want them to be is very time consuming and requires a great deal of patience.

One aspect of character improvement you have a large amount of control over is the remodeling of weapons. Remodeling requires that you collect specific items in certain amounts. It also requires the assistance of a Junk Shop or the **Junk Shop** ability. Remodeling isn't expensive, but it can be difficult to find the items you need to remodel your weapons.

One of the best ways to find these items is to collect cards, which you can do by playing Triple Triad with various people in the game. Then after collecting some cards, you can use the **Card Mod** ability to transform the cards into the necessary items. However, some items you'll have to find, steal, or get by defeating enemies. Refer to each individual character's section for more information on upgrading that character's weapons.

Things to keep in mind about improving your characters:

- There are items and abilities that can increase a characters stats over time or immediately. **"Up"** items (i.e. Str Up, Spr Up) can raise a specific stat by one point. Characters can Junction **"Bonus"** abilities (i.e. HP Bonus, Mag Bonus) that boost a particular stat each time the Junctioned character goes up a level. You can even use the **Devour** ability to slowly raise some stats by eating just the right enemies.

- As the spells you collect improve, you should take a moment and examine each character's stats to ensure that your party is optimally Junctioned. If you don't want to waste time, you can have the game do this for you automatically by selecting the "Auto" function.

- Characters who don't take part in battles, don't receive experience points. You should avoid letting a single character get too far behind everyone else.

- Although Weapons Monthly Magazines will tell you about new weapons, you don't have to have them to remodel any particular weapon. All you need is the proper items in your inventory, and the option to remodel will appear whether or not you've seen the weapon in a magazine. So, technically, you could get the best weapons in the game as early as Disc Two as long as you know what items you're looking for and where to find them.

The Draw System

You'll soon learn that Final Fantasy VIII's Draw System is unique in a lot of ways. Magic Points (MP) are a thing of the past. A magic user is no longer limited to the spells his/her class or job type can learn. Rather, magic is "drawn" from enemies, Draw Points, and refined from items. Outside of battle, you can stock magic for later use. In battles, you can draw magic for immediate use or completely stock up on powerful spells that you can later Junction with a Guardian Force.

Before you get started, you should learn about Draw Points. These are blue/white or purple/white points found in various locations around the world. A character Junctioned with a Draw command can stock magic from a Draw Point for later use. Each Draw Point is unique. Some have weak magic, while others contain forbidden spells that are much more difficult to find. After using a Draw Point, it may take a while before you can draw from it again. This varies a great deal from Draw Point to Draw Point. Some refill almost immediately, while others may never fill again.

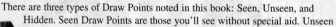

There are three types of Draw Points noted in this book: Seen, Unseen, and Hidden. Seen Draw Points are those you'll see without special aid. Unseen Draw Points are those that are tucked away behind something, like a book shelf. Although Unseen Draw Points may not be visible to you, it doesn't mean that they're invisible. They are typically the hardest kind to find. Hidden Draw Points are usually out in the open, but they're invisible to the naked eye. To locate them, you must either randomly search an area, or Junction the **Move-Find** ability on an active character, which turns all Hidden Draw Points into Seen Draw Points. Knowing these terms will help you a great deal in using this book. Draw Points tend to provide anywhere from 1 to 15 of a spell. This is often determined by the Draw Point's refill rate and by the length of time since you last drew magic from it.

Refining magic from items requires special Guardian Force abilities. There are many different types, such as **T Mag-RF** and **Mid Mag-RF**. T Mag-RF enables you to refine Thunder magic from some items. Mid Mag-RF enables you to refine mid-level spells from low-level spells. For example, you can transform 5 Thunder spells into one Thundara spell using the Mid Mag-RF ability. Overall, this is the most efficient way to build up your magic stock, because it often enables you to get spells way before you could draw them from an enemy.

The most common way to build up your magic stock is to draw them from enemies. During battle, you can use the **Draw** command to absorb magic from an enemy. The number drawn from an enemy varies from as much as 9 to as little as 1. It's possible that an attempt at drawing may fail. This is usually due to a character's low magic skill, but can sometimes be caused by the type of magic. Higher level magic is much tougher to draw than lower level magic.

Some more things you should know about the Draw System:

- As monsters level up, their spell inventory changes. Higher level monsters carry better magic than their lower level cohorts.

- You can find Draw Points on the World Map. Check places like train tunnels, bends along an island coast, tips of peninsulas, and bridges. These Draw Points are ALWAYS hidden, and you can't see them even if you have the Move/Find ability equipped.

- Enemies can draw magic from your party members. This is a very rare occurrence, but some enemies can draw magic from you and cast it on your party. Others simply draw magic from you and "eat" it. It's also possible for a stock of a spell to be completely blown away.

- There is a limit as to how much magic you can carry. A character can carry 100 of a single spell and 32 different spells. If you start to get overloaded, give some of your weaker magic to inactive characters, or refine it into stronger magic. You can also throw spells away by simply using the ● button.

Acquiring and Using Items

There are a ton—and I do mean a ton—of items in Final Fantasy VIII. Items come in all sorts of forms, and can be used in many ways. However, the most significant change is that you can refine some items into other items. It typically takes a large stock of an item to do any refining, but acquiring items has also been made easier from other Final Fantasy games.

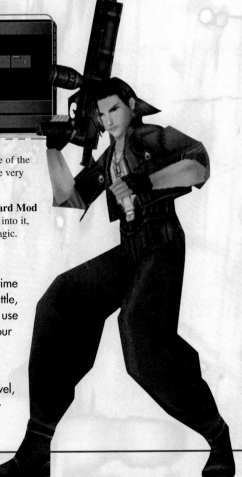

Most items are gained after battles. Defeated enemies will often drop one or more of an item. The item an enemy drops depends on its level and pure luck. Eventually, you'll also learn how to steal items from your enemies using the **Mug** ability. This makes it all the more easier to quickly amass a large stock of some of the easier-to-find items. Keep in mind that the items you can steal from an enemy can be very different from the items that they drop.

A more efficient way of getting items is to refine them from cards. Using the **Card Mod** ability, you can quickly acquire hard-to-find items. If you're willing to put the effort into it, you can actually upgrade weapons earlier and teach Quistis several types of Blue Magic.

Other things you should know about items:

- The maximum number you can hold of any one item is 100. Any time you have 100 of an item, and you acquire more of that item in battle, the additional items are lost. If you have 100 of an item you don't use much, consider refining it into something else or selling some of your stock.

- Enemies can have as many as four items that they randomly drop. The items an enemy drops depends on its level. To determine its level, simply **Scan** the enemy in battle to check its level. Using this information, you can then refer to the Bestiary to determine which item the enemy will drop at that particular level.

Basics of Battling

Battles play a huge role in all Final Fantasy games. The fate of an entire world often relies upon the outcome of a single battle against a seemingly unstoppable foe. In the early stages of the game, you'll have a good chance to learn how battles work and how to develop a routine you use for certain situations. As you delve deeper into the game, you should work on your speed and setup. By the end of the game, you should be able to fly through menus and quickly locate any item, spell, or ability. It may not seem like much, but the speed at which you act can make a huge difference in some cases.

At the beginning of a battle there are several things that can happen:

First Strike	Your party has the jump on the enemy and can attack first, or run away in some cases.
Struck First	The enemy has the jump on your party, and can attack first or run away.
Back Attack	Either the good guys or the bad guys have sneaked up on the other, resulting in a free shot at their opponents' backs. Any attack against a character's backside causes twice the normal damage.

All of these situations are random occurrences, but you can increase or decrease the odds with certain Guardian Force abilities. Obviously, catching an enemy in either of these situations is a great advantage, but being caught in such situations can be deadly.

When a character's HPs have been reduced to a fourth of his/her normal amount, the gauge will turn yellow as a warning that you desperately need to heal that character. More importantly, it also indicates that the character in question is set to perform a **Limit Break**. However, these Limit Breaks differ a bit from Final Fantasy VII, where Limit Breaks were built up over time as an enemy repeatedly struck a character. This is great for you, because it enables you to use it to your advantage.

By keeping a character's HPs in the yellow, that character can almost always use his/her Limit Break every turn. Don't get too excited though; by doing so, you are risking death so this tactic isn't recommended during tougher fights.

Now just because your character's HPs are in the yellow doesn't mean that the Limit Break will always be available. Instead, there's just a chance that it will appear. The odds are directly linked to the amount of HPs a character has remaining. For example, a character with 50 HPs will almost always get a Limit Break whereas a character with 500 HPs will not. So how do you beat the system? It's easy. When a character's ATB (Active Time Bar) fills, tap the ⬤ button if that character's Limit Break doesn't appear. In effect, this skips the character and gives him/her a second chance. However, don't press too quickly, or you may miss the Limit Break if it appears. Each character's Limit Breaks are different. Refer to the individual character sections for more details.

During battle, there are many abnormal status effects that can be afflicted on your party and on the enemy. The following is a list of the various types:

Status Effect	Symptom	Cure
Silence	Victim can no longer use magic or summon GFs	Echo Screen (item), Esuna (magic)
Confusion	Victim loses all sense of reality and begins randomly attacking any target, even itself)	Remedy (item), Esuna (magic
Poison	Victim loses HPs each time it performs an action during battle	Antidote (item), Esuna (magic)
Berserk	Victim loses control and goes into a mad rage; character can only use physical attacks and cannot pick targets. Attack strength and player speed is increased slightly	Remedy (item), Esuna (magic)
Slow	Victim's speed is cut in half	Remedy (item), Esuna (magic), Haste (magic)
Blind	Victim loses sight, and hit rate is drastically reduced	Eye Drops (item), Esuna (magic)
Slow Death	A counter appears over the victim's head. If it reaches zero before the end of the battle, the character is knocked out	Dispel (magic)
Petrify	Victim is turned to stone	Soft (item), Esuna (magic)
Zombie	Victim becomes an undead creature	Holy Water (item), Esuna (magic)
Slow Petrify	A counter appears over the victim's head. If it reaches zero before the end of the battle, the character is petrified	Soft (item), Esuna (magic)
Sleep	Victim is put to sleep and cannot act; HPs are not restored	Esuna (magic)
Curse	Victim cannot use Limit Breaks	Holy Water (item), Esuna (magic)
Defense Cut	Victim receives double damage from physical attacks	Esuna (magic)

Other things you should know about battles:

- You can escape from battles by holding down the R2 and L2 buttons on your controller. However, you cannot escape from all battles.

- Pressing the ● button skips a "ready" character so that you can get to another character whose ATB has filled.

- Holding down the ● button will automatically select the attack option and target the closest enemy. If you have the Cursor: Memory option selected in the Configuration menu, it will select the character's last action. Very, very handy.

- You can remove an enemy's positive status effects (such as Haste, Regen, Double, Reflect, Triple, Protect, Shell, and Aura) by using Dispel magic.

The SeeD Rank

Earning Gil is done a bit differently in Final Fantasy VIII than it was in Final Fantasy VII. Once Squall becomes a SeeD, Balamb Garden pays him a regular salary. In the past, you had to pick up Gil after hard-fought battles. The amount he's paid is based on his SeeD Rank, which is a numeric ranking based on his actions taken throughout the game.

The Dollet Field Exam close to the start of the game determines Squall's initial SeeD Rank. There are seven categories Squall is rated on during the exam. Each one is worth the same amount, but the scores are determined very differently. You'll find the details on each category and how its score is determined in the following information.

As the game progresses, Squall's SeeD Rank will fluctuate depending on his actions. It can rise or fall depending on the decisions you've made, your actions during some battles, and how many enemies you've defeated. It can take some time for your SeeD Rank to increase to the well-paid levels, but you can quickly raise it by taking a series of SeeD Written Tests.

Written Tests are found in your submenu under the Tutorial heading. Each test is comprised of 10 true/false questions based on the world of Final Fantasy VIII. You must answer all 10 questions correctly to raise Squall's SeeD Rank by one. There is no penalty for failing a Written Test, and you can take each test as many times as necessary to pass.

Each Written Test is assigned a level. Squall can take tests up to the level he is currently at himself. For example, if Squall is at Level 15 he can take Written Tests of Level 15 or lower. There are a total of 30 tests, and you can only pass each test once, so don't take any tests you don't have to when maxing out Squall's salary. You may want to retake some tests later if Squall's SeeD Rank takes a sudden dive.

SeeD Ranking Chart

This table discusses how Squall's initial SeeD Rank is determined. SeeD Rank fluctuations are not all based on similar parameters.

Conduct

The Dollet Mission Event determines your Conduct score. The points are determined by how much time remains on the clock when you reach the beach during the evacuation.

Remaining Time	Points
25:00+	100
24:59~24:00	90
23:59~23:00	80
22:59~20:00	70
19:59~19:00	60
18:59~17:00	50
16:59~15:00	40
14:59~10:00	30
9:59~6:00	20
5:59~3:00	10
2:59~0:00	0

Judgement

Judgement is based on the Fire Cavern Event. The less time there is on the clock when you defeat Ifrit, the better your score will be.

Remaining Time	Points
0:00~0:07	100
0:08~0:29	90
0:30~0:59	80
1:00~1:59	70
2:00~2:59	60
3:00~9:59	50
10:00~10:59	40
11:00~11:59	30
12:00~12:59	20
13:00~13:59	10
14:00~14:59	5
15:00+	0

Attack

The number of enemies your party defeated during the Dollet Mission Event determines your Attack score. This number does *not* include enemies defeated by Guardian Forces. Even if an enemy's HP reaches zero more than once during a battle (ie. X-ATMO92), only the first time will contribute to the total.

Enemies Defeated	Points
75+	100
25~74	80
15~24	50
10~14	20
0~9	0

Spirit

It's possible to only fight X-ATM092 once during the Dollet Field Exam. After the initial escape from X-ATM092 at the Communications Tower, you'll run for two screens. When you reach the screen with the downward slope, press the ⬤ button to walk instead of run. This will keep the party from being stunned and avoids a second battle against X-ATM092.

Times Escaped	Points
1	100
2	70
3~4	50
5~9	30
10	0

Attitude

Many things determine attitude:

1) The number of people you talk to during the Dollet Field Exam. There is a one point deduction per conversation. This includes talking to people in Balamb. If you talk to Biggs, you will lose two points

Note

You are not required to initiate conversation at ANY time. The only exception however, occurs when you're with Seifer in Dollet's town square.

2) A one point deduction is taken each time you attempt to go toward the Communication Tower before Seifer commands you to do so.

3) Each time you jump off the cliff shortcut to reach the Communication Tower (Selphie's shortcut), you receive a five point deduction.

4) You lose 10 points if you fail to save the dog while passing through Dollet's town square during your escape from Dollet. Speak with the dog to help it escape.

5) If you run into the Cafe to escape from the X-ATM092, you lose 20 points.

Total Deductions	Points
0	100
1~8	80
9~13	70
14~17	50
18~24	30
25+	10

Bonus

You will receive a 100 point bonus if you destroy the X-ATM092 (bring its HP to zero). Depending on your level, it has anywhere from 5500 to 6500 HP. It is only possible to destroy it on the bridge.

SeeD Rank Salary Chart

The following table shows how much Squall is paid at each rank from 1 to A.

SeeD Rank	Salary (G)
1	500
2	1000
3	1500
4	2000
5	3000
6	4000
7	5000
8	6000
9	7000
10	8000
11	9000
12	10000
13	11000
14	12000
15	12500
16	13000
17	13500
18	14000
19	14500
20	15000
21	15500
22	16000
23	16500
24	17000
25	17500
26	18000
27	18500
28	19000
29	19500
30	20000
A	30000

SeeD Written Test Answers

The following table lists all of the answers for every SeeD Written Tests.

Test Level 1
Yes No Yes Yes Yes No No Yes No No

Test Level 2
Yes No Yes Yes Yes No Yes Yes No No

Test Level 3
No No Yes No Yes Yes Yes No Yes No

Test Level 4
No Yes Yes Yes No No Yes Yes No No

Test Level 5
No No No Yes Yes No No Yes Yes Yes

Test Level 6
Yes No Yes Yes No No Yes Yes No Yes

Test Level 7
Yes Yes Yes Yes Yes Yes No Yes Yes No

Test Level 8
No Yes No No Yes Yes No No Yes No

Test Level 9
No Yes No No No No No No Yes Yes

Test Level 10
Yes No No No No No No No Yes No

Test Level 11
Yes Yes No Yes Yes No Yes No No Yes

Test Level 12
No Yes No No Yes No Yes No Yes No

Test Level 13
Yes No No No Yes No No No No No

Test Level 14
Yes Yes Yes Yes No Yes Yes No Yes No

Test Level 15
Yes Yes No No No No No Yes No Yes

Test Level 16
Yes No No Yes No Yes No No Yes No

Test Level 17
Yes No No Yes No No Yes No No

Test Level 18
Yes No No No Yes No No No No No

Test Level 19
Yes No No Yes No No No No No Yes

Test Level 20
Yes Yes No No Yes No Yes Yes No No

Test Level 21
Yes Yes Yes Yes No No Yes No Yes No

Test Level 22
No No No Yes No No No Yes Yes No

Test Level 23
Yes No No No Yes Yes Yes Yes Yes

Test Level 24
Yes Yes No Yes Yes No No No Yes

Test Level 25
Yes No Yes Yes Yes No No Yes No No

Test Level 26
Yes Yes No Yes No No Yes No Yes No No

Test Level 27
No Yes No No No Yes No Yes No

Test Level 28
Yes No No Yes Yes No Yes No No

Test Level 29
No No Yes Yes Yes No No No Yes No

Test Level 30
No Yes No No No Yes No No No

Useful Commands You Should Know

Run from Battle

Press and hold R2 + L2 until the party runs or you see a message saying you can't run.

Soft Reset

Pause the game and press and hold L1 + L2 + R1 + R2 + Select and press the Start button. The game will fade out and return to the title screen.

Discard Magic

In the Magic Menu inside the Main Menu, select the use option and highlight a spell, and then press the ● button to discard the highlighted magic.

Removing Junctioned Magic

In the Junction screen, highlight a Junctioned magic and press the ● button.

Remove Battle Displays

During a battle, hold the Select button to make all of the battle display boxes disappear. When you release the button, the boxes will reappear.

Battle Menus

Turn on extra text boxes to assist with targeting by pressing the L1 button during a battle. Pressing L1 a second time turns off the extra boxes.

View Statuses

In battle when you attempt to remove abnormal status effects using magic, items, or abilities a side box appears showing one of the abnormal status effects on the character. You can view the other abnormal effects by presssing the ● button, which causes the window to cycle through the abnormal statuses.

Auto Pilot for Ragnarok

While riding in the Ragnarok, open the large World Map and highlight your destination. Press the ● button and choose "Yes" and the Ragnarok will pilot itself. You may cancel the auto pilot option by pressing the ● button.

Automatic Attack & Draw

In the Configuration Menu, set the Cursor option to Memory. During battle, you can then repeat the action you last took with a character by simply holding down the ● button. This is extremely handy when stocking up on magic.

Scan Camera Controls

After using Scan magic, you will see a model of the enemy you targeted. You may manipulate the model using the commands below:

Rotate model	**Directional Pad or Analog Stick (not all models rotate)**
Zoom	**Hold R1 or L1 and use Directional Pad or Analog Stick**
Reset	**Press L1 and L2 simultaneously**

Squall Leonhart

Squall uses a sword called the Gunblade. This rare weapon takes many, many years to master and is therefore rarely used. Currently, there is only one other Gunblade user in Balamb Garden—Seifer Almasy. With the Gunblade, Squall can unleash his special skill, Renzokuken, a deadly series of punishing attacks sometimes followed by a powerful ending move. In the eyes of others, Squall is seen as a silent, cold person. Having this perceived image is fine by him.

Age: 17
Height: 5' 8"
DoB: August 23
Blood Type: AB
Weapon: Gunblade
Special Skill: Renzokuken

Squall's Vital Stats by Level

LV	HP	Str	Vit	Mag	Spr	Spd	Luck
1	223	1	1	2	1	20	15
10	616	8	8	8	7	22	16
20	1044	15	14	15	13	24	16
30	1464	21	19	21	18	25	17
40	1877	27	24	27	22	27	18
50	2281	32	28	31	26	29	19
60	2678	36	32	35	29	30	19
70	3067	40	35	39	32	32	20
80	3449	43	37	42	33	34	21
90	3822	46	39	44	35	35	21
100	4187	47	41	45	36	37	22

Using Squall's Gunblade

As Squall attacks an enemy, you can significantly raise the damage caused by the attack by pressing the R1 button just before he makes contact. The timing is tricky at first, but soon it will become second nature. A good audio clue is to listen for the swipe of Squall's Gunblade. When you hear it, press R1. This can also be used to enchance Seifer's Gunblade attacks at the beginning of the game.

Squall's Limit Break: Renzokuken

The Renzokuken is a series of Gunblade attacks that cause big damage. When the Limit Break begins, a bar appears at the bottom of the screen. As the light moves across the bar, press R1 when the light enters the small box near the end. Pressing R1 at the right time results in a much stronger attack. If you miss, Squall will still attack, but the attack will be much weaker.

This function can be set to Auto in Squall's Status Screen if you're not comfortable with pressing R1. You can also turn off the indicator box, and attempt to press R1 at the proper time without the indicator's assistance.

At the end of Squall's Renzokuken, an ending attack will sometimes randomly occur. There are four possible ending attacks. Which ending attacks Squall can perform depend upon the weapon he's carrying at that time.

Rough Divide

Squall finishes his Limit Break by charging at a single enemy and performing a rising slash.

Fated Circle

After leaping into the air, Squall twirls his Gunblade and releases a shockwave of energy that hits all enemies.

Blasting Zone

A column of light shoots out of Squall's Gunblade, which he uses to crush his foes.

Lion Heart

Squall knocks a single enemy into the air, and then unleashes a devastating flurry of attacks. This is Squall's strongest Limit Break in the game.

Weapons

Revolver (Basic)
Cost: 100 Gil
Atk: 11
Hit: 255
Limit Break: Rough Divide

Items	Dropped By	Stolen From	Card Mod
M-Stone Piece (x2)	Bite Bug, Funguar, Buel, Jelleye, Glacial Eye, Creeps, Belhelmel, Blobra. T-Rexaur, Blobra, Bomb, Vysage, Lefty, Righty, Elastoid, Gesper, Blitz, Death Claw, Abyss Worm, Gayla, Armadodo (Level 1-19)	Bite Bug, Blobra, Buel	Bite Bug (1 for 1), Funguar (1 for 1)
Screw (x2)	Geezard, GIM47N (rare)	Geezard	Geezard 1 for 5

Shear Trigger

Cost: 200 Gil
Atk: 14
Hit: 255
Limit Breaks: Rough Divide, Fated Circle

Items	Dropped By	Stolen From	Card Mod
Steel Pipe (x1)	Wendigo (rare), GIM47N (Level 1-29, rare)	Wendigo	Elastoid (1 for 1)
Screw (x4)	Geezard, GIM47N (rare)	Geezard	Geezard (1 for 5)

Cutting Trigger

Cost: 400 Gil
Atk: 18
Hit: 255
Limit Breaks: Rough Divide, Fated Circle

Items	Dropped By	Stolen From	Card Mod
Mesmerize Blade (x1)	Mesmerize	Mesmerize	Mesmerize (1 for 1)
Screw (x8)	Geezard, GIM47N (rare)	Geezard	Geezard (1 for 5)

Flame Saber

Cost: 600 Gil
Atk: 20
Hit: 255
Limit Breaks: Rough Divide, Fated Circle, Blasting Zone

Items	Dropped By	Stolen From	Card Mod
Betrayal Sword (x1)	Forbidden	Blitz	Forbidden (1 for 1)
Turtle Shell (x1)	Armadodo (Level 30-100), Adamantoise (Level 1-29)	Armadodo	Adamantoise (3 for 1), X-ATM092 (2 for 1)
Screw (x4)	Geezard, GIM47N (rare)	Geezard	Geezard (1 for 5)

Twin Lance

Cost: 800 Gil
Atk: 22
Hit: 255
Limit Breaks: Rough Divide, Fated Circle, Blasting Zone

Items	Dropped By	Stolen From	Card Mod
Dino Bone (x1)	T-Rexaur	T-Rexaur	T-Rexaur (2 for 1), Armadodo (1 for 1), Sacred (1 for 100)
Red Fang (x1)	Hexadragon, Chimera	Hexadragon, Chimera	Hexadragon (3 for 1)
Screw (x12)	Geezard, GIM47N (rare)	Geezard	Geezard (1 for 5)

Punishment

Cost: 1000 Gil
Atk: 24
Hit: 255
Limit Breaks: Rough Divide, Fated Circle, Blasting Zone

Items	Dropped By	Stolen From	Card Mod
Chef's Knife (x1)	Tonberry	Tonberry	Tonberry (1 for 1), Tonberry King (1 for 1)
Star Fragment (x2)	Iron Giant, T-Rexaur (rare), Tri-Face (rare, Level 30-100), Chimera (Level 20-100, rare), Hexadragon (Level 30-100), Red Dragon (Level 1-44, rare)	Iron Giant	Iron Giant (3 for 1)
Turtle Shell (x1)	Armadodo (Level 30-100), Adamantoise (Level 1-29)	Armadodo	Adamantoise (3 for 1), X-ATM092 (2 for 1)
Screw (x8)	Geezard, GIM47N (rare)	Geezard	Geezard (1 for 5)

Lion Heart

Cost: 2000 Gil
Atk: 30
Hit: 255
Limit Breaks: Rough Divide, Fated Circle, Blasting Zone, Lion Heart

Items	Dropped By	Stolen From	Card Mod
Adamantine (x1)	Adamantine	BGH251F2 (at FH)	Minotaur (1 for 10)
Dragon Fang (x4)	Blue Dragon, Hexadragon (Level 1-29), Grendel (Level 1-29)	N/A	N/A
Pulse Ammo (x12)	N/A	N/A	N/A

Note Pulse Ammo can be obtained using the Ammo-RF ability. One Energy Crystal refines into 10 Pulse Ammo and a Laser Cannon refines into 5 Pulse Ammo. ·

Rinoa Heartilly

A member of the Timber resistance group "Forest Owls," Rinoa fights against the Galbadian President, Vinzer Deling, whose dictatorship has caused great suffering in her homeland for far too long. Rinoa is very emotional, and tends to go with her gut feeling when acting. Her best friend is her dog, Angelo, who often rushes into battle to help Rinoa when she's in trouble.

Age: 17
Height: 5' 3½"
DoB: March 3
Blood Type: ?
Weapon: Blaster Edge
Special Skill: Combine (Angelo)

Rinoa's Vital Stats by Level

LV	HP	Str	Vit	Mag	Spr	Spd	Luck
1	217	1	0	8	3	20	16
10	610	10	5	15	8	22	17
20	1038	19	10	22	14	24	17
30	1458	27	14	29	19	25	18
40	1871	35	18	35	24	27	19
50	2275	42	21	41	28	28	19
60	2672	48	24	46	31	30	20
70	3061	54	26	51	34	32	20
80	3443	59	28	55	36	33	21
90	3816	64	30	59	38	35	22
100	4181	67	31	63	39	36	22

Rinoa's Limit Break: Combine

Rinoa actually has two different types of Limit Breaks: Angelo and Angel Wing. She begins the game with Angelo, but will receive the Angel Wing Limit Break during Disc Three.

Angelo

Rinoa's pet dog, Angelo, comes to her aid in times of need. Angelo can also show up randomly during battles without being called or just to lend a helping hand. Rinoa can teach Angelo new tricks by finding or purchasing copies of **Pet Pals Magazine**. Each issue contains one new trick. Read the magazine, and the trick will be added to Angelo's status screen within Rinoa's status screen in the Main menu.

To teach Angelo a trick, access the Angelo status screen and select a trick with an empty or partly filled bar next to it. Tricks with full red bars have already been learned, and can be used in battle. As Rinoa explores the world, the trick will slowly be learned. Keep listening for a confirmation noise, which indicates that Angelo has mastered the trick. You can then select another trick to learn, if one is available.

Angel Wing

Angel Wing is similar to the Berserk status effect. The main difference is that instead of only performing physical attacks, Rinoa will only use magic. Basically, you lose control of Rinoa for the remainder of the battle even if she's K.O.'ed and then revived. Her magic power and speed are boosted slightly to provide her more power. The spells she uses are picked randomly and targeted randomly. Any magic she casts does not come from your stocked magic.

Angelo's Tricks

Trick Name	Learned In...	Trick Effect
Angelo Rush	Starts With	Damages one enemy/random counterattack
Angelo Recover	Pet Pals Vol.2	Restore HP to a party member with low HP/random event
Angelo Reverse	Pet Pals Vol.4	Revive party member from KO/random event
Angelo Search	Pet Pals Vol.5	Find items on the battlefield/random event
Angelo Cannon	Starts With	Damages all enemies/when called
Angelo Strike	Pet Pals Vol.1	Damage one enemy/when called
Invincible Moon	Pet Pals Vol.3	Make all party members invincible/when called
Wishing Star	Pet Pals Vol.6	Damage all enemies/when called

Rinoa's Weapons

Pinwheel	Items	Dropped By	Stolen From	Card Mod
Cost: 100 Gil **Atk:** 11 **Hit:** 99	M-Stone Piece (x3)	Bite Bug, Funguar, Buel, Jelleye, Glacial Eyes, Creeps, Belhelmel, Blobra, T-Rexaur, Blobra, Bomb, Vysage, Lefty, Righty, Elastoid, Gesper, Blitz, Death Claw, Abyss Worm, Gayla, Armadodo (Level 1-19)	Bite Bug, Blobra, Buel	Bite Bug (1 for 1), Funguar (1 for 1)

Valkyrie	Dropped By	Stolen From	Card Mod	
Cost: 200 Gil **Atk:** 14 **Hit:** 101	Shear Feather (x1)	Thrustaevis, Death Claw	Thrustaevis, Death Claw	Thrustaevis (1 for 1)
Items	Magic Stone (x1)	Bite Bug, Funguar, Buel, Jelleye, Glacial Eye, Creeps, Belhelmel, Blobra, Geezard, Abyss Worm, Ochu (all above Level 20-29) Ochu (Level 1-29)	Grat, Buel, Jelleye	Grat (1 for 1), Buel (1 for 1), Jelleye (1 for 1)

Rising Sun	Items	Dropped By	Stolen From	Card Mod
Cost: 400 Gil **Atk:** 18 **Hit:** 103	Saw Blade (x1)	Belhelmel	Belhelmel	Belhelmel (1 for 1)
	Screw (x8)	Geezard, GIM47N (rare)	Geezard	Geezard (1 for 5)

Cardinal	Items	Dropped By	Stolen From	Card Mod
Cost: 800 Gil **Atk:** 24 **Hit:** 104	Cockatrice Pinion (x1)	Cockatrice	Cockatrice	Cockatrice (1 for 1), Iguion (1 for 1)
	Mesmerize Blade (x1)	Mesmerize	Mesmerize	Mesmerize (1 for 1)
	Sharp Spike (x1)	Grand Mantis, Death Claw	Grand Mantis	Grand Mantis (1 for 1)

Shooting Star	Items	Dropped By	Stolen From	Card Mod
Cost: 1000 Gil **Atk:** 28 **Hit:** 107	Windmill (x2)	Thrustaevis, Abyss Worm, Death Claw (rare), GIM52A (rare)	Thrustaevis, Abyss Worm	Abyss Worm (1 for 1)
	Regen Ring (x1)	Torama (Level 30-100), Chimera (Level 30-100, rare), Turtapod (Level 30-100, rare), Mesmerize (Level 30-100, rare), Lefty (Level 30-100, rare)	Torama, Biggs (2nd fight)	Chimera (10 for 1)
	Force Armlet (x1)	Ochu (Level 30-100, rare), Forbidden (Level 30-100, rare), Edea (2nd fight)	N/A	N/A
	Energy Crystal (x2)	Elnoyle, Behemoth (rare), Red Dragon (rare, Level 35-100)	N/A	Elnoyle (10 for 1)

Quistis Trepe

The whip is Quistis' weapon of choice. But when faced with a dangerous situation, she relies more upon Blue Magic. Quistis is much admired in Balamb Garden, and her admirers have even formed a fan club known as the "Trepies." She's a bit of a child prodigy considering she's the youngest instructor at the Garden. However, her actions toward her students sometimes betray her age and undermine her authority, as she lacks the stern demeanor of most Garden staff.

Age: 18
Height: 5' 6"
DoB: October 4
Blood Type: A
Weapon: Chain Whip
Special Skill: Blue Magic

Quistis' Vital Stats by Level

LV	HP	Str	Vit	Mag	Spr	Spd	Luck
1	216	1	1	1	2	19	14
10	582	8	6	8	8	21	15
20	980	15	11	14	13	22	15
30	1370	21	16	20	18	24	16
40	1753	26	20	25	22	25	17
50	2127	31	23	29	26	27	18
60	2494	36	26	33	29	28	18
70	2853	39	28	36	31	30	19
80	3205	42	29	39	33	31	20
90	3548	45	30	41	34	33	20
100	3883	46	30	42	34	34	21

Quistis' Limit Break: Blue Magic

Blue Magic is basically the same as an enemy skill. If you're a Final Fantasy veteran, this should seem very familiar. Final Fantasy V had the Blue Mage job class. Final Fantasy VI (III in the states) had a character named Gau, who would leap onto the enemies' backs, and learn their attacks. In Final Fantasy VII, there was an Enemy Skill Materia that enabled a character to learn an enemy skill after getting hit with it. Obtaining Blue Magic is done a bit differently in Final Fantasy VIII, but the basic idea remains the same.

By finding special items, you can teach Quistis a new Blue Magic skill. These items can be dropped by or stolen from monsters, made using the Card Mod ability, or refined from other items.

Blue Magic List

Item	Blue Magic	Drop/Steal From	Card Mod	Refine Item
Spider Web	Ultra Waves	Caterchipiller	Caterchipiller	N/A
Coral Fragment	Electrocute	Cockatrice, Creeps, Blitz	Creeps	N/A
Curse Spike	LV?Death	Forbidden, Imp, Malboro, Tri-Face	Tri-Face	N/A
Black Hole	Degenerator	Gesper, Wendigo	Diablos, Gesper	N/A
Water Crystal	Aqua Breath	Chimera, Fastitocalon-F, Fastitocalon, Grand Mantis, Chimera	Fastitiocalon, Fastitocalon-F	N/A
Missile	Micro Missile	Death Claw, GIM52A	N/A	N/A
Mystery Fluid	Acid	Gayla	Gayla	N/A
Running Fire	Gatling Gun	BGH251F2, Iron Giant, SAM08G	SAM08G	N/A
Inferno Fang	Fire Breath	Hexadragon, Ruby Dragon	Ruby Dragon	N/A
Malboro Tentacle	Bad Breath	Malboro	Malboro	N/A
Whisper	White Wind	Adamantoise	N/A	N/A
Laser Cannon	Homing Laser	Belhelmel, Elastoid, Mobile Type 8	N/A	N/A
Barrier	Mighty Guard	Behemoth	Behemoth	N/A
Power Generator	Ray-Bomb	Blitz	N/A	N/A
Dark Matter	Shockwave Pulsar	N/A	N/A	Curse Spike (100 for 1)

Quistis' Weapons

Chain Whip

Cost: 100 Gil
Atk: 12
Hit: 103%

Items	Dropped By	Stolen From	Card Mod
M-Stone Piece (x2)	Bite Bug, Funguar, Buel, Jelleye, Glacial Eye, Creeps, Belhelmel, Blobra. T-Rexaur, Bomb, Vysage, Lefty, Righty, Elastoid, Gesper, Blitz, Death Claw, Abyss Worm, Gayla, Armadodo (Level 1-19)	Bite Bug, Blobra, Buel	Bite Bug (1 for 1), Funguar (1 for 1)
Spider Web (x1)	Caterchipillar	Caterchipillar	Caterchipillar (1 for 1)

Slaying Tail

Cost: 200 Gil
Atk: 15
Hit: 104%

Items	Dropped By	Stolen From	Card Mod
Magic Stone (x2)	Bite Bug, Funguar, Buel, Jelleye, Glacial Eye, Creeps, Belhelmel, Blobra, Geezard, Abyss Worm, Ochu (all above Level 20-29) Ochu (Level 1-29),	Grat, Buel, Jelleye	Grat (1 for 1), Buel (1 for 1), Jelleye (1 for 1)
Sharp Spike (x1)	Grand Mantis, Death Claw	Grand Mantis	Grand Mantis (1 for 1)

Red Scorpion

Cost: 400 Gil
Atk: 20
Hit: 105%

Items	Dropped By	Stolen From	Card Mod
Ochu Tentacle (x2)	Ochu	Ochu	Ochu (1 for 1)
Dragon Skin (x2)	Anacondaur, Blue Dragon	N/A	N/A

Save the Queen

Cost: 800 Gil
Atk: 25
Hit: 107%

Items	Dropped By	Stolen From	Card Mod
Malboro Tentacle (x2)	Malboro	Malboro	Malboro (4 for 1)
Sharp Spike (x4)	Grand Mantis, Death Claw	Grand Mantis	Grand Mantis (1 for 1)
Energy Crystal (x4)	Elnoyle, Behemoth (rare), Red Dragon (rare, Level 35-100)	N/A	Elnoyle (10 for 1)

Zell Dincht

Zell, a master of close-combat fighting skills, uses kicks and punches to defeat his enemies. Zell also has a great passion for the hot dogs that are sold in Balamb Garden's cafeteria. Never one to cause problems to others, Zell's abundant energy, wild temper, and reactionary style sometimes get him into trouble. People in his hometown of Balamb view him as a "comic-bookish" type of hero, or a klutzy, poorly behaved person.

Age: 17
Height: 5' 5"
DoB: March 17
Blood Type: B
Weapon: Glove
Special Skill: Duel

Zell's Vital Stats by Level

LV	HP	Str	Vit	Mag	Spr	Spd	Luck
1	252	2	1	1	0	20	14
10	627	9	7	7	5	22	15
20	1035	16	12	14	9	23	15
30	1435	22	17	19	14	25	16
40	1828	27	21	24	17	26	17
50	2212	32	25	29	20	28	17
60	2589	36	28	33	22	29	18
70	2958	40	30	36	24	31	18
80	3320	43	32	38	26	32	19
90	3673	45	33	40	26	34	20
100	4018	47	33	42	27	35	20

Zell's Limit Break: Duel

Relying completely on his powerful fists, Zell has developed a fighting style that's all his own. When his HP drops, Zell goes into high gear and nails his opponents with a powerful custom-made combo.

When the game begins, Zell only knows five basic attacks. Throughout the game, Zell can learn new attacks by locating issues of a magazine called **Combat King**. Each issue will teach Zell a new move.

Combat King Locations

Combat King 001	In a cell on the first floor of the D-District Prison
Combat King 002	Defeat Fujin and Raijin in Balamb
Combat King 003	Get from Zell's girlfriend in Balamb (see Secrets)
Combat King 004	Get from an Esthar Soldier in Esthar (see Disc Three walkthrough)
Combat King 005	Found in Lunatic Pandora during Disc Three (see Disc Three walkthrough)

NOTE *You can buy all the Combat Kings during Disc Three from the Esthar Book Store as long as you have taught the Tonberry GF the Familiar ability.*

When the Duel Limit Break is selected, a window appears at the bottom of the screen showing all of the available attacks. To the right is the time limit for the combo. If you don't enter an ending attack before the time limit expires, the combo will end on its own. As you enter attacks, the main window will disappear and reappear with a new set of attacks. Typically, there are two to three options in each window. Sometimes only two moves appear in the window, but you'll notice a blank spot at the bottom. At these times, you can input the Punch Rush (🔘 🔘) rather than the two options that appear in the box.

Initially, this may seem difficult, but after learning the attacks you will have no trouble. The following chart lists combo strings that lead to ending attacks. Use these to boost your speed, because you'll know exactly what to press next before the options even appear. You can also set Zell's Duel attacks to Auto in Zell's Status Screen.

Duel Attacks

Attack Name	Movement	Found in...
Punch Rush	🔘 🔘	Learned
Booya	→ ←	Learned
Heel Drop	↑ ↓	Learned
Mach Kick	← → 🔘	Learned
Dolphin Blow	L1 R1 L1 R1	Combat King 001
Meteor Strike	↓ 🔘 ↑ 🔘	Combat King 002
*Burning Rave	↓ ↓ ↓ 🔘	Learned
*Meteor Barret	↑ 🔘 ↓ 🔘 🔘	Combat King 003
*Different Beat	🔘 🔘 🔘 🔘 ↑	Combat King 004
*My Final Heaven	↑ → ↓ ← 🔘	Combat King 005

*Notes ending moves

Burning Rave Combos

Meteor Barret Combos

Different Beat Combos

My Final Heaven Combos

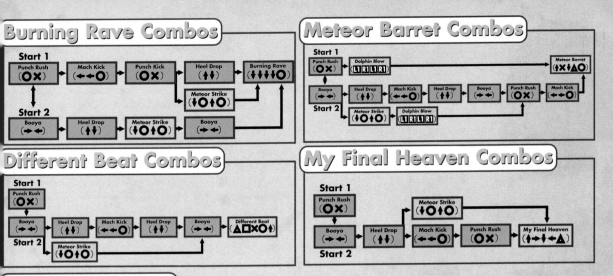

Zell's Weapons

Metal Knuckle

Cost: 100 Gil
Atk: 12
Hit: 98%

Items	Dropped By	Stolen From	Card Mod
Fish Fin (x1)	Fastitocalon-F, Fastitocalon	Fastitocalon-F	N/A
M-Stone Piece (x4)	Bite Bug, Funguar, Buel, Jelleye, Glacial Eye, Creeps, Belhelmel, Blobra, T-Rexaur, Bomb, Vysage, Lefty, Righty, Elastoid, Gesper, Blitz, Death Claw, Abyss Worm, Gayla, Armadodo (Level 1-19)	Bite Bug, Blobra, Buel	Bite Bug (1 for 1), Funguar (1 for 1)

Maverick

Cost: 200 Gil
Atk: 15
Hit: 99

Items	Dropped By	Stolen From	Card Mod
Dragon Fin (x1)	SAM08G (Level 29-100), Grendel	Grendel	Grendel (1 for 1)
Spider Web (x1)	Caterchipillar	Caterchipillar	Caterchipillar (1 for 1)

Gauntlet

Cost: 400 Gil
Atk: 20
Hit: 101%

Items	Dropped By	Stolen From	Card Mod
Dragon Skin (x1)	Anacondaur, Blue Dragon, Grendel (Level 1-19, rare)	N/A	N/A
Fury Fragment (x1)	Red Dragon, Blue Dragon, Grendel (Level 20-100)	Blue Dragon	Blue Dragon (4 for 1)

Ehrgeiz

Cost: 800 Gil
Atk: 25
Hit: 103%

Items	Dropped By	Stolen From	Card Mod
Adamantine (x1)	Adamantine	BGH251F2 (at FH)	Minotaur (1 for 10)
Dragon Skin (x4)	Anacondaur, Blue Dragon	N/A	N/A
Fury Fragment (x1)	Red Dragon, Blue Dragon, Grendel (Level 20-100)	Blue Dragon	Blue Dragon (4 for 1)

Selphie Tilmitt

Selphie is a recent transfer student to Balamb Garden. She grew up in Trabia Garden, located deep in the mountains on the northern continent. Her outgoing personality and sincerity have earned her many friends at Balamb and Trabia Gardens. Currently, she is busy trying to organize the Garden Celebration between training sessions. When fighting, Selphie uses giant Nunchaku and special magic that includes several unique spells.

Age: 17
Height: 5' 1½"
DoB: July 16
Blood Type: B
Weapon: Nunchaku
Special Skill: Slot

Selphie's Vital Stats by Level

LV	HP	Str	Vit	Mag	Spr	Spd	Luck
1	211	1	1	5	2	15	18
10	559	7	6	11	8	17	19
20	937	14	10	17	13	20	20
30	1307	20	15	22	18	21	21
40	1670	25	18	27	23	24	21
50	2024	30	21	32	27	26	22
60	2371	34	24	36	30	28	23
70	2710	38	26	40	33	30	24
80	3042	41	27	43	35	33	25
90	3365	43	28	46	37	34	26
100	3680	45	28	49	38	37	26

Selphie's Limit Break: Slot

Early in the game, Selphie's Limit Break is extremely valuable because it enables you to access spells you probably won't see elsewhere for quite some time. In addition, Selphie has several types of magic that can't be found anywhere else in the game:

Full-Cure

In early Boss fights, this spell will come in handy as it completely restores your entire party's HP.

Wall

This spell casts Protect and Shell on all party members. It's a great defensive spell, but kind of rare.

Rapture

Rather than causing damage to an opponent, Rapture attaches angel wings to the enemy's back and flies it right out of the battle. This spell is also rare, and doesn't work against Bosses.

The End

This is Selphie's strongest Limit Break, and perhaps the best one in the game. When Selphie casts this spell, the enemy is taken to a serene field of flowers, where it is put to rest. The End works on regular enemies and Bosses, however, it doesn't affect undead enemies. The End is the most difficult Limit Break to get in Selphie's Slot menu. Your chances of getting it increase when Selphie's level is very high, and when she's in danger of getting knocked out.

When you select Slot, a menu opens in the bottom-left corner of the screen. You'll then see a spell with a number next to it. The spell shown is what will be cast if you choose the cast option; the number indicates how many times the spell will be cast. If you want, choose the "Do Over" command to receive a different spell and number. Targeting of the spells is completely random, but Selphie will not cast protective/curative magic on enemies or attack magic on allies.

Selphie's Weapons

Flail

Cost: 100 Gil
Atk: 12
Hit: 98%

Items	Dropped By	Stolen From	Card Mod
M-Stone Piece (x2)	Bite Bug, Funguar, Buel, Jelleye, Glacial Eye, Creeps, Belhelmel, Blobra, T-Rexaur, Blobra, Bomb, Vysage, Lefty, Righty, Elastoid, Gesper, Blitz, Death Claw, Abyss Worm, Gayla, Armadodo (Level 1-19)	Bite Bug, Blobra, Buel	Bite Bug (1 for 1), Funguar (1 for 1)
Bomb Fragment (x1)	Bomb	Bomb	Bomb (1 for 1)

Morning Star

Cost: 200 Gil
Atk: 15
Hit: 99%

Items	Dropped By	Stolen From	Card Mod
Steel Orb (x2)	Wendigo, GIM47N (Level 1-29, rare)	Wendigo	Wendigo (1 for 1)
Sharp Spike (x2)	Grand Mantis, Death Claw	Grand Mantis	Grand Mantis (1 for 1)

Crescent Wish	Items	Dropped By	Stolen From	Card Mod
Cost: 400 Gil **Atk:** 20 **Hit:** 100%	Inferno Fang (x1)	Red Dragon (Level 1-44)	Red Dragon	Red Dragon (10 for 1)
	Life Ring (x1)	Turtapod, Torama (Level 1-19), Mesmerize	N/A	Turtapod (5 for 1)
	Sharp Spike (x4)	Grand Mantis, Death Claw	Grand Mantis	Grand Mantis (1 for 1)

Strange Vision	Items	Dropped By	Stolen From	Card Mod
Cost: 200 Gil **Atk:** 25 **Hit:** 255%	Adamantine (x1)	Adamantine	BGH251F2 (at FH)	Minotaur (1 for 10)
	Star Fragment (x3)	Iron Giant, T-Rexaur (rare), Tri Face (rare, Level 30-100), Chimera (Level 20-100, rare), Hexadragon (Level 30-100), Red Dragon (Level 1-44, rare)	Iron Giant (3 for 1)	Iron Giant
	Curse Spike (x2)	Creeps (Level 20-29), Imp, Malboro, Forbidden, Grand Mantis (Level 1-29, rare), Tri-Face	Tri-Face	Tri-Face (1 for 1)

Irvine Kinneas

Irvine is touted as an expert marksman who can use special ammo to attack enemies. He puts on airs and attempts to convince those around him that he's a misunderstood loner, an image he uses to his advantage when courting female students. However, when placed in a pressure situation, he tends to shed his tough exterior and quickly loses his composure.

Age: 17
Height: 6' 0"
DoB: November 24
Blood Type: A
Weapon: Gun
Special Skill: Shot

			Irvine's Vital Stats by Level				
LV	**HP**	**Str**	**Vit**	**Mag**	**Spr**	**Spd**	**Luck**
1	213	1	1	1	0	19	13
10	579	8	6	8	6	21	14
20	977	14	12	14	11	23	15
30	1367	20	16	20	15	25	15
40	1750	25	20	25	19	27	17
50	2124	30	23	30	22	29	17
60	2491	34	26	33	25	31	18
70	2850	37	28	36	27	33	19
80	3202	40	30	39	28	35	20
90	3545	43	31	41	28	37	21
100	3880	45	31	42	28	39	21

Irvine's Limit Break: Shot

When in trouble, Irvine loads his weapon with special ammunition and assaults his opponents with a hail of bullets. After selecting Shot, choose the type of ammo you want Irvine to use. Consider your enemy before choosing. Do you need the wide-spread damage of Shotgun Ammo, or a powerful punch against a tough beast?

When the Shot Limit Break begins, two windows appear. The one on the left shows which enemy(s) you're targeting. Move the cursor up and down to switch targets while shooting. The window on the right indicates how much ammo is remaining, and the time before the Limit Break ends.

Normal Ammo (Normal Shot)

Inflicts a moderate amount of damage on one enemy, and reloads at an average speed. You can shift your aim between several targets while using this type of Ammo.

Shotgun Ammo (Scatter Shot)

Similar to Normal Ammo, Shotgun Ammo hits every enemy on-screen with each shot.

Dark Ammo (Dark Shot)

Similar to Normal Ammo, but each time you hit an enemy you have a chance of causing several abnormal status effects (Sleep, Blind, Poison, Silence, etc.)

Fire Ammo (Flame Shot)

This fire elemental ammo causes damage to all enemies on-screen. Effective against enemies weak against fire, but doesn't work well on enemies resistant to fire magic. It will heal enemies that absorb fire magic.

Demolition Ammo (Canister Shot)

Although it has a slow load time, it packs a strong punch. Its downside is that you can only target one enemy at a time, although you can still cycle through targets.

Fast Ammo (Quick Shot)

Think machine gun. It's not very strong, but you can quickly unload about 25 rounds into a group of enemies. This ammo's speed makes up for its lack of power. Just make sure you have a healthy supply, or you'll quickly run out.

AP Ammo (Armor Shot)

Armor Piercing (AP) Ammo is much better than the similar Demolition Ammo. It's stronger than Demolition Ammo and the firing rate is much faster.

Pulse Ammo (Hyper Shot)

This is by far the best ammo you can find. It causes maximum damage to a single enemy, and has a great fire rate. Unfortunately, it's difficult to come by.

You can find, buy, or refine ammo. You need to refine most of the good stuff from rare items. Just make sure you keep an ample supply around, because you don't want to run out in the middle of a critical battle.

Ammo-RF List

1 Screw = 8 Normal Ammo
1 Normal Ammo = 1 Fast Ammo
1 Shotgun Ammo = 2 Fast Ammo
1 Bomb Fragment = 20 Fire Ammo
1 Red Fang = 40 Fire Ammo
1 Fuel = 10 Fire Ammo
1 Poison Powder = 10 Dark Ammo
1 Venom Fang = 20 Dark Ammo
1 Missile = 20 Demolition Ammo
1 Running Fire = 40 Demolition Ammo
1 Cactus Thorn = 40 Demolition Ammo
1 Sharp Spike = 10 AP Ammo
1 Chef's Knife = 20 AP Ammo
1 Laser Cannon = 5 Pulse Ammo
1 Energy Crystal = 10 Pulse Ammo
1 Power Generator = 20 Pulse Ammo

Note

You can save some ammo by watching the damage each shot causes. If your shots stop causing damage, the enemy no longer has any HP. Press the △ button to stop shooting.

Irvine's Weapon List

Valiant

Cost: 100 Gil
Atk: 12
Hit: 105%

Items	Dropped By	Stolen From	Card Mod
Steel Pipe (x1)	Wendigo (rare), GIM47N (Level 1-29, rare)	Wendigo	Elastoid (1 for 1)
Screw (x4)	Geezard, GIM47N (rare)	Geezard	Geezard (1 for 5)

Ulysses

Cost: 200 Gil
Atk: 15
Hit: 108%

Items	Dropped By	Stolen From	Card Mod
Steel Pipe (x1)	Wendigo (rare), GIM47N (Level 1-29, rare)	Wendigo	Elastoid (1 for 1)
Bomb Fragment (x1)	Bomb	Bomb	Bomb (1 for 1)
Screw (x2)	Geezard, GIM47N (rare)	Geezard	Geezard (1 for 5)

Bismarck

Cost: 400 Gil
Atk: 20
Hit: 110%

Items	Dropped By	Stolen From	Card Mod
Steel Pipe (x1)	Wendigo (rare), GIM47N (Level 1-29, rare)	Wendigo	Elastoid (1 for 1)
Dynamo Stone (x4)	Blitz (Level 30-100)	Elastoid (Level 1-29)	Blitz (1 for 1), Quezacotl (1 for 100)
Screw (x8)	Geezard, GIM47N (rare)	Geezard	Geezard (1 for 5)

Exeter

Cost: 800 Gil
Atk: 25
Hit: 115%

Items	Dropped By	Stolen From	Card Mod
Dino Bone (x1)	T-Rexaur	T-Rexaur	T-Rexaur (2 for 1), Armadodo (1 for 1), Sacred (1 for 100)
Moon Stone (x1)	Elnoyle (Level 1-39, rare), Imp (Level 40-100), Torama (Level 40-100)	Elnoyle	N/A
Star Fragment (x1)	Iron Giant, T-Rexaur (rare), Tri-Face (Level 30-100, rare), Chimera (Level 20-100, rare), Hexadragon (Level 30-100), Red Dragon (Level 1-44, rare)	Iron Giant	Iron Giant (3 for 1)
Screw (x18)	Geezard, GIM47N (rare)	Geezard	Geezard (1 for 5)

Laguna Loire

Laguna is an energetic man with a big heart. Although a bit of a klutz, he's a strong leader who inspires a great deal of loyalty and respect from those around him. His weapon of choice is a machine gun, which can fire multiple shots at enemies posing a threat to his party members. Although he dreams of someday starting a writing career, he's currently serving in the Galbadian Army.

Laguna's Vital Stats by Level

LV	HP	Str	Vit	Mag	Spr	Spd	Luck
1	184	2	1	2	1	22	14
10	577	9	8	8	7	24	15
20	1005	16	14	15	13	25	15
30	1425	22	19	21	18	27	16
40	1838	28	24	26	22	28	17
50	2242	33	28	31	26	30	18
60	2639	37	32	35	29	31	18
70	3028	41	35	39	32	33	19
80	3410	44	37	42	33	34	20
90	3783	46	39	44	35	36	20
100	4148	48	41	46	36	37	21

Age: 27
Height: 5' 9"
DoB: January 3
Blood Type: B
Weapon: Machine Gun
Special Skill: Desperado

Laguna's Limit Break: Desperado

Laguna tosses a hand grenade, and then empties a few clips of ammo at his enemy before bailing out. This attack hits multiple enemies.

Kiros Seagill

One of Kiros' most distinguishing features are the sharp blades, called Katal, which he wears on both arms. His fighting style is also unique, just like his weapon. He has a very caring personality and a sharp wit. Little is known about Kiros, except that he fights alongside Laguna in Galbadia's Army.

Kiros' Vital Stats by Level

LV	HP	Str	Vit	Mag	Spr	Spd	Luck
1	160	1	1	2	2	30	15
10	517	8	7	9	8	32	16
20	905	14	12	16	14	34	17
30	1285	20	16	23	20	36	18
40	1658	25	20	28	24	37	18
50	2022	30	24	34	29	39	19
60	2379	34	26	38	32	41	20
70	2728	37	28	42	35	42	21
80	3070	40	30	45	38	44	22
90	3403	42	31	48	40	46	23
100	3728	43	31	50	41	48	23

Age: 23
Height: 6' 4"
DoB: July 6
Blood Type: O
Weapon: Katal
Special Skill: Blood Pain

Kiros' Limit Break: Blood Pain

Using his deadly Katal, Kiros goes into a frenzy of quick attacks, causing incredible damage to a single opponent.

Ward is a big, powerful man. He carries with him an unusually heavy weapon, the Harpoon, which he throws at attacking enemies. Just like Kiros, Ward has been assigned to fight alongside Laguna in the Galbadian Army. His devotion to his friends is unwavering.

Age: 25
Height: 7' 0"
DoB: February 25
Blood Type: A
Weapon: Harpoon
Special Skill: Massive Anchor

Ward's Limit Break: Heavy Anchor

Tossing his anchor high into the air, Ward leaps after it and rides the anchor back down into the ground. The resulting shockwave damages all enemies in the area.

Ward's Vital Stats by Level

LV	HP	Str	Vit	Mag	Spr	Spd	Luck
1	210	2	3	2	1	15	10
10	657	10	9	8	6	16	10
20	1145	18	15	13	11	18	11
30	1625	25	20	19	16	19	11
40	2098	31	25	23	20	20	12
50	2562	37	29	27	23	21	12
60	3019	42	33	30	26	23	13
70	3468	47	37	32	28	24	13
80	3910	51	40	34	29	25	13
90	4343	54	42	35	30	27	14
100	4768	56	44	36	30	27	14

Seifer has gained a reputation in Balamb Garden as a show-off and a snob. With his friends Fujin and Raijin, he acts as the Garden's Disciplinary Committee. Seifer is the only other Gunblade user at Balamb Garden besides Squall. The two have a heated rivalry that leads them both into trouble at times.

Age: 18
Height: 6' 2"
DoB: December 22
Blood Type: O
Weapon: Gunblade
Special Skill: Fire Cross

Seifer's Limit Break: Fire Cross

Seifer hits an opponent with a Fire spell, and then follows the attack with a blast of energy from his Gunblade.

Seifer's Vital Stats by Level

LV	HP	Str	Vit	Mag	Spr	Spd	Luck
1	275	3	2	2	5	15	12
10	812	10	8	9	10	18	13
20	1400	17	14	15	16	21	13
30	1980	23	19	21	20	24	14
40	2553	29	24	26	25	27	15
50	3117	34	28	30	28	30	16
60	3674	38	32	34	32	33	16
70	4223	41	34	38	34	36	17
80	4765	44	37	41	36	39	18
90	5298	46	38	43	37	42	18
100	5823	48	39	45	38	45	19

Very little is known about Edea, other than the fact that she has inherited the Sorceress Power at some point in her life. She only recently appeared for the first time, and seems to be working with Vinzer Deling, the Galbadian President. Her true intentions are unclear, but it seems unlikely that she will bring peace to the warring nation of Galbadia.

Age ?
Height: ?
DoB: ?
Blood Type: ?
Weapon: —
Special Skill: Ice Strike

Edea's Limit Break: Ice Strike

Edea uses her powerful sorceress magic to create a gigantic ice javelin, which she hurls into her opponents.

Edea's Vital Stats by Level

LV	HP	Str	Vit	Mag	Spr	Spd	Luck
1	209	0	0	11	8	16	10
10	566	6	2	18	14	18	11
20	954	12	5	25	20	19	11
30	1334	18	7	31	25	21	12
40	1707	23	10	36	30	22	12
50	2071	27	12	41	34	24	13
60	2428	31	14	45	37	25	13
70	2777	34	16	48	40	27	14
80	3119	37	17	51	42	28	14
90	3452	39	18	54	44	30	15
100	3777	41	20	55	45	31	15

Enemies

(Training Center only)
Grat, T-Rexaur

Enemies

(Outdoor)
Bite Bug

(Plains/Forests)
Glacial Eye (Plains)
T-Rexaur (Forests)
Caterchipillar (Forests)
Fastitocalon-F (Beaches)

Draw Points

Cure (Front Gate)
Esuna (Library)
Blizzard (Training Center)

Save Points

Hall, Training Center
Dormitory

Rare Cards

Quistis (Trepe Groupies #1,
#2, #3/Cafeteria, classroom)
MiniMog (Jogger, Hall)

Magazines

Occult Fan I (Library/Book
Shelves)

1

Follow Quistis to the classroom

2

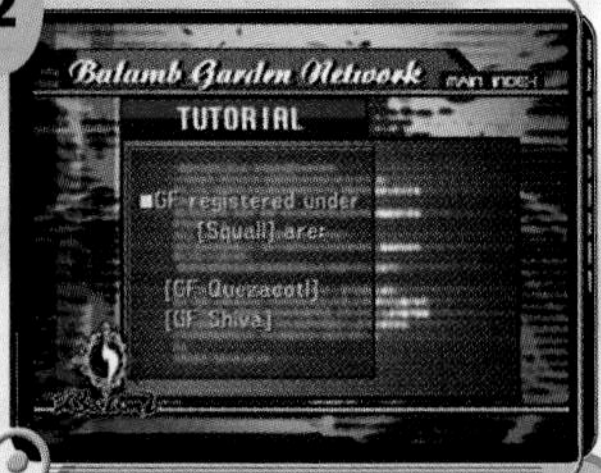

Get Shiva and Quezacotl from the Study Panel

3

Speak with Quistis in the classroom

4

Meet Quistis at the Front Gate

SeeD Ranking

As you begin the game, you begin earning or losing points toward your SeeD Ranking that you'll be given later in the game. The SeeD Rankings are broken down into several categories: Conduct, Judgement, Attack, Spirit, and Attitude. Your SeeD Ranking is determined by many factors; the choices you make, the time you spend exploring between missions, how well you obey orders, and by the number of enemies you defeat. If you want to achieve a high SeeD Rank later, you'll need to abide by these factors for now. Check out the SeeD Ranking secrets on p.9 for more information.

Exploring the Garden

The Classroom

At the start of the game simply follow Squall's instructor, Quistis Trepe, until she releases everyone from class. Speak with the other students, and then return to Squall's desk and access the Study Panel. Select the Tutorial section titled "new" and you'll automatically receive your first two Guardian Forces (GF), **Quezacotl** and **Shiva**. Before you equip your two new GFs, take some time to go through the Tutorial section and learn all about the basic controls and concepts in FFVIII.

After you finish the Tutorial section, you should consider looking through the rest of the choices on the Study Panel. Once you've had your fill, shut down the Study Panel and exit the classroom.

Starter Deck

After passing the SeeD exam later, you'll want to begin playing cards with people you'll find all over the world. However, you can't start playing until you have at least five cards. You could wait until you find five cards on the battlefield, but you can get a mediocre starting deck of Level 1 cards by stopping and talking to the person standing on the 2nd floor walkway. This deck isn't very strong, but it will become a decent one with the addition of a few stronger cards, which won't take long.

Touring the SeeD Garden

The Garden is very large and full of all kinds of activity. There are 10 major areas that you'll visit quite often, as well as several minor locations that you'll only see at specific points in the story. The following information provides a brief rundown of the major locations and what you'll find at each one.

Dormitory

This is where you'll find Squall's room. At various times during the game, you'll be asked to return here. You can use Squall's bed to restore any lost Hit Points (HP) for your party members or GFs, or save your game using the Save Point.

Parking

Any and all vehicles used by SeeD are stored here. You'll typically only come here when you need a set of wheels.

Training Center

Those wishing to brush up on their fighting skills can visit the Training Center at any time. There are monsters roaming around freely inside the Training Center, so use caution when entering. This is a great place to build up Squall and his GFs at the beginning of the game.

Library

Not only can you meet a lot of interesting people here, you can also pick up useful information and a magazine. Make sure you stop in often.

Front Gate

The great outdoors beckons at the end of this long corridor. If you're not driving to your next objective, you must exit the Garden through the Front Gate. By the way, when you're looking for a game of cards, this is a great place to find challengers.

Infirmary

You'll remember the Infirmary from the beginning of the game. Dr. Kadowaki, the residing physician, is always here to give advice or play a game of cards.

Occult Fan I

Hidden in the second bookcase is a copy of Occult Fan I. This bizarre magazine hints at strange occurrences throughout the world and can help you discover secret events or sub-quests later in the game.

Quad

The Quad is the home of the Garden Festival, but there's not much going on here... yet. Stop by and join the Garden Festival committee if you like.

Cafeteria

Hot dogs are a staple of the SeeD diet. The Cafeteria has hot dogs occasionally, but they always go fast. This is a great area to meet up with people. You should definitely stop by if you're looking to meet someone new.

Classroom

The classrooms are all located on the second floor, however, Squall only has access to Quistis' classroom. This is also the best place to learn more about the game by accessing the Study Panel at Squall's desk in the back.

Cid's Office

Headmaster Cid runs the SeeD Garden from his third floor office. You can only visit his office when he permits it, so don't bother looking for an entrance, because there isn't one yet.

NOTE

If you do not take the transfer student on the tour, there will be no mention of Cid's office at this point in the game. At any rate, you'll be unable to reach this area until later in the game.

Draw Points

Squall begins the game without any stocked magic. Fortunately, there are several **Draw Points** throughout the Garden. Visit them all to get a headstart on your magic supply.

Most Draw Points can be used an infinite amount of times, but you must wait for the Draw Point to refill after each Draw. However, some Draw Points can only be used once. Most of the time, it takes a while for the Draw Point to refill, so don't wait around. An easy way to tell whether or not you can draw from a Draw Point is by its color. Full Draw Points are purple, while empty Draw Points are Blue.

Leaving the Garden

Meet Quistis at the Front Gate when you're ready to go. Once she joins your party, you'll want to equip her with one of the GF's you received earlier. It isn't necessary to equip her with a GF, but without one she'll only be able to attack during battle.

Once outside, you should take some time to prepare for the Fire Cavern. First, you should look for a few enemies in particular that have some valuable magic. **Bite Bugs** live in the grassy areas and have **Scan** and **Fire** magics, which enables you to examine an enemy's HP and weaknesses. **Glacial Eyes** also live in the plains, and they have **Blizzard**, **Scan**, and **Cure** magic. Stockpile both types of magic, because they'll be extremely helpful in the Fire Cavern. Along the beach south of the Garden you'll find **Fastitocalon-Fs**, which also have **Blizzard** magic, but they are also worth 3 AP each.

Leaving the Garden (Cont.)

By the time you enter the Fire Cavern, you should have a large supply of Blizzard and Cure magic. Remember that both Quistis and Squall can hold 100 of each type of magic, and there's no limit as to how much magic you can draw from a single monster.

It's also a good idea to boost Squall's and Quistis' vital stats by stocking up on a couple of other spells. Using Quezacotl to junction 100 Sleep spells to a character's Magic boosts the Magic stat by a whopping 12 points. This will help immensely during the first Boss fight.

Additionally, you can teach Quezacotl **T Mag-RF** (Thunder Magic-Refine), which uncovers the skill **Mid Mag-RF** (Mid-Level Magic-Refine). Learning the Mid Mag-RF ability will enable you to refine one Blizzara from five Blizzard spells. This is particularly useful in the Fire Cavern, because most of the enemies inside have a weakness against Ice magic. Blizzara is even more useful in defeating the Fire Cavern's Boss.

World Map Draw Points

Scattered around the World Map are invisible Draw Points. You'll find one such Draw Point hidden at the entrance to the train tunnel just east of Balamb. This one contains the **Esuna** spell, which you won't see much of until later in the game. Always check train tunnels and other odd places on the World Map for Draw Points.

Blue Magic: Ultra Waves

Quistis' Limit Breaks are based on Blue Magic, which is a type of magic used by monsters. By collecting special items, Quistis learns new types of Blue Magic, which she can later use in battle. Your first chance to teach Quistis a new Blue Magic is on your way to the Fire Cavern.

You can find an enemy known as Caterchipillar in the forest outside the Fire Cavern. This enemy uses a Blue Magic called **Ultra Waves** that attacks multiple targets. Defeat a Caterchipillar, and it may drop a special item—**Spider Web**. Use the item outside of battle to teach Quistis the Blue Magic: Ultra Waves.

FIRE CAVERN

1

Select a time limit for the test

2

Locate and defeat the GF Ifrit

3

Return to Balamb Garden

Enemies

Ifrit (Boss)
Bomb
Red Bat
Buel

Draw Points

Fire

Rare Cards

Ifrit (defeat Boss)

A cave set in a hillside east of Balamb Garden represents the Fire Cavern. Your goal is to defeat the Boss inside the Fire Cavern under the constraints of a time limit that you choose for yourself. Hopefully, you've prepared well by stocking up on lots of magic and training your GFs.

The Time Limit & Your SeeD Ranking

As Squall approaches the entrance to the cavern, he is asked to choose a time limit for the test. The choices are 10, 20, 30, or 40 minutes. Obviously, the more time you have, the easier the test will be to complete. However, if you want to get a high SeeD Rank at graduation, you'll want to have as little time left on the clock as possible at the end of the battle with Ifrit. Ten minutes should suffice; don't worry though, it's more time than it seems.

The Fire Cavern is short and easy to navigate and the Boss isn't tough if you know its one weakness. Plus, you only need to reach the end of the cavern and defeat the Boss in the time that you chose before entering the cavern. You can take as much time as you like exiting the cavern.

If you do choose 10 minutes, don't pay too much attention to Quistis' comments as you run through the cavern. She doesn't say much that you really need to hear, and you'll need to conserve some time for the Boss fight. Also, try to avoid long, drawn-out battles. Use **Blizzard** to eliminate any tough enemies you meet and move on quickly. Lastly, avoid drawing from enemies on your way to the Boss fight, and instead wait until you're on your way out. Most of them won't have anything you need right now anyway.

Elemental Warfare

The Fire Cavern is full of monsters that have a weakness to Ice magic. Use spells like Blizzard and Blizzara to easily destroy your enemies.

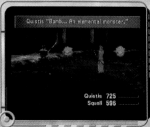

GUARDIAN FORCE ALERT!

IFRIT

GF	HP	1068	AP	20	— —
	EXP	— —	Weak vs. Ice/Absorbs Fire		

Ifrit is the toughest enemy you've faced thus far, but this GF isn't as tough as you might think. This Boss is an Elemental and has a single weakness you can exploit: **Ice** magic. Before the battle, make sure one of your characters can summon **Shiva**, who is an Ice Elemental. Also, make sure the other one has **Blizzard** or **Blizzara** spells that he/she can cast.

At the start of the battle, immediately summon Shiva and hit Ifrit with Ice magic, ignoring the use of any physical attacks. If Shiva has learned the **Boost** ability, don't forget to use it because it can make the battle much quicker. If you're trying to get a higher SeeD Rank, you need to watch Ifrit's HP. When it gets close to 100 HP, just wait for the clock to wind down to about 20-25 seconds and then use Blizzard magic and physical attacks to bring the battle to an end. After winning this battle, you receive a **G-Returner**, **Ifrit's Card**, **20 AP**, and Ifrit becomes one of your GFs.

On Your Way Out

Bombs are great cards! Use Quezacotl's **Card** ability to convert a few Bombs into cards, or try to win a few from battles. Also, make sure you hit the **Fire** Draw Point on your way back through the cavern. There's no time limit on your way out.

1

Change uniforms in Squall's dorm room

2

Go to the first floor lobby (Hall) and meet the others

3

Drive west to Balamb

4

Board the assault boat at the dock

After the battle with Ifrit in the Fire Cavern, it's time to return to Balamb Garden and prepare for the SeeD Field Exam.

Changing Uniforms

The first place you should visit upon your return to Balamb Garden is Squall's room in the Dormitory section of the Garden. To change uniforms, inspect his bed and then inspect the bed again to rest up before your next challenge. There's also a **Save Point** here; I suggest you use it. Make sure you return to the main Hall when you're ready to move on.

Traveling

The team will be taking the Garden Car to Balamb to meet up with the others. You probably saw Balamb earlier; it's the city to the west of Balamb Garden. Just stick to the road and you'll find it. Once there, don't waste any time boarding the assault boat. You've got a job to do!

NOTE
You cannot exit the vehicle on your way to Balamb.

DOLLET (SeeD FIELD EXAM)

Enemies

Galbadian Soldier (in town)
Anacondaur
Galbadian Soldier
Geezard
Elite Soldier (on mountain)
Galbadian Soldier
Elite Soldier
Biggs (Boss)
Wedge (Boss)
Elvoret (Boss; Comm Tower)

Draw Point

Blind (Comm Tower)

Save Points

Beach, Comm Tower

1 Follow Seifer to Dollet's Central Square

2 Scout the area and then wait for the Galbadian Army to arrive

3 Rescue a Dollet Soldier from an Anacondaur

4 Meet the messenger from "A" Squad

5 Enter the Communications Tower

6 Battle Biggs and Wedge

7 Defeat Elvoret

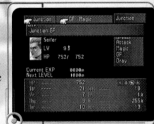
8 Head back to the beach

9 Escape from X-ATM092

The SeeD Field Exam takes place in a town known as Dollet, which is currently under siege by Galbadian Forces. Your job is to help rid the town of any remaining Galbadian soldiers.

Check Your GFs

Zell and Seifer are now in your party. They don't come equipped with GFs, so you'll need to assign them one if you want them to perform tasks other than attack. At the least, give Zell a GF so he can begin drawing magic and boosting his stats through Junctioning.

NOTE

You can access Quistis, although she's not currently in your party. You should go ahead and give her magic to either Squall or Zell using the *"Switch" option* in the Main Menu. It's certainly much easier than having Zell draw a bunch of magic you already have stocked elsewhere.

You're Being Graded

Your actions are being watched closely by your SeeD instructors. Act quickly, concentrate on completing your objective, avoid stopping to talk, follow orders, outwit your opponents, and finish battles quickly to get the highest grade possible.

Passing Through

It's difficult to get lost in Dollet. Simply head up the street and follow any order Seifer gives you. During any long pauses, avoid talking to any characters unless it's an order, or wait around until something happens.

Selphie

You can follow Selphie off the cliff if you want, but it might be wiser to walk around so you can get a better look at your surroundings. Such knowledge may be useful a little later. Plus, if you jump off the cliff, you'll have 5 points deducted from your SeeD Ranking. Also, make sure you equip her with one of your three GFs before going anywhere. At this point, Selphie will have whatever Magic Seifer had drawn.

BIGGS

HP	467~705	AP	4	––
EXP	––	––		

WEDGE

HP	416~640	AP	4	––
EXP	––	Immune to poison		

At the beginning of this fight, you'll only battle against Biggs because Wedge is off on patrol at the moment. Biggs' attacks aren't much stronger than that of a typical Elite Soldier. However, you can draw **Esuna** magic from Biggs, which is extremely useful for Junctioning and is extremely helpful for removing negative status effects in battles. You should try to draw as much Esuna from Biggs as possible.

Wedge will show up as soon as you cause a large amount of damage to Biggs or once a few minutes have passed. With the two present, you can stock up on magic to your heart's content, because Wedge has a **Cure** spell that you can draw to stockpile, or use on a party member when their HP's get low. When you're ready to end the fight, focus on Biggs or call upon your strongest GF. Once you inflict damage equal to both characters' HP, they're blown away and the real Boss fight begins.

33

GUARDIAN FORCE ALERT!

Elvoret

	HP	1563~3523	AP	10	
EXP		--	Immune to Poison/Strong Def. vs Magic (High Spirit)		--

First, start the battle by drawing **Siren** from Elvoret. Siren is a new GF that you can Junction after the fight, but ONLY if you draw the new GF out of Elvoret. This Boss is much tougher than Biggs and Wedge. Fortunately, it also has **Cure** magic you can rely on when your HPs are low.

Elvoret also has a spell you won't see much called **Double**. This spell enables you to cast a single spell twice in the same turn. This is very handy for later battles, and it Junctions well with several stats. However, Elvoret has a very high defense against magic spells, so avoid using Double unless you want to double up on Cures. Focus on using your strongest GFs, and then rely on your physical attacks only if you have to. For winning this battle, you receive two **Elixirs**, two **Cottages**, three **G-Returners**, and **Weapons Mon Mar** (the March edition of Weapons Monthly).

X-ATM092

	HP	5072~5770	AP	50	
EXP		--	Weak vs. Thunder/ Immune to Poison		--

You now have exactly 30 minutes to reach the transport on the beach back to Balamb and a large, solid steel monster is trying to ensure that Squall and the others become permanent residents. The X-ATM092 is built tough—real tough. In fact, it's nearly invincible, but it does have one weakness. Like so many other creatures, X-ATM092 is an Elemental although not in the traditional sense. As a machine, it's weak against Thunder magic. This makes Quezacotl, the Thunder GF, your new best friend.

Hit X-ATM092 with **Quezacotl** and **Thunder** magic until it falls, which is after you've caused about 1200 points of damage. When this occurs, you have no option but to escape (hold the L2 and R2 buttons on your controller). If you don't escape, the Boss will get back up and heal itself entirely, meaning you'll have to waste several more minutes knocking it back down again.

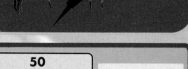

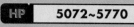

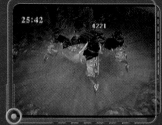

There is one trick though: Although the Boss is "invincible," it does have a set amount of HP. If you can deplete its HP before it can repair itself, you'll receive AP (a whopping 50 AP at that) as though you'd destroyed it even though it still repairs itself.

TIP If you're really good, and Quezacotl's compatibility is near 1000 and it has learned SumMag+10%, 20%, and 30%, and the Boost ability, you can actually receive 400 AP by fighting X-ATM092 eight times and depleting its HP during each battle. Keep in mind, though, that you'll lose some points toward your SeeD Ranking.

X-ATM092 (Cont.)

Each time you run from X-ATM092, it will repair itself and begin chasing the team back to the transport. When it catches you, you're forced to fight it again. With a 30 minute time limit, you can only afford to fight it a few times. Fortunately, there is only one spot where you must fight. The rest of the times you can dodge the Boss if you react quickly and just keep moving.

The one time you must fight occurs when X-ATM092 first appears; everything else can be dodged. There are three tricky spots to be aware of. The first is the cliff Selphie jumped down earlier. On this screen, you should ALWAYS use the D-pad on your controller and not the Analog Stick. When using the Analog Stick, Squall tends to get hung up on the curved path. With the D-Pad, the game automatically compensates and pushes Squall and the others around the obstacle.

The second tricky spot is the leftmost, downward mountain path. About halfway down the path, use the ▲ button to WALK down the path. Walking will prevent you from losing your balance when the Boss' heavy footsteps leave the party immobile and vulnerable.

The third trouble spot is the bridge, where X-ATM092 leaps over the party to cut them off. When this happens, run back the way you came—but not too fast! X-ATM092 will jump back over the party again attempting to cut them off a second time. Turn back around and keep going toward the transport.

Enemies

Outdoor Enemies

Bite Bug (Plains/Forests)
Glacial Eye (Plains)
T-Rexaur (Forests)
Caterchipillar (Forests)
Fastitocalon-F (Beaches)

Draw Points

Thunder (Town Square)
Cure (Dock)

Save Points

Balamb Hotel

Rare Cards

Zell (Zell's Mom; Zell must be in your party)

Magazines

Timber Maniacs (Train Platform)
Timber Maniacs (Balamb Hotel)

Other Locations

Item Shop
Balamb Junk Shop
Balamb Hotel

1 Exit the assault boat and speak with Quistis

2 Return to Balamb Garden

After their narrow escape from Dollet, the team gets dropped off in Balamb for a little R&R before returning to the Garden to receive their SeeD Rankings.

Homecoming

Balamb is Zell's hometown. Make sure you stop by and say "hello" to his mother, who just so happens to be a card player.

NOTE

While exploring Zell's home, you can find a practical joke. After checking the magazine stack in the living room, you'll find an old copy of Timber Maniacs. In actuality, you haven't found anything at all, but this is your reward for being thorough in your searches.

Queen of Cards

There's a mysterious woman near the train station known as the "Queen of Cards." She can give you information on the current status of the card game, plus she can spread new rules for a fee. You can even challenge her to a game, which sometimes pays off big because she tends to use the "Direct" and "All" trading rules. (For more information on the Card Game, refer to page 161.)

Timber Maniacs!

You can find your first issue of **Timber Maniacs** on the train platform right next to the signpost in the foreground.

Where to Go?

There isn't much for you to do here. Look around, play some cards, rest up, save… whatever you feel like doing. When you're finished, return to Balamb Garden to get your test score.

BALAMB GARDEN (Post Exam)

Enemies

Training Center only
Grat
T-Rexaur
Granaldo (Boss)
Raldo (Boss)
Diablos (Boss)

Outdoor Enemies
Bite Bug (Plains/Forests)
Glacial Eye (Plains)
T-Rexaur (Forests)
Caterchipillar (Forests)
Fastitocalon-F (Beaches)

Draw Points
Cure (Front Gate)
Esuna (Library)
Blizzard (Training Center)

Save Points
Hall
Training Center
Dormitory

Rare Cards
MiniMog (Jogger, Hall)
Quistis (Trepe Groupie #1,
#2, #3/Cafeteria, classroom)
Seifer (Cid/Cid's Office)

1 Go to the Hall and meet with Quistis, Xu, and Cid.

2 Locate Seifer near the Library

3 Go to the Second Floor to get Squall's grades

4 Speak with Cid

5 Return to the second floor to see your SeeD Rank Report

6 Change clothes in Squall's Dorm and go to the ball

7 Return to Squall's room and change clothes again

8 Meet Quistis in the Training Center and go to the Secret Area inside

9 Battle Granaldo and the Raldos

10 Return to Squall's Dorm room

11 Go to the Front Gate to learn about your first mission

12 Save your game and use the Magical Lamp if you're ready

13 Catch a train in Balamb

With the SeeD Field Exam now over, the team heads back to Balamb Garden to get their SeeD Rankings and to prepare for their next assignment.

What To Do?

Stop and talk with Quistis, Xu, and Cid in the main Hall, and then find Seifer outside the Library. When it's time to get your SeeD Rank, you'll hear an announcement over the intercom. Simply follow the instructions given to you. After graduation, return to Quistis' classroom.

Battle Meter

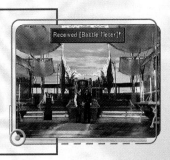

Talk to Cid right after graduation and he'll give you a **Battle Meter**. You can access it in the Information section of the Tutorial. The Battle Meter provides information on how you're performing.

The Battle Meter indicates how far you've walked, the number of battles you've fought, how many battles you've won, and how many battles you've run from.

SeeD Rank

After graduation, you'll receive your initial SeeD Rank based on your actions in the Fire Cavern, around the Garden, and during the Field Exam. A good starting rank is typically around a six. From this point forward, you'll receive regular paychecks from SeeD based on your SeeD Rank. The higher your rank, the more you're paid. Your SeeD Rank will fluctuate throughout the game based upon your actions. Fulfilling your orders flawlessly and efficiently can sometimes boost your rank, whereas a failed mission or incorrect decision can lower it.

There are also tests you can take to increase your SeeD Rank. Each test that you flawlessly pass raises your SeeD Rank by one. You can take the first test at Squall's Study Panel in Quistis' classroom or by accessing the Tutorial section from the Main Menu.

You can take other tests in the Tutorial section. There are a total of 30 tests that you can take, however, Squall cannot take a test higher than his current level. For example, if Squall is at Level 14, he can only take the first 14 tests. The highest SeeD Rank anyone can obtain is "A," which is the equivalent of Level 30.

Test Answers You'll find the answers to all of the questions in the SeeD Rank section (p. 9) of this book.

Meeting Quistis

Upon meeting Quistis at the Training Center, you should equip her with at least one GF. The Training Center is full of dangerous creatures. The "**Secret Area**" Quistis spoke of is in the very back of the Training Center, down the hall and above the **Save Point**.

Granaldo

HP	1314~9700	AP	5	Flying Monster
EXP	– –	Weak vs. Wind		

Raldos

HP	111~6700	AP	3	– –
EXP	– –	– –		

Granaldo and its sidekicks, three Raldos, have two useful spells: Protect and Shell. Stock up as much as you can on both of them. As you attack, focus on eliminating all three Raldos first. Initially, they don't attack directly, but if you defeat Granaldo before them, the Raldos go into high gear and use their super-speed to decimate your party.

On the other hand, Granaldo isn't nearly as powerful when fighting alone. In fact, Granaldo is weak against Sleep spells. Put this Boss to sleep with its own magic, and then pummel it into submission with attack magic. If the Raldos are still alive while Granaldo is sleeping, they'll wait harmlessly to be picked up by Granaldo.

In the Morning

Check Squall's desk in his new room to find the April edition of Weapons Monthly (**Weapons Mon Apr**). If you'd like, this is a good time to visit Quistis' classroom and take the first test at Squall's Study Panel. You can also take the test by accessing the Tutorial section from the Main Menu. This is also a good time to play cards; try to get the **MiniMog** and **Quistis** Cards.

Selphie's Diary

If you're working on the Garden Festival Committee, you should check out Selphie's new and improved "School Festival Committee" web page via Squall's Study Panel. From this site, you can read about Selphie's thoughts on her latest missions, the progress on the Garden Festival, and you can peek at her on-line diary.

First Mission

Meet everyone at the Front Gate to receive your new assignment. Also, make sure you remember the password phrase given to you by the Garden Faculty member: "But the owls are still around." You'll need the password phrase when you arrive at Timber. After the meeting, speak with Cid and he'll give you a **Magical Lamp**.

The Magical Lamp

GUARDIAN FORCE ALERT!

Diablos

	HP	1600~80,8000	AP	20	
GF	EXP	– –		Weak vs. Wind	**Flying Monster**

The Magical Lamp, which you receive from Cid, can be used at any time, however, you should save your game before using it. This lamp acts as a portal to a different dimension, one where the GF Diablos is waiting for its next challenge. When you use the lamp, you are automatically thrust into battle against Diablos. This Boss is very tough, so you may want to build up your party a bit before attempting the fight.

This GF uses Time-based magic to drain its opponents' HP. Gravija siphons three-fourths of each party member's HP, leaving them near death and ready for Diablos' finishing blow.

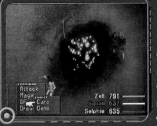

You can use one of two strategies for this fight. First, you can draw Diablos' Demi magic and use it against the GF. Although it won't cause as much damage to Diablos as it does to your team, it may be your strongest attack at this point. Demi won't finish off this beast, so continue to pummel Diablos' HPs with a physical attack or attack magic.

Regarding the second strategy, Diablos' Gravija magic will lower your party's HP to the point that they can use their Limit Breaks. In particular, Selphie's is useful because she can continue to cast Full-Cure spells on the party after each Gravija attack. However, you may need to use the "● button trick" until her Limit Break is ready (if Selphie's Limit Break doesn't appear when it's her turn to attack, keep pressing the ● button until it appears). You may also have to utilize the "Do Over" option several times to get a Full-Cure. Choose "Do Over" instead of "Cast" to turn down the spell in the hopes that the next spell will be the one you want. It's kind of like re-rolling dice. After winning the battle, Diablos joins you and you receive its card!

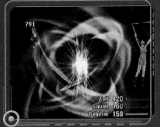

Seifer's Card

Before leaving the Garden, you should challenge Cid to a game of cards. The Headmaster has the rare **Seifer Card** in his deck, but be careful because Cid is no slouch at cards. If you don't challenge Cid now, you probably won't get another chance for quite some time.

Enemies
Funguar
Geezard

Draw Points
Cure (Timber Forest)
Water (Timber Forest)

Save Points
Galbadia Hotel

Magazines
Pet Pals Vol. 1
(SeeD Train Cabin)

1

Buy a train ticket in Balamb and board the train headed for Timber

2

Enter the SeeD cabin

3

As Laguna, navigate the forest and locate the armored vehicle

4

Visit the Galbadia Hotel's bar and watch the show

5

Speak with the hotel concierge to visit Julia's room

Upon receiving your first assignment, go to Balamb and speak with a conductor and pay 3,000 Gil for a train ticket. When you board the train, speak with Zell and Selphie. However, a mysterious vision leaves them with unanswered questions.

Where to Go

This is the first time you'll met Laguna Loire and his two companions, Kiros and Ward. Continue forward through the forest, and then cross the log over the river. When you find the armored vehicle on the path, get inside of it to automatically drive to Deling City.

When you arrive at Deling City, you should head for the **Galbadia Hotel** by walking east. Once there, visit the lounge downstairs. It's here where you'll meet an amazing pianist named **Julia**. Speak with both Kiros and Ward before and after Julia plays the piano. After the concert, speak with the hotel concierge to find Julia's room. Keep speaking with Julia until the scene switches back to Squall and company aboard the train.

FOREST OWLS

1

Meet the Forest Owl member at the train station and give the password phrase

2

Wake up the Forest Owl's leader at the back of the train

3

Go to the Strategy Room to learn about your mission

4

Speak with Watts to begin the mission

5

Kidnap the President

6

Speak to Rinoa to confront the President

7

Battle the Fake President and Gerogero

Enemies
Fake President (Boss)
Gerogero (Boss)

Save Points
Forest Owl's Base

Rare Cards
Angelo (Watts)

Magazines
Pet Pals Vol. 2 (Rinoa's Bed/post meeting)

The Password

Upon arriving at Timber Station, you'll be approached by a person who recites the code words, "Oh, the forest of Timber sure has changed!" You must reply by saying the password phrase, "But the Owls are still around." Now simply follow your escort to the waiting train. Once you're introduced to Zone and Watts, they'll ask you to go meet "the princess." Go to the last room in the train to find a familiar face.

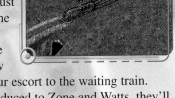

Anarchist Monthly

When you have the time, check the bulletin board in the Strategy Room. Inside, you'll find several issues of a magazine known as **Anarchist Monthly**. This magazine will provide lots of information on the Galbadian dictator, Vinzer Deling.

43

Rinoa's Limit Breaks

Rinoa's Limit Breaks involve her pet dog, Angelo. Like most dogs, Angelo can learn tricks with Rinoa's assistance. These tricks are then randomly used in battle or when Rinoa calls upon Angelo. Her dog begins the game knowing two tricks, but you can learn several others by collecting issues of **Pet Pals magazines**.

Each issue of Pet Pals magazine teaches a new trick. You found one earlier on the train to Timber, and you can find a second issue lying on Rinoa's bed after the strategy meeting.

Use the magazines by reading them in your inventory. Then enter Rinoa's status menu in the main menu and flip through the pages until you reach Angelo's screen. Tricks with a full red bar are learned tricks and can be used in battle. Empty bars represent unlearned tricks. To learn an unlearned trick, highlight the unlearned trick and exit the main menu. As Rinoa walks around, the trick is slowly learned. When you hear a tone while walking around, you'll know the trick has been fully learned and you can choose another.

The Kidnapping

After re-introducing yourself to Rinoa, you'll follow her to the strategy room where you'll receive details of the Forest Owl's mission.

The plan consists of the following steps:

1. Catch up to the **2nd escort car** and sneak onboard

2. Proceed cautiously across the roof of the **2nd escort car**

3. Proceed across the roof of the **President's car**

4. Uncouple the **1st escort** car

5. Have the **dummy car** and your **team** move in after uncoupling the escort car

6. Uncouple the **2nd escort** car

7. Escape with the **President's car**

Step 1: When the base catches up to the President's train, simply follow Rinoa onto the last car.

Step 2: The 2nd escort car is the one that's supposed to be equipped with heat and motion detectors. Simply stand still at first and watch the soldiers below. When they open their windows, they'll discover that neither of their sophisticated sensors is working, so quickly run across and ignore the whole "stop-and-go" plan.

Step 4: During this step, Selphie and Zell will serve as your lookouts. When they yell that a soldier is on its way back, don't waste a second getting back on top of the train car. When both soldiers head back the other way, you can drop down and finish the job. The codes are randomly given to Squall at this point. Remember that you only have five seconds to enter each code.

Step 3: The third step is simple, because there's no one to stop your progress.

Step 6: Uncoupling the 2nd escort car is tougher than the first. Selphie and Zell are busy, so this time you don't have a lookout. You must keep an eye on the guards by pressing the R1 button. If either guard is on its way back, you should climb up (regardless of how far off the guard is) just to be safe. You now have five codes to enter, but you still have a full five seconds to enter each code.

Step 5: This part is all up to the guys back at the base. As long as you perform your task within the given time limit, they'll have time to merge with the President's car.

Step 7: If you've done your job, this step will occur automatically. If not, you'll have to start again at the last train car you were entering the codes for.

NOTE

Should you complete the mission without getting caught, your SeeD rank will increase one level. However, if you fail any step, you'll be given the chance to start over or to end the game. Starting over places you back at the last car you were entering the codes for, but you lose your chance to boost your SeeD Rank. By choosing to end the game, you can reload your last saved game and try to earn the bonus again.

After completing the mission, you'll appear in the Forest Owl's train. Prepare your party and then talk to Rinoa when you're ready to confront the President.

Fake President	HP	52~778	AP	– –	– –
	EXP	– –		– –	

Gerogero	HP	350~3650	AP	20	– –
	EXP	– –	Very Weak vs Holy/Weak vs Fire & Earth/Immune to Poison		

WARNING!

To use some of the following Boss strategies, you must have one of your characters equip the Item command before entering the Boss fight.

Also, since Zell and Selphie have lost their Junctions, you'll need to reapply their Junctions before talking to Rinoa.

This Boss has two forms. The first form, disguised as the Fake President, isn't very strong or quick, so take your time to draw and use its Cure magic to heal a party member who is low on HP. The second form, however, is much deadlier. Its physical attacks are strong, but what really makes it powerful is its wide array of abnormal status attacks. Fortunately, Gerogero carries Esuna magic, which is capable of removing any abnormal status effects. NEVER LEAVE AN ABNORMAL STATUS EFFECT ON A CHARACTER!! If you do so during this battle, Gerogero may hit all three characters with Berserk or Silence, in effect limiting you to nothing but physical attacks.

Because Gerogero is an undead creature, it has a weakness to Holy and Curative magic. You probably won't have any Holy magic yet, so instead you'll need to rely upon Cure and Cura. You can cast Double on everyone, and then constantly hit Gerogero with Cure and Cura. Gerogero also has a weakness to Fire, so Ifrit should be particularly effective in this battle.

There is a one-hit kill option in this battle. Using a Phoenix Down, Elixir, or a X-Potion on Gerogero will destroy this Boss instantly. Because curative magic and items have reverse effects against the undead, a Phoenix Down—which normally restores life—causes instant death. The X-Potion and Elixir—which heal a person entirely—removes all HP of the undead. At this point of the game, you're probably more likely to have a Phoenix Down because Elixirs and X-Potions are more difficult to find. Keep in mind that a Phoenix Down has a chance of failing, whereas the X-Potion and Elixir do not.

TIMBER

1

Debrief in the Strategy Room, and then speak with Watts to go to Timber

2

Speak with the locals to locate the Pub

3

Defeat the Galbadian Soldiers outside the Pub

4

Assist the Pub's Owner by moving the Drifter

5

Go through the back alley to the TV Station

6

Meet up with Rinoa and follow her to the Pub Owner's home

7

Speak with Zone to get tickets for the train to Dollet

8

Board the train to Dollet, and get off at the East Academy Station

9

Pass through the small forest to the northwest

Enemies

Galbadian Soldier
Elite Soldier

Draw Points

Blizzaga (Timber Maniacs/Supply Room)
Cure (Outside Pub)
Scan (Back Alley)

Save Points

Timber Hotel
Back Alley
Train Platform (Hidden)

Magazines

Pet Pals Vol.3 (Pet Shop)
Pet Pals Vol.4 (Pet Shop)
Girl Next Door (Timber Maniacs/Magazine Stack)
Timber Maniacs (Timber Maniacs/Artist's Office)

MidMag-RF

If you haven't started using (or even learned) the **MidMag-RF** ability, it's time you did. Using this ability, you can take all of those Fire, Thunder, and Blizzard spells you've been stocking and refine them into **Fira**, **Thundara**, and **Blizzara** spells. Not only do these spells hit harder, they also boost a character's stats more than the basic level one spell does.

This is a particularly good time to refine these spells, because Timber is swarming with Galbadian Soldiers that carry the same types of magic.

Free Potion

Speak to the guy on the bridge that overlooks the train tracks and he'll eventually give you a free Potion. Any time you see him thereafter, he'll give you more free Potions as long as Rinoa or Quistis is in your party.

Magazines Galore

There are a lot of magazines to find in Timber. At the Pet Shop, you can purchase **Pet Pals Vol. 3 and 4**. At the Timber Maniacs office, it shouldn't be any surprise that you can find an

old copy of **Timber Maniacs** lying on the floor, but you may be a little shocked to find a copy of **"Girl Next Door"** hidden in the magazine stacks in the lobby. Make sure you get all four of these magazines; each one is worth it.

The Souvenir Shop

There's a small souvenir shop near the train to Balamb. Although the shop doesn't have much to offer, you should pay it a visit and speak to its owner. If your party needs to be healed, she can provide you with clues to the location of the infamous **Owl's Tears**. If you're lost, she can show you her "easy-to-read" map of Timber. She can also give you a bit of information about Zone's taste in reading materials, which may come in handy some day.

Owl's Tears

Since you can't stay at the local hotel, you'll need to find an alternate way to refresh your party. You can find the **Owl's Tears** at the small house next to the Dollet train station. The old man living inside will let you drink all you want, which is a good thing because the Owl's Tears completely restore your team's HP and

you can't stay at the hotel just yet. To get the Owl's Tears, simply go to the faucet on the left side of the room.

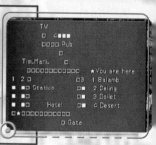

If you're really persistent, however, you can find **500 Gil** in the old man's cupboard. This is the old man's secret savings, so if you take it he won't let you have any more Owl's Tears. The choice is yours to make.

Moving the Drifter

There's a drifter blocking the Pub's back door, which subsequently blocks your progress. There are two ways to move the drifter: buy him a drink or give him one of his missing cards.

There are six drinks from which to choose, but the drifter only likes one of the six. Upon speaking with the woman at the bar, you learn that the drifter likes bitter drinks. Now observe the drifter to check out the drink he's currently holding. The following chart makes finding the correct drink a little easier:

	Red	Green	Yellow
Sweet	Mimett	Tantal	Curiel
Bitter	Krakka	Reagan	Sylkis

Answer: The drifter only likes Reagan; he'll turn down anything else. (By the way, you might remember the various drink names from *Final Fantasy VII*. These were the names given to the different greens you could feed a Chocobo.)

If you would rather not spend 100 Gil buying the drifter a drink, you can simply tell him about the **monster card** you found after the fight outside the Pub. He's so elated upon hearing this information that he moves out of the way. In addition, he lets you keep the card and gives you another card just for kicks!

Finding Galbadia Garden

Disembark from the train at the first stop, the East Academy, when you are given the option.

Looking directly to the northwest from the East Academy Station, you'll see a small wooded area set between two mountains. This is the wooded area everyone has been talking about. To reach Galbadia Garden, simply pass through the forest.

Enemies

Esthar Soldier (Human)
Esthar Soldier (Cyborg)
Gesper
Elastoid

Draw Points

Sleep (Entrance)
Confuse (Upper Level)
Cure (Second Level/Under Rock)

Save Points

Second Level/Second Crossroad

Enter the woods near Gabadia Garden

Battle the Esthar Sodliers

Find your way through the mysterious maze

Battle another set of Esthar Soldiers on the edge of a cliff

Upon entering the forest Squall, Quistis, and Selphie fall into another trance. Although Laguna has left Timber, his situation has not improved.

The Excavation Site

This area is comprised of a couple of large loops. Whenever you come to a crossroad, you'll typically want to take the path that leads off the top of the screen (unless you want to backtrack a bit).

This area is also spotted with various traps you can set for the Esthar Soldiers. However, keep in mind that when you set a trap, you're blocking your own way in that same direction. Make sure you thoroughly explore the area before choosing to set traps.

Blue Magic: Degenerator

While running around, you're bound to bump into a monster known as a Gesper. These bumbling cyborgs may not seem like much of a threat, but they have a killer attack called **Degenerator** that can eliminate a character, no matter how powerful, in a single hit. The plus side is that Gespers carry the **Black Hole** item, which they sometimes drop. With **Black Hole**, Quistis can learn the awesome Degenerator magic.

The Old Keys & Other Things

There are many things to find while exploring the excavation site. Some of these items might seem pointless, but you should take the time to seek them out nonetheless.

You can find two **Old Keys** scattered throughout the second level of the excavation site. You can't see either key on the ground, but if you search the ground in the right area they aren't too difficult to find. The first is located near the beginning of the lower level, close to the Confuse Draw Point. Climb down the ladder, and stay near the left-hand side as you walk down the tunnel. The second Old Key is at the first crossroad close to a pile of debris. You can't keep the keys; regardless of what you do, Laguna always happens to lose them. Don't bother looking around for them again, because they're gone for good.

In another area, you'll find three gray panels on the ground. Laguna can tamper with a lever from one of the panels to set a trap for the Esthar Soldiers. Once you pull the lever, you won't be able to cross the panels again.

Lastly, you'll find a detonation device lying on the ground near the area's end. The device is linked to a couple of nearby boulders. Push the red switch first, and then try the blue switch. This will cause the boulders to fall into a hole in the floor elsewhere. Don't mess the order up, or the boulders will only end up blocking Laguna's path.

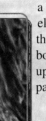

Beyond the detonation switch, you'll find a boulder stuck in the side of the wall. Move the boulder to reveal a Cure Draw Point.

Human or Cyborg

There are two types of Esthar Soldiers in the excavation site: Human and Cyborg. The human soldiers are wimps and are easily defeated. On the other hand, the Cyborgs are tough and extremely powerful.

You can differentiate between the two by their stance and color. Always eliminate the Cyborg soldiers first, because of the greater threat that they pose.

Soul Crush

In the last battle, Ward and Kiros are hit with an attack called **Soul Crush** that reduces their HP to one point each. When you return to the "normal world," make sure you heal Quistis and Selphie (especially if both are currently in your party) because if they only have one HP each, they may be skirting death in the next battle.

GALBADIA GARDEN

Outside Enemies

Plains
Belhelmel
Geezard
Blood Soul

Forests
Wendigo
Ochu
Anacondaur
Funguar
Cockatrice

Draw Points

Haste (Unseen; Center Hall)
Double (Hidden; Auditorium)
Shell (Athletic Track)
Life (Locker Room)

Save Points

Center Hall
Second Floor Center Hall
Back Hall

1 Find Galbadia Garden beyond the forest

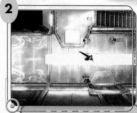

2 Enter the Garden and locate the 2nd floor reception room

3 Speak with everyone until Squall leaves the room

4 Return to the Center Hall and speak with Fujin and Raijin

5 Go to the Front Gate and find Quistis

6 Meet the rest of the party at the Front Gate

7 Talk to Headmaster Martine and Irvine will join the party

8 Go to Galbadia Station and catch the train to Deling City

Power Up!

The forest you passed through to reach Galbadian Garden is a great place to build experience. Most of the monsters in this area (especially the rare Ochu) are worth a lot of Exp and AP—almost as much as the T-Rexaurs from the beginning of the game. This is especially helpful if you're trying to build up Diablos' Mug ability, which requires 200 AP.

Where's the Reception Room?

Upon entering Galbadia Garden, just keep walking forward until you find a hall with several people undergoing forced exercise. Notice the staircase behind them? The Reception Room is at the top of the stairs.

Level 6 Boss Cards

If you have the patience to play a lot, you can win the entire set of Level 6 Boss cards from one person in Galbadia Garden.

There are three people inside a classroom off the east branch of the center path talking about cards. The female of the group has a complete set of the Level 6 Bosses. Of course, getting them all is no small task. She's quite an accomplished player, possessing the best deck you've encountered thus far.

Irvine's Limit Break

Typically, Irvine doesn't need special ammunition to use his gun. However, his Limit Break requires the use of special ammunition that can be bought or refined from items.

Initially, you'll probably have two types of ammunition: Normal Ammo and Shotgun Ammo. The type of ammunition used determines the effectiveness of the attack. Normal Ammo hits a single target, while Shotgun Ammo attacks all targets on-screen. You can buy both types of ammo from town shops.

During Irvine's Limit Break, you must fiercely press the R1 button to shoot as many times as possible in the allotted time. You may go through 10 rounds of ammunition each time, so it's important to have plenty of ammo on hand. If you don't plan wisely, Irvine's Limit Break might get cut short.

Hop the Train

In order to get anywhere, you must board the train at the Far East Galbadia Train Station located southwest of Galbadia Garden. There's a vehicle blocking the tracks, but it will leave when you board the train.

Enemies

(Outside)
Thrustaevis
Wendigo
Geezard

Draw Points
Thundara (City Square)

Save Points
Galbadia Hotel Lobby

Magazines
Timber Maniacs (Galbadia Hotel/Under Bed)

1

Exit the train and ride the escalators up to the streets of Deling City

2

Ride a bus to Caraway's Mansion

3

"Your objective is to go to the [Tomb of the Unknown King], look for traces of this lost student, and return with his ID number."

Speak with the guard outside Caraway's Mansion to get your next assignment

4

Exit the city and head for the Tomb of the Unknown King

Time to Upgrade?

Stole 2 [Steel Pipes]

By now, you may have the option to begin remodeling your characters' weapons. To get the necessary items, you can refine cards into items. For example, you can refine an Elastoid card, which you may have picked up during Laguna's last adventure, into a Steel Pipe. The Steel Pipe is a necessary item for remodeling Squall's Gunblade and Irvine's shotgun. You can also get **Saw Blades** from Belhelmels, which are necessary to remodel Rinoa's weapon to the **Rising Sun**.

Also, if you have the **Mug** ability, you can steal all of the Steel Pipes you need from Wendigos, which can be found around Deling City.

Transportation

Deling City has a great public transportation system. Speak with the blue-clad attendants to hop onto a bus when it arrives. The bus will then circle the city.

If you have trouble finding **Caraway's Mansion**, just hop on the bus in front of the Train Station and get off the bus at the very first stop.

Caraway's Quest

The guard outside of Caraway's Mansion asks you to retrieve a code number from the **Tomb of the Unknown King**. Fortunately, Caraway was nice enough to supply you with a map. You can also purchase a "current location displayer" for 5,000 Gil. This item shows exactly where you are on the tomb map. It helps a little bit, but you don't really need it. Also, make sure you reject the guard's offer to supply you with a hint—this quest isn't tough.

Caraway's Guard
"The [Tomb of the Unknown King] to the northeast."

TOMB OF THE UNKNOWN KING

1

Find the Tomb of the Unknown King

2

Locate the blue sword and get the missing student's I.D. No.

3

Battle Sacred

4

Open the floodgate

5

Lower the drawbridge

6

Enter the central structure

7

Defeat Sacred and Minotaur

8
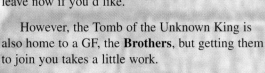
Return to Deling City

Enemies

Armadodo
Blobra
Buel

Outside

Thrustaevis
Funguar

Draw Points

Protect (Entrance)
Float (Dam Room)
Cura (Hidden; Bridge Control Room)

Save Points

Entrance
Sacred's Chamber (Hidden)
Bridge Control Room (Hidden)

Finding the Tomb

There's a long peninsula northeast of Deling City. At the very end of the peninsula is the Tomb of the Unknown King, which you won't be able to see from Deling City. It's a long walk, so you might want to rent a car.

The Code Number

At the first intersection you reach inside the tomb, you'll see a sword with a blue hilt lying on the ground. Upon inspecting the sword, you'll receive a random **Student ID No.** This is the Code Number you're looking for, so you can leave now if you'd like.

However, the Tomb of the Unknown King is also home to a GF, the **Brothers**, but getting them to join you takes a little work.

Finding Your Way

The layout of the tomb is simple, but it can be very confusing until you get your bearings straight. What makes this area so confusing is that, unlike other maps, when you enter a new screen the perspective is always over Squall's shoulder. This really doesn't present a problem until you start to backtrack and forget that left is now right and right is now left.

A simple strategy to follow is to go to the right at every intersection. By doing so, you stay on the outer loop and you can hit all of the rooms along the outside in the proper order. Also, following this route will eventually return you back to the entrance.

What to Do Inside

After finding the Code Number, you have the optional challenge of finding the Brothers and defeating them. This task requires that you take several steps. First, you must find Sacred and defeat it, which causes it to run away. This also opens up the other two rooms on the outer ring of the maze, which you must locate next and flip two switches. Flipping one switch opens a dam, while the other switch lowers a bridge that you can't see just yet. This enables you to gain access to the center of the maze.

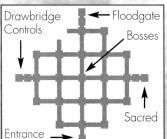
Drawbridge Controls — Floodgate
Bosses
Sacred
Entrance

To get there, return to the entrance and then head straight into the center of the maze to find the bridge you lowered earlier. Inside the center room you'll fight the Brothers, so make sure you save first.

GUARDIAN FORCE ALERT!

Sacred

HP	855~36,375	AP	20
EXP	--	Weak vs Poison & Wind/ Immune to Earth	--

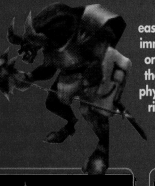

The fight against Sacred is easy. Use Sacred's Protect magic immediately and cast it on everyone in your party. This will reduce the effect of Sacred's powerful physical attacks. Sacred also carries the Life spell, so make sure you stock up on it as much as possible. The Life spell is very important to have during battles, plus it Junctions really well.

Casting Float on this Boss will cut off its regenerating HP. This effect doesn't last long, so you may have to cast Float several times during the battle. After the initial prep work, continue to recast Protect whenever necessary and whittle away at the Boss' HP with GFs and physical attacks until Sacred runs away.

GUARDIAN FORCE ALERT!

Sacred	GF	HP	855~36,375	AP	20	– –
		EXP	– –	Weak vs Poison & Wind/ Immune to Earth		

Minotaur	GF	HP	578~27,218	AP	20	– –
		EXP	– –	Weak vs Wind & Poison/ Absorbs Earth		

If you don't have a healthy supply of Float spells, this could turn out to be a long, hard battle. Float serves two purposes in this battle: 1. When cast on both Bosses, it eliminates their HP regeneration ability as long as the spell lasts; 2. It protects your party from the devastating Mad Cow Special when cast on your party members. This works because Sacred and Minotaur are both Earth Elementals. When they are in contact with the ground, the earth slowly restores their HP. However, if you pick them up off the ground, they no longer have that advantage. The Mad Cow Special is also an Earth-based attack. Therefore, if the party isn't touching the ground, the attack passes harmlessly below them.

Physical attacks work well in this battle, but you'll make quicker work of each Boss by using boosted GF attacks. If you decide to work on each Boss individually, you should focus on Minotaur, because its attacks are much stronger. Winning this Boss fight gets you the Sacred Card and the Minotaur Card, plus you can now Junction with the Brothers GF from this point forward.

HP Boost

Between Deling City and the Tomb of the Unknown King, you'll come across some nasty birds called Thrustaevises. Depending on this creature's level, it may have the **Tornado** spell in its drawable inventory. Tornado junctions really well to just about any stat, but at this point it's best used to boost everyone's HP. If the Thrustaevises in the area don't have the Tornado spell (due to its current level), you can steal **Windmills** from them, which can be refined into 20 Tornado spells each.

Enemies

Outside
Thrustaevis
Wendigo
Geezard

Sewers
Creeps
Red Bat
Grand Mantis

Draw Points

Thundara (City Square)
Esuna (Sewers)
Zombie (Sewers)
Bio (Hidden; Sewers)

Save Points

Galbadia Hotel Lobby
Caraway's Mansion
Outside Presidential Residence
Sewers (Entrance/Exit)

Magazines

Timber Maniacs (Galbadia Hotel/Under Bed)
Weapons Monthly May Issue (Sewers)

1 Return to Caraway's Mansion and give the I.D. No. to the guard

2 Enter the Mansion and speak with General Caraway

3 Tour the city and get the details for the mission to come

4 Return to the mansion and split into two groups: Sniper Team and Gateway Team

5 Move both teams to their designated areas

6 Take the Gateway Team back to Caraway's Mansion

7 Have Rinoa climb the stacked boxes and find the way inside the Presidential Residence

8 Find a way for the Gateway Team to escape from Caraway's Mansion

9 Take Squall and Irvine into the Presidential Residence

10 Find Rinoa and save her from the Iguions

11 Locate the hatch leading to the clock tower and prepare for the attack

12 Get the Gateway Team through the sewers and throw the switch at the top of the gateway arch

13 Approach the Sorceresses' float and defeat her

Got the Code?

When you return to Deling City, you should immediately head for Caraway's Mansion with the Code Number from the Tomb of the Unknown King.

The way you input the code is unique, so pay attention. You must give the "ones" first, "tens" second, and "hundreds" third (if necessary). For example, if the code is 135, you would enter the 5, then the 3, and finally the 1.

Weapons Monthly

When either Rinoa or Squall and Irvine are placed at the base of the Presidential Residence, you can access a manhole leading into the sewers before climbing the stacked boxes. Follow the path to its end to find the **May issue of Weapons Monthly** (Weapons Mon May).

Switching Around

You'll do a lot of switching between parties during this part of the game. Also, don't forget to switch Junctions each time—you don't want to leave anyone defenseless!

Exiting the Mansion

There's only one way out of Caraway's trap and you must find it. There is one small clue. Check out the painting hanging on the wall. Everything you need to know is right there before you. If you still can't figure it out, check out the section called **"The Answer"** at the end of this section (see pg. 62). Otherwise, do your best to solve this puzzle on your own.

Also, take some time to talk to Zell and Selphie as they explore the room. Their comments are meant to assist you and to make you laugh.

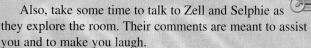

Getting Through the Sewers

You'll spend a fair amount of time below Deling City, and getting around isn't easy. There are a lot of locked gates and dead ends along the way. However, you should check every gate to make absolutely sure you can't go through.

If you can't figure out where to go, you can also use the water wheels to go up or down a level. Just stand in front of one and press the ⚪ button to grab hold. Keep in mind, though, that the water wheels are a one-way ride, so there's no going back.

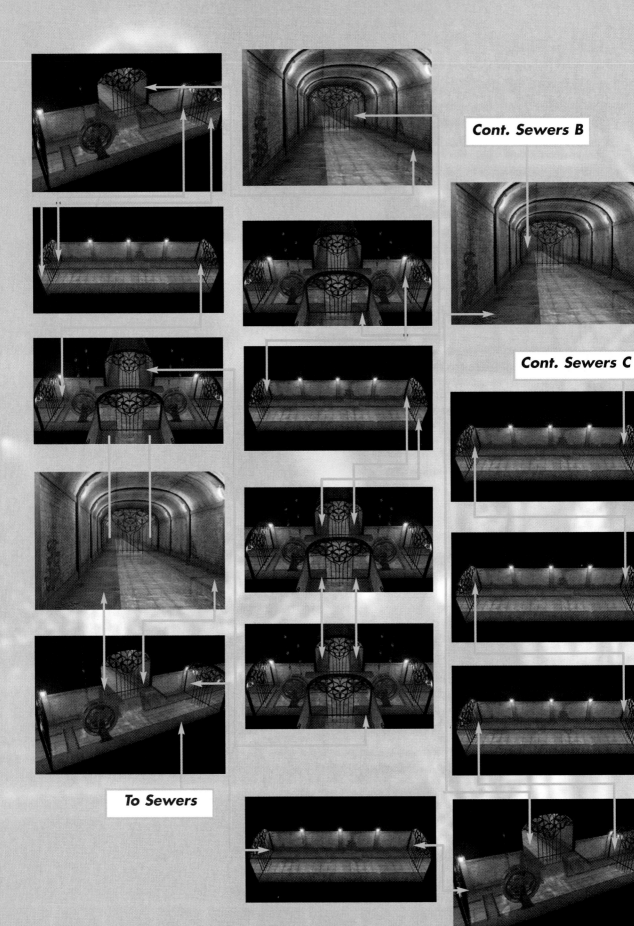

Cont. Sewers B

Cont. Sewers C

To Sewers

Blue Magics: Lvl? Death & Electrocute

You can find two more Blue Magics in the sewers below Deling City. Keep your eye out for a creature called Creeps. At Levels 20 to 29, Creeps carry the **Curse Spike** item, which teaches Quistis the **Lvl? Death** magic. You'll have other opportunities to get a Curse Spike later in the game, but this is your first opportunity. Also, you can steal **Coral Fragments** from Creeps. Coral Fragments can teach Quistis the **Electrocute Blue Magic**.

GUARDIAN FORCE ALERT!

Iguions

	HP	127~1747	AP	10	
GF	EXP	— —	Weak vs Earth & Holy/ Immune to Fire & Poison		— —

To get this Boss fight off to a good start, you should draw the GF Carbuncle from either of the two Iguions. Don't miss this opportunity!!

The Iguions aren't tough. Neither one has much HP, so a strong GF can knock them out in a single shot. However, Ifrit is essentially worthless in this battle, because both Iguions are immune to Fire magic. If you have the Brothers GF, use it because the Iguions are weak against earth magic.

Watch out for the Iguions' Magma Breath. It causes a large amount of damage, and sometimes places a Stone curse spell on its victim. You can easily remove this effect by using Esuna, which you can draw from the Bosses.

If Squall and Irvine get turned to stone, it's game over! Also, make sure you stock up on the Break spell; it Junctions nicely and can turn enemies to stone.

Seifer

	HP	176~1150	AP	— —	
	EXP	— —	Weak vs Poison		— —

Apparently, Seifer hasn't been working on his fighting skills since he joined Edea. His physical attack is weak, unless he uses his Gunblade properly (which rarely happens).

Seifer's Fira spell is his strongest attack, but you can easily counter it by using your new GF Carbuncle if

Squall is equipped with it. If not, just summon your strongest GFs and Seifer will bow out of the fight soon enough.

Edea

HP	1300~7000	AP	20		--
EXP	--		\ --		

As you would expect, Edea uses a lot of magic—very strong magic at that. Fortunately, Rinoa and Irvine join Squall for this battle, so things should be much easier.

At the start, have the character equipped with Carbuncle summon the GF to cast Reflect on the entire party. Edea will counter this by casting Dispel, but the spell only affects one person at a time. Therefore, she usually ends up spending the next three actions using Dispel. Meanwhile have your other two characters summon GFs or use physical attacks while the third character immediately begins to summon Carbuncle again.

Although your third party member will never get to attack directly, that character's actions will ensure that Edea never gets to attack with anything more powerful than her Astral Punch once Carbuncle arrives the first time.

Edea carries very strong magic: Cura, Dispel, Double, and Life. Not only is this group of magic strong, but it junctions well to your stats. After casting Carbuncle, you may also want to draw from Edea to stock up on magic. Even if you lose this fight against Edea, you can progress further. However, losing the battle means missing out on 20 AP.

The Answer

To escape Caraway's trap, you must take a glass from the shelves near the door. As the painting suggests, place the glass in the statue's hands. Upon doing so, a secret passage opens that leads to the sewers below Deling City.

WINHILL

1

Kiros
"You seem well."

Visit the Pub and talk to Kiros

2

Follow the road to the Item Shop

3

Laguna
"Including Buchubuchus and Bunbuns that Assistant Commander Ellone oh-so-hates..."

Return to the Pub and speak with Raine

4

Laguna
"Time for a little break..."
(Rest)
(Keep working)

Take a nap in Laguna's bed

Enemies

Caterchipillar
Bite Bug

Draw Points

Curaga (Laguna's bed-room—Hidden)
Dispel (Boat Dock)
Drain (Road)
Reflect (Road—Hidden)

Save Points

Laguna's bedroom

Shop

Item Shop

Laguna's Job

Leave the Pub and head down across the bridge. Follow the road straight through to the end of the town to the Item Shop. Laguna's job is to defeat any monsters he finds in the village. After completing the first patrol, return to the Pub, go up to the second floor, and report your progress to Raine. Return to Laguna's room to rest.

Kiros 3681
Laguna 474

Bonus Gil

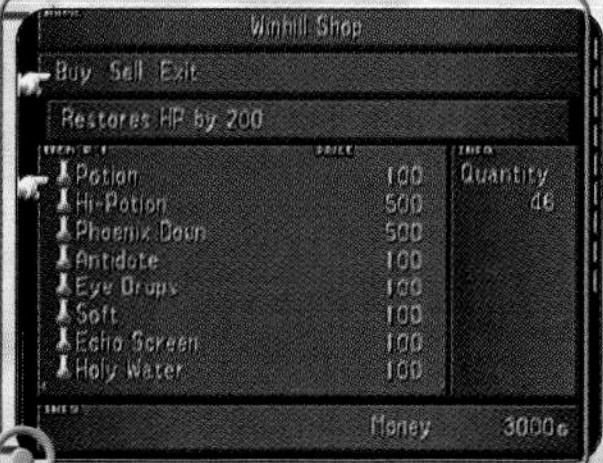

Notice that Laguna has 3000 Gil on him. You can spend the money on items at the item shop. Anything purchased is added to your inventory, so Squall will have access to it later. However, you can't add the 3000 Gil to Squall's stash.

Winhill Shop
Buy Sell Exit
Restores HP by 200
Potion   100   Quantity
Hi-Potion   500   46
Phoenix Down   500
Antidote   100
Eye Drops   100
Soft   100
Echo Screen   100
Holy Water   100
                Money   3000G

D-DISTRICT PRISON

Enemies

Wendigo
GIM47N
GIM52A
Guard
Thrustaevis
Geezard
Belhelmel
Elite Soldier

(Outside)
Blood Soul
Belhelmel
Geezard

(Beaches)
Fastitocalon-F's
Righty
Lefty

Draw Points

Berserk (9th Floor Cell)
Thundaga (11th Floor Cell)

Items

Str Up (2nd Floor Cell)
Pet Nametag
(2nd Floor Cell)
Tent (4th Floor Cell)
Pet House (3rd Floor Cell)

Save Points

1st Floor Cell (Hidden)
6th Floor Cell
10th Floor Cell
Large Control Room
(Hidden)

Magazines

Combat King 001
(1st Floor Cell)

Shops

Item Shop (Man from
Garden, 8th Floor Cell)

As Zell go up to the 8th floor and retrieve the party's weapons

Battle Biggs and Wedge to break out of the cell

Follow the Moombas up to the 13th floor and rescue Squall

Use the elevator by pressing the red button on the control panel

Rescue Zell from the Prison Guards

Split into two parties and take Squall's party to the top of the prison

Take Irvine's party to the 3rd floor

Exit the top of the prison and defeat the remaining Guards

Help Squall safely cross the collapsing bridge

Split into two teams: one headed to Balamb Garden and one headed to the Missile Base

Steal the Galbadian train and head for Balamb

Drive the stolen vehicle along the road to the Missile Base south of Deling City

Retrieving the Weapons

As you begin, make sure you Junction Zell with GFs and some magic. You may need to switch Junctioned abilities with another character using the Switch option. The halls are full of enemies, and you don't want to get caught unprepared. The party's weapons are being held on the floor above (the 8th Floor) by two guards. After defeating them, Zell will return the weapons to their rightful owners.

Blue Magic: Micro Missile

One of the robotic guards inside the prison is the GIM52A. This robotic fiend uses the Micro Missile attack, which Quistis can also use providing she finds the right item, the **Missile**. You can steal a Missile from a GIM52A, or you can hope one will be dropped after a battle with one of the robots.

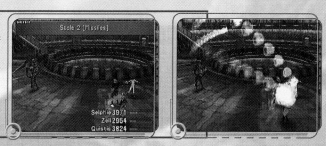

Biggs	HP	1467~2235	AP	10	--
	EXP	--	--	

Wedge	HP	1416~2139	AP	--	--
	EXP	--	*Immune to Poison*	

Biggs and Wedge are a bit tougher than they were during the fight on the Dollet Communications Tower, but not by much. You can easily finish them off with a couple of strong GFs, but don't neglect to stock up on Reflect and Regen before the battle is won. Also, if you have the Mug ability, you should steal from them since they're carrying good items.

If you want to have a little fun, try casting Zombie on both Biggs and Wedge. You can then instantly kill them by using a couple of Phoenix Downs or Life spells. However, it's more fun to cast Regen on both of the "Zombied" Bosses, which acts like poison. You can also speed up the effect by casting Haste on them. As noted earlier, this is an easy fight, so don't be afraid to goof around a little.

Another fun trick is to cast Confuse on either character. If Wedge is confused and attacks Biggs, Biggs will immediately counterattack Wedge while yelling at him. If the attack is the other way around, Wedge will yell at Biggs to "Stop picking on me."

Special Card Games

On your way up the floors to save Squall, there are several prisoners who will play cards with you—but at a price. Fortunately, however, each one has an item to give you if you win. On the 5th and 11th Floors, you'll find prisoners who will give you a random item if you can defeat them. The person on the 5th Floor charges 500 Gil per game, while the person on the 11th Floor charges 200 Gil per game. The items you'll receive vary from a **Potion** to much better items like an **HP Up**.

A prisoner on the 10th Floor has a better prize for 300 Gil. Defeat this prisoner and you'll receive an upgrade for your Battle Meter called the **Character Report**. This gives you specific information on each of your characters, so you can see which character you're using the most and who's fought the best. Access the Character Report using the Information headings under the Tutorial section of the Main Menu.

Check All Cells

The prison is full of items for you to pick up. Once the alarms sound, nearly every cell is unlocked. Check behind every door to find useful items, card playing inmates, Draw Points, and Save Points. However, you must be careful while exploring, because the halls are full of monsters and Galbadian guards.

Oomba Moombas

Depending on the selections you make when a choice is given, several Moombas may appear out of nowhere to help you in various ways. A couple of Moombas will give you valuable items. Other Moombas will offer to create a shortcut for you on one of the prison floors. What this does is remove the barrier in between the staircases so that you don't have to go all the way around the perimeter. So how do you get the Moombas to appear? When given a choice, stand your ground, be brave, and fight for what is just. If you lack courage, lie, or submit to authority, the Moombas won't appear.

The Lift

After leaving the Torture Room, press the red button on the lift's control panel when Zell instructs you to do so. When the control room reaches the bottom level, head to the right through the doorway. Continue forward until you reach another doorway, and press the ⊘ button to cause the doorway to implode.

Elite Soldier	HP	148~4940	AP	2	— —
	EXP	30 (+5)		Weak vs Poison	

GIM52As	HP	1431~19400	AP	3	— —
	EXP	30 (+8)		Immune to Poison	

All of the fights you faced while pushing your way through the prison should have prepared you for this dangerous battle. The Elite Soldier acts as support for the two GIM52As, which makes eliminating the Elite Soldier your top priority. With their leader out of the way, it's just a matter of dealing with the GIM52As and any support magic cast on them.

Use Dispel magic (which you can draw from the GIM52As) to remove any support magic like Protect that the Elite Soldier might have cast on them. Then hit both GIM52As hard with Thunder magic and Quezacotl.

A Narrow Escape

After the Boss fight, and when you find Squall hanging from the bridge, you need to hold right on the directional button to guide him to safety. If you fail, it's Game Over!

GALBADIA MISSILE BASE

1 Use an ID Card on the left door to enter the base

2 Speak with the Maintenance Soldiers on the Observation Deck

3 Speak with the Maintenance Soldier in the Missile Launch Bay

4 Return to the Maintenance Soldiers on the Observation Deck

5 Disable the terminal in the circuit room to cause a blackout

6 Assist with pushing the Missile Launcher into place

NOTE

Upon exiting the circuit room, keep your cool and be cooperative with the soldiers. If you make it into the Missile Launch Bay without getting caught, continue to follow the remainder of the objectives. If you do get caught, refer to the text under the section entitled "Busted!"

7 Alter the Error Ratio on the Missile Control Panel

8 Fight the Command Leader in the Launch Control Room

9 Examine the three panels and disable the Missile Launch control panel

0 Set the self-destruct sequence

11 Exit the base

12 Defeat BGH251F2 (Boss)

Enemies

Command Soldier
Command Leader
Geezard
G-Soldier
Elite Soldier
SAM08G
BGH251F2 (Boss)

Draw Points

Full-Life (Missile Launcher Bay)
Blind (Observation Deck)
Blizzara (Circuit Room)

Save Points

Base Entrance
Outside Missile Launch Bay

Magazines

Weapons Mon Jun (defeat BGH251F2)

Getting Inside

There's a place to scan an ID Card between the two doors inside the first building. Don't worry about finding an ID Card. A member of your party will have found one inside the stolen vehicle earlier.

What To Do

Your goal is to sneak through the base and sabotage the missile launch. To do so, speak with all the soldiers scattered throughout the base and follow their orders. You'll get the chance to sabotage the terminal in the circuit room, alter the missiles' error ratio, disable the launch mechanism, and set the base to self-destruct.

Along the way, you'll have several options while talking to the soldiers. It's best to always play it cool so you can keep your identity a secret until you reach the Launch Control Room. By doing so, you can quietly go about the process of sabotaging the base.

Setting the Missiles Off Course

The Missile Control Panel is located next to the Missile Launch Bay's door. Inspect it and you'll be given a close-up view of the panel's screen. First, select "Target." Next, select "Set Error Ratio" and hold right on the directional button to set the Error Ratio to maximum. Select "Data Upload," and then select "Yes" to upload the data.

Control Panel Secret

You can toy around a bit with the Missile Control Panel. Choose to go to the Equipment inspection screen and you'll see the equipment used by the Galbadian Army. Hold down both the ⬤ and ⬤ buttons and press up or down on the control pad. The scene will switch to either a dancing Galbadian Soldier or Elite Soldier. Pretty strange stuff.

Setting the Time Limit

When setting the auto self-destruct mechanism, you're given the choice of 10 to 40 minutes. You should only need 10 minutes if you weren't found out. If you were found out, you shouldn't need more than 20 minutes. Choosing a time limit of 20 minutes or less enables you to use the door in the room with the self-destruct device. This door is a quick shortcut to the base's exit and much easier than backtracking through the base.

Busted!

If you get caught, you're forced to face random encounters inside the base and you won't be able to change the missiles' error ratio at first. Instead, you'll have to set the self-destruct mechanism and then fight your way back into the base while the self-destruct countdown continues. During this time, it helps to have Diablos' **Enc Half** or **Enc None** abilities to limit the random encounters you face. If you are forced into a random battle, you should immediately escape from it so as to limit the amount of time wasted.

To access the missiles' Control Panel, you must get an **ID Card** and a **password** from the downed Soldier next to the Launch Control Room stairs. The downed Soldier will only appear once you reach the base's entrance. Quickly return to the Control Panel, get the Soldier's ID and password ("EDEA"), and then access the Control Panel. Go to "Target," select "Set Error Ratio," and set it to maximum. Choose "Data Upload" and then exit the Control Panel. Upon exiting the base, you'll have a very short amount of time to fight the upcoming Boss.

Raising the SeeD Rank

You have two opportunities to increase your SeeD Rank in this event. First, get through this entire section without getting caught by the guards. Second, exit the base and defeat the Boss within 10 minutes.

BGH251F2

HP	4200~8400	AP	20	— —
EXP	— —		Immune to Poison	

BGH251F2 is a heavy-duty battle tank with extremely powerful attacks. However, as solid is it might look, it's weak against Thunder, Earth, and Water magic, which makes destroying it much easier.

To cut down on the damage caused by this Boss' attacks, you can draw Protect from it. However, if you're short on time, it's better to just hit the Boss hard with Quezacotl and other GFs (preferably not Brothers due to the length of the GF's animation). After destroying the Boss, the crew (two Galbadian Soldiers and an Elite Soldier) will remain behind to continue the fight. They're not powerful enemies, so finishing them off isn't difficult.

TRY AGAIN...
You will lose this battle and the game will end if: 1) The time expires while fighting the Boss; 2) Your party members are all defeated in the battle; 3) You did not set the Error Ratio to maximum on the Control Panel.

BALAMB GARDEN

Enemies

(Balamb Garden)
Grat
Caterchipillar
Bite Bug
Granaldo
Glacial Eye
Bomb
Grendel
T-Rexaur

(MD Levels)
Buel
Tri-Face
Blood Soul
Blobra
Oilboyle (Boss)

Draw Points
Cure (Front Gate)
Demi (Cafeteria—Hidden)
Blizzard (Training Center)
Esuna (Library)
Full-Life (MD Level)

Save Points
Squall's Room
Training Center
MD Level

Items
Mega Potion (Collapsed man outside Gate Booth)
X-Potion (SeeD at Quad)
Gysahl Greens (SeeD in Cafeteria)
Tent (SeeD in Parking Lot)
Remedy (SeeD in Training Center)
Mega Phoenix (SeeD Candidate in Library, with Zell)
Remedy (SeeD Candidate in Library, without Zell)

Shops
Item Shop (Man from Garden—Training Center)

1. Help the SeeDs in each area of Balamb Garden

2. Find Xu on the 2nd Floor

3. Speak with Cid in his office

4. Enter the MD Level

5. Defeat the Oilboyles

6. Start the ancient machinery

Finding Headmaster Cid

No one knows where Headmaster Cid is except Xu, but she's nowhere to be found. Before she appears, there's a series of tasks you must perform.

There are SeeDs fighting off monsters in each branch of Balamb Garden: Library, Training Center, Parking Lot, Dormitory, Cafeteria, Quad, and Infirmary. You must visit each area and help them out before Xu will appear near the elevator. You can then speak with her on the second floor. After finding her, she'll take you to see Cid.

Tip Make sure you speak with the SeeDs you assist. Most of them will give you an item.

An Old Friend

You'll find Nida, the other SeeD who graduated with Squall, in front of the Infirmary. Be sure you stop by to say hello.

Getting Around Underground

The following are a few tips to help you navigate the MD Level of Balamb Garden:

• The elevator controls don't work, so you'll have to find another way out. Check the floor to find an access panel that you can open.

• After exiting the elevator, you'll need to open a large hatch at the end of the hall.

• Use the large valve wheel to open the doors in the previous room. It takes a great deal of effort to move the wheel. See if you can tap the ● button fast enough to move it using just Squall. Exit the room and go down the new ladder.

• After climbing up the ladder and turning on the computer, you'll need to go down into the pit below. Look for a green light on a gate in the railing that leads to a ladder.

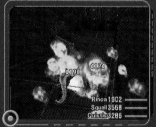

• There's a large lever next to the Save Point. Throw the lever to open the bay doors on the other side of the bridge. Head across the bridge to fight the Bosses, two Oilboyles, and then climb down the ladder at the bridge's end.

• All that's needed to start the large gears in motion is a couple of twists on the center column in the control panel. You can ignore all of the other parts.

Oilboyles

HP	1068	AP	20	
EXP	— —		*Weak vs. Ice/Absorbs Fire*	— —

The Oilboyles have one major weakness: Fire. With this knowledge in hand, you can finish this battle quickly by summoning Ifrit a couple of times (once if Ifrit is beefed up). It also helps if you took Squall's advice earlier and equipped everyone with the Elem-Atk-J ability with Fire, Fira, or Firaga.

The only thing you really need to worry about are the different status attacks the Oilboyles cast. If a character gets hit with an abnormal status effect, simply draw the Esuna spell from an Oilboyle and cast it on the affected party member.

Enemies

NORG (Boss)

Draw Point

Bio (NORG Pod—Hidden)

1 Go to the 2nd Floor deck

2 Return to Cid's Office

3 Awaken in Dormitory and head for the Directory

4 Head for the Basement and confront NORG

5 Visit Cid in the Infirmary

6 Speak with Xu near the Directory

7 Go to the 2nd Floor deck and meet White SeeDs

8 Find Ellone in the Library

NORG

HP	4400~12200	AP	20
EXP	— —		Weak vs. Wind/Immune to Posison

NORG's vast wealth has afforded him a virtual fortress known as the NORG Pod. The Garden Master locks himself inside the pod, and uses the pod's left and right Orbs to cast a variety of magic at his foes. The trick to fighting the NORG Pod is to balance the acts of attacking the central door where NORG is hiding, and attacking the Orbs so that NORG can't use the Pod's magic. The Pods shift colors to show their readiness. Blue signifies the least ready, yellow means the Pod is warming up, while Red signals that the Orb is ready to cast magic. By attacking the Orbs, you can force them to shift back one or two colors. By following this tactic, you can essentially keep them from ever casting magic as long as you're willing to dedicate a couple of characters to attacking them.

GUARDIAN FORCE ALERT!

NORG (Cont.) GF

HP	4400~12,200	AP	20		--
EXP	--		Weak vs Wind/ Immune to Poison		

There are two ways to go about this fight. The slower approach is to have two of your characters focus on attacking the NORG Orbs so that they're constantly a blue color. Meanwhile, have the third character focus on the NORG Pod and, later, NORG. A faster way is to summon the GF Carbuncle at the beginning of the battle. Carbuncle's Reflect spell will protect the party from most of the magic the Left Orb uses and from some of NORG's magic. One of your characters should then focus on attacking the Right Orb. The Right Orb uses Dispel magic to remove the Reflect spell from your characters, so you must keep it at blue or yellow to avoid having to constantly summon Carbuncle. The other two characters can then focus on the NORG Pod and NORG.

Most GFs work really well in this battle. They won't inflict much damage to the Pods, but NORG is weak defensively without his NORG Pod for protection. Also, make sure you use the Mug ability if you have it. NORG and the two Orbs have rare items ripe for plunder. Last, but certainly not least, make sure you draw the Leviathan GF from NORG. You don't want to miss this awesome GF!

Hidden Draw Point

After the battle with NORG, you can draw **Bio** from the wreckage. By standing in front of the wreckage, you can see a Draw Point hidden in the ball of light. You don't need to be close to the Draw Point; just stand with Squall's toes against the very front of NORG's Pod and use the Draw Point normally.

Enemies

SAM08G
GIM47N
Elite Soldier
BGH251F2 (Boss)
Galbadian Soldier

Draw Points

Full-Life (Crane Arm with
    Old Fisherman—Hidden)
Regen (Train Tracks)
Shell (FH Junk Shop)
Haste (Train Station)
Ultima (Mayor Dobe's
    House—Unseen)

Save Points

Train Tracks

Rare Cards

Quezacotl (Mayor Dobe)
Seifer (Cid)

Magazines

Timber Maniacs (Grease
    Monkey's House/on floor)
Timber Maniacs (FH Hotel/
    Magazines in room)
Occult Fan III (Master Fisherman/
    Below Garden)

1

2

3

Visit the Mayor's house

Follow the train tracks
through the town to the
Train Station

Defeat BGH251F2 (Boss)

4

Return to Balamb Garden

Battle Cid

If you didn't get the **Seifer Card** from Cid earlier in the game, this is your chance. Speak with him after he gives Squall his orders and Cid will play cards, albeit hesitantly.

Occult Fan III

On the path below the one leading to Balamb Garden's observation deck you'll find a Master Fisherman. Speak with him and when you get the opportunity select, "What are you talking about?" and he'll reward you with a copy of Occult Fan III.

Quezacotl Card & Martine

After speaking with the Mayor, why not challenge him to a game of cards? If you're lucky, you can win the **Quezacotl GF Card** from him. Also, check to the right of the Mayor's house to find Martine, the Headmaster of Galbadia Garden you met earlier. He's an excellent card player and has all of the **Level 7 Boss Cards** at his disposal. You can try to win them all, if you have the patience!

Blue Magic: Gatling Gun

On your way to the train station during the attack, you'll most likely run into a SAM08G enemy. Steal an item called **Running Fire** from one of these nasty looking robots and you'll be able to teach Quistis the **Gatling Gun Blue Magic**.

BGH251F2

HP	5100~7800	AP	20	
EXP	— —		Weak vs Thunder, Water, & Earth/ Immune to Poison	— —

BGH251F2 somehow managed to survive the explosion of the Missile Base and has made its way here. This Boss is already badly beaten up, but it's still a threat. Handle it the same way you did in the previous fight: strong Thunder based magic, Quezacotl, and physical attacks.

Also, make sure you use the Mug ability to steal a piece of Adamantine from BGF251F2. It may not have an immediate use, but it will come in handy later when you remodel your weapons.

The Master Fisherman

When you first enter FH, you should drop down below the path connecting FH to Balamb Garden and find the Master Fisherman. He'll give you a copy of **Occult Fan III**, and then ask you to meet him at the Inn later. Comply with his request, and you'll learn a lot more about FH and the people in it. Also, you'll receive a **Megalixir** if you stick around to hear his entire story. You must visit the Master Fisherman when you first arrive at FH. Otherwise he'll disappear and you'll miss your chance to meet him.

The Long Lost Son

After fighting BGH251F2, leave the Train Station area and then return there again. New people will now be in the area, including a person you may have heard of if you've been talking to everyone. The man on the left side of the area is the son of one of the cafeteria workers back at Balamb Garden. Speak with him and convince him to return to Balamb Garden.

1

Visit Selphie at the Quad

2

Talk to Cid on the Bridge

3

Go to the Mayor's House

4

Explore to the right of the stage and examine the magazine on the ground

5

Make your way back to the Bridge

6

Pilot Balamb Garden north to Balamb

Choosing Instruments

Before the big show can begin, you must assign instruments to Quistis, Selphie, Irvine, and Zell. Before choosing one for Zell, you should have him play all eight parts to get an idea of what each piece sounds like. After hearing them all, try to put together a score that sounds good to you. The two best match-ups are as follows:

Irish Jig	Slow Dance
Guitar	Sax
Violin	Electric Guitar
Flute	Piano
Tap	Bass Guitar

BALAMB

1 "You guys look suspicious. What are you doing here?"

Talk your way past the guard

2 Zell "Ma, you're safe!"

Visit Zell's house and talk to Ma Dincht

3 Galbadian Soldier "Have some respect for the captain! The captain is currently on patrol!"

Go to the Hotel to see the Commander

4 Galbadian Soldier "Oh, the captain? Yeah, he was just fishing here."

Talk to the Soldier next to the dog at the dock

5 Ma Dincht "Just now, a man came in and asked if he could use the kitchen..."

Check Zell's house for the Captain

6 Station Staff "Don't look at me! An important-looking Galbadian man came and ordered the soldiers some time."

Look for the Captain at the Train Station

7 Talk to the dog on the dock

8 Follow the dog back to the Train Station

9 "I was patrolin', just like you told me. I even look up that search dog, sleepin' on the job, ya know?!"

Chase Raijin back to the Hotel

10 Fight Raijin and Fujin

11 Selphie "Um... Can we maybe go to Trabia Garden?"

Pilot Balamb Garden northeast to Trabia Garden.

Enemies

G-Soldier
Fujin (Boss)
Raijin (Boss)

Draw Points

Cure (Dock)
Thunder (Town Square)

Save Points

Zell's room

Magazine

Combat King 002
(defeat Fujin & Raijin)

Rare Cards

Zell (Zell's Mom—Zell must be in your party)

Shops

Item Shop
Junk Shop

Disembarking

When you arrive at Balamb, pilot Balamb Garden onto the beach and then park anywhere on the island where there aren't any trees. (To disembark, press the ⬤ button.) You can't enter Balamb through the port, so don't even bother trying. Once you're ready to board Balamb Garden, walk up next to it and press the ⬤ button to get back inside.

Leaving Town

If you want to leave the town before you liberate it, you can do so by helping out the **Big Bad Rascal**. While visiting Zell's mother, speak with him and he'll leave the house. Then visit the neighbors next door to find him consoling the Hotel Owner's daughter. He will then head to the town entrance to check on the Hotel Owner and his wife. You can assist him by causing a

distraction. Talk to the guard while he talks to the Hotel Owner, and then meet him back in town. After expressing his appreciation for your assistance, he will offer to cause a distraction for you if you ever need to get out of town.

Zell's Room

Since you can't stay at the hotel, Zell will finally cave in and let you visit his room. All you need to do is try to go up the stairs in his house.

You can get a special reaction from each party member the first time you visit Zell's room. Also, make sure that you check out his punching bag.

The Search for the Captain

The Captain is difficult to find because he moves around so much; however, he's left a long line of clues for you to follow. After finding Ma Dincht and speaking with the guards at the Hotel, you can begin your search. Follow the line of clues in this order:

- The Dock

- Zell's house

- Train Station

- The Dock

- Train Station

- The Hotel

Other Ways to Find the Captain

Besides tracking the Captain down using the various clues found around Balamb, you can also use two other tactics to locate him.

If you simply wait around for a really long time (15 minutes or so) and don't do anything, you can approach the hotel and the Captain will be back from his patrol. You can also talk to the dog on the dock, and it will lead you back to the hotel instead of the train station.

Another way is to locate the hidden reporter. Around the dock area, you'll find a reporter hiding underneath the vehicle closest to the screen. You can pay the reporter for clues to the Captain's whereabouts. The fee increases depending on the type of clue you desire (gold, silver, or bronze). If you purchase a "gold" clue, the reporter will lead you straight to the captain's current location.

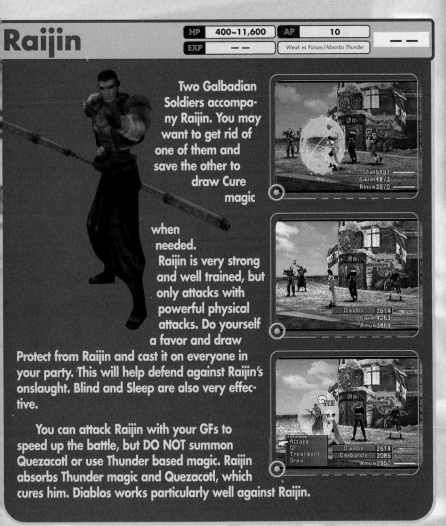

HP	400~11,600	AP	10	
EXP	— —		Weak vs Poison/Absorbs Thunder	— —

Raijin

Two Galbadian Soldiers accompany Raijin. You may want to get rid of one of them and save the other to draw Cure magic when needed.

Raijin is very strong and well trained, but only attacks with powerful physical attacks. Do yourself a favor and draw Protect from Raijin and cast it on everyone in your party. This will help defend against Raijin's onslaught. Blind and Sleep are also very effective.

You can attack Raijin with your GFs to speed up the battle, but DO NOT summon Quezacotl or use Thunder based magic. Raijin absorbs Thunder magic and Quezacotl, which cures him. Diablos works particularly well against Raijin.

GUARDIAN FORCE ALERT!

Fujin	GF	HP	300~8700	AP	10	– –
		EXP	– –		*Weak vs Poison/Absorbs Wind*	

Raijin		HP	5400~22,600	AP	12	– –
		EXP	– –		*Weak vs Poison/Absorbs Lightning*	

Raijin comes back strong for round two and his partner in crime, Fujin, joins in this time. Start off by drawing Protect from Raijin and casting it on your party. Also, make sure you immediately draw the Pandemona GF from Fujin. Although Fujin uses strong magic, resist the urge to summon Carbuncle during this battle, as Reflect will only work against you. Fujin's strongest spell passes right through Reflect, so all Reflect does is prevent you from healing your characters.

Raijin's HPs are less in this battle, but his attack power is much higher. He's also learned a new attack called the Raijin Special that typically causes around 800 points of damage if your characters aren't protected. This makes him the greater threat, so focus your assault on him. Fujin, on the other hand, has Cure magic, so you should try to keep her around, as you may need to draw it later in the battle.

If you mugged Raijin in the last battle, you should do so again. He has two more Str Up items ripe for the picking. Also, if you resort to magic or GFs, you should once again avoid using Quezacotl. Raijin still absorbs Thunder magic, and Fujin absorbs Wind magic, so avoid using spells such as Thunder and Aero.

NOTE If you accidentally have Thunder or Wind magic Junctioned to a character's attack, you can have that character draw magic from one enemy and use it on the other. For example, you can draw Aero from Fujin and cast it on Raijin, or you can draw Thunder from Raijin and cast it on Fujin. By using this tactic, you can avoid exhausting your own magic reserves.

TRABIA GARDEN

1 Talk to Selphie and her friend near the gargoyle statue

2 Wait for Selphie at the basketball court on the left side of Trabia Garden

3 Walk down to the beach

4 Pilot Balamb Garden to the Orphanage

Getting to Trabia Garden

Trabia Garden is on the large continent to the north of Balamb. To get there, you must pilot the Garden to a beach on the large continent and then

walk (or ride) through the mountains to Trabia Garden, which is well hidden by the mountain range. Use the in-game map feature in conjunction with the map shown here to help locate it.

Chocobo Forest

Just north of Trabia Garden you'll find the first of seven Chocobo Forests. These small, dome-shaped forests are where Chocobos live. Refer to the "Chocobos" section of this guide to find out exactly where it's at and how you can get your very own **Chocobo** and **Chicobo**.

Enemies

(Outside)
- Mesmerize
- Bite Bug
- Gayla
- Snow Lion

(Forests)
- Blue Dragon
- Bite Bug
- Snow Lion
- Gayla

Draw Points

- Thundaga (in front of statue)
- Zombie (Cemetery—Hidden)
- Aura (Festival Stage—Hidden))

Save Points

- Classroom

Rare Cards

- Selphie (Selphie's friend near gargoyle statue)

Magazine

- Weapons Mon Aug (in front of statue)
- Timber Maniacs (Cemetery)

Blue Magic: Acid

Outside of Trabia Garden, you'll find the Gayla monster. It carries **Mystery Fluid** (which it sometimes drops), or you can steal it from the beast. Either way, once you acquire a Mystery Fluid, you can teach Quistis the **Blue Magic, Acid**.

Hidden Treasure

Speak with the Trabia Garden student holding a book in the classroom to learn about a **hidden treasure**. The book says the treasure is buried five steps south of the gargoyle statue. The statue is back at the front gate. Stand in front of it, and walk approximately five steps forward and search the ground. You'll find the **August issue of Weapons Monthly**.

Optional Side Quests!!

You've come to a point in the game where you can opt to continue with the main story, or take a moment to complete a few Side Quests. Optional events (a.k.a. Side Quests) enable you to find new GFs and powerful items that you normally wouldn't find, but they do require you to turn your attention away from your main objectives for a bit. If you're curious about what you can do now, flip to the "Side Quests" (see p. 166) section of this book and check out the Shumi Village, Winhill, and Centra Ruins events, to name a few.

1

Head for Edea's House

2

Board Balamb Garden and head for Galbadia Garden

3

Form a party and head for the Quad

4

Return to the bridge

5

Take Zell's party into the Quad

6

Find Squall at the Front Gate

7

Fight off soldiers in the 2nd Floor Classroom

8

Return to the bridge to see Dr. Kadowaki

9

Go to the second floor Observation Deck

10

Battle the Galbadian Paratrooper

Enemies

GIM52A
Paratrooper
Elite Soldier
Galbadian Soldier

Finding the Orphanage

Edea's House is far to the south at the very tip of the Centra continent on the Cape of Good Hope. To find it, simply circle the southernmost continent until you find a peninsula with a lighthouse and a small white building. You can inspect the building when you get there, but you can't go inside.

The Hovering Ship

To the northeast of Edea's House, you'll see a large hovering ship. This is actually Galbadia Garden, which has been transformed in the same style as Balamb Garden. Save your game and then board Balamb Garden. Head straight for Galbadia Garden to initiate an encounter.

Giving Orders

If you give too many orders, or forget to give a crucial order, Nida will scold Squall. To avoid this from happening, stick to the basics: preparing for the attack, defending Balamb Garden, and taking care of the junior classmen. If you want, go ahead and throw in a few more. The comment about the hot dogs is worth choosing!

Free Item

Make sure you check on everyone on the second floor of the Garden. Squall will order those standing around to get to their positions. However, one student, on the second floor, will give you a useful item—a **Cottage**.

Shifting Characters

Once again, you'll be shifting between characters as you did in Deling City. Make sure you use the Switch command, and then Junction your GFs and magic each time to your other party members to avoid leaving a party member undefended.

Easy Victory

The Garden is full of Galbadia's best machines and soldiers. You can easily defeat these enemies by Junctioning **Death** as a Status-Attack Junction and **Thunder** as an Elemental-Attack Junction. The Death Junction will kill most soldiers in a single hit. The Thunder Junction will increase the damage inflicted to most machines.

Squall's Battle

When an opposing soldier pins down Squall, don't try to run and don't threaten the enemy. Doing so will only cause an injury to Squall. Instead, choose to **"Look around for another option"** and examine the Emergency Exit door and select the option to **"Press the button for the emergency exit."**

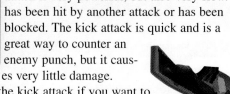

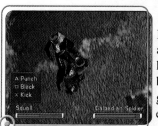

Once you're in the battle, you have four controls. The normal three are Punch (button), Block (button), and Kick (button). The punch attack is very powerful, but also very slow. You should only use it when the enemy has been hit by another attack or has been blocked. The kick attack is quick and is a great way to counter an enemy punch, but it caus- es very little damage. You'll need to use more than the kick attack if you want to win the battle.

The block option (button) enables you to block an enemy attack. You should use this a lot to counter kicks. The fourth hidden attack is the **Deathblow** (button). After blocking several enemy attacks, you'll get the chance to use the Deathblow. This attack is extremely powerful and can near- ly knock out the enemy with a single hit. Weaken the enemy a bit with kicks and punches, and then block until you get the Deathblow to finish off the enemy.

Enemies

Elite Soldier
Galbadian Soldier
Death Claw
Creeps
Jelleye
Slapper

Draw Points

(Galbadia Garden)
Aura (on ground outside)
Protect (hockey rink)
Life (Locker Room)
Shell (basketball courts)
Haste (Center Hall, downstairs)

Save Points

(Galbadia Garden)
Entrance
Center Hall Downstairs
Center Hall (upstairs)
Master Room

Get the three Card Keys

Obtain the Cerberus GF
(Optional)

Battle Seifer

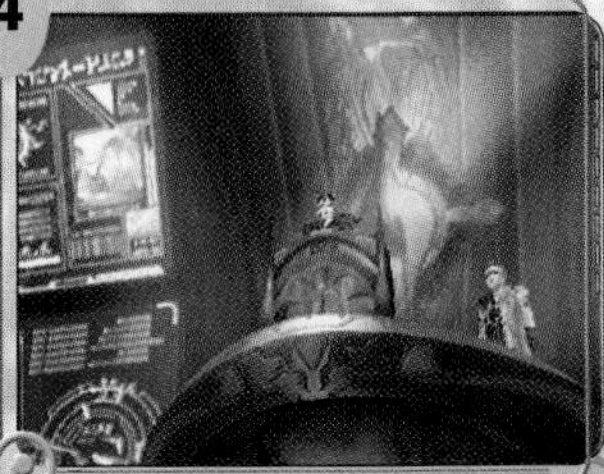

Go to the Auditorium and
battle Edea

Getting Around in Galbadia Garden

You're not a welcome visitor in Galbadia Garden, a fact made clear by the roaming monsters and locked doors. Your goal is to find three students who have the **Card Keys** you need to get through the locked doors.

Card Key 1 is located on the second floor and should be your first target. You can use this key to enter a locked room on the bottom floor, which leads to the hockey rink. There's another student on the other side of the rink hiding in a classroom. This student has **Card Key 2**. You can use this key to enter the door on the third floor, which leads to an area that should look familiar.

Go the main hall and head to the left. You'll find the last key, **Card Key 3** in a classroom. Take the key up to the elevator next to the Reception Room you visited on your first trip to Galbadia Garden.

Cerberus

HP	7100~10,000	AP	30	
EXP	– –		Immune to Wind/Absorbs Thunder	– –

(Optional)

In the center of the main hall you'll see a large beast. It's up to you whether or not you battle Cerberus, but if you don't you'll miss an opportunity to get a new GF.

Before the battle, make sure no one in your party has Thunder Elemental-Attack Junctioned; otherwise, that person will be unable to use physical attacks because they will heal Cerberus.

Cerberus isn't tough as long as you can keep it from using its Triple spell on itself. To do so, simply counter the Triple spell with Dispel. This severely limit Cerberus' attack options.

Also, make sure you stock up on Triple if you haven't already, because it Junctions quite well. Don't forget to steal the Spd-J Scroll from this Boss before the end of the battle.

Seifer

HP	1300~10,300	AP	20	
EXP	– –		Weak vs Poison	– –

Seifer has improved a great deal since your last encounter. He now uses his Gunblade better, plus he has a wicked special attack called Demon Slice that causes around 1,500 points of damage.

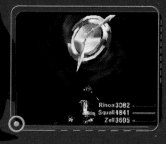

You should begin the battle by drawing Haste from Seifer and casting it on your party members. Then use whatever you want to defeat Seifer. This really isn't a tough battle as long as you keep everyone's HP in check. When Seifer's HP gets low, he'll begin using Hi-Potions, however they won't be strong enough to save him!

Seifer		HP	1200~7400	AP	– –	– –
		EXP	– –	Weak vs Poison		

Edea	GF	HP	500~16,000	AP	50	– –
		EXP	– –	– –		

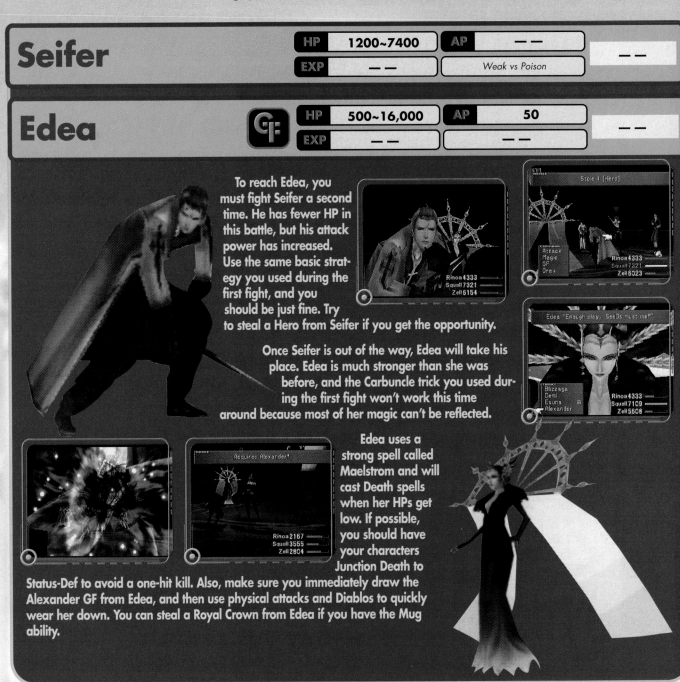

To reach Edea, you must fight Seifer a second time. He has fewer HP in this battle, but his attack power has increased. Use the same basic strategy you used during the first fight, and you should be just fine. Try to steal a Hero from Seifer if you get the opportunity.

Once Seifer is out of the way, Edea will take his place. Edea is much stronger than she was before, and the Carbuncle trick you used during the first fight won't work this time around because most of her magic can't be reflected.

Edea uses a strong spell called Maelstrom and will cast Death spells when her HPs get low. If possible, you should have your characters Junction Death to Status-Def to avoid a one-hit kill. Also, make sure you immediately draw the Alexander GF from Edea, and then use physical attacks and Diablos to quickly wear her down. You can steal a Royal Crown from Edea if you have the Mug ability.

EDEA'S HOUSE

1

2

3

1 Go to Sorceress Edea's House

2 Speak with Cid and Edea

3 Visit Rinoa in the Infirmary

4

5

6

4 Fight off the Ruby Dragon

5 Return to Edea's House

6 Get a letter and directions from Edea

Draw Points

Curaga (Bedroom)
Magazines
Timber Maniacs
(Bedroom/on floor)
Weapons Monthly July
Issue (Training Center/
on ground)

Rare Cards

Leviathan (CC Joker/
Training Center)
Carbuncle (CC Heart/
Bridge)
Gilgamesh (CC King/
Dormitory)
Edea (Edea/Edea's House)

Challenge CC Members

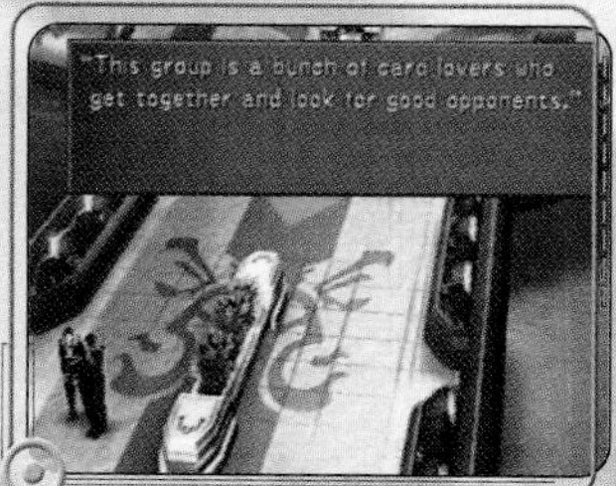

Are you ready to take on the best of the best? The CC group is a collection of seven card-playing fanatics. Each person has a solid set of cards, and knows how to work the rules in their favor. By defeating each of them, you can collect some rare cards and bulk up your collection of cards for modifying later on if necessary. This is your first opportunity to challenge them. If you're ready, check the "Side Quests" section for more information on the CC group.

What's Happened To NORG?

Check the basement level to discover that NORG's "egg" has apparently hatched. There are two apologetic Shumi looking around, but no one has anything to say about the hatched "egg" yet.

Edea's Card

While visiting Edea's House, make sure you challenge Edea to a game of cards. She's tough, but you'll want to get **Edea's Card** from her.

Also, if you haven't received the **Seifer Card** from Cid yet, this is a good time to do so.

The Big Movie

After speaking with Rinoa, you'll be sent back into the past again. This time you're forced into a mini-game against a Ruby Dragon. Laguna has two options during the battle: Defend (button) and Attack (button). (If you have a turbo controller, you can set the Attack button to auto-fire to quickly win the battle.)

Battle the Ruby Dragon by defending against its short, quick attack, and then rapidly tap the Attack button to counterattack as the enemy prepares a longer, slower attack. Continue to repeat this pattern until the Ruby Dragon is defeated.

After the fight, you're forced down a hill where you'll battle the Ruby Dragon a second time. You can either fight immediately, or take a moment to ensure that your party members are properly equipped. You should definitely take a moment to equip Kiros and Ward, because they aren't Junctioned with any GFs. There's also a **Save Point** to the left. This is not a Boss fight, although the Ruby Dragon is a powerful enemy.

Ruby Dragon

The Ruby Dragon is a Fire Elemental, so summon Shiva if you have the GF equipped or use Ice Magic. Demi is also a very effective spell. You can also Junction Ice Magic to your attack and Fire to your defense if you want the added insurance, but you shouldn't need it. Be sure not to cast any Fire or Wind based magic, as it will cure the Ruby Dragon.

WHITE SeeD SHIP

1 Find the White SeeD Ship

2 Speak with Zone and Watts

3 Talk with the Leader a second time

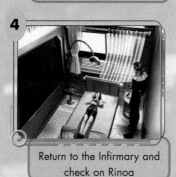

4 Return to the Infirmary and check on Rinoa

Draw Points
Holy (Cabin)

Save Points
Deck (Hidden)

Rare Cards
Shiva (Zone)

Magazines
Timber Maniacs (Bridge)

Finding the Ship

Return to Edea's House and speak with Edea. She'll tell you to look for the White SeeD Ship, which is in a hidden location somewhere around the Centra Continent. She'll also give you a letter that will enable you to board the White SeeD Ship once you locate it.

Edea's Letter

You can make a little extra Gil with Edea's Letter. Take it to a shop and you can sell it for 125 Gil. It isn't much, but it can help if you're short on cash. Return to Edea's House and speak with Edea again. She'll scold you and then hand over another letter. You can continue to sell her letters and get new ones to your heart's content. Granted this isn't a great money maker, but it's kind of humorous.

The White SeeD Ship is hidden in a cove north of Edea's House. Check your map and compare it to the one shown here. The ship isn't tall, so keep your eyes open for its silver sails and brown body.

Finding the Ship (Cont.)

You'll notice a chain of islands that somewhat resembles skeletal fingers. You'll find a small channel flowing through the islands on the east side of this land formation. Pass through the channel heading east and immediately turn south. This is where you'll find the hidden White SeeD Ship.

Girl Next Door

Did you get that copy of the **Girl Next Door** magazine from Timber Maniacs way back on Disc One? Now's your chance to use it! Visit Zone on the bridge of the SeeD Ship and talk to him several times. Eventually, he'll notice that you have a copy of Girl Next Door (assuming you do indeed have it) and asks if you'll

give it to him. You can turn him down, ask him for Gil, or just give it to him for free. Be a chum and give it to Zone for free.

In return Zone will give you a **Rename Card** and the **Shiva Card**. Not a bad trade. (If you didn't get the Girl Next Door magazine, it's inside the Timber Maniacs building in the front lobby, which is located in Timber. You can always get it now, and then return to the White SeeD Ship.)

GREAT SALT LAKE

1

2

3

Enter Great Salt Lake

Defeat Abadon

Locate the hidden door

Enemies

Vysage
Righty
Lefty

Draw Points

Meteor (High Ledge—Hidden)
Thundaga (Monster Skull)

Save Points

Cliff (to the right of the Boss)

Navigating the Lake

There are two paths through the Great Salt Lake. The easy path takes you through the bottom of the lake and contains no surprises.

However, the upper path is home to two **Draw Points**. Getting there is easy, although you may miss it at first. There's a large monster's skull on the ground near the entrance. Climb across the skull, and then use the monster's spine as a path to the ledges above. Continue using the bones as paths until you find both Draw Points. When you reach the end of the upper path, you must jump down to the lower path and continue forward.

Abadon

HP	510~17,010	AP	40	
EXP	— —		Weak vs Fire & Holy	Undead Monster

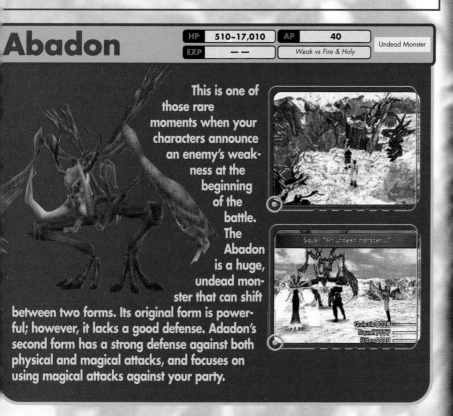

This is one of those rare moments when your characters announce an enemy's weakness at the beginning of the battle. The Abadon is a huge, undead monster that can shift between two forms. Its original form is powerful; however, it lacks a good defense. Adadon's second form has a strong defense against both physical and magical attacks, and focuses on using magical attacks against your party.

Abadon (Cont.)

HP	510~17,010	AP	40	Undead Monster
EXP	— —		Weak vs Fire & Holy	

Abadon causes a lot of bad status effects. Its claw attack in its original form can cause Curse. The second form tends to often cast Confuse and Blind. If you have Treatment equipped, it will come in handy, but those of you who don't can draw Esuna from Abadon.

Although Abadon is weak against Fire and Holy magic, neither will cause as much damage as the Recover ability. Use it on Abadon to cause 9999 points of damage against this Boss. Also, Alexander's Revive ability (if you have it) can instantly kill Abadon. You can also accomplish this by using a Phoenix Down, just like the Gerogero Boss fight earlier in the game. Also, avoid casting Curaga against the Boss, because it doesn't cause much damage. However, if Cure or Curaga is all that you have, then use them.

Dead End?

After the Boss fight, you must follow the trail right into the next screen and watch the background. Notice the shape that is being outlined? Obviously, there's something hidden there. Have Squall search the background to find what you've been looking for.

ESTHAR

As Laguna

1

Ride the elevator to Esthar

2

Speak with the Security Guards twice

3

Talk to both of the other prisoners several times

4

Listen in on Dr. Odine's conversation

5

Head back downstairs to find Dr. Odine

6

Ride the elevator to the control room in Dr. Odine's Lab

As Squall

7

Unlock the doors to Ellone's room and visit her.

8
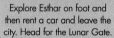
Explore Esthar on foot and then rent a car and leave the city. Head for the Lunar Gate.

9

Speak with the Lunar Gate Staff member to board the waiting capsules

As Zell

1

Return to Dr. Odine's Lab in Esthar and speak with Dr. Odine

1
Catch Lunatic Pandora at one of the checkpoints

OCS Display Test

There's a control panel on the side of the walkway near the entrance to Esthar. If you wish, stop and examine the control panel to run a test on the surrounding panels. This helps explain how Esthar keeps itself hidden from the rest of the world.

Enemies

SAM08G
Galbadian Soldier
Elite Soldier
GIM52A
(Laguna)
Esthar Soldier (Human)
Esthar Soldier (Cyborg)
Gesper
Elastoid

Draw Points

Death (Outside Pandora Lab)
Double (Dr. Odine's Lab)
Flare (Dr. Odine's Lobby)
Blizzard (Presidential Palace Area)
Tornado (Shopping Mall)
Curaga (Inner Skyway Area)
Quake (Dr. Odine's Lab)

Save Points

Outside Pandora Lab
Dr. Odine's Lab (Hidden)
Outside to right of Presidential Palace (Hidden, near Lift)
Near Airstation

Magazines

Weapons Monthly First Issue (on floor/Pandora Lab in the Past)
Pet Pals Vol.5 (Esthar Pet Store)
Pet Pals Vol.6 (Esthar Pet Store)
Occult Fan IV (Presidential Secretary/Presidential Residence)
Combat King 004 (Esthar Soldier/Middle of City)

Rare Cards

Ward (Dr. Odine)

Laguna's Visit

Make sure you equip Ward and Kiros right away for their first battle. Each party member's Junctions have been dropped, with the exception of Squall's/Laguna's. As you fight, be very careful against the Gesper. This creature has the powerful Degenerator attack. The Gesper can eliminate one of your characters with a single hit from this attack.

As you pass through the Lunatic Pandora Lab, make sure you listen to Dr. Odine's conversation. You'll overhear a reference to a copy of **Weapons Monthly**. As you pass through the lab a second time, you'll see it on the ground near the bottom of the screen. This is the first issue of Weapons Monthly ever to be published.

At Dr. Odine's Lab, you can't get in the door in front of you. Ride the elevator up to the control room above, and use the brown switches on the wall to unlock the door below. Return to the ground floor to find **Ellone**.

Exploring Esthar

The quickest way around Esthar comes courtesy of the lifts found virtually everywhere. These lifts will take you to all of the major attractions throughout the city, and you don't need to visit most of the side paths. Don't forget to stop at the **Shopping Mall**, where you'll find a lot of good items for sale. This is especially true if you have the GF Tonberry's **Familiar** ability, which adds a lot of items to each shop's inventory.

Free Items

Sometimes the shops in Esthar will give you free items. Cloud's Shop will give you a Hi-Potion and an X-Potion. Johnny's Shop gives you a Hi-Potion and a Mega-Potion. Karen's Shop will randomly give you a Hi-Potion, and then a Mega-Phoenix later. The best item is the Rosetta Stone that Cheryl's Shop is giving away.

To leave Esthar, you can either rent a car or simply walk out. If you have the money, it's worth paying the 3500 Gil to rent a car. You have a lot of distance to cover, and there are a lot of nasty creatures outside. If you choose to walk, you should use the elevator located in the center of the Rent-A-Car station.

Occult Fan IV & Combat King 004

During your first visit to Esthar (while dropping off Rinoa), you should seek out the Presidential Aide wearing white and blue in front of the Airstation. After speaking with him, return to the Presidential Palace. Just outside the room where you left Rinoa and Odine, you'll find the Presidential Secretary standing outside the door. Speak with him, and

he'll complain about the President's growing collection of magazines. When he walks away, you can find the **Occult Fan IV** lying on the ground where he was standing.

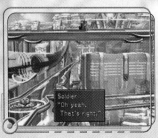

Once again during your first visit to Esthar, you should seek out a lone Esthar Soldier on a high catwalk in the center of the city. After speaking with him, proceed with the game. When Zell returns to Esthar later, speak with the soldier a second time before visiting Odine's Lab. The soldier will say, "I'm done with this," and will leave behind the **Combat King 004**.

On the Way to Lunar Gate

There are four places you can visit in the area outside of Esthar: Lunatic Pandora Laboratory, Sorceress Monument, Lunar Gate, and Tears' Point. All four locations are now highlighted on the World Map.

Before you head for Lunar Gate, however, you should take a quick detour and go to Tears' Point. There's a valuable item at Tears' Point known as the **Solomon Ring**. To use it, you'll need 18 items: six **Steel Pipes**, six **Remedy+**, and six **Malboro Tentacles**. This item enables you to summon the GF **Doomtrain**. Also, there are two Draw Points along the way. One contains Life, while the other has Reflect.

You can get the necessary items by stealing Steel Pipes from Wendigos, using the Medicine Level Up ability to create Remedy+, and by stealing (or winning) Malboro Tentacles from Malboros. You don't have to fight Doomtrain, and once you summon it, it joins you without putting you through another grueling test.

Blue Magic: Bad Breath

Outside Esthar, you may take part in a battle with a creature called a Malboro. These nasty plants have a wicked status attack called Bad Breath, which hits your entire party with nearly every abnormal status effect in the game. The only plus side is that you can steal or win **Malboro Tentacles** from these creatures. This item enables Quistis to learn the **Blue Magic, Bad Breath**.

Catching Lunatic Pandora

You only have 20 minutes to reach Lunatic Pandora before it completely passes over the city. This won't be an easy task if you don't know the city well, because you only have pictures of three areas to go by. If you miss Lunatic Pandora at one of the contact points, you must rush to the next one. The following information will guide you from each contact point to the next.

As soon as you leave Dr. Odine's Lab, press the ⬤ button to access the picture of where Lunatic Pandora will arrive next. Doing so should help you considerably. The first thing you will notice is that the lifts are all on the fritz for some reason, which means you must walk around the city. Also, you'll notice that Galbadian forces have now infested the city, so there will be random encounters.

Each time you reach the entry point of Lunatic Pandora, you'll fight some Galbadian troops. They serve as a diversionary tactic to draw you away from Lunatic Pandora as it continues to pass through the city. If you fail to defeat the troops quickly, Lunatic Pandora will pass you by and you'll have to head to the next contact point.

Contact Point #1 (Center of the City)

Arrives between 15:00 and 12:00

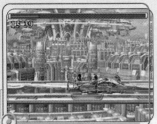

From Dr. Odine's Lab, head off the right side of the screen to the Central Gate and then take the path out through the top. Go up the stairs on the next screen and out the left side to reach the first contact point.

Contact Point #2 (Skyway Crossing)

Arrives between 10:00 and 5:00

From the first contact point, head off the right side of the screen and back down the stairs. Exit via the path at the bottom, which places you back at the Central Gate. Head to the right through the Shopping Mall to an intersection two screens further. Go to the left from the intersection to find the second contact point.

Contact Point #3 (North of the Shopping Mall)

Arrives between 3:00 and 0:00

From the second contact point, head back to the right and then down at the crossroads. This will place you at the third—and final—contact point. You must defeat the Galbadian guards in order to enter Lunatic Pandora at this contact point before the timer reaches 0:00.

Once inside Lunatic Pandora, it doesn't matter which way you go. What happens next is unavoidable, so don't think you did anything wrong.

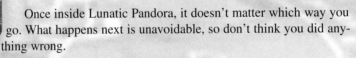

LUNAR BASE

1

Talk to Piet in the Lunar Dock, and then pick up Rinoa

2

Place Rinoa in the Med Lab, and follow Piet to the Control Room

3

Examine the monitor, and then find Ellone on the second floor

4

Return to the Med Lab

5

Go to the Control Room

6

Locate the locker room on the second floor

7

Put on a spacesuit and go out the airlock

8

Return to the Control Room and speak with everyone

9

Speak with Ellone and evacuate the Lunar Base

10

Make a daring rescue

Draw Points

Meteor (Ellone's Room)
Meltdown (next to the Escape Pod)

Save Points

Med Lab,
Next to the Escape Pod

Rare Cards

Laguna (Ellone)
Alexander (Pier)

Alexander & Laguna Cards

While on the Lunar Base, you can acquire the **Alexander Card** by challenging Piet and the **Laguna Card** by challenging Ellone. This task may prove to be tough, because almost every rule is in effect on the Lunar Base.

Space Rescue

Squall must attempt a daring rescue. All you must do to help is to line up the victim with Squall's open arms. This is fairly easy, because you have plenty of time to line up for the grab.

Simply push toward the tumbling person until that person is lined up directly with the center of the screen. As the victim draws closer to Squall, it will be much easier to make smaller adjustments. You have a limited amount of booster jet fuel, which you can use by pressing the ● button. The boosters move you a lot faster, but your supply of fuel is very limited and should be used sparingly.

RAGNAROK

1

Find the clue on how to defeat the Propagators

2

Eliminate the Purple Propagators

3

Destroy the Red Propagators

4

Eradicate the Yellow Propagators

5

Exterminate the Green Propagators

6

Find the Bridge

7

Go to the passenger deck to regroup

8

Return to the Bridge

9

Fly to the Sorceress Memorial

Enemies
Propagator

Draw Points
Life (Catwalk)
Cura (Aisle)
Full-Life (downstairs corridor—Hidden)

Save Points
Entrance (Air Room)
Hanger

Clearing the Ragnarok

Just your luck. The Ragnarok is full of nasty monsters known as Propagators. These creatures aren't that tough, but they're very strong and difficult to kill off—permanently. By inspecting the computer terminals in the ship, you'll discover that although Propagators may have a nasty nature, they do help each other out. If one gets killed, its partner will eventually come and revive it. This being the case, the only way to keep a Propagator from regenerating is to kill them in pairs.

There are a total of eight Propagators on board the Ragnarok, with four color variations: Yellow, Green, Red, and Purple. The different colors mark the different pairs. Therefore, to clear the ship of Propagators you must eliminate them in colored pairs. Once you grasp this concept, the actual task isn't nearly as tough.

Note When in battle, casting Blind and Silence on the Propagators severely limits their chances of inflicting any damage to your party members. You can make this easier by Junctioning 100 Pain spells to either Rinoa's or Squall's weapon.

Start with the Purple Propagator, the one you first saw on your way into the ship inside the Hangar area. After eliminating it, head through the cargo doors and take a quick left through the door in the corridor before the Red Propagator can attack you. The Purple Propagator is in the next room.

After defeating the Purple Propagators, return to the previous room and eliminate the first Red Propagator. Now head back to the Hangar where you defeated the first Purple Propagator, and climb the stairs to the catwalk above. Apparently, this Red Propagator has made the catwalk its new home.

With both the Red and Purple Propagators eliminated, it's time to take on the Yellows. Return to the Air Room where you first entered the Ragnarok to find the first of the Yellow Propagators. After eliminating it, pass through the rooms you've already cleared to find the Passenger Deck. (The Passenger Deck is located through the doorway to the left of the Green Propagator standing on the elevator platform. Inside is an extremely aggressive Yellow Propagator.

After eliminating the first six Propagators, it's time to finish off the Green Propagators. Start with the one resting on the elevator platform next to the Passenger Deck. Only one left! Head back down to the Hangar where you started this whole process, and you'll see a small door on the right side of the back wall. The last of the Propagators is waiting inside.

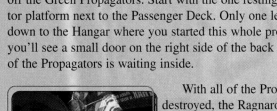

With all of the Propagators destroyed, the Ragnarok is yours to do with as you wish. Ride the elevator platform to the bridge and take the Ragnarok back home.

SORCERESS MEMORIAL & EDEA'S HOUSE

Enemies

Memorial
Turtapod

Esthar
Turtapod
Imp
Torama
Iron Giant

Draw Points

Stop (Memorial Steps)

Rare Cards

Squall (Laguna)

1

Enter the Memorial

2

Find Rinoa and free her

3

Flee from the Memorial

4

Fly to Edea's House

5

Follow Angelo to the flower field

6

Return to the Presidential Palace in Esthar

7

Speak with the President

8

Enter Lunatic Pandora at Tears' Point

Landing at Esthar

In case you haven't already noticed, you can land the Ragnarok at Esthar's Airstation. Look for a building with a landing pad on top. When you're over the building, a message appears with the name "Esthar/Airstation." Press the ● button as you normally would to land and your party will appear outside the Airstation complex in Esthar. This is much easier than parking the Ragnarok outside Esthar and walking across town.

Check Your Party

Upon returning to Esthar, immediately check each party members' Junctions. Zell and Rinoa are forced into your party, so they may not be Junctioned with GFs. Because the city is overrun with creatures, it would be a bad idea not to switch Junctions.

Also, it's been a while since Rinoa was last in your party. You should check her status and make sure Angelo is learning a new trick. Rinoa may also be several levels behind your other characters, so take good care of her during any upcoming battles.

Last, but not least, Rinoa has a new type of Limit Break. With her new sorceress powers, she can choose to use the **Angel Wing** instead of calling on Angelo. Angel Wing enables Rinoa to cast a continuous chain of spells without having them removed from her inventory. The down side is that you never know what spell will be next, plus you lose control of Rinoa for the remainder of the battle. The effect is similar to having a party member "berserked," except that in this case Rinoa uses magical attacks instead of physical attacks. This effect also causes Rinoa's magic strength to increase, thus inflicting more damage.

Squall Card

Challenge Laguna to a game of cards in his chamber, or once you're on board the Ragnarok. If you're lucky, you can win the **Squall Card** from him.

LUNATIC PANDORA

1. Battle Fujin and Raijin

2. Ride the elevators

3. Fight Mobile Type 8

4. Challenge Seifer

Enemies

- Behemoth
- Elnoyle
- Imp
- Iron Giant
- Torama
- Fujin (Boss)
- Raijin (Boss)
- Mobile Type 8 (Boss)

Items

- LuvLuv G (Dead End Tunnel)
- Spd-J Scroll (Crystal Halls)
- Combat King 005 (Crystal Halls, in panel)
- Phoenix Pinion (Crystal Halls, in panel)
- Power Generator (Crystal Halls, in panel)

Draw Points

- Curaga (Elevator Lobby)
- Meteor (Staircase)
- Holy (Crystal Halls)
- Silence (Crystal Halls—Hidden)
- Ultima (Crystal Halls—Hidden)
- Confuse (Crystal Halls)

Save Point

- Near Entrance

Fujin (2nd rnd.)	HP	5300-18,200	AP	8	– –
	EXP	– –		– –	

Raijin (2nd rnd.)	HP	5400-22,600	AP	12	– –
	EXP	– –	Weak vs. Ice/Poison		

Once again you must battle Fujin and Raijin. In essence, this battle is similar to the previous one; however, the two Bosses have grown stronger over time.

Fujin now has the Sai attack, which reduces a character to a single HP. You can counter this by having one of your characters equipped with the Recover ability, or you can draw Curaga magic from Fujin. She also spends a lot of time casting support magic. You may want to cast Reflect on both Bosses and on your party to help counter her barrage of magic.

Begin this battle by summoning the Doomtrain GF. Its negative status attack will leave Fujin and Raijin nearly paralyzed for the remainder of the battle. Diablos and Cactuar also inflict major damage.

Navigating Lunatic Pandora

Finding your way around Lunatic Pandora is a lot easier than it may seem at first. Find either Elevator Two or Elevator Three and ride down to the central hall where three elevators meet. Use Elevator One to reach a new area, and then just go straight ahead. There are a lot of side paths scattered throughout the area, but all eventually lead to a dead end.

The Laguna Effect

Depending on the actions you took while exploring the Excavation Site (a.k.a. Lunatic Pandora's Excavation Site), you may be able to locate some useful items and Draw Points. The following covers the action taken by Laguna in the past and the result in the present:

As Laguna: Pick up the first Old Key near the ladder in the lower level.

Later Effect: You can now access an Ultima Draw Point hidden in a doorway past the floor panels.

As Laguna: Remove a lever from the middle floor panel to set a trap for the Esthar Soldiers.

Later Effect: The floor panel is now open and inside is a Silence Draw Point.

As Laguna: Find the second Old Key at the first intersection.

Later Effect: The door at the base of the long ladder is now open. Inside you can find a LuvLuvG item.

As Laguna: Find the gray detonator, and press the red switch prior to pushing the blue switch.

Later Effect: Both boulders fall into gaps in the floor, which enables you to get to some of the secrets listed here. It also enables you to reach a copy of Combat King 005.

As Laguna: Move the rock away from a tunnel wall to reveal a Cure Draw Point.

Later Effect: Searching the spot where the Draw Point once was, reveals a hidden Spd-J Scroll.

Easy Battles

You'll soon notice that random encounters inside Lunatic Pandora are too easy to be real. All the monsters you will encounter are level one monsters. So, although the battles are easy, your characters won't receive much experience from the battles.

Also, keep this in mind if you want to steal useful items like **Energy Crystals** from Behemoths. You may need to use the **Lvl Up** ability to strengthen your enemies.

Blue Magic: Mighty Guard

You're sure to run into a Behemoth or two while exploring Lunatic Pandora. Behemoths carry a useful item called **Barrier**, which enables Quistis to learn the protective **Blue Magic, Mighty Guard**. You can either steal this item, or wait for a Behemoth to drop one.

Mobile Type 8

HP	30,400-46,400	AP	40	
EXP	— —		**Weak vs Thunder**	**Flying Monster**

Like most machines, the Mobile Type 8 has a weakness to Thunder magic, so this is a good time to use Quezacotl. However, don't forget to steal items from all three parts of this Boss (its main body and its probes). All three have great items ripe for the taking.

This Boss has two forms. The first is its normal form in which all three pieces are attached. This form isn't too dangerous, but it does counterattack whenever it's hit in the main body. This counterattack, Twin Homing Laser, only causes around 600 points of damage, so it isn't much of a concern.

When the Boss shifts to its second form, it is preparing to use its ultimate attack, the Corona. This attack drains all three party members down to a single HP. When this occurs, immediately cease all attacks as a counterattack from one of the probes could kill one of your characters in this weakened state. Quickly begin healing or use your Limit Breaks, as each character should get the opportunity to use them. Using Limit Breaks is risky, but you may be able to defeat the Boss before it can counterattack, thereby eliminating the need to heal everyone.

To quickly heal, draw Curaga from the Left Probe. This probably won't fully heal everyone, but it should be enough to keep everyone alive for now. If you use Limit Breaks, you should be able to destroy the Boss quickly as long as the Limit Breaks used are good ones. Whatever you do, act quickly or this Boss will quickly finish you off with its follow-up attack, Medigo Flame. This attack causes around 2000 points of damage to each party member.

Seifer

HP	3700~34,500	**AP**	40		--
EXP	--		*Weak vs. Poison*		

Although Seifer is stronger than ever, this isn't a tough battle. Seifer is carrying the Aura spell, which you should draw from him. A character affected by the Aura spell can easily get his/her Limit Break, regardless of how high his/her HP is at the time. Stock up on this spell while you have the chance, and cast it on each of your party members.

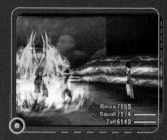

Using Aura, you can quickly beat Seifer into submission. Don't move too fast though, or you'll miss the chance to steal from Seifer.

Gilgamesh

As the battle with Seifer begins, Odin will appear if you took the time to find this semi-GF earlier in the game. Don't get too confident though; Seifer has a nasty surprise in store for Odin.

A new semi-GF, **Gilgamesh**, will appear and take the fallen Odin's place. After a few moments, Gilgamesh will appear and end the battle with Seifer. From this point forward, Odin will no longer appear randomly, but Gilgamesh will take up where Odin left off.

LUNATIC PANDORA

Where to Go

There's been a slight change to this area. In the area where you earlier fought Mobile Type 8, you'll now discover that the structure to the right of the path has dropped a bridge. Cross over and then climb up the structure to reach a ledge above. This leads to your next battle.

Adel

| HP | 6000~51,000 | AP | -- | -- |
| EXP | -- | | -- | |

As you might have guessed, Adel is a bit rusty after all those years of confinement. It also doesn't help that she's a little preoccupied with Rinoa. This battle is a bit tricky, because you can't use attacks that will damage both Rinoa and Adel. Well, you can, but it isn't recommended. However, those who are brave enough to tempt fate can steal some Megalixirs from the helpless Rinoa. Just don't hurt her too much. If Rinoa gets killed during the battle, it's game over!

Start the battle by drawing Regen from Rinoa and casting it on everyone in your party (including Rinoa). Casting Regen will protect you from Adel's attacks by healing your party periodically. Also, make sure you steal the Samantha Soul from Adel, and then focus on attacking her.

Just use normal attacks, and don't worry about Adel's Ultima spell. It really doesn't cause that much damage. Adel will periodically absorb some of Rinoa's hit points in order to restore herself. If you haven't cast the Regen spell on Rinoa, then make sure that you cast a Cure spell on her after Adel has absorbed Rinoa's hit points a few times. As long as you attack quickly, this won't be much of a factor. Make sure you focus on stealing items, and then concentrate on attacking Adel. Also, don't forget to recast the Regen spell when it runs out.

Enemies

Behemoth
Elnoyle
Imp
Iron Giant
Torama
Fujin (Boss)
Raijin (Boss)
Mobile Type 8 (Boss)

Draw Points

Curaga (Elevator Lobby)
Meteor (Staircase)
Holy (Crystal Halls)
Triple (Edea's House)
Ultima (Crystal Halls—Unseen)
Silence (Crystal Halls—Unseen)

Items

LuvLuvG (Dead End Tunnel)
Spd-J Scroll (Crystal Halls)
Combat King 005 (Crystal Halls)
Phoenix Pinion (Crystal Halls, in panel)
Power Generator (Crystal Halls, in panel)

Save Points

Near Entrance
Crystal Halls
"Bone Hall" (Lunatic Pandora—Hidden)
Commencement Room

Sorceress Battles

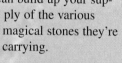

Upon arriving in the time-compressed world, you're greeted by a long chain of fights against unnamed Sorceresses. None of them are very powerful, however, when given a chance they can cause some serious havoc. Quickly eliminate them using standard physical attacks. You may want to steal from them all, because you can build up your supply of the various magical stones they're carrying.

The final Sorceress fight is the only one you must worry about. Take this opportunity to stock up on **Holy**

magic, but watch out for the Sorceress' counterattack, which causes between 1000 and 2000 points of damage. When the Sorceress begins to count down from five, she is preparing to cast **Ultima**. When this occurs, quickly heal your party. During the countdown, the Sorceress will not counterattack, so unload with everything you have.

What to Do Next

Your options are limited in the time-compressed world. You can no longer enter any towns, but you can still check out dungeons, Chocobo Forests, and you can explore a bit. The Ragnarok still exists, but finding it isn't easy. Before you explore Edea's House, check your characters and make sure you're satisfied with your characters' levels, spell stocks, and items. To exit Edea's House and Ultimecia's Castle, you must use one of three portals near the castle's entrance.

When climbing the gigantic chain outside the castle, you'll notice three portals set in stone arches. Face a portal and press the ● button to leap across the chasm and land on the portal's edge. Each portal takes you to a different spot on the World Map. The lowest portal places you in Galbadia's Wilburn Hill area, near the destroyed Missile Base.

The middle portal leads to Centra's Serengetti Plains, close to the Centra Ruins. The highest portal takes you to the coast of Esthar on the edge of Grandidi Forest, which is close to the sacred Chocobo Forest.

Finding the Ragnarok

The Ragnarok is still around and full of people from the C.C. Group, provided that you defeated the C.C. Group's King earlier in the game. It's a long trek, but you can win some rare cards that you may have missed throughout your journey from the C.C. Group's members. You can also use the Ragnarok to find the Queen of Cards, who's hiding somewhere on the World Map.

While the journey to the Ragnarok isn't tough, it is very long and slow. After going through the second portal outside Ultimecia's Castle, you'll arrive in Centra's Serengetti Plains area just a bit north of the Centra Ruins. Check the World Map and you'll see a red dot southeast of your position. The red dot signifies the Ragnarok. To reach it, you need to find transportation across the ocean, and without the Garden, you must rely on Chocobos.

While on foot, head to the northwest and wrap your way around the bay to the Chocobo Forest on the northeast tip of the Centra continent. Get a Chocobo and return the way you came. Ride the Chocobo to the southern border until you spot a beach. Ride across the ocean to the continent below, which will take you very, very close to Edea's House.

From Edea's House, travel to the east along the mountains. However, keep an eye out for a small pass through the middle of the mountain range.

On the other side, you'll find the Kashkabald Desert and the **Ragnarok**. There's a fourth portal near the Ragnarok. Upon entering this portal, a new portal will appear in front of Ultimecia's Castle. Now you can travel to this location any time you wish.

Finding the Queen of Cards

After finding the Ragnarok, you can begin your hunt for the Queen of Cards and explore the world. The Queen of Cards is hiding in the Abadan Plains, just to the south of Esthar.

You'll find her near the escape pod crash site (the same place where you found Piet on Disc Three). Keep in mind that there's no visible sign of the crash from the World Map. To locate it, you must scour the southern tip of the plains until you enter the area.

Enemies

All monsters present (even some old Bosses)

Draw Points

Flare (Outside—Hidden)
Meteor (Terrace—Hidden)
Slow (Fountain)
Dispel (Chapel)
Ultima (Armory—Hidden)
Holy (Treasure Vault)
Cura (Destroyed Hall)
Curaga (Storage Room)
Full-Life (Prison Cell—Hidden)
Aura (Wine Cellar—Hidden)
Meltdown (Art Gallery)
Triple (Clock Tower Balcony)
Stop (Top of Clock Tower)

Save Points

Outside the entrance
Destroyed Hall
Clock Tower Base (Hidden)
Outside Ultimecia's Room

1

Battle Sphinxara in the Front Foyer

2

Cause the giant chandelier to fall and destroy the trap door below

3

Fight Tri-Point in the Wine Cellar

4

Have the secondary party pull the lever below the chandelier

5

Cross the chandelier with the main party and fight Krysta

6

Go to the gallery and solve the painting puzzle

7

Challenge Trauma in the gallery

8

Enter the open cell in the dungeon and get the Prison Key

9

Defeat the Red Giant inside the cell

10

Get the Armory Key from the shaky bridge

11

Enter the armory and do battle with Gargantua

12

Search the fountain to find the Treasure Vault Key

13

Enter the Treasure Vault and solve the chest puzzle

14

Conquer Catoblepas in the Treasure Vault

15

Climb the clock tower and swing across the bell to reach a hidden area

16

Fight Tiamat on the destroyed balcony

17 0:54

Save your game and have your secondary party ring the bell in the stairwell to the right of the Front Foyer

18 0 25

Have your primary party rush to the Chapel in under forty-five seconds to challenge the mighty Omega Weapon (optional)

19

(This is it... Ultimecia is here.)
(Get it over with. Fight her now)
(It's too early to face her)

Climb the Clock Tower and find Ultimecia's hideaway

20
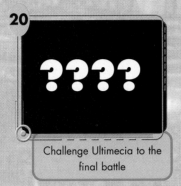
????

Challenge Ultimecia to the final battle

Sealed Abilities

Upon entering Ultimecia's Castle, nearly all of your party members' abilities are sealed off. This means you won't be able to use Draw Points, draw magic from enemies, use Save Points, revive fallen characters, use magic, items, and GF Abilities, or perform Limit Breaks. In battle, your party members will only have the Attack command. Outside of battle, you can perform some basic tasks, like Junctioning and rearranging Magic, but you won't be able to use GF abilities or heal characters with items or magic.

The parties' powers have been sealed by Ultimecia's servants.

"Release which seal?"
[Item]
[Magic]
[GF]
[Draw]
[Command Ability]
[Limit Break]
[Resurrection]
[Save]

It should be fairly obvious that you don't want to fight the mighty Ultimecia with your party in this condition. Therefore, you'll need to "unlock" your abilities. To do so, you must explore the castle and solve a series of puzzles to lure out Ultimecia's servants. There are a total of eight puzzles, and it won't be easy defeating the Bosses without the use of your full powers.

Rather than dragging you around the castle from Boss to Boss, the following will guide you through each Boss individually. This will give you a chance to figure things out on your own; you can then refer to this guide if you have trouble locating or defeating a particular Boss. As a reference, the Bosses are listed in the order you should fight them.

What Are Those Green Circles?

The green circles seen throughout the castle are **switch points**. These switches aren't levers, but instead a place where you can switch between your two parties. This will become necessary to solve some of the puzzles.

Make sure that when you switch between parties, you also switch junctioned abilities. You definitely don't want to enter a fight with only the Attack command unless you absolutely have to do so.

[Party Switch Point]
Switch to the other party
Change party members
Cancel

Getting Along Without

Although you can't use magic, you can still Junction spells to your Elem-Atk and Stat-Atk. Initially, you may want to Junction **Drain** to each party member's Stat-Atk. Therefore, on each hit a character takes, he/she will heal himself/herself. This will help keep their HPs up during tough battles. You can also Junction useful spells like **Pain**, **Sleep**, and **Death** so that you get the benefits of the magic without having to cast the spells.

Many of the Bosses use a specific elemental attack. If you customize your defenses before these fights, you can actually get the Boss to heal you instead of hurt you. You may also want to look at each Boss in the Bestiary (see pg. 194) so that you can better prepare for the battle if you decide not to read the individual strategies.

A large part of how well you will perform is determined by the order in which you choose to release your party's abilities. I suggest starting off with **Magic** or **GF Abilities**. Magic and GF Abilities will give you the ability to heal your party with Cure magic or the Recover ability. Plus, it provides the added punch you'll need for some of the tougher Bosses with higher defenses.

Don't forget about the Save Point outside on the steps of the castle. After exiting the front door, your abilities that were removed inside the castle return, so you can regularly save and heal your party. You may need to visit here often at first. However, remember that as soon as you re-enter the castle, your abilities—except those you've previously released—will be sealed up again.

Sphinxaur/Sphinxara

HP	10,000	AP	30		--
EXP	--		--		

This is the easiest of Ultimecia's servants, and should be your first target. You can see the Sphinxaur from just inside the front door. It resides at the top of the stairs in the Front Foyer. Ascend the stairs and approach Sphinxaur to enter combat.

At this point, you should only be able to use the Attack Command. This Boss has low HP, it's slow, and its attacks are weaker than you might expect. It can summon creatures to assist it, but they're typically weak creatures like Jelleyes. Additionally, this Boss likes to use Ice magic, so you may want to junction Blizzaga to each party member's Elem-Def.

Tri-Point

HP	2400~22,400	AP	30	
EXP	– –		– –	*Flying Monster*

To reach Tri-Point, head up the stairs in the Front Foyer and go through the door at the top. This places you above a huge chandelier. As you walk on the chandelier, it will plummet to the room below. The force of the impact disperses your party, but it also destroys a rusted trap door below the chandelier. Open the trap door to the Wine Cellar below to find Tri-Point.

This Boss only seems tough, so if you plan carefully you won't have any problems. Junction as much Thunder magic as possible to each character's Elem-Def. Each time you attack this Boss with physical attacks, it will counterattack with its Mega Spark. This is a Thunder-based attack that hits everyone, causing big damage. However, if your party is prepared to absorb Thunder magic, it will heal your party instead of harm it.

Tri-Point has an elemental weakness to either Fire or Ice, but switches between the two each time it gets hit. To avoid this problem, just make sure your party is prepared to absorb the Mega Spark, and then beat Tri-Point into submission.

WARNING! *Do not fight Krysta until after you've released either Magic or your GFs. Personally, I wouldn't try this fight until I could summon GFs, but let your own style of play dictate your decision.*

115

Krysta

HP	5200~16,000	AP	30	
EXP	– –		*Immune to Ice*	*Flying Monster*

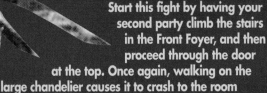

Start this fight by having your second party climb the stairs in the Front Foyer, and then proceed through the door at the top. Once again, walking on the large chandelier causes it to crash to the room below. On the right side of the screen, you'll notice a green circle next to a lever. Have your second party stand in the circle in order to flip the lever. Switch to your main party and have them find their way up the stairs to the top of the chandelier. With the second party holding the lever, the main party can cross the chandelier without it falling. You'll find Krysta on the other side of the terrace.

Krysta doesn't have a lot of HP, but its crystalline body provides an extremely high defense against physical or magic attacks. This Boss also counterattacks any physical or magic attack with a punch that can cause close to 3000 hit points of damage. You can counter this attack by summoning powerful GFs. Diablos and Cactuar (or Demi for magic users) works really well in this battle. After summoning both GFs, the battle may be over before it actually begins. If you use magic, cast Meltdown before using spells such as Tornado, Meteor or Ultima.

Also, Krysta won't counterattack summoned creatures. In effect, this means that it will just stand motionless throughout most of the fight. However, be aware of Krysta's final attack—an Ultima spell.

Go through the door on the right side of the balcony in the Front Foyer, and follow the path to an art gallery. You'll find two floors worth of paintings in the gallery. Upon examining them, you'll discover that all but one painting has a title. Your task is to discover the title of the large painting by combining the titles of other paintings in the gallery.

At first, this may seem like an impossible task, however, it's really quite simple. Following are the lists of all 12 titles:

• IGNUS
(Fire)

• INANDANTIA
(Flood)

• IUDICIUM
(Judgment)

• INTERVIGILIUM
(Sleep)

• VIGIL
(Watchman)

• VIVIDARIUM
(Garden)

• VIATOR
(Messenger)

• VENUS
(Love)

• XIPHIAS
(Swordfish)

• XERAMPELINAE
(Red Clothes)

• XYSTUS
(Tree-lined Road)

• INAUDAX
(Cowardice)

NOTE

It is imperative that you inspect all of the paintings even though you have this list. Otherwise, the titles will not appear when you go to name the large painting.

It is extremely difficult to look at a painting and decipher its name with only the choices to work with. As luck would have it, though, there's a clue nearby. Climb the steps to the second floor and check out the **clock etched into the floor** below. This is your clue. Can you figure it out from here?

If you don't understand, look at the numbers the hands are pointing to: VIII, IIII, and VI. All three numbers correspond with one of the paintings around you. Now try again to figure it out on your own.

Here is one last clue if you still don't see the relationship. The numbers represent the letters in three of the titles. The "V" represents the letter "V" and the "I" represents the letter "I."

HERE'S THE ANSWER! Quickly look away if you want to figure this out on your own. In essence, the "V" on two of the numbers indicates that you should use only titles that have a "V" in them. The "I"s represent the exact number of "I"s in the titles.

Thus, VIII stands for VIVIDARIUM, IIII stands for INTERVIGILIUM, and VI stands for VIATOR. Enter the three titles in the order you would read a clock: hour, minute, and second. So the answer is VIVIDARIUM ET INTERVIGILIUM ET VIATOR, or In the Garden Sleeps a Messenger.

Trauma

HP	5555~34,114	AP	30	Flying Monster
EXP	— —		Weak vs Wind	

After solving this puzzle, you'll find that a new Boss, Trauma, has appeared behind you. Trauma has a lot of HP and a solid defense against physical attacks. It can also create Dromas, which are miniature versions of itself.

Trauma's main attack is its Mega Pulse Cannon, a devastating attack that hits each of your characters hard. The Dromas also have Pulse Cannons, however, they're not as powerful.

Begin the battle by summoning Doomtrain if possible. This will probably eliminate any Dromas, plus it should weaken Trauma's defenses. Follow this up with the Pandemona and Cactuar GFs to really attack Trauma's remaining defenses. Any non-summoning character should use physical attacks or act as a "medic" for the others.

Red Giant

HP	30,000	AP	30	— —
EXP	— —		— —	

Beyond the art gallery, you'll find a room with a staircase leading into a dungeon. While inside the dungeon, pass through the left door to enter a cell with a decaying corpse. There's a shining key (the Prison Key) in the corpses' hand. You need the Prison Key to get out of the cell once you're locked inside. The only problem is that taking the key makes the Red Giant appear, and this Boss isn't going to let you leave without a fight.

Start the fight by summoning Doomtrain. This should blind the Boss and weaken its defenses. With the Boss blinded, it will have a difficult time hitting your party. Plus, with its defenses weakened, physical attacks will prove effective. Finish this Boss off with GFs, such as Quezacotl and Cactuar.

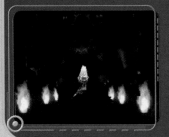

Gargantua

HP	10,100~15,400	AP	42
EXP	– –		– –

From the Front Foyer, follow the hall on the bottom-left of the screen until you reach a shaky bridge. While on the bridge, you'll notice an item. Every step you take shakes the bridge, causing the item to move closer and closer to the edge. To keep the bridge motionless, press and hold the ⬤ button to walk instead of run. This will enable you to pick up the item. If you're using the Analog joystick, push it slightly to the right to make your party walk.

The item, the Armory Key, is used to unlock the armory in the dungeon room. If you fail to stop running and the key falls from the bridge, all is not lost. Return to the dungeon and check the water trough closest to the door. You should find a shiny object in the water. This is the Armory Key, which was washed along the stream to this point.

You'll find a Vysage waiting in the back of the armory; however, this is no ordinary Vysage. After defeating all three parts, including Lefty and Righty, a lumbering behemoth, known as Gargantua, will crawl out of the ground. Gargantua is similar to Krysta, because of its power and magic attacks. It will respond to physical attacks with its Counter Twist counterattack, which causes around 2000 points of damage, so you'll need to use magic or GFs.

Also, be prepared to cure abnormal status effects, because Gargantua uses Berserk on your party. This leaves your party no other option but to use physical attacks, which the Boss can counterattack.

To be really prepared for this battle, Junction Earth magic to your party's Elem-Def and Berserk to their Stat-Def. By doing so, Gargantua will have a tough time causing damage to your characters.

Catoblepas

HP	10,500~60,000	AP	30
EXP	– –	Weak vs Earth & Water/ Absorbs Thunder	– –

Search the fountain outside the Chapel to find the Treasure Vault Key, which unlocks the Treasure Vault. To find the Treasure Vault, take the top left exit in the Front Foyer. It's tucked away on the left side in the tilted hallway.

Inside the Treasure Vault, there's a treasure box puzzle. Your goal is to have all four boxes open at the same time. As a guide, we'll number the boxes from 1~4, going from right to left.

#1 moves 1 & 2

#2 moves 1, 2, & 3

#3 moves 2, 3, & 4

#4 moves 3 & 4

Step 1: Shut box #1

Step 2: Shut box #4

Step 3: Shut box #2

Step 4: Open box #3

In four easy steps, all four boxes should open and the Boss, Catoblepas, will appear in the middle of the room.

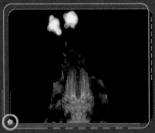

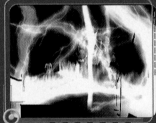

Catoblepas has the most HP of all of the Bosses you've fought thus far in Ultimecia Castle. You must protect your party from Thunder magic to lessen the damage caused by the Boss' Thundaga attacks.

Start the battle by summoning Doomtrain to blind and slow the Boss, plus this will reduce its defenses. This will make the rest of the battle a breeze.

Leviathan and Brothers work well in this battle, however, you should avoid using Quezacotl because Quezacotl actually heals Catoblepas, as does any Thunder magic. Also, note that this Boss has Meteor, which you should draw. The Meteor spell works well against this Boss if you have a strong magic user, which you should at this point in the game.

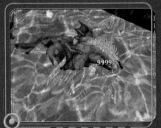

After landing the final blow, Catoblepas will unleash one final Meteor spell, so keep an eye on each party member's HPs.

Tiamat

HP	21,200~89,600	AP	30	Flying Monster
EXP	– –		Strong vs Fire & Thunder/ Immune to Wind	

Climb the Clock Tower until you reach a large swinging bell. On the left side of the tower, stand near the edge and press the ⊗ button to jump onto the bell when it is close to your party. Your party will jump off the bell and onto a small ledge. Pass through the hole in the wall to find Tiamat.

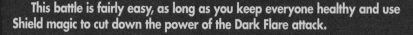

Tiamat is a GF gone bad, due to Ultimecia's control. It acts (and looks) a lot like Bahamut, but it isn't as powerful. Tiamat's only attack is its Dark Flare attack, which is very powerful. When it's not attacking, it simply waits for its next opportunity to use Dark Flare.

Because Dark Flare takes a long time to charge, take this opportunity to protect your party with the Shield spell. Also, heal each party member and hit Tiamat with everything you've got.

Start the battle by summoning Doomtrain to slow Tiamat and weaken its defenses. This will make the already slow countdown to Dark Flare even slower. Follow this up by summoning any powerful GFs except Ifrit, Quezacotl, and Pandemona. If you have Eden don't be afraid to use it. You should have plenty of time to summon Eden between Dark Flares.

This battle is fairly easy, as long as you keep everyone healthy and use Shield magic to cut down the power of the Dark Flare attack.

NUTHIN' BUT THE BEST

This is an optional battle. You do not need to defeat Omega Weapon in order to finish the game or "unlock" your party's abilities. Omega Weapon is extremely challenging and the rewards for defeating it are minimal. It's more of a test to see just how good of a player you truly are... so how good are you?

Also, after defeating Omega Weapon, a new heading, "Proof of Omega," appears in the Tutorial section of the Main Menu.

Omega Weapon

HP	111,105~1,161,000	AP	250
EXP	— —		— —

Weak vs. Ice/Absorbs Fire

There's another switch point near the fountain. Leave your main party at the switch point, and take control of your party. Exit the Front Foyer via the door on the upper-right side of the room. There's a large bell in the ceiling of the very next room. To summon Omega Weapon, you must ring the bell. To do so, have the leader of your secondary party pull the rope at the base of the stairs.

Upon doing so, a timer will appear in the corner of the screen. The timing indicates the time you have to find Omega Weapon and to initiate the battle. Quickly run your secondary party to the switch point in the same room and take control of your main party. Then run to the Chapel where the organ is to find the hulking Omega Weapon. To initiate combat, simply run into the Boss.

Preparations for Battle

This is no ordinary battle, so you must plan ahead of time. Before you ring the bell, take some time to refine some items from cards, rearrange your spells and items, upgrade your weapons, and make sure everyone is healthy.

Use your Card Mod ability to refine 100 Megalixirs from the Bahamut card, 100 LuvLuvGs from the Chubby Chocobo card, and 10 Holy Wars from the Gilgamesh card. Move the Megalixirs and Holy Wars to the front of your item inventory, along with any Mega Phoenixes in your inventory. Use the 100 LuvLuvGs on the three characters in your main party so that each character is at full compatibility (1000) with each of the GFs he/she is equipped with. You'll need your GFs to arrive quickly in the upcoming battle.

Examine your party's Junctions. Junction 100 Death spells to each party member's Stat-Def. Omega Weapon uses a Level 5 Death spell that can wipe out the entire party in a single shot, so be prepared for it. Check your party's Command Abilities. Make sure everyone can summon GFs and draw magic. Additionally, have at least two magic users, two people who can use items, and you may want to equip the Recover and Revive abilities.

Also, check your Character Abilities and remove any Bonus or Mug abilities. Replace these with abilities that increase your characters' vital statistics with a focus on Speed, Strength, and Magic. You may also want to equip abilities like Auto-Potion or Auto-Haste, but stay away from equipping Auto-Reflect.

Make sure Squall has his ultimate weapon, Lion Heart. This enables him to perform the Lion Heart Limit Break, which can cause close to 100,000 points of damage to Omega Weapon. If Zell and Irvine are in your party, upgrade their weapons as well because they will use them in their Limit Breaks. The female characters probably won't use their weapons throughout the entire battle, so upgrading isn't necessary.

Check your GFs. Make sure Cerberus, Eden, and Doomtrain are all Junctioned to a character taking part in the battle. Also, Junction each GF on a different character so that you can cast all three simultaneously. Also, make sure Eden IS NOT Junctioned to Squall; he'll have other things to do besides summoning GFs.

Make sure that you have a small supply of Aura spells (at least 18) in the Magic inventory of a character equipped with the Magic Command Ability. You should also have a supply of Full-Life and Curaga spells just in case you need them.

That should do it! If you find you've forgotten something once you enter the battle, you can always try to regroup for a second assault.

An Epic Battle

Let me start off by recommending a party. I like Zell, Rinoa, and Squall for this battle. Give Zell Eden and the Item Command Ability. Give Rinoa the Magic Command Ability and Doomtrain. Give Squall Cerberus and the Magic Command Ability. Granted, a lot more goes into this setup, but these are the only specifics. You don't have to set up your party in this fashion, it just happens to be my personal favorite.

As the battle begins, quickly summon Doomtrain, Cerberus, and Eden, however, DO NOT boost Doomtrain. Doing so will heal the Boss, but it will also weaken its defenses. This will enable you to cause double the damage using physical attacks, such as Squall's Limit Break. Cerberus will set up your spell casters with Double and Triple, which you'll use next. Eden will deal out the first dose of major damage. Attempt to boost Eden as high as possible to inflict maximum damage.

After the GFs do their work, have a spell caster use Aura on each party member, or at least the two characters without Eden. Now the two characters not using Eden will be able to dominate Omega Weapon with repeated Limit Breaks. With any luck, Squall will use the Lion Heart Limit Break several times in a row.

With Aura in place, have the character equipped with the Item Command Ability use Holy War on the party. This will make everyone temporarily invincible. It's important to do this *after* Aura is cast, because Holy War blocks magic. Without the Aura spell, you'll need to rely more on GFs and strong magic.

If you followed my suggestion, Zell will constantly summon Eden after using Holy War and Squall and Rinoa will begin using their Limit Breaks. Make sure that if you choose Rinoa, only select the Combine Limit Break. You can't afford to lose control of her for the remainder of the battle.

Everyone should keep this up until either the Holy War or Aura spell wears off. Aura will typically end before the Holy War effect. During the remaining seconds of the Holy War effect, you may want to stock up on Ultima, Holy, Flare, and Meteor spells from Omega Weapon. This is your best shot to get a full 100 Ultimas.

When the effect of Holy War ends, quickly recast Aura on everyone and use another Holy War. Follow the same tactics and continue recasting any time you need to. This battle will take a long time, however, if you use this strategy you won't lose unless something goes horribly wrong.

For defeating Omega Weapon, you receive a Three Stars. Not much of a prize for such a tough fight, but the chance to stock up on strong spells is well worth the effort.

The Organ & the Floodgate Key

There's one more task to undertake. If you choose to follow these steps, you can find a rare **Rosetta Stone**, which might come in handy before you challenge Ultimecia.

First you must find the **Floodgate Key.** Follow the top-left hall from the Front Foyer and you'll eventually reach a room with two elevators. To get the elevators to operate, you must load both sides simultaneously. The trick is that the higher party must weigh more than the lower party; otherwise, the elevators won't work. Place all the males in the higher elevator, while placing all the females in the lower elevator. You don't have to put all the guys in one, but you should have at least two guys to one girl.

After the lighter party gets lifted up, enter the room to find a small storage area. On the floor, you'll find the **Floodgate Key.** Take the Floodgate Key to the Dungeon and use it to unlock the lever in the middle of the room. Move the lever to close the floodgate, which stops the flow of water.

Now head for the organ in the Chapel area. You may have been wondering what this was for. There's a dark hall to the right of the fountain in front of the Chapel. Inside the hall you'll find a gate made of spears. These spears retract when the organ is played properly. To play it properly, you must hit all eight keys (buttons) simultaneously. Once you've done so, go check the gate. If some of the spears are still up, return to the organ and try it again.

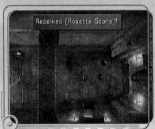

When the gate is completely lowered, you can pass through it to find a short canal. By closing the floodgate earlier, you drained the canal of water, so you can walk around inside of it. (If the canal is full of water, you need to go back and shut the floodgate.) In the dry canal, you'll find a box containing a **Rosetta Stone.** You'll also find a door that leads to the cell in the Dungeon.

Ultimecia Awaits

Ultimecia awaits your arrival beyond the Clock Tower. The battles ahead are difficult, but not as tough as Omega Weapon. If you have trouble, just rely on the strategy in the Omega Weapon section. Otherwise, have fun and experiment a little.

If you need additional help, check out the BradyGAMES website at www.bradygames.com for a helpful FAQ. Good luck and enjoy the incredible ending. You've certainly earned it!

ITEMS LIST

Recovery Items

Name	Description	#of Items	Ability	Refines to...
Potion	Restores HP by 200	3	Med LV Up	Potion+
Potion+	Restores HP by 400	3	Med LV Up	Hi-Potion
Hi-Potion	Restores HP by 1000	3	Med LV Up	Hi-Potion+
Hi-Potion+	Restores HP by 2000	3	Med LV Up	X-Potion
X-Potion	Fully restores HP	3	Med LV Up	Mega-Potion
Mega-Potion	Restores HP by 1000 to all members	20	Forbid Med-RF	Elixir
Phoenix Down	Removes KO status	50	Med LV Up	Mega Phoenix
Mega Phoenix	Removes KO status from all members	3	Tool-RF	Phoenix Pinion
Elixir	Fully restores abnormal status and HP	10	GFAbl Med-RF/ Med LV Up	Doc's Code/ Megalixir
Megalixir	Fully restores abnormal status and HP to all	—	—	—

Status Items

Name	Description	#of Items	Ability	Refines to...
Antidote	Cures Poison	1	ST Mag-RF	Bio
Soft	Cures Petrify	1	ST Mag-RF	3 Break
Eye Drops	Cures Darkness	1	ST Mag-RF	Blind
Echo Screen	Cures Silence	1	ST Mag-RF	2 Silence
Holy Water	Cures Zombie, Curse	1	L Mag-RF	2 Zombie
Remedy	Cures abnormal status	10/1	Med LV Up/ Supt Mag-RF	Remedy+/5 Esuna
Remedy+	Cures abnormal status and Magic effect	10	Med LV Up	Elixir

Battle Items

Name	Description	#of Items	Ability	Refines to...
Hero trial	Occasionally makes character invincible	10	Med LV Up	Hero
Hero	Makes character invincible	10	Med LV Up	Holy War-trial
Holy War-trial	Occasionally makes all party members invincible	10	Med LV Up	Holy War
Holy War	Makes all party members invincible	5	GFAbl Med-RF	Knight's Code
Shell Stone	Same effect as Shell	1	Supt Mag-RF	Shell
Protect Stone	Same effect as Protect	1	Supt Mag-RF	Protect
Aura Stone	Same effect as Aura	1	Supt Mag-RF	Aura
Death Stone	Same effect as Death	1	L Mag-RF	Death

Name	Description	#of Items	Ability	Refines to...
Holy Stone	Same effect as Holy	1	L Mag-RF	Holy
Flare Stone	Same effect as Flare	1	F Mag-RF	Flare
Meteor Stone	Same effect as Meteor	1	Forbid Mag-RF	Meteor
Ultima Stone	Same effect as Ultima	1	Forbid Mag-RF	Ultima
Gysahl Greens	Summons Chicobo	—	—	—
Phoenix Pinion	Summons Phoenix	20/1	GFAbl Med-RF/ F Mag-RF	Phoenix Spirit/ Firaga
Friendship	Summons Moomba	—	—	—

Stayover Items

Name	Description	#of Items	Ability	Refines to...
Tent	Fully restores abnormal status and HP to all	4/1	Recov Med-RF/ L Mag-RF	Mega-Potion/ 10 Curaga
Pet House	Restores HP to all GF	1	GF Recov Med-RF	2 G-Returner
Cottage	Same effect as Tent plus restores all GF	2/1	Recov Med-RF/ L Mag-RF	Mega-Potion/ 20 Curaga

GF Recovery Items

Name	Description	#of Items	Ability	Refines to...
G-Potion	Restores 200 HP to GF	—	—	—
G-Hi-Potion	Restores 1000 HP to GF	—	—	—
G-Mega-Potion	Restores 1000 HP to all GF	—	—	—
G-Returner	Revives GF from KO	—	—	—
Rename Card	Changes GF's name	—	—	—

GF Ability Items

Name	Description	#of Items	Ability	Refines to...
Amnesia Greens	Makes GF forget an ability	—	—	—
HP-J Scroll	GF learns HP-J ability	10	GFAbl Med-RF	Giant's Ring
Str-J Scroll	GF learns Str-J ability	10	GFAbl Med-RF	Power Wrist
Vit-J Scroll	GF learns Vit-J ability	10	GFAbl Med-RF	Orihalcon
Mag-J Scroll	GF learns Mag-J ability	10	GFAbl Med-RF	Force Armlet
Spr-J Scroll	GF learns Spr-J ability	10	GFAbl Med-RF	Hypno Crown
Spd-J Scroll	GF learns Spd-J ability	10	GFAbl Med-RF	Jet Engine
Luck-J Scroll	GF learns Luck-J ability	1	Forbid Med-RF	Luck Up
Aegis Amulet	GF learns Eva-J ability	2/1	Forbid Med-RF/ Time Mag-RF	Spd Up/ 100 Haste
Elem Atk	GF learns Elem-Atk-J ability	1	Forbid Med-RF	4 Elixir
Elem Guard	GF learns Elem-Defx4 ability	1	Forbid Med-RF	4 Elixir
Status Atk	GF learns ST-Atk-J ability	1	Forbid Med-RF	4 Elixir
Status Guard	GF learns ST-Defx4 ability	1	Forbid Med-RF	4 Elixir
Rosetta Stone	GF learns Abilityx4 ability	1	Tool-RF	Shaman Stone
Magic Scroll	GF learns Magic ability	1	Tool-RF	10 Wizard Stone

Name	Description	#of Items	Ability	Refines to...
GF Scroll	GF learns GF ability	1	Tool-RF	10 Wizard Stone
Draw Scroll	GF learns Draw ability	1	Tool-RF	10 Wizard Stone
Item Scroll	GF learns Item ability	1	Tool-RF	10 Wizard Stone
Gambler Spirit	GF learns Card ability	1	Tool-RF	10 Wizard Stone
Healing Ring	GF learns Recover ability	1	Recov Med-RF/ Tool-RF/GF Recov Med-RF/L Mag-RF	20 Mega-Potion/ 30 Cottage/ 20 G-Mega-Potion/ 100 Curaga
Phoenix Spirit	GF learns Revive ability	1	Recov Med-RF/ GF Recov Med-RF/ F Mag-RF/L Mag-RF	100 Phoenix Down/ 40 G-Returner/ 100 Firaga/100 Full-Life
Med Kit	GF learns Treatment ability	1	ST Med-RF/Forbid Med-RF/Supt Mag-RF	20 Remedy/ 2 Megalixir/100 Esuna
Bomb Spirit	GF learns Kamikaze ability	1	F Mag-RF	100 Firaga
Hungry Cookpot	GF learns Devour ability	1	Tool-RF	Shaman Stone
Mog's Amulet	GF learns MiniMog ability	1	Tool-RF	Shaman Stone
Steel Pipe	GF learns SumMag +10% ability	1	Tool-RF/ST Mag-RF	Aura Stone/20 Berserk
Star Fragment	GF learns SumMag +20% ability	1	Tool-RF/Forbid Mag-RF	2 Meteor Stone/ 5 Meteor
Energy Crystal	GF learns SumMag +30% ability	1/1/50/1	Ammo-RF/Tool-RF/ GF Abl Med-RF/ Forbid Mag-RF	10 Pulse Ammo/ 2 Ultima Stone/ Samantha Soul/ 3 Ultima
Samantha Soul	GF learns SumMag +40% ability	20/1	GF Abl Med-RF/ Time Mag-RF	Elem Atk/60 Triple
Healing Mail	GF learns GFHP+10% ability	1	Recov Med-RF/ GF Recov Med-RF/ L Mag-RF	6 Hi-Potion/ Pet House/20 Curaga
Silver Mail	GF learns GFHP+20% ability	1/5	GF Recov Med-RF/ GF Abl Med-RF	2 Pet House/ Gold Armor
Gold Armor	GF learns GFHP+30% ability	1/5	GF Recov Med-RF/ GF Abl Med-RF	4 Pet House/ Diamond Armor
Diamond Armor	GF learns GFHP+40% ability	1/1/5	Tool-RF/GF Recov Med-RF/GF Abl Med-RF	50 Cottage/16 Pet House/Elem Guard
Regen Ring	GF learns HP+20% ability	1	Recov Med-RF/ Tool-RF/GF Recov Med-RF/L Mag-RF	8 Phoenix Down/ 5 Tents/6 G-Returner/ 20 Full-Life
Giant's Ring	GF learns HP+40% ability	10/1	GF Abl Med-RF/ Supt Mag-RF	Gaea's Ring/60 Protect
Gaea's Ring	GF learns HP+80% ability	1	Forbid Med-RF	HP Up
Strength Love	GF learns Str+20% ability	1	Tool-RF	2 Aura Stone
Power Wrist	GF learns Str+40% ability	1/10	Tool-RF/GF Abl Med-RF	10 Aura Stone/ Hyper Wrist
Hyper Wrist	GF learns Str+60% ability	10	Forbid Med-RF	Str Up
Turtle Shell	GF learns Vit+20% ability	1	Tool-RF/Supt Mag-RF	10 Protect Stone/ 30 Protect

Name	Description	#of Items	Ability	Refines to...
Orihalcon	GF learns Vit+40% ability	1/10	Tool-RF/GF Abl Med-RF	30 Protect Stone/Adamantine
Adamantine	GF learns Vit+60% ability	5/20	Forbid Med-RF/ GF Abl Med-RF	Vit Up/Steel Curtain
Rune Armlet	GF learns Spr+20% ability	1	Tool-RF/Supt Mag-RF	10 Shell Stone/40 Shell
Force Armlet	GF learns Spr+40% ability	1/10	Tool-RF/GF Abl Med-RF	30 Shell Stone/Magic Armlet
Magic Armlet	GF learns Spr+60% ability	10/20	Forbid Med-RF/ GF Abl Med-RF	Spr Up/Moon Curtain
Circlet	GF learns Mag+20% ability	1	Tool-RF	2 Aura Stone
Hypno Crown	GF learns Mag+40% ability	1/10	Tool-RF/GF Abl Med-RF	10 Aura Stone/Royal Crown
Royal Crown	GF learns Mag+60% ability	10/20	Forbid Med-RF/ GF Abl Med-RF	Mag Up/Status Atk
Jet Engine	GF learns Spd+20% ability	50/10	Forbid Med-RF/ GF Abl Med-RF	Spd Up/Rocket Engine
Rocket Engine	GF learns Spd+40% ability	5/1	Forbid Med-RF/ Time Mag-RF	Spd Up/50 Triple
Moon Curtain	GF learns Auto-Shell ability	1	Supt Mag-RF	100 Shell
Steel Curtain	GF learns Auto-Protect ability	1	Supt Mag-RF	100 Protect
Glow Curtain	GF learns Auto-Reflect ability	2/1	GF Abl Med-RF/ Supt Mag-RF	Monk's Code/100 Reflect
Accelerator	GF learns Auto-Haste ability	1	Time Mag-RF	100 Haste
Monk's Code	GF learns Counter ability	1	Forbid Med-RF	Str Up
Knight's Code	GF learns Cover ability	1	Forbid Med-RF	Vit Up
Doc's Code	GF learns Med Data ability	1	Forbid Med-RF	Megalixir
Hundred Needles	GF learns Return Damage ability	1	Forbid Med-RF	Spd Up
Three Stars	GF learns Expendx3 ability	1	Time Mag-RF	100 Triple
Ribbon	GF learns Ribbon ability	1	GF Abl Med-RF	Status Guard

Ammo Items

Name	Description	#of Items	Ability	Refines to...
Normal Ammo	Regular Ammo	1	Ammo-RF	Fast Ammo
Shotgun Ammo	Ammo that attacks all opponents	1	Ammo-RF	2 Fast Ammo
Dark Ammo	Ammo with status changing effect	—	—	—
Fire Ammo	Ammo with Fire element	—	—	—
Demolition Ammo	Ammo 3 times more powerful than Normal Ammo	—	—	—
Fast Ammo	Ammo for rapid fire	—	—	—
AP Ammo	Armor-piercing ammo	—	—	—
Pulse Ammo	Ammo that contains powerful energy	5	Forbid Mag-RF	Ultima

Tool Items

Name	Description	#of Items	Ability	Refines to...
M-Stone Piece	Stone with a little Magic power	1	T Mag-RF/I Mag-RF/ F Mag-RF/L Mag-RF/ Time Mag-RF/ST Mag-RF/Supt Mag-RF	5 Thunder/5 Blizzard/ 5 Fire/5 Cure/5 Slow/ 5 Silence/5 Esuna
Magic Stone	Stone with Magic power	1	T Mag-RF/I Mag-RF/ F Mag-RF/L Mag-RF/ Time Mag-RF/ST Mag-RF/Supt Mag-RF	5 Thundara/5 Blizzara/ 5 Fira/5 Cura/5 Haste/ 5 Berserk/5 Dispel
Wizard Stone	Stone with strong Magic power	1	T Mag-RF/I Mag-RF/ F Mag-RF/L Mag-RF/ Time Mag-RF/ST Mag-RF/Supt Mag-RF	5 Thundaga/5 Blizzaga/ 5 Firaga/5 Curaga/ 5 Stop/5 Bio/20 Dispel
Ochu Tentacle	Strong, flexible tentacle	1	ST Med-RF/ST Mag-RF	3 Eyedrops/30 Blind
Healing Water	Water with life force	1	Recov Med-RF/Tool-RF/ GF Recov Med-RF/ L Mag-RF	2 Hi-Potion/2 Tent/ 2 G-Hi-Potion/20 Cura
Cockatrice Pinion	Feather with petrifying power	1	ST Med-RF/ST Mag-RF	3 Soft/20 Break
Zombie Powder	Powder with Zombie effect	1	ST Med-RF/L Mag-RF	3 Holy Water/ 20 Zombies
Lightweight	Shoes to make you light on your feet	100/1	GF Abl Med-RF/ Time Mag-RF	Accelerator/20 Haste
Sharp Spike	Long, sharp claw	1	Ammo-RF	10 AP Ammo
Screw	Use to remodel weapons	1	Ammo-RF	8 Normal Ammo
Saw Blade	Serrated blade	1	L Mag-RF/Supt Mag-RF	10 Death/20 Dispel
Mesmerize Blade	Long, sharp blade	1	Recov Med-RF/ GF Recov Med-RF/ L Mag-RF	2Mega Potion/ G-Hi-Potion/20 Regen
Vampire Fang	Fang that makes Vampire attack	1	Supt Mag-RF	20 Drain
Fury Fragment	Stone that contains morale	1	Tool-RF/Supt Mag-RF	2 Aura Stone/5 Aura
Betrayal Sword	Sword that betrays allies	1	ST Med-RF/ST Mag-RF	Remedy/20 Confuse
Sleep Powder	Induces sleep	1	ST Med-RF/ST Mag-RF	Remedy/20 Sleep
Life Ring	Ring with life force	1	Recov Med-RF/ GF Recov Med-RF/ L Mag-RF	2 Phoenix Down/ 2 G-Returner/20 Life
Dragon Fang	Dragon's fang with recovery force	1/100/1	ST Med-RF/ GF Abl Med-RF/ Supt Mag-RF	Remedy/Med Kit/ 20 Esuna

Blue Magic Items

Name	Description	#of Items	Ability	Refines to...
Spider Web	Quistis learns Blue Magic, Ultra Waves	1	Time Mag-RF	20 Slow
Coral Fragment	Quistis learns Blue Magic, Electrocute	1	T Mag-RF	20 Thundara
Curse Spike	Quistis learns Blue Magic, LV?Death	1/100/1	ST Med-RF/Tool-RF*/ ST Mag-RF	Remedy/Dark Matter/10 Pain
Black Hole	Quistis learns Blue Magic, Degenerator	1	Time Mag-RF	30 Demi
Water Crystal	Quistis learns Blue Magic, Aqua Breath	1	I Mag-RF	50 Water
Missile	Quistis learns Blue Magic, Micro Missiles	1	Ammo-RF	20 Demolition Ammo
Mystery Fluid	Quistis learns Blue Magic, Acid	1	ST Mag-RF	10 Meltdown
Running Fire	Quistis learns Blue Magic, Gatling Gun	1	Ammo-RF	40 Demolition Ammo
Inferno Fang	Quistis learns Blue Magic, Fire Breath	1	Tool-RF/F Mag-RF	2 Flare Stone/20 Flare
Malboro Tentacle	Quistis learns Blue Magic, Bad Breath	1/100/1	ST Med-RF/GF Abl Med-RF/ST Mag-RF	2 Remedy/Moon Curtain/40 Bio
Whisper	Quistis learns Blue Magic, White Wind	1/1/100/1	Tool-RF/GF Recov Med-RF/GF Abl Med-RF/L Mag-RF	Cottage/4 G-Hi-Potion/ Healing Ring/50 Curaga
Laser Cannon	Quistis learns Blue Magic, Homing Laser	1	Ammo-RF	5 Pulse Ammo
Barrier	Quistis learns Blue Magic, Mighty Guard	50/1	GFAbl Med-RF/ Supt Mag-RF	Aegis Armlet/40 Shell
Power Generator	Quistis learns Blue Magic, Ray-Bomb	1	Ammo-RF/Tool-RF/	20 Pulse Ammo
Dark Matter	Quistis learns Blue Magic, Shockwave Pulsar	1	GF Abl Med-RF/ Forbid Mag-RF	Shaman Stone/Luck J-Scroll/ 100 Ultima

Indicates that the GF Siren must be at level 100 to change 100 Curse Spikes into 1 Dark Matter.

Compatibility Items

Name	Description	#of Items	Ability	Refines to...
Bomb Fragment	Stone with Fire element	1/100/1	Ammo-RF/GF Abl Med-RF/F Mag-RF	20 Fire Ammo/Bomb Spirit/ 20 Firaga
Red Fang	Dragon's fang with Fire element	1	Ammo-RF/F Mag-RF	40 Fire Ammo/20 Firaga
Arctic Wind	Contains Ice element wind	1	I Mag-RF	20 Blizzara
North Wind	Contains strong Ice element wind	1	I Mag-RF	20 Blizzaga
Dynamo Stone	Stone with Thunder element	1	T Mag-RF	20 Thundaga
Shear Feather	Bird's feather that flies on wind	1	T Mag-RF	20 Aero

Name	Description	#of Items	Ability	Refines to...
Venom Fang	Poisonous monster fang	1	ST Med-RF/Ammo-RF/ ST Mag-RF	10 Antidote/20 Dark Ammo/20 Bio
Steel Orb	Steel orb with gravitational power	1	Time Mag-RF	15 Demi
Moon Stone	Holy moon stone with monsters living inside	1	Tool-RF/Forbid Mag-RF	2 Holy Stone/20 Holy
Dino Bone	Large dinosaur bone	1	Time Mag-RF	20 Quake
Windmill	Windmill containing wind energy	1	T Mag-RF	20 Tornado
Dragon Skin	Durable dragon skin	100/1	GF Abl Med-RF/ Supt Mag-RF	Glow Curtain/20 Reflect
Fish Fin	Fish's fin	1	I Mag-RF	20 Water
Dragon Fin	Very hard dragon's scale	1	Time Mag-RF	20 Double
Silence Powder	Powder containing Silence	1	ST Med-RF/ST Mag-RF	3 Echo Screen/ 20 Silence
Poison Powder	Powder containing Poison	1	ST Med-RF/Ammo-RF	3 Antidote/ 10 Dark Ammo
Dead Spirit	Contains Death	1	Tool-RF/L Mag-RF	2 Death Stone/ 20 Death
Chef's Knife	Tonberry's knife	1	Ammo-RF/L Mag-RF	20 AP Ammo/30 Death
Cactus Thorn	Cactuar's thorn	1/100	Ammo-RF/GF Abl Med-RF	40 Demolition Ammo/ Hundred Needles
Shaman Stone	Stone with mystical power	1/10/1	Tool-RF/Forbid Med-RF*/GF Abl Med-RF	LuvLuvG/Hero Trial/ Rosetta Stone

* The GF Doomtrain must be at level 100 to change 10 Shaman Stones into 1 Hero Trial.

Event Items

Name	Description	#of Items	Ability	Refines to...
Fuel	Fuel for a rental car	1	Ammo-RF	10 Fire Ammo
Girl Next Door	Naughty Magazine	—	—	—
Sorceress' Letter	Edea's introduction letter	—	—	—

Special Items

Name	Description	#of Items	Ability	Refines to...
Chocobo's Tag	Changes Chocobo's name	—	—	—
Pet Nametag	Changes pet's name	—	—	—
Solomon Ring	Mysterious old ring used to summon Doomtrain	—	—	—
Magical Lamp	Mysterious old lamp used to summon Diablos	—	—	—

Power Up Items

Name	Description	#of Items	Ability	Refines to...
HP Up	Raises HP by 10	2	GF Abl Med-RF	HP-J Scroll
Str Up	Raises Strength by 1	2	GF Abl Med-RF	Str-J Scroll
Vit Up	Raises Vitality by 1	2	GF Abl Med-RF	Vit-J Scroll
Mag Up	Raises Magic by 1	2	GF Abl Med-RF	Mag-J Scroll
Spr Up	Raises Spirit by 1	2	GF Abl Med-RF	Spr-J Scroll
Spd Up	Raises Speed by 1	2	GF Abl Med-RF	Spd-J Scroll
Luck Up	Raises Luck by 1	2	GF Abl Med-RF	Luck-J Scroll
LuvLuv G	Raises compatibility with all GF by 20	—	—	—

Special Magazines

Items	Description	Location
Weapons Mon 1st	Weapons research Magazine, First Issue	Lunatic Pandora Lab in the past with Laguna
Weapons Mon Mar	Weapons research Magazine, March Issue	Battle with Elvoret at the Dollet Comm Tower
Weapons Mon Apr	Weapons research Magazine, April Issue	Squall's dorm room after graduation
Weapons Mon May	Weapons research Magazine, May Issue	Sewers in Deling City
Weapons Mon Jun	Weapons research Magazine, June Issue	Battle with BGH251F2 at the Galbadian Missile Base
Weapons Mon Jul	Weapons research Magazine, July Issue	On the ground in the Balamb Garden Training Center after the Galbadian Garden battle
Weapons Mon Aug	Weapons research Magazine, August Issue	In front of the gargoyle statue in Trabia Garden
Combat King 001	Magazine for fighters, Dolphin Blow Issue	Bottom floor of the D District Prison
Combat King 002	Magazine for fighters, Meteor Strike Issue	Given to you after Fujin and Rajin in Balamb
Combat King 003	Magazine for fighters, Meteor Barret Issue	Girl who has a crush on Zell, Balamb Hotel
Combat King 004	Magazine for fighters, Different Beat Issue	Second visit to Esthar, from Esthar Soldier
Combat King 005	Magazine for fighters, My Final Heaven Issue	While exploring Lunatic Pandora as Squall
Pet Pals Vol. 1	Magazine for dog lovers, Angelo Strike Issue	Train bound for Timber
Pet Pals Vol. 2	Magazine for dog lovers, Angelo Recover Issue	Rinoa's bed in the Forest Owl's base
Pet Pals Vol. 3	Magazine for dog lovers, Invincible Moon Issue	Purchased at the Timber Pet Shop
Pet Pals Vol. 4	Magazine for dog lovers, Angelo Reverse Issue	Purchased at the Timber Pet Shop
Pet Pals Vol. 5	Magazine for dog lovers, Angelo Search Issue	Purchased at the Timber Pet Shop
Pet Pals Vol. 6	Magazine for dog lovers, Wishing Star Issue	Purchased at the Timber Pet Shop
Occult Fan I	World's Mysteries Magazine, Scoop Issue	Bookcases inside the Balamb Garden Library
Occult Fan II	World's Mysteries Magazine, Photo Issue	Dollet; challenge the Pub manager to cards
Occult Fan III	World's Mysteries Magazine, Magic Issue	First arrive at FH find the Master Fisherman
Occult Fan IV	World's Mysteries Magazine, Report Issue	Presidential Aide in Esthar's Presidential Palace

Timber Maniacs

You'll find Timber Maniacs magazines dropped all over the world. After reading an issue of Timber Maniacs, you can read a special article on Laguna, on Squall's study panel in Balamb Garden. Check Selphie's web page and read the section about Laguna.

Area	Location
Balamb Station	Near the train signal
Balamb Hotel	Inside the guest room
Timber Maniacs	On the floor in the office
Timber Hotel	On a table in the guest room
FH	In the Grease Monkey's house
FH Hotel	Inside the guest room

Area	Location
Trabia Garden	In the graveyard
Dollet Pub	On a table in the Pub
Dollet Hotel	Inside the guest room
Shumi Village	Artisan's house
White SeeD Ship	On the floor in the bridge
Edea's House	On the ground inside the house

FINAL FANTASY VIII GUARDIAN FORCES

FINAL FANTASY VIII introduces us to the *Guardian Force* (GF), a new type of creature that a character can summon. You'll acquire several of these creatures throughout the game, relying on them heavily throughout its entirety. Guardian Forces will assist you in battles, strengthen your characters with new abilities and Junctioned magic, and they will help you acquire new magic, items, and even cards.

Guardian Forces

From Final Fantasy II to Final Fantasy VII, summoned creatures have always been there to lend a helping hand in the heat of battle. Final Fantasy VIII has pushed the summoned creature's role even further with the introduction of Guardian Forces. They're still the same powerful creatures you've come to know and love, and you'll see a lot of familiar faces, but this time their role is much larger than it has been in the past.

Rather than just assisting in battle, Guardian Forces actually determine the vital stats and abilities of the character they're Junctioned with. Face it, without a GF backing him up, Squall is pretty much an ordinary guy thrown into an extraordinary circumstance. Granted GFs don't do it all on their own, but they're the basis on which a character is built upon.

Junctioning with a GF

Junctioning may sound complicated at first, however, it's really quite simple. Open the Main menu and select the Junction option, and then select a character. At first, only the Junction option will be highlighted, because a GF must be Junctioned to a character before the other options become available.

Choose to Junction and select the GF option. A list of all of the GFs you've had join you thus far will be shown. Those in white are available for Junctioning. Grayed out GFs are already Junctioned to the character you've chosen. GFs whose names are opaque are already Junctioned to a different character. These GFs cannot be selected until they have been removed from the character they're currently Junctioned to.

After selecting a GF, back out of the screen using the ⬤ button. You must next Junction magic to your character's stats using the GF's Junction abilities, assuming that the GF has at least one. Junction abilities increase a vital stat by enabling you to Junction stocked magic to the stat. Different types of magic have different effects on the various stats. You don't have to Junction magic yourself. If you want, you can select the Auto option, and then choose to have the game prioritize increasing a character's Attack Power (Atk), Magic Power (Mag), or Defense (Def). The game will then automatically choose from the character's stocked magic, and make appropriate Junctions based on what you've chosen.

Note Always double-check the game's decisions when using the Auto Junction command. The game doesn't make any decisions based on your surroundings, and may equip spells to your attack or defense that you'd rather it didn't.

After boosting the character's stats, it's time to set the character's abilities. The top three abilities are Command abilities. These are the options available to the character during a battle. Character's start the game with the Attack ability, but must be given additional Command abilities. Be very careful when setting these abilities. You'll almost always want everyone in your party to have the ability to **Draw Magic**. Also, it's important to have at least one person who can use **Magic** and one who can use **Items**.

The two abilities below the Command abilities are the Character abilities. These give your character additional bonuses to vital stats and other benefits. You can eventually have as many as four Character abilities equipped on a character, but at the beginning of the game you'll have to make due with just two.

Now your character is ready for battle. Over time, you'll get a feel for setting up your characters to take full advantage of the abilities you've chosen.

GF Growth

GFs grow throughout the game in a way that's very similar to your own characters. Just as your characters gain experience and go up levels, so do your GFs. Any GFs Junctioned to characters in a battle receive an amount of experience equal to what the character they're Junctioned to receives. However, if more than one GF is equipped on a character, the experience gets divided into equal shares between the GFs.

Besides Exp (Experience Points), GFs also gain AP (Ability Points). AP is learned to teach GFs new abilities and comes in much smaller portions than Exp. AP is earned after any battle during which a GF was Junctioned to a character in the battle. If more than one GF is Junctioned to a character, the GFs still receive the full AP amount rather than having to split it among them equally.

Items can also teach GFs some abilities. In fact, you can only get some abilities by using these rare items. Overall, it's much more effective to use an item to learn an ability than to wait for a GF to earn a bunch of AP.

As GFs grow in strength, their Attack Power and HP also grow. The maximum level for any GF is 100. Teaching a GF certain GF Abilities, like HP+10%, can alter both a GF's Attack Power and HP. The effect of these abilities is cumulative, so it's best to teach a GF as many of these abilities as possible.

A Love/Hate Relationship

Guardian Forces are like any pet. The more they like a character, the quicker they'll respond to his/her call. This is known as a Guardian Forces' **Compatibility**. Never overlook this when Junctioning a GF with a character. If a GF has a particularly low compatibility with a character, it may take an eternity for the GF to appear in battle. While waiting for the GF to appear, it will absorb damage targeted at the Junctioned character.

In tougher battles, a low compatibility is a mark for death. You should try to get all of the GFs you use regularly up to at least a compatibility rating of 800, but try hard to get the rating closer to 1000, which is the maximum.

The compatibility rating can be raised in many ways. The easiest (and best) way is by summoning a GF. This raises the compatibility rating in most all cases by 20 points. If a GF is an elemental, you can also raise the compatibility by having a character cast magic of the same elemental type as the Junctioned GF. Healing GFs using curative GF Medicines will also raise a GF's compatibility slightly. Lastly, you can find and use lots of items outside of battle as a sort of sacrifice that boost a GF's compatibility with a character.

A GF's compatibility rating can also be lowered. This is typically due to the fact that you haven't been using a Junctioned GF, and have been using other Junctioned GFs regularly. GFs are as jealous as they are loyal.

Teaching an Old GF a New Trick

Every GF begins the game with its basic set of abilities. Some abilities will have already been learned, while others will need a little work. There will also be some abilities that you can't even see until you've taught a GF some of its starting abilities.

Only one ability can be learned at a time, so teaching a GF a full 22 abilities can take some time. In some cases, you may no longer need an ability as it may have lost its effect. For example, once a GF learns the ST-Def-Jx2, the ST-Def-J ability no longer has any effect. You can use an item known as **Amnesia Greens** to make the GF forget the ST-Def-J ability, which in turn enables you to replace it with a new ability by using an item whenever you choose to do so.

You can guide your GFs on what they learn by accessing the GF section in the Main menu. Pay close attention to each GF, and try to personalize them to fit your style of play. In the beginning, focus on **SumMag+** abilities and **Boost** to strengthen the GFs' attacks. Then focus on Junction abilities to strengthen your party's vital stats.

Note *For more information on GF Items and how Junctioned Magic affects character stats, check out the Items and Magic Lists.*

Quezacotl

Elemental:	Thunder
Starting Level:	1
Starting HP:	300

Found At: Access Squall's study panel from his desk in the classroom at Balamb Garden. Select the **Tutorial** option and Quezacotl will automatically be added to your GF inventory along with Shiva.

GF's Attack: Thunder Storm

Quezacotl's attack is elemental Thunder based. It's particularly good against any type of machine/robotic enemy.

Useful Abilities: One of Quezacotl's best abilities is the **Card Mod**. This ability enables you to refine items from Cards, and makes it much easier to upgrade weapons and to teach Quistis new types of Blue Magic. The **Card** command ability is also useful at the beginning of the game. Your starting deck is fairly weak, but the Card ability will enable you to immediately add some powerful Cards to your deck by changing enemies into cards.

Quezacotl's Vital Statistics

Level	HP	Atk. Power
1	300	275
10	754	572
20	1266	902
30	1786	1232
40	2314	1562
50	2850	1892
60	3394	2222
70	3949	2552
80	4506	2882
90	5074	3212
100	5650	3542

Quezacotl's Ability List

Ability	AP Needed	Leads To	Ability	AP Needed	Leads To
HP-J	50	N/A	Mag+20%	60	Mag+40%, Elem-Atk-J
Vit-J	50	Elem-Def-J	Mag+40%	120	N/A
Mag-J	Learned	N/A	SumMag+10%	40	SumMag+20%
Elem-Atk-J	160	N/A	SumMag+20%	70	SumMag+30%
Elem-Def-J	100	Elem-Defx2	SumMag+30%	140	N/A
Elem-Defx2	130	N/A	GFHP+10%	40	GFHP+20%
Magic	Learned	N/A	GFHP+20%	70	N/A
GF	Learned	N/A	Boost	10	N/A
Draw	Learned	N/A	T Mag-RF	30	Mid Mag-RF
Item	Learned	N/A	Mid Mag-RF	60	N/A
Card	40	Card Mod	Card Mod	80	N/A

SHIVA

Elemental:	Ice
Starting Level:	1
Starting HP:	298

Found At: Access Squall's study panel from his desk in the classroom at Balamb Garden. Select the **Tutorial** option and Shiva will automatically be added to your GF inventory along with Quezacotl.

GF's Attack: Diamond Dust

Shiva's attack is elemental Ice based. The attack is very powerful against fire elemental creatures.

Useful Abilities: Shiva's **Vitality+** and **Spirit+** abilities are useful for improving a character's stats at the beginning of the game. These abilities enable one of your characters to have a strong defense against physical and magic attacks without having a lot of powerful magic for Junctioning to Vitality or Spirit. The **Doom** ability is also useful until you gain the ability to draw or refine Death spells later in the game. This ability enables you to cast Slow Death on a single enemy, which is handy when facing some strong monsters.

Shiva's Vital Statistics

Level	HP	Atk. Power
1	298	263
10	734	564
20	1226	897
30	1726	1230
40	2234	1564
50	2750	1897
60	3274	2230
70	3806	2563
80	4346	2897
90	4894	3230
100	5450	3563

Shiva's Ability List

Ability	AP Needed	Leads To	Ability	AP Needed	Leads To
Str-J	50	Elem-Atk-J	Vit+20%	60	Vit+40%
Vit-J	50	Vit+20%	Vit+40%	120	N/A
Spr-J	Learned	N/A	Spr+20%	60	Spr+40%, Elem-Def-J
Elem-Atk-J	160	N/A	Spr+40%	120	N/A
Elem-Def-J	100	Elem-Defx2	SumMag+10%	40	SumMag+20%
Elem-Defx2	130	N/A	SumMag+20%	70	SumMag+30%
Magic	Learned	N/A	SumMag+30%	140	N/A
GF	Learned	N/A	GFHP+10%	40	GFHP+20%
Draw	Learned	N/A	GFHP+20%	70	N/A
Item	Learned	N/A	Boost	10	N/A
Doom	60	(Gained at LV 10)	I Mag-RF	30	N/A

IFRIT

Elemental:	Fire
Starting Level:	1
Starting HP:	305

Found At: Ifrit is located at the end of the Fire Cavern. You must defeat this GF before it will join you in battle.

GF's Attack: Hell Fire

Ifrit's attack is elemental Fire based. It's most effective against Ice elemental creatures.

Useful Abilities: Ifrit's **HP-J** ability is a must-have early in the game. This ability provides at least one of your characters with a solid HP base, which in turn gives you the stamina for long fights and the ability to resist powerful attacks. The **Str Bonus** ability is great if you can learn it while your characters are still at low levels. Each time a character equipped with the Str Bonus ability levels up, the Str Bonus ability increases that character's Strength by one point. If you equip it on one character long enough, that character will be a real powerhouse by the end of the game.

Ifrit's Vital Statistics

Level	HP	Atk. Power
1	305	298
10	804	607
20	1366	950
30	1936	1293
40	2514	1636
50	3100	1980
60	3694	2323
70	4296	2666
80	4906	3009
90	5524	3352
100	6150	3695

Ifrit's Ability List

Ability	AP Needed	Leads To	Ability	AP Needed	Leads To
HP-J	50	N/A	Str+40%	120	Str Bonus
Str-J	Learned	N/A	Str Bonus	100	N/A
Elem-Atk-J	Learned	N/A	SumMag+10%	40	SumMag+20%
Elem-Def-J	100	Elem-Defx2	SumMag+20%	70	SumMag+30%
Elem-Defx2	130	N/A	SumMag+30%	140	N/A
Magic	Learned	N/A	GFHP+10%	40	GFHP+20%
GF	Learned	N/A	GFHP+20%	70	GFHP+30%
Draw	Learned	N/A	GFHP+30%	140	N/A
Item	Learned	N/A	Boost	10	N/A
Mad Rush	60	(Gained at LV 10)	F Mag-RF	30	N/A
Str+20%	60	Str+40%	Ammo-RF	30	(Gained at LV 10)

Elemental:	None (casts Silence
Starting Level:	3
Starting HP:	391

Found At: You must draw Siren during the Boss fight with Elvoret on top of the Dollet Communications Tower.

GF's Attack: Silent Voice

Siren's attack is non-elemental. This makes it safer to use than previous GFs, but its attack power is less than most other GFs. The attack does have a side effect in that it attempts to affect enemies with the Silence status.

Useful Abilities: By far one of Siren's best abilities is the **Move-Find** ability. With this ability, you can see hidden Save Points and Draw Points as you explore the various locations. However, Draw Points on the World Map will remain invisible even if Move-Find is equipped. Without it, you'll have to rely on maps or just plain guesswork. **Treatment** is another great ability. With this ability, you can instantly cure almost any type of abnormal status effect. Siren is also one of the few Guardian Forces with the **ST-Atk-J** and **ST-Def-Jx2** abilities. These abilities enable you to Junction magic that causes or defends against abnormal status effects with your attack and defense. When used properly, these abilities are extremely helpful and powerful throughout the entire game.

Siren's Vital Statistics

Level	HP	Atk. Power
3	391	223
10	724	393
20	1206	634
30	1696	875
40	2194	1115
50	2700	1356
60	3214	1596
70	3736	1837
80	4266	2078
90	4804	2318
100	5350	2559

Siren's Ability List

Ability	AP Needed	Leads To	Ability	AP Needed	Leads To
Mag-J	Learned	N/A	Mag Bonus	100	N/A
ST-Atk-J	Learned	N/A	Move-Find	40	N/A
ST-Def-J	Learned	N/A	SumMag+10%	40	SumMag+20%
ST-Def-Jx2	130	N/A	SumMag+20%	70	SumMag+30%
Magic	Learned	N/A	SumMag+30%	140	N/A
GF	Learned	N/A	GFHP+10%	40	GFHP+20%
Draw	Learned	N/A	GFHP+20%	70	N/A
Item	Learned	N/A	Boost	10	N/A
Treatment	100	(Gained at LV 12)	L Mag-RF	30	N/A
Mag+20%	60	Mag+40%	ST Med-RF	30	N/A
Mag+40%	120	Mag Bonus	Tool-RF	30	N/A

BROTHERS

Elemental:	Earth
Starting Level:	7
Starting HP:	670

Found At: The Brothers GF is located in the Tomb of the Unknown King. You must defeat one of the minotaur brothers (Sacred) first, and then defeat the two of them together to have them join you.

GF's Attack: Brotherly Love

The Brothers' attack is elemental Earth based. This makes the attack worthless against flying creatures, because those types of creatures don't touch the ground.

Useful Abilities: The Brothers' **HP+** and **HP Bonus** abilities are great to have at any time. Of course, the earlier you get the HP Bonus ability the better, because the character equipped with this ability gains 30 extra HP each time he/she levels up. **Defend** is an underrated ability that enables you to avoid damage from any attack, however, you'll probably want to pass it up for other useful abilities.

Brothers' Vital Statistics

Level	HP	Atk. Power
7	670	529
10	824	632
20	1406	977
30	1996	1322
40	2594	1667
50	3200	2012
60	3814	2357
70	4436	2702
80	5066	3047
90	5704	3392
100	6350	3737

Brothers' Ability List

Ability	AP Needed	Leads To	Ability	AP Needed	Leads To
HP-J	Learned	N/A	HP+40%	120	HP+80%
Str-J	50	Elem-Atk-J	HP+80%	240	HP Bonus
Spr-J	50	Elem-Def-J	Cover	100	N/A
Elem-Atk-J	160	N/A	HP Bonus	100	N/A
Elem-Def-J	100	N/A	SumMag+10%	40	SumMag+20%
Magic	Learned	N/A	SumMag+20%	70	SumMag+30%
GF	Learned	N/A	SumMag+30%	140	N/A
Draw	Learned	N/A	GFHP+10%	40	GFHP+20%
Item	Learned	N/A	GFHP+20%	70	GFHP+30%
Defend	100	N/A	GFHP+30%	140	N/A
HP+20%	Learned	N/A	Boost	10	N/A

DIABLOS

Elemental:	None
Starting Level:	9
Starting HP:	730

Found At: Speak with Headmaster Cid before leaving for Timber and he'll give you a cursed Magical Lamp. Use the lamp in your inventory, and you'll get teleported into battle against Diablos. You must defeat Diablos before it will join your party.

GF's Attack: Dark Messenger

Diablos' non-elemental attack may not seem like much at the start. You can expect it to cause less than 100 points of damage to most creatures when you first get Diablos. After the GF gets some experience, its attack quickly becomes one of the most lethal attacks in the game. There are a lot of enemies that are immune to Diablos' attack.

Useful Abilities: Mug is one of the best abilities in the entire game. This ability enables you to steal useful and, oftentimes, rare items from your enemies. Until you gain this ability, you'll never truly appreciate its usefulness. With it, you can upgrade weapons faster, teach Guardian Forces rare abilities, and create hard-to-find magic and items through refining. Diablos' **Abilityx3** ability is also useful. It enables a character to equip three GF abilities instead of the normal two.

Diablos' Vital Statistics

Level	HP	Atk. Power
9	730	9% of Opponent's Max HP
10	784	10% of Opponent's Max HP
20	1326	20% of Opponent's Max HP
30	1876	30% of Opponent's Max HP
40	2434	40% of Opponent's Max HP
50	3000	50% of Opponent's Max HP
60	3574	60% of Opponent's Max HP
70	4156	70% of Opponent's Max HP
80	4746	80% of Opponent's Max HP
90	5344	90% of Opponent's Max HP
100	5950	100% of Opponent's Max HP

Note *Regardless of Diablos' level, the maximum amount of Hit Points Diablos can inflict on any enemy is 9999.*

Diablos' Ability List

Ability	AP Needed	Leads To	Ability	AP Needed	Leads To
HP-J	50	HP+20%	HP+80%	240	N/A
Mag-J	Learned	N/A	Mag+20%	60	Mag+40%
Hit-J	120	N/A	Mag+40%	120	N/A
Abilityx3	Learned	N/A	Mug	200	N/A
Magic	Learned	N/A	Enc-Half	30	Enc-None
GF	Learned	N/A	Enc-None	100	N/A
Draw	Learned	N/A	GFHP+10%	40	GFHP+20%
Item	Learned	N/A	GFHP+20%	70	GFHP+30%
Dark	100	N/A	GFHP+30%	140	N/A
HP+20%	60	HP+40%	Time Mag-RF	30	N/A
HP+40%	120	HP+80%	ST Mag-RF	30	N/A

CARBUNCLE

Elemental:	None (casts Reflect)
Starting Level:	16
Starting HP:	1220

Find At: You must draw Carbuncle during the Boss fight with the Iguions (Disc One).

GF's Attack: Ruby Light

Carbuncle doesn't actually attack the enemy. Instead, it casts Reflect on your entire party. This is a handy defensive maneuver, and is usually available before Reflect or Triple magic begins to appear.

Useful Abilities: Carbuncle's most valuable abilities are **ST-Atk-J**, **ST-Def-J** and **Abilityx3**. All three abilities are somewhat rare and extremely useful under any conditions, just as they are with Diablos and Siren. The **Vit Bonus** and **Counter** abilities are also worthwhile. The Vit Bonus increases a Junctioned character's Vitality by one point each time the character levels up. This enables you to create a character with a powerful defense against physical attacks. Counter gives your character the chance to randomly counterattack an enemy when attacked.

CARBUNCLE'S VITAL STATISTICS

Level	HP	Atk. Power
1	N/A	N/A
16	1220	N/A
20	1326	N/A
30	2086	N/A
40	2714	N/A
50	3350	N/A
60	3994	N/A
70	4646	N/A
80	5306	N/A
90	5974	N/A
100	6650	N/A

CARBUNCLE'S ABILITY LIST

Ability	AP Needed	Leads To	Ability	AP Needed	Leads To
HP-J	50	HP+20%	HP+20%	60	HP+40%
Vit-J	Learned	N/A	HP+40%	120	N/A
Mag-J	50	ST-Atk-J	Vit+20%	60	Vit+40%
ST-Atk-J	160	N/A	Vit+40%	120	Vit Bonus
ST-Def-J	100	ST-Def-Jx2	Vit Bonus	100	N/A
ST-Def-Jx2	130	N/A	Counter	200	Auto-Reflect
Abilityx3	Learned	N/A	Auto-Reflect	250	N/A
Magic	Learned	N/A	GFHP+10%	40	GFHP+20%
GF	Learned	N/A	GFHP+20%	70	GFHP+30%
Draw	Learned	N/A	GFHP+30%	140	N/A
Item	Learned	N/A	Recov Med-RF	30	N/A

Leviathan

Elemental:	Water
Starting Level:	17
Starting HP:	1349

Find At: Leviathan must be drawn from the Boss NORG during the battle at Balamb Garden (Disc Two).

GF's Attack: Tsunami

Leviathan's attack is elemental Water based. This is by far the strongest Water attack you'll find, so it comes in handy fighting the few creatures with a weakness to Water magic.

Useful Abilities: Without a doubt, Leviathan's most useful ability is **Recover**. It enables you to completely restore a single character's HP without using magic. Also, Leviathan cannot be Silenced, so you can use the Recover ability at times when you wouldn't be able to use items or magic. The **Spr Bonus** ability is also handy if you can get it at an early level. Equipping this on a low level character early in the game will give that character an extremely strong defense against magic later on.

LEVIATHAN'S VITAL STATISTICS

Level	HP	Atk. Power
1	N/A	N/A
17	1349	963
20	1546	1075
30	2206	1445
40	2847	1815
50	3550	2185
60	4234	2555
70	4926	2925
80	5626	3295
90	6334	3666
100	7050	4036

LEVIATHAN'S ABILITY LIST

Ability	AP Needed	Leads To	Ability	AP Needed	Leads To
Spr-J	Learned	N/A	Spr Bonus	100	N/A
Magic	Learned	N/A	Auto-Potion	150	N/A
GF	Learned	N/A	SumMag+10%	40	GFHP+20%
Draw	Learned	N/A	SumMag+20%	70	SumMag+30%
Item	Learned	N/A	SumMag+30%	140	N/A
Mag-J	50	Elem-Atk-J	GFHP+10%	40	GFHP+20%
Elem-Atk-J	160	N/A	GFHP+20%	70	GFHP+30%
Elem-Defx2	130	N/A	GFHP+30%	140	N/A
Recover	200	N/A	Boost	10	N/A
Spr+20%	60	Spr+40%	Supt Mag-RF	20	GF Recov Med-RF
Spr+40%	120	Spr Bonus	GF Recov Med-RF	30	N/A

PANDEMONA

Elemental:	Wind
Starting Level:	19
Starting HP:	1442

Find At: You can draw Pandemona from Fujin during the Boss fight with Fujin and Raijin (Disc 2).

GF's Attack: Tornado Zone

Pandemona's attack is elemental Wind based. There are a lot of enemies with a weakness to Wind magic, and there's not much to choose from when it comes to Wind based magic. Pandemona's Tornado Zone is a welcome addition.

Useful Abilities: Pandemona's abilities provide a character with superhuman speed. With **Spd-J**, **Spd+20/40%**, and **Initiative** you'll be able to finish battles before the enemy even draws its weapon. If you're willing to devote enough space, you can also equip Pandemona's **Str-J** and **Str+20/40%** abilities to create a speedy powerhouse of a character.

PANDEMONA'S VITAL STATISTICS

Level	HP	Atk. Power
1	N/A	N/A
19	1442	1052
20	1506	1092
30	2146	1466
40	2794	1840
50	3450	2213
60	4114	2587
70	4786	2961
80	5466	3335
90	6154	3708
100	6850	4082

PANDEMONA'S ABILITY LIST

Ability	AP Needed	Leads To	Ability	AP Needed	Leads To
Str-J	Learned	N/A	Str+40%	120	N/A
Spd-J	120	Spd+20%	Spd+20%	150	Spd+40%
Elem-Atk-J	Learned	N/A	Spd+40%	200	N/A
Elem-Def-J	Learned	N/A	Initiative	160	N/A
Elem-Defx2	130	N/A	SumMag+10%	40	SumMag+20%
Magic	Learned	N/A	SumMag+20%	70	SumMag+30%
GF	Learned	N/A	SumMag+30%	140	N/A
Draw	Learned	N/A	GFHP+10%	40	GFHP+20%
Item	Learned	N/A	GFHP+20%	70	GFHP+30%
Absorb	80	N/A	GFHP+30%	140	N/A
Str+20%	60	Str+40%	Boost	10	N/A

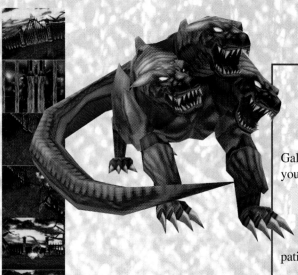

CERBERUS

Elemental:	None (casts Double & Triple)
Starting Level:	23
Starting HP:	1490

Find At: You can challenge Cerberus while you're in the main hall of Galbadia Garden (Disc Two). You must defeat Cerberus before it will join you.

GF's Attack: Counter Rockets

This isn't actually an attack, but it does cast Double and Triple magic on your entire party. This is handy, but you'll want to get the GF's compatibility up so that Cerberus arrives quickly at the beginning of a battle.

Useful Abilities: Let's face it: Cerberus has one of the best sets of abilities you'll find. Its various Junction abilities enable you to raise a variety of statistics. The **ST-Atk-J** and **ST-Def-Jx4** abilities also enable you to cause havoc on the enemy with sneaky abnormal status attacks, while keeping the Junctioned character nearly impervious to abnormal statuses. Add on the speed boosting abilities, and it's hard to find a better GF.

CERBERUS' VITAL STATISTICS

Level	HP	Atk. Power
1	N/A	N/A
10	N/A	N/A
23	1490	N/A
30	1876	N/A
40	2434	N/A
50	3000	N/A
60	3574	N/A
70	4156	N/A
80	4746	N/A
90	5344	N/A
100	5950	N/A

CERBERUS' ABILITY LIST

Ability	AP Needed	Leads To	Ability	AP Needed	Leads To
Str-J	Learned	N/A	GF	Learned	N/A
Mag-J	50	ST-Atk-J	Draw	Learned	N/A
Spr-J	50	ST-Def-J	Item	Learned	N/A
Spd-J	120	Spd+20%	Spd+20%	150	Spd+40%
Hit-J	Learned	N/A	Spd+40%	200	Auto-Haste
ST-Atk-J	160	N/A	Auto-Haste	250	N/A
ST-Def-J	100	ST-Def-Jx2	Expendx2-1	250	N/A
ST-Def-Jx2	130	ST-Def-Jx4	Alert	200	N/A
ST-Def-Jx4	180	N/A	GFHP+10%	40	GFHP+20%
Abilityx3	Learned	N/A	GFHP+20%	70	GFHP+30%
Magic	Learned	N/A	GFHP+30%	140	N/A

ALEXANDER

Elemental:	Holy
Starting Level:	25
HP:	1925

Find At: You must draw Alexander from Edea during the Boss fight inside Galbadia Garden (Disc Two).

GF's Attack: Holy Judgement

Alexander's attack is elemental Holy based. It's extremely effective against the undead or creatures affected with Zombie. This attack isn't very powerful at first, but if you put time into building up Alexander, you can make good use of its attack by Junctioning Zombie magic to a character's weapon using the Status Attack Junctioning ability. Basically, this enables you to force an elemental weakness onto an enemy.

Useful Abilities: The **Med LV Up** ability may not seem like much, but you'll probably need it for the UFO Side Quest and to use the Solomon Ring. Alexander's **Revive** ability is great during later parts of the game, like the fight with Ultima Weapon. This ability enables you to quickly revive and cure a K.O.'ed character. The **Elem-Def-Jx4** is also a great ability, but it may take you a while to get it. I suggest putting it off until you've earned the 200 AP necessary to learn the Revive ability.

ALEXANDER'S VITAL STATISTICS

Level	HP	Atk. Power
1	N/A	N/A
10	N/A	N/A
25	1925	1350
30	2266	1542
40	2954	1920
50	3650	2298
60	4354	2676
70	5066	3054
80	5786	3432
90	6514	3810
100	7250	4188

ALEXANDER'S ABILITY LIST

Ability	AP Needed	Leads To	Ability	AP Needed	Leads To
Spr-J	Learned	N/A	Spr+40%	120	N/A
Elem-Atk-J	160	N/A	Med Data	200	Med LV Up
Elem-Defx2	Learned	N/A	SumMag+10%	40	SumMag+20%
Elem-Defx4	180	N/A	SumMag+20%	70	SumMag+30%
Abilityx3	Learned	N/A	SumMag+30%	140	N/A
Magic	Learned	N/A	GFHP+10%	40	GFHP+20%
GF	Learned	N/A	GFHP+20%	70	GFHP+30%
Draw	Learned	N/A	GFHP+30%	140	N/A
Item	Learned	N/A	Boost	10	N/A
Revive	200	N/A	High Mag-RF	60	N/A
Spr+20%	60	Spr+40%	Med LV Up	120	N/A

DOOMTRAIN

Elemental:	Poison (casts abnormal status)
Starting Level:	28
HP:	2521

Find At: You can find a ring called the Solomon Ring at Tears' Point in Esthar. Also, you need to gather six of the following items: Malboro Tentacles, Remedy+, and Steel Pipes and use the ring. Doomtrain will accept the items and join your party. (First available during Disc Three.)

GF's Attack: Runaway Train

Doomtrain's attack is elemental Poison based. This makes it particularly useful against human enemies, like Galbadian Soldiers. The attack also attempts to cause several abnormal status effects including Poison, Darkness, Silence, Berserk, Sleep, Doom, Curse, Petrify, Confuse, and VIT 0. Sometimes it's worth casting even if the enemy is immune to or absorbs Poison damage just to inflict some of the abnormal statuses.

Useful Abilities: Doomtrain has four very useful abilities in **Elem-Atk-J**, **ST-Atk-J**, **Elem-Def-Jx4**, and **ST-Def-Jx4**. All of these are a bit hard to come by and to get them on a single GF is truly incredible. The **Forbid Med-RF** is great, but it is difficult to get the items for it. Junk Shop, on the other hand, is a bit more practical, but shouldn't really be a priority until Disc Four.

DOOMTRAIN'S VITAL STATISTICS

Level	HP	Atk. Power
1	N/A	N/A
10	N/A	N/A
28	2521	1931
30	2686	2028
40	3514	2509
50	4350	2990
60	5194	3471
70	6046	3953
80	6906	4434
90	7774	4915
100	8650	5396

DOOMTRAIN'S ABILITY LIST

Ability	AP Needed	Leads To	Ability	AP Needed	Leads To
Elem-Atk-J	Learned	N/A	SumMag+10%	40	SumMag+20%
ST-Atk-J	Learned	N/A	SumMag+20%	70	SumMag+30%
Elem-Defx4	180	N/A	SumMag+30%	140	SumMag+40%
ST-Def-Jx4	180	N/A	SumMag+40%	200	N/A
Magic	Learned	N/A	GFHP+10%	40	GFHP+20%
GF	Learned	N/A	GFHP+20%	70	GFHP+30%
Draw	Learned	N/A	GFHP+30%	140	GFHP+40%
Item	Learned	N/A	GFHP+40%	200	N/A
Darkside	100	N/A	Boost	10	N/A
Absorb	80	N/A	Junk Shop	Learned	N/A
Auto-Shell	250	N/A	Forbid Med-RF	200	N/A

BAHAMUT

Elemental:	None
Starting Level:	35
HP:	3274

Find At: Once you have the Ragnarok in Disc Three, you can begin searching for the Deep Sea Research Center in the southwest corner of the World Map. Inside, you must answer Bahamut's questions correctly and then defeat the GF before it will join you.

GF's Attack: Mega Flare

Bahamut's non-elemental attack isn't extremely powerful, however, the attack animation is long and enables you to boost the GF close to the 250 maximum.

Useful Abilities: Obviously, **Abilityx4** makes getting this GF well worth the effort. The **Rare Item** ability is also nice to have if you're into collecting absolutely everything the game has to offer. It's also nice to equip a second person with the **Mug** ability if you're out to build up your item stock.

BAHAMUT'S VITAL STATISTICS

Level	HP	Atk. Power
1	N/A	N/A
10	N/A	N/A
20	N/A	N/A
35	3274	1451
40	3714	1614
50	4600	1940
60	5494	2266
70	6396	2593
80	7306	2919
90	8224	3245
100	9150	3571

BAHAMUT'S ABILITY LIST

Ability	AP Needed	Leads To	Ability	AP Needed	Leads To
Ability x4	Learned	N/A	Rare Item	250	N/A
Magic	Learned	N/A	SumMag+10%	40	SumMag+20%
GF	Learned	N/A	SumMag+20%	70	SumMag+30%
Draw	Learned	N/A	SumMag+30%	140	SumMag+40%
Item	Learned	N/A	SumMag+40%	200	N/A
Str+60%	Learned	N/A	GFHP+10%	40	GFHP+20%
Mag+60%	Learned	N/A	GFHP+20%	70	GFHP+30%
Mug	200	N/A	GFHP+30%	140	GFHP+40%
Move-HP Up	200	N/A	GFHP+40%	200	N/A
Auto-Protect	250	N/A	Boost	10	N/A
Expendx2-1	250	N/A	Forbid Mag-RF	Learned	N/A

JUMBO CACTUAR

Elemental:	None
Starting Level:	20
HP:	1766

Find At: Cactuar Island is a small, desert island east of the Centra Ruins. In the desert sands, you'll see a small green creature that randomly appears. This small creature is the Jumbo Cactuar, an ancient Cactuar that has grown to enormous proportions. Use the Ragnarok to land on the island and chase down the Jumbo Cactuar. Defeat it and you'll get the Cactuar GF.

GF's Attack: 1,000 Needles

Cactuar's attack is the second most powerful GF attack in the game. The damage inflicted is directly related to the Cactuar's level. **1,000 Needles** causes 1,000 points of damage for every 10 levels of Cactuar's experience. So at level 100, the attack causes 10,000 points of non-elemental damage. Also, the damage from Cactuar's attack cannot be reduced by a high defense or support magic, plus Boosting isn't necessary.

Useful Abilites: Cactuar's big prize is its five Bonus abilities. They should enable you to customize your characters just about any way you want. Unfortunately, you get Cactuar so late in the game you may not really get to enjoy the full benefit of the bonuses.

JUMBO CACTUAR'S VITAL STATISTICS

Level	HP	Atk. Power
1	N/A	N/A
10	N/A	N/A
20	1766	2000
30	2536	3000
40	3314	4000
50	4100	5000
60	4894	6000
70	5696	7000
80	7324	9000
90	7324	9000
100	8150	10,000

JUMBO CACTUAR'S ABILITY LIST

Ability	AP Needed	Leads To	Ability	AP Needed	Leads To
Eva-J	200	Eva+30%	Move-HP Up	200	N/A
Luck-J	200	Luck+50%	HP Bonus	Learned	N/A
Magic	Learned	N/A	Str Bonus	Learned	N/A
GF	Learned	N/A	Vit Bonus	Learned	N/A
Draw	Learned	N/A	Mag Bonus	Learned	N/A
Item	Learned	N/A	Spr Bonus	Learned	N/A
Defend	100	N/A	Auto-Potion	150	N/A
Kamikaze	100	N/A	Expendx2-1	250	N/A
Eva+30%	150	Expendx2-1	GFHP+10%	40	GFHP+20%
Luck+50%	200	N/A	GFHP+20%	70	GFHP+30%
Initiative	160	N/A	GFHP+30%	140	N/A

TONBERRY KING

Elemental:	None
Starting Level:	30
HP:	2596

Find At: You must fight and defeat 18 plus Tonberrys at the Centra Ruins. After defeating enough Tonberrys, the Tonberry King will appear. Defeat the Tonberry King and it will join you as a GF.

GF's Attack: Chef's Knife

Tonberry's attack targets a single creature at random. The attack isn't very powerful at first, but it becomes much more valuable over time. The animation for the attack is relatively short, so you won't be able to do much Boosting.

Useful Abilities: Once you have Tonberry on your side, your shopping experiences will be much more enjoyable. The **Familiar** ability adds items to every shop, some of which are relatively difficult to find. **Call Shop** is also nice, because it lets you revisit any shop you've been to in the past. This is extremely handy in Disc Four. The **LV Down** and **LV Up** abilities are also kind of fun. Use them to beef up weaker monsters or to give more pathetic creatures a fearsome bite. Adjusting creatures' levels enables you to customize your battles and choose when you want a tough battle or gain a rare item from an enemy.

TONBERRY KING'S VITAL STATISTICS

Level	HP	Atk. Power
1	N/A	N/A
10	N/A	N/A
20	N/A	N/A
30	2596	1492
40	3394	1830
50	4200	2167
60	5014	2505
70	5836	2842
80	6666	3180
90	7504	3517
100	8350	3855

TONBERRY KING'S ABILITY LIST

Ability	AP Needed	Leads To	Ability	AP Needed	Leads To
Magic	Learned	N/A	SumMag+10%	40	SumMag+20%
GF	Learned	N/A	SumMag+20%	70	SumMag+30%
Draw	Learned	N/A	SumMag+30%	140	N/A
Item	Learned	N/A	GFHP+10%	40	GFHP+20%
LV Down	Learned	N/A	GFHP+20%	70	GFHP+30%
LV Up	Learned	N/A	GFHP+30%	140	N/A
Eva+30%	Learned	N/A	Boost	10	N/A
Luck+50%	Learned	N/A	Haggle	150	Sell-High
Initiative	160	N/A	Sell-High	150	N/A
Move-HP Up	200	N/A	Familiar	150	Call Shop
Auto-Potion	150	N/A	Call Shop	200	N/A

Doink

EDEN

Elemental: None

Starting Level: 30

HP: 4786

Find At: After defeating Bahamut at the Deep Sea Research Center, you'll be able to head deeper underwater. Well below the surface you'll encounter Ultima Weapon, if you have enough steam power left to reactivate the excavation site. Eden, the ultimate GF, must be drawn from Ultima Weapon during the battle.

GF's Attack: Eternal Breath

Eden's attack is simply the most powerful attack in the game. On its own, it can cause around 13,000 points of damage. The attack animation is very long and easily allows for Boosting to a full 250. This tends to increase the damage to about 35,000 points of damage.

Useful Abilities: Devour is one of the coolest abilities you'll find. Sure it's a little silly, but with it you actually have the potential to max out several of a character's stats by eating the right type of creatures (refer to the Bestiary for more information). Of course, this process could literally take months, but true Final Fantasy diehards are always up for a good challenge—right?

EDEN'S VITAL STATISTICS

Level	HP	Atk. Power
1	N/A	N/A
10	N/A	N/A
20	N/A	N/A
30	4786	5425
40	6314	6300
50	7850	7175
60	9334	8050
70	9999	8925
80	9999	9600
90	9999	10,675
100	9999	11,550

EDEN'S ABILITY LIST

Ability	AP Needed	Leads To	Ability	AP Needed	Leads To
Spd-J	Learned	N/A	Expendx3-1	250	N/A
Eva-J	Learned	N/A	SumMag+10%	40	SumMag+20%
Hit-J	Learned	N/A	SumMag+20%	70	SumMag+30%
Magic	Learned	N/A	SumMag+30%	140	SumMag+40%
GF	Learned	N/A	SumMag+40%	200	N/A
Draw	Learned	N/A	GFHP+10%	40	GFHP+20%
Item	Learned	N/A	GFHP+20%	70	GFHP+30%
Mad Rush	60	N/A	GFHP+30%	140	GFHP+40%
Darkside	100	N/A	GFHP+40%	200	N/A
Devour	Learned	N/A	Boost	10	N/A
Luck+50%	200	N/A	GFAbl Med-RF	30	N/A

GF Ability Lists

Junction Abilities

Ability	Effect	Item
HP-J	Junctions magic to character's Hit Points	HP-J Scroll
Str-J	Junctions magic to character's Strength	Str-J Scroll
Vit-J	Junctions magic to character's Vitality	Vit-J Scroll
Mag-J	Junctions magic to character's Magic	Mag-J Scroll
Spr-J	Junctions magic to character's Spirit	Spr-J Scroll
Spd-J	Junctions magic to character's Speed	Spd-J Scroll
Eva-J	Junctions magic to character's Evasion	Aegis Amulet
Hit-J	Junctions magic to character's Hit %	N/A
Luck-J	Junctions magic to character's Luck	Luck-J Scroll
Elem-Atk-J	Junctions elemental magic to character's Elemental Attack	Elem Atk
Elem-Def-J	Junctions elemental magic to character's Elemental Defense	N/A
Elem-Defx2	Junctions 2 elemental magics to character's Elemental Defense	N/A
Elem-Defx4	Junctions 4 elemental magics to character's Elemental Defense	Elem Guard
ST-Atk-J	Junctions status magic to character's Status Attack	Status Atk
ST-Def-J	Junctions status magic to character's Status Defense	N/A
ST-Defx2	Junctions 2 status magics to character's Status Defense	N/A
ST-Defx4	Junctions 4 status magics to character's Status Defense	Status Guard
Abilityx3	Sets 3 Party and/or Character Abilities to a character	N/A
Abilityx4	Sets 4 Party and/or Character Abilities to a character	Rosetta Stone

Command Abilities

Ability	Effect	Item
Magic	Enables use of Magic in battle	Magic Scroll
GF	Enables use of GF in battle	GF Scroll
Draw	Enables use of Draw in/out battle	Draw Scroll
Item	Enables use of Item in battle	Item Scroll
Card	Transforms enemy into a card	Gambler Spirit
Doom	Casts Death on an enemy	N/A
Mad Rush	Casts Berserk, Protect, and Haste on all allies	N/A
Treatment	Cures Poison, Petrify, Darkness, Silence, Zombie, Sleep, Berserk, Slow, Stop, Curse, Slow Petrify, Confuse, and Vit 0	Med Kit
Defend	Reduces damage from physical attacks to 0 and cuts magic damage in half	N/A
Darkside	Triples damage inflicted by Attack, but with each use, the character loses 1/10 of their maximum HP	N/A
Recover	Restores all HP to one party member	Healing Ring
Absorb	Drains HP from target; causes damage if used against Undead	N/A
Revive	Restores one party member from K.O. status	Phoenix Spirit
LV Down	Cuts target's level by half	N/A
LV Up	Doubles target's level	N/A
Kamikaze	Inflicts major damage, but knocks the character out	Bomb Spirit
Devour	Allow consumption of enemies	Hungry Cookpot
MiniMog	Restores HP to all GF; costs character's average level x 100 Gil to use	Mog's Amulet

Character Abilities

Ability	Effect	Item
HP+/20/40/80%	Increase HP by 20, 40, or 80%; effect is cumulative	Regen Ring, Giant's Ring, Gaea's Ring
Str+20/40/60%	Increase Strength by 20, 40, or 60%; effect is cumulative	Strength Love, Power Wrist, Hyper Wrist
Vit+20/40/60%	Increase Vitality by 20, 40, or 60%; effect is cumulative	Turtle Shell, Orihalcon, Adamantine
Mag+20/40/60%	Increase Magic by 20, 40, or 60%; effect is cumulative	Circlet, Hypno Crown, Royal Crown
Spr+20/40/60%	Increase Spirit by 20, 40, or 60%; effect is cumulative	Rune Armlet, Force Armlet, Magic Armlet
Spd+20/40%	Increase Speed by 20 or 40%; effect is cumulative	Jet Engine, Rocket Engine
Eva+30%	Increase Evade by 30%	N/A
Luck+50%	Increase Luck by 50%	N/A
Mug	Changes Attack command into Mug; allows character to steal items from enemies	N/A
Med Data	HP recovery from items doubles during battles	Doc's Code
Counter	Character counterattacks when hit with a physical attack	Monk's Code
Return Damage	When damaged, character returns 1/4 of the damage to the opponent	Hundred Needles
Cover	Take physical damage in place of an almost disabled ally; damage is reduced by 1/2	Knight's Code
Expendx2-1	Reduces the number of magic used in Double from 2 to 1	N/A
Expendx3-1	Reduces the number of magic used in Triple from 3 to 1	Three Stars
HP Bonus	When a character levels up, HP gains an additional 30 points	N/A
Str Bonus	When a character levels up, Strength gains an additional point	N/A
Vit Bonus	When a character levels up, Vitality gains an additional point	N/A
Mag Bonus	When a character levels up, Magic gains and additional point	N/A
Spr Bonus	When a character levels up, Spirit gains an additional point	N/A
Auto-Reflect	Automatically activates Reflect in battle; doesn't expire with time or K.O. status	Glow Curtain
Auto-Shell	Automatically activates Shell in battle; doesn't expire with time or K.O. status	Moon Curtain
Auto-Protect	Automatically activates Protect in battle; doesn't expire with time or K.O. status	Steel Curtain
Auto-Haste	Automatically activates Haste in battle; doesn't expire with time or K.O. status	Accelerator
Initiative	ATB gauge is always full when battle begins	N/A
Move-HP Up	Recovers HP by walking on the World Map	N/A
Auto-Potion	Uses recovery items automatically when damaged in battle; uses Potion and Hi-Potion from item stock	N/A

Party Abilities

Ability	Effect
Alert	Prevents enemy's Back Attack and First Strike, and increases the party's chances for Back Attack and First Strike
Enc-Half	Reduces the encounter rate by half
Enc-None	No random encounters with enemies
Rare Item	Rare items become easier to obtain after battle
Move-Find	Hidden Save Points and Draw Points become visible

GF Abilities

Ability	Effect	Item
SumMag+10/20/30/40%	Increases GF's attack damage by 10, 20, 30, or 40%; effect is cumulative	Steel Pipe, Star Fragment, Energy Crystal, Samantha Soul
GFHP+10/20/30/40%	Increases GF's HP by 10, 20, 30, or 40%; effect is cumulative	Healing Mail, Silver Mail, Gold Armor, Diamond Armor
Boost	Increase damage during GF's attack	N/A

Menu Abilites

Ability	Effect
Haggle	Buy items at shops for a discount
Sell-High	Sell items to shops for a higher price than usual
Familiar	Enables you to buy a better variety of items at shops
Call Shop	Call any shops you've visited from the menu screen
Junk Shop	Call a Junk Shop from the menu
T Mag-RF	Refine Lightning/Wind magic from items
I Mag-RF	Refine Water/Ice magic from items
F Mag-RF	Refine Fire magic from items
L Mag-RF	Refine Life/Recovery magic from items
Time Mag-RF	Refine Time/Space magic from items
ST Mag-RF	Refine Status magic from items
Supt Mag-RF	Refine Support magic from items
Forbid Mag-RF	Refine Forbidden magic from items
Recov Mag-RF	Refine Recovery magic from items
ST Med-RF	Refine Status Recovery Medicine from items
Ammo-RF	Refine Ammunition from items
Tool-Rf	Refine Tools from items
Forbid Med-RF	Refine Forbidden Medicine from items
GFRecov Med-RF	Refine Recovery Medicine for GF from items
GFAbl Med-RF	Refine GF Ability Medicine from items
Mid Mag-RF	Refine Mid-Level magic from Low-Level magic
High Mag-RF	Refine High-Level magic from Mid-Level magic
Med LV Up	Refine rare medicines from common medicines
Card Mod	Refine items from cards

Acquiring Missed GFs

If you missed any GF on your way through the game, you can get them during Disc Four at Ultimecia's Castle. After defeating Sphinxaur, choose to unlock the Draw ability. You'll then be able to draw the following GFs from the corresponding Bosses.

Siren = Tri-Point
Leviathan = Trauma
Pandemona = Red Giant
Carbuncle = Krysta
Cerberus = Gargantua
Alexander = Catoblepas
Eden = Tiamat

Other Guardian Forces

Odin

You must search out Odin's lair inside the Centra Ruins and defeat him if you want him to join your cause. Odin is not a controllable GF. Once he joins you, he'll randomly appear at the start of about 1 in every 10 battles (except Boss fights). Riding through the battlefield on his mighty steed, Odin uses his sword Zantetsuken to cut your enemies in two. This attack kills all enemies on the battlefield. This is sort of a blessing and a curse. It's great when Odin appears and cuts down a powerful creature like a Malboro, but if you're trying to stock up on magic or steal an item from a rare creature it's a bit of a nuisance.

Phoenix

You can only summon Phoenix by using a Phoenix Pinion during a battle. When the Phoenix appears, it revives any K.O.ed characters and restores some of their HP. Phoenix Pinions are hard to come by, but once you've summoned Phoenix there is a random chance that it will appear again later when your party is in trouble.

Boko the Chocobo

As you probably already know, Chocobos are back in Final Fantasy VIII. And once again you can summon a Chocobo to aid you in battle. You won't be able to do this until you've solved a puzzle in at least one of the many Chocobo Forests scattered around the world. During a battle, use a Gysahl Green to lure the Chocobo into attacking your enemies.

MiniMog

MiniMog is more of a GF ability than a GF. By using Mog's Amulet, you can teach a GF the MiniMog ability. When called upon, MiniMog will perform a dance that restores all of your GFs HP. This is great to have at the end of the game when Bosses actually begin targeting GFs. Each time you use MiniMog in battle, it'll cost you Gil. The amount varies based on your character's average level times 100 Gil. So if your average level is 20, it'll cost you 2000 Gil.

Moomba

Moombas are decent fighters due to their massive paws and razor-sharp claws, but it sure doesn't seem like fighting is the first thing they have on their minds. You can call upon a Moomba by using a Friendship item in battle.

Gilgamesh

Near the end of Disc Three, Gilgamesh will appear if you already have Odin at that point. Gilgamesh is a lot like Odin in that you can't control him and he appears randomly. The biggest difference is that Gilgamesh can appear at any point during a battle (even Boss fights). What happens depends on which of his four sword attacks he selects:

Zantetsuken	Cuts all enemies in half, resulting in death
Masamune	Extremely strong attack against all enemies
Excaliber	Strong attack against all enemies
Excalipoor	Causes 1 point of damage to each enemy

Note: Remember the Masamune from Final Fantasy VII? That's the same name used for Sephiroth's incredible sword.

Magic List

The following is a complete list of the magic you can Draw/Stock in Final Fantasy VIII, and the effects caused when the magic is Junctioned to a character.

Magic List Legend

*All of the following tables are based on Junctioning 100 of a spell.

Effect on Attributes	All increases in these categories are based on actual number of points
Elemental Attack/Defense	All increases in these categories are based on percentages
Status Attack/Defense	All increases in these categories are based on percentages
Name	The name of the spell Junctioned
HP	Character's Hit Points
Str	Character's Strength
Vit	Character's Vitality
Mag	Character's Magic
Spr	Character's Spirit
Spd	Character's Speed
Eva	Character's Evasion rate
Hit	Character's Hit Percentage
Luck	Character's Luck
% Change	The percentage by which a stat increases
Fire	Elemental Fire Attack/Defense
Ice	Elemental Ice Attack/Defense
Thunder	Elemental Thunder Attack/Defense
Earth	Elemental Earth Attack/Defense
Poison	Elemental Poison Attack/Defense (Elemental) Poison Status Attack/Defense (Status)
Wind	Elemental Wind Attack/Defense
Holy	Elemental Holy Attack/Defense
Status Effect	Any abnormal statuses caused by Junctioned magic when attacking
Status Defense	Any abnormal statuses defended against due to Junctioned Magic

Magic Effects

Life Magic

Cure	Restores a small amount of HP/one ally
Cura	Restores some HP/one ally
Curaga	Restores a lot of HP/one ally
Death	Randomly causes immediate death/one enemy
Holy	Inflicts Holy magic damage/one enemy
Life	Restores some HP and revives from KO/one ally
Full-Life	Fully restores HP and revives from KO/one ally
Regen	Restores small amounts of HP at regular intervals/one ally
Zombie	Causes Zombie status (undead)/one enemy

Fire Magic

Fire	Causes minor elemental Fire damage/one enemy
Fira	Causes elemental Fire damage/one enemy
Firaga	Causes major elemental Fire damage/one enemy
Flare	Causes major non-elemental damage/one enemy

Ice Magic

Blizzard	Causes minor elemental Ice damage/one enemy
Blizzara	Causes elemental Ice damage/one enemy
Blizzaga	Causes major elemental Ice damage/one enemy
Water	Causes elemental Water damage/one enemy

Thunder Magic

Thunder	Causes minor elemental Thunder damage/one enemy
Thundara	Causes elemental Thunder damage/one enemy
Thundaga	Causes major elemental Thunder damage/one enemy
Aero	Causes elemental Wind damage/one enemy
Tornado	Causes elemental Wind damage/all enemies

Time/Space Magic

Haste	Speeds up target's ATB Gauge/one ally
Slow	Slows down target's ATB Gauge/one enemy
Stop	Stops target's ATB Gauge/one enemy
Quake	Cause elemental Earth damage/all enemies
Demi	Reduces enemy's HP by 1/4/one ally
Double	Allows target to cast 2 of the same spell consecutively/one ally
Triple	Allows target to cast 3 of the same spell consecutively/one ally

Support Magic

Esuna	Removes Poison, Petrify, Blind, Silence, Berserk, Sleep, Curse, Slow, Stop, Slow Petrify, Confuse, Zombie, and Vit 0/one ally
Dispel	Removes Haste, Regen, Protect, Shell, Aura, Reflect, Float, Double, and Triple/one enemy
Protect	Reduces physical attack damage by 1/2
Shell	Reduces magic attack damage by 1/2
Reflect	Reflects magic back at caster's party/one ally
Drain	Remove HP from target and give to caster/one enemy
Aura	Limit Break can be used more often/one ally

Forbidden Magic

Meteor	Bombards enemies with meteors causing random non-elemental damage/random enemies
Ultima	Cause a large amount of non-elemental damage/all enemies

ST Magic

Bio	Causes elemental Poison damage and adds Poison status to target/one enemy
Break	Causes non-elemental damage and adds Petrify status to target/one enemy
Blind	Causes Blind status, impairing accuracy of physical attacks/one enemy
Silence	Causes Silence status, disabling target from using Magic, Draw, and GF commands
Berserk	Causes Berserk status, forcing character to auto-matically initiate physical attacks each turn/one enemy
Sleep	Causes Sleep status, disabling target temporarily/one enemy
Confuse	Causes Confuse status, forcing target to use random commands and targeting decisions/one enemy
Pain	Causes Poison, Silence, and Blind status
Meltdown	Causes non-elemental damage and Vit 0 status, lowering targets defenses/one enemy

Other Magic

Float	Lifts target off ground, avoiding elemental Earth magic
Scan	Analyze target's vital information

Life Magic

Effect on Attributes

Name	HP	Str	Vit	Mag	Spr	Spd	Eva	Hit	Luck
Cure	200	4	15	4	15	3	4	2	2
Cura	500	8	28	8	28	4	5	3	3
Curaga	2200	20	65	20	65	10	10	10	10
Death	1800	22	22	38	58	10	10	10	38
Holy	3800	55	28	45	48	10	18	24	14
Life	1200	8	50	10	50	4	3	3	4
Full-Life	4800	20	80	20	85	8	10	8	20
Regen	2600	18	70	18	60	8	8	8	8
Zombie	800	15	24	15	12	2	2	2	2

Elemental Attack

Name	% Change	Fire	Ice	Thunder	Earth	Poison	Wind	Water	Holy
Cure	-	-	-	-	-	-	-	-	-
Cura	-	-	-	-	-	-	-	-	-
Curaga	-	-	-	-	-	-	-	-	-
Death	-	-	-	-	-	-	-	-	-
Holy	100	-	-	-	-	-	-	-	Yes
Life	-	-	-	-	-	-	-	-	-
Full-Life	-	-	-	-	-	-	-	-	-
Regen	—	—	—	—	—	—	—	—	—
Zombie	-	-	-	-	-	-	-	-	-

Elemental Defense

Name	% Change	Fire	Ice	Thunder	Earth	Poison	Wind	Water	Holy
Cure	-	-	-	-	-	-	-	-	-
Cura	-	-	-	-	-	-	-	-	-
Curaga-	-	-	-	-	-	-	-	-	-
Death	-	-	-	-	-	-	-	-	-
Holy	200(100*)	-	-	-	-	-	-	-	Yes
Life	30	Yes	Yes	Yes	Yes	Yes	Yes	Yes	Yes
Full-Life	40	Yes	Yes	Yes	Yes	Yes	Yes	Yes	Yes
Regen	—	—	—	—	—	—	—	—	—
Zombie	-	-	-	-	-	-	-	-	-

Status Attack / Status Defense

Name	% Change	Status Effect	% Change	Status Protection
Cure	-	-	-	-
Cura	-	-	-	-
Curaga	-	-	-	-
Death	100	Death	100	Death
Holy	-	-	40	Death, Bio, Berserk, Zombie, Sleep, Cursed, Confuse, Drain.
Life	-	-	20	Death
Full-Life	-	-	40	Death
Regen	—	—	—	—
Zombie	100	Zombie	100	Zombie

Fire Magic

Effect on Attributes

Name	HP	Str	Vit	Mag	Spr	Spd	Eva	Hit	Luck
Fire	100	10	4	10	4	8	6	10	8
Fira	200	15	8	15	8	12	8	16	12
Firaga	1400	30	16	30	16	14	10	20	14
Flare	3200	56	26	44	26	12	10	26	12

Elemental Attack

Name	% Change	Fire	Ice	Thunder	Earth	Poison	Wind	Water	Holy
Fire	50	Yes	-	-	-	-	-	-	-
Fira	80	Yes	-	-	-	-	-	-	-
Firaga	100	Yes	-	-	-	-	-	-	-
Flare	-	-	-	-	-	-	-	-	-

Elemental Defense

Name	% Change	Fire	Ice	Thunder	Earth	Poison	Wind	Water	Holy
Fire	50	Yes	-	-	-	-	-	-	-
Fira	80	Yes	-	-	-	-	-	-	-
Firaga	150(50*)	Yes	-	-	-	-	-	-	-
Flare	80	Yes	Yes	Yes	-	-	-	-	-

Status Attack / Status Defense

Name	% Change	Status Effect	% Change	Status Protection
Fire	-	-	-	-
Fira	-	-	-	-
Firaga	-	-	-	-
Flare	-	-	-	-

Ice Magic

Effect on Attributes

Name	HP	Str	Vit	Mag	Spr	Spd	Eva	Hit	Luck
Blizzard	100	10	4	10	4	8	6	10	8
Blizzara	200	15	8	15	8	12	8	16	12
Blizzaga	1400	30	16	30	16	14	10	20	14
Water	300	20	14	44	14	12	10	18	13

Elemental Attack

Name	% Change	Fire	Ice	Thunder	Earth	Poison	Wind	Water	Holy
Blizzard	50	-	Yes	-	-	-	-	-	-
Blizzara	80	-	Yes	-	-	-	-	-	-
Blizzaga	100	-	Yes	-	-	-	-	-	-
Water	100	-	-	-	-	-	-	Yes	-

Elemental Defense

Name	% Change	Fire	Ice	Thunder	Earth	Poison	Wind	Water	Holy
Blizzard	50	-	Yes	-	-	-	-	-	-
Blizzara	80	-	Yes	-	-	-	-	-	-
Blizzaga	150(50*)	-	Yes	-	-	-	-	-	-
Water	150(50*)	-	-	-	-	-	-	Yes	-

Status Attack / Status Defense

Name	% Change	Status Effect	% Change	Status Protection
Blizzard	-	-	-	-
Blizzara	-	-	-	-
Blizzaga	-	-	-	-
Water	-	-	-	-

Thunder Magic

Effect on Attributes

Name	HP	Str	Vit	Mag	Spr	Spd	Eva	Hit	Luck
Thunder	100	10	4	10	4	8	6	10	8
Thundara	200	15	8	15	8	12	8	16	12
Thundaga	1400	30	16	30	16	14	10	20	14
Aero	300	17	10	16	10	20	18	22	15
Tornado	3000	48	24	42	24	33	32	38	14

Elemental Attack

Name	% Change	Fire	Ice	Thunder	Earth	Poison	Wind	Water	Holy
Thunder	50	-	-	Yes	-	-	-	-	-
Thundara	80	-	-	Yes	-	-	-	-	-
Thundaga	100	-	-	Yes	-	-	-	-	-
Aero	80	-	-	-	-	-	Yes	-	-
Tornado	100	-	-	-	-	-	Yes	-	-

Elemental Defense

Name	% Change	Fire	Ice	Thunder	Earth	Poison	Wind	Water	Holy
Thunder	50	-	-	Yes	-	-	-	-	-
Thundara	80	-	-	Yes	-	-	-	-	-
Thundaga	150(50*)	-	-	Yes	-	-	-	-	-
Aero	80	-	-	-	-	-	Yes	-	-
Tornado	200(100*)	-	-	-	-	-	Yes	-	-

Status Attack / Status Defense

Name	% Change	Status Effect	% Change	Status Protection
Thunder	-	-	-	-
Thundara	-	-	-	-
Thundaga	-	-	-	-
Aero	-	-	-	-
Tornado	-	-	-	-

Time Magic

Effect on Attributes

Name	HP	Str	Vit	Mag	Spr	Spd	Eva	Hit	Luck
Haste	500	12	16	20	20	50	20	10	10
Slow	500	12	16	20	20	40	20	10	10
Stop	20	18	20	30	24	48	25	20	10
Quake	20	40	20	40	20	7	7	30	12
Demi	16	34	18	36	18	12	8	14	10
Double	200	15	6	18	6	10	10	40	2
Triple	2400	70	10	70	10	70	40	150	30

Elemental Attack

Name	% Change	Fire	Ice	Thunder	Earth	Poison	Wind	Water	Holy
Haste	—	—	—	—	—	—	—	—	—
Slow	—	—	—	—	—	—	—	—	—
Stop	—	—	—	—	—	—	—	—	—
Quake	100	—	—	—	Yes	—	—	—	—
Demi	—	—	—	—	—	—	—	—	—
Double	—	—	—	—	—	—	—	—	—
Triple	—	—	—	—	—	—	—	—	—

Elemental Defense

Name	% Change	Fire	Ice	Thunder	Earth	Poison	Wind	Water	Holy
Haste	—	—	—	—	—	—	—	—	—
Slow	—	—	—	—	—	—	—	—	—
Stop	—	—	—	—	—	—	—	—	—
Quake	200(100*)	-	-	-	Yes	-	-	-	-
Demi	—	—	—	—	—	—	—	—	—
Double	—	—	—	—	—	—	—	—	—
Triple	—	—	—	—	—	—	—	—	—

Status Attack / Status Defense

Name	% Change (Attack)	Status Effect	% Change (Defense)	Status Protection
Haste	—	—	—	—
Slow	100	Slow	100	Slow
Stop	100	Stop		
Quake	—	—	100	Stop
Demi	—	—	—	—
Double	—	—	—	—
Triple	—	—	—	—

Support Magic

Effect on Attributes

Name	HP	Str	Vit	Mag	Spr	Spd	Eva	Hit	Luck
Esuna	500	6	36	12	36	3	3	3	10
Dispel	1000	12	38	16	60	8	8	8	14
Protect	400	6	40	10	18	3	3	3	14
Shell	400	6	18	10	40	3	3	3	14
Reflect	2000	14	46	20	72	10	10	8	16
Drain	400	13	30	20	24	6	5	5	4
Aura	3400	70	22	24	24	10	5	50	40

Elemental Attack

Name	% Change	Fire	Ice	Thunder	Earth	Poison	Wind	Water	Holy
Esuna	-	-	-	-	-	-	-	-	-
Dispel	-	-	-	-	-	-	-	-	-
Protect	-	-	-	-	-	-	-	-	-
Shell	-	-	-	-	-	-	-	-	-
Reflect	-	-	-	-	-	-	-	-	-
Drain	-	-	-	-	-	-	-	-	-
Aura	-	-	-	-	-	-	-	-	-

Elemental Defense

Name	% Change	Fire	Ice	Thunder	Earth	Poison	Wind	Water	Holy
Esuna	-	-	-	-	-	-	-	-	-
Dispel	-	-	-	-	-	-	-	-	-
Protect	20	Yes	Yes	Yes	-	-	-	-	-
Shell	20	Yes	Yes	Yes	Yes	Yes	Yes	Yes	Yes
Reflect	-	-	-	-	-	-	-	-	-
Drain	-	-	-	-	-	-	-	-	-
Aura	-	-	-	-	-	-	-	-	-

Status Attack / Status Defense

Name	Status Attack % Change	Status Effect	Status Defense % Change	Status Protection
Esuna	-	-	20	Bio, Petrify, Blind, Silence, Berserk, Sleep, Slow, Stop, Curse, Confuse
Dispel	-	-	50	Drain
Protect	-	-	-	-
Shell	-	-	-	-
Reflect	-	-	25	Bio, Petrify, Blind, Silence, Berserk, Sleep, Slow, Stop, Confuse
Drain	100	Drain	100	Drain
Aura	-	-	200	Curse

ST Magic

Effect on Attributes

Name	HP	Str	Vit	Mag	Spr	Spd	Eva	Hit	Luck
Bio	700	24	15	24	15	5	5	4	4
Break	1000	20	20	34	35	10	10	10	12
Blind	100	6	5	12	10	3	3	30	2
Silence	100	6	5	12	10	4	3	3	2
Berserk	300	13	8	14	8	5	5	4	3
Sleep	100	6	5	12	10	4	10	3	2
Confuse	700	22	18	28	18	18	8	8	8
Pain	2800	42	38	60	45	4	4	4	40
Meltdown	1500	24	80	20	20	3	4	12	8

Elemental Attack

Name	% Change	Fire	Ice	Thunder	Earth	Poison	Wind	Water	Holy
Bio	100	-	-	-	-	Yes	-	-	-
Break	-	-	-	-	-	-	-	-	-
Blind	-	-	-	-	-	-	-	-	-
Silence	-	-	-	-	-	-	-	-	-
Berserk	-	-	-	-	-	-	-	-	-
Sleep	-	-	-	-	-	-	-	-	-
Confuse	-	-	-	-	-	-	-	-	-
Pain	-	-	-	-	-	-	-	-	-
Meltdown	-	-	-	-	-	-	-	-	-

Elemental Defense

Name	% Change	Fire	Ice	Thunder	Earth	Poison	Wind	Water	Holy
Bio	150(50*)	-	-	-	-	Yes	-	-	-
Break	-	-	-	-	-	-	-	-	-
Blind	-	-	-	-	-	-	-	-	-
Silence	-	-	-	-	-	-	-	-	-
Berserk	-	-	-	-	-	-	-	-	-
Sleep	-	-	-	-	-	-	-	-	-
Confuse	-	-	-	-	-	-	-	-	-
Pain	-	-	-	-	-	-	-	-	-
Meltdown	-	-	-	-	-	-	-	-	-

Status Attack / Status Defense

Name	Status Attack % Change	Status Effect	Status Defense % Change	Status Protection
Bio	100	Bio	100	Bio
Break	100	Petrify	100	Petrify
Blind	100	Blind	100	Blind
Silence	100	Silence	100	Silence
Berserk	100	Berserk	100	Berserk
Sleep	100	Sleep	100	Sleep
Confuse	100	Confuse	100	Confuse
Pain	100	Bio, Darkness, Silence	100	Bio, Darkness, Silence
Meltdown	-	-	-	-

Forbidden Magic

Effect on Attributes

Name	HP	Str	Vit	Mag	Spr	Spd	Eva	Hit	Luck
Meteor	4600	75	34	52	34	30	30	40	22
Ultima	6000	100	82	100	95	60	60	60	60

Elemental Attack

Name	% Change	Fire	Ice	Thunder	Earth	Poison	Wind	Water	Holy
Meteor	-	-	-	-	-	-	-	-	-
Ultima	-	-	-	-	-	-	-	-	-

Elemental Defense

Name	% Change	Fire	Ice	Thunder	Earth	Poison	Wind	Water	Holy
Meteor	150(50*)	-	-	-	Yes	-	Yes	-	-
Ultima	100	Yes	Yes	Yes	Yes	Yes	Yes	Yes	Yes

Status Attack / Status Defense

Name	% Change	Status Effect	% Change	Status Protection
Meteor	-	-	-	-
Ultima	-	-	-	-

Other Magic

Effect on Attributes

Name	HP	Str	Vit	Mag	Spr	Spd	Eva	Hit	Luck
Float	200	8	15	8	15	16	8	12	20
Scan	100	5	5	5	5	3	3	3	3

Elemental Attack

Name	% Change	Fire	Ice	Thunder	Earth	Poison	Wind	Water	Holy
Float	-	-	-	-	-	-	-	-	-
Scan	-	-	-	-	-	-	-	-	-

Elemental Defense

Name	% Change	Fire	Ice	Thunder	Earth	Poison	Wind	Water	Holy
Float	50	-	-	-	Yes	-	-	-	-
Scan	-	-	-	-	-	-	-	-	-

Status Attack / Status Defense

Name	% Change	Status Effect	% Change	Status Protection
Float	-	-	-	-
Scan-	-	-	-	-

An asterisk (*) next to an item indicates absorption.

Triple Triad is Final Fantasy VIII's challenging card game. This is a mini-game like none you've ever seen. Throughout the course of the game, you can collect special cards based on the minor enemies, Bosses, Guardian Forces, and major characters from Final Fantasy VIII. With your deck, you can challenge almost anyone to a game of cards. What are the benefits? Using the **Card Mod** ability, you can refine the cards you've won into valuable and rare items.

How Do I Play?

First, you need a good starting deck, and you can get one from a person in Balamb Garden at the start of the game. The cards aren't that great, but they're better than nothing at all.

Challenging people to a card game is easy. Approach a person in normal fashion, and press the ⬤ button. If the person is a card player, they'll most likely accept your challenge. If not, they'll converse with you normally.

If you've been given an assignment, it's best to wait to play cards on your own free time. The Garden looks down on SeeDs that goof off while on assignments. There's no such thing as too many of one card. If nothing else, use the Card Mod ability to turn your extras into items and sell them for Gil.

Basic Strategy

The biggest challenge Triple Triad presents is the always-changing set of rules. So, while it may seem like a good idea to always play your best hand, many times this is not the case.

When the rules are basic (Same, Open, Sudden Death, and Elemental), all you need are strong cards to win. You can simply over-power your opponent by playing cards that he/she simply cannot beat. However, if some of the more advanced rules (Plus, Same Wall, and Random) are in effect, it's best to back off a bit and try to win the game through strategy, rather than brute force.

Always play defensively. There's no reason to take each card your opponent plays. Play a waiting game with your opponent and plan ahead. Let your opponent trap his/her own cards, and then force certain moves by strategically placing your cards.

Corners typically offer the best defense, while the center spot is obviously the worst. In some cases, though, you may find it beneficial to play a card in the center at the start of the match to limit your opponent's options. This works well against tougher opponents.

Try not to spread the Random rule—it's a killer. And although Open may seem like the best rule in the game, your opponent gains as much from it as you do. Skilled opponents may gain too much from being able to see your hand.

Card-Related Side Quests

There are three card-related Side Quests: The Queen of Cards, the CC Group, and the Alien Encounter. If you want to find all the cards, check out the "Side Quests" section in this book.

Level 1: Monster Cards

Level 2: Monster Cards

GRAT

Level: 2
Elemental: N/A
Class: Monster
Card Mod: 1 = 1 Magic Stone

BUEL

Level: 2
Elemental: N/A
Class: Monster
Card Mod: 1 = 1 Magic Stone

MESMERIZE

Level: 2
Elemental: N/A
Class: Monster
Card Mod: 1 = 1 Mesmerize Blade

GLACIAL EYE

Level: 2
Elemental: Ice
Class: Monster
Card Mod: 1 = 1 Arctic Wind

BELHELMEL

Level: 2
Elemental: N/A
Class: Monster
Card Mod: 1 = 1 Saw Blade

THRUSTAEVIS

Level: 2
Elemental: Wind
Class: Monster
Card Mod: 1 = 1 Shear Feather

ANACONDAUR

Level: 2
Elemental: Poison
Class: Monster
Card Mod: 1 = 1 Venom Fang

CREEPS

Level: 2
Elemental: Thunder
Class: Monster
Card Mod: 1 = 1 Coral Fragment

GRENDEL

Level: 2
Elemental: Thunder
Class: Monster
Card Mod: 1 = 1 Dragon Fin

JELLEYE

Level: 2
Elemental: N/A
Class: Monster
Card Mod: 1 = 1 Magic Stone

GRAND MANTIS
Level: 2
Elemental: N/A
Class: Monster
Card Mod: 1 = 1 Sharp Spike

Level 3: Monster Cards

FORBIDDEN

Level: 3
Elemental: N/A
Class: Monster
Card Mod: 1 = 1 Betrayal Sword

ARMADODO

Level: 3
Elemental: Earth
Class: Monster
Card Mod: 1 = 1 Dino Bone

TRI-FACE

Level: 3
Elemental: Poison
Class: Monster
Card Mod: 1 = 1 Curse Spike

FASTITOCALON

Level: 3
Elemental: Earth
Class: Monster
Card Mod: 1 = 1 Water Crystal

SNOW LION

Level: 3
Elemental: Ice
Class: Monster
Card Mod: 1 = 1 North Wind

OCHU

Level: 3
Elemental: N/A
Class: Monster
Card Mod: 1 = 1 Ochu Tentacle

SAMO8G

Level: 3
Elemental: Fire
Class: Monster
Card Mod: 1 = 1 Running Fire

DEATH CLAW

Level: 3
Elemental: Fire
Class: Monster
Card Mod: 1 = 1 Sharp Spike

CACTUAR

Level: 3
Elemental: N/A
Class: Monster
Card Mod: 1 = 1 Cactus Thorn

TONBERRY
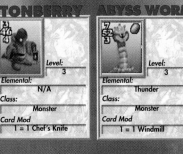
Level: 3
Elemental: N/A
Class: Monster
Card Mod: 1 = 1 Chef's Knife

ABYSS WORM

Level: 3
Elemental: Thunder
Class: Monster
Card Mod: 1 = 1 Windmill

Level 4: Monster Cards

TURTAPOD
Level: 4
Elemental: N/A
Class: Monster
Card Mod: 5 = 1 Healing Mail

VYSAGE

Level: 4
Elemental: N/A
Class: Monster
Card Mod: 1 = 1 Wizard Stone

T-REXAUR

Level: 4
Elemental: N/A
Class: Monster
Card Mod: 2 = 1 Dino Bone

BOMB

Level: 4
Elemental: Fire
Class: Monster
Card Mod: 1 = 1 Bomb Fragment

BLITZ

Level: 4
Elemental: Thunder
Class: Monster
Card Mod: 1 = 1 Dynamo Stone

WENDIGO

Level: 4
Elemental: N/A
Class: Monster
Card Mod: 1 = 1 Steel Orb

TORAMA

Level: 4
Elemental: N/A
Class: Monster
Card Mod: 5 = 1 Life Ring

IMP

Level: 4
Elemental: N/A
Class: Monster
Card Mod: 1 = 1 Wizard Stone

BLUE DRAGON

Level: 4
Elemental: Poison
Class: Monster
Card Mod: 4 = 1 Fury Fragment

ADAMANTOISE
Level: 4
Elemental: Earth
Class: Monster
Card Mod: 3 = 1 Turtle Shell

HEXADRAGON
Level: 4
Elemental: N/A
Class: Monster
Card Mod: 1 = 1 Sharp Spike

Level 5: Monster Cards

IRON GIANT
Level: 5
Elemental: N/A
Class: Monster
Card Mod: 3 = 1 Star Fragment

BEHEMOTH
Level: 5
Elemental: Earth
Class: Monster
Card Mod: 10 = 1 Barrier

CHIMERA
Level: 5
Elemental: Water
Class: Monster
Card Mod: 10 = 1 Regen Ring

PUPU
Level: 5
Elemental: N/A
Class: Monster
Card Mod: 1 = 1 Hungry Cookpot

ELASTOID
Level: 5
Elemental: N/A
Class: Monster
Card Mod: 1 = 1 Steel Pipe

GIM47N
Level: 5
Elemental: N/A
Class: Monster
Card Mod: 1 = 10 Fast Ammo

MALBORO
Level: 5
Elemental: Poison
Class: Monster
Card Mod: 4 = 1 Malboro Tentacle

RUBY DRAGON
Level: 5
Elemental: Fire
Class: Monster
Card Mod: 10 = 1 Inferno Fang

ELNOYLE
Level: 5
Elemental: N/A
Class: Monster
Card Mod: 10 = 1 Energy Crystal

TONBERRY KING
Level: 5
Elemental: N/A
Class: Monster
Card Mod: 1 = 1 Chef's Knife

WEDGE, BIGGS
Level: 5
Elemental: N/A
Class: Monster
Card Mod: 1 = 1 X-Potion

Level 6: Boss Cards

FUJIN, RAIJIN
Level: 6
Elemental: N/A
Class: Boss
Card Mod: 1 = 1 X-Potion

ELVORET
Level: 6
Elemental: Wind
Class: Boss
Card Mod: 1 = 10 Death Stones

X-ATM092
Level: 6
Elemental: N/A
Class: Boss
Card Mod: 2 = 1 Turtle Shell

GRANALDO
Level: 6
Elemental: N/A
Class: Boss
Card Mod: 1 = 1 G-Returner

GEROGERO
Level: 6
Elemental: Poison
Class: Boss
Card Mod: 10 = 1 Circlet

IGUION
Level: 6
Elemental: N/A
Class: Boss
Card Mod: 1 = 1 Cockatrice Pinion

ABADON
Level: 6
Elemental: N/A
Class: Boss
Card Mod: 1 = 30 Dark Ammo

TRAUMA
Level: 6
Elemental: N/A
Class: Boss
Card Mod: 1 = 30 Demolition Ammo

OILBOYLE
Level: 6
Elemental: N/A
Class: Boss
Card Mod: 1 = 30 Fire Ammo

SHUMI TRIBE
Level: 6
Elemental: N/A
Class: Boss
Card Mod: 5 = 1 Gambler Spirit

KROYSTA
Level: 6
Elemental: N/A
Class: Boss
Card Mod: 1 = 10 Holy Stones

Level 7: Boss Cards

PROPAGATOR
Level: 7
Elemental: N/A
Class: Boss
Card Mod: 1 = 1 G-Mega-Potion

JUMBO CACTUAR
Level: 7
Elemental: N/A
Class: Boss
Card Mod: 1 = 1 Cactus Thorn

TRI-POINT
Level: 7
Elemental: Thunder
Class: Boss
Card Mod: 40 = 1 Jet Engine

GARGANTUA
Level: 7
Elemental: N/A
Class: Boss
Card Mod: 10 = 1 Strength Love

MOBILE TYPE 8
Level: 7
Elemental: N/A
Class: Boss
Card Mod: 1 = 10 Shell Stones

SPHINXARA
Level: 7
Elemental: N/A
Class: Boss
Card Mod: 1 = 1 G-Mega-Potion

TIAMAT
Level: 7
Elemental: N/A
Class: Boss
Card Mod: 1 = 10 Flare Stones

BGH251F2
Level: 7
Elemental: N/A
Class: Boss
Card Mod: 1 = 10 Protect Stones

RED GIANT
Level: 7
Elemental: N/A
Class: Boss
Card Mod: 1 = 5 Meteor Stones

CATOBLEPAS
Level: 7
Elemental: N/A
Class: Boss
Card Mod: 1 = 1 Rename Card

ULTIMA WEAPON
Level: 7
Elemental: N/A
Class: Boss
Card Mod: 1 = 1 Ultima Stone

Level 8: GF Cards

CHUBBY CHOCOBO

Level: 8
Elemental: N/A
Class: GF
Card Mod
1 = 100 LuvLuvGs

ANGELO

Level: 8
Elemental: Wind
Class: GF
Card Mod
1 = 100 Elixirs

GILGAMESH

Level: 8
Elemental: N/A
Class: GF
Card Mod
1 = 10 Holy Wars

MINIMOG

Level: 8
Elemental: Ice
Class: GF
Card Mod
1 = 100 Pet Houses

CHICOBO

Level: 8
Elemental: Poison
Class: GF
Card Mod
1 = 100 Gysahl Greens

QUEZACOTL

Level: 8
Elemental: Thunder
Class: GF
Card Mod
1 = 100 Dynamo Stones

SHIVA

Level: 8
Elemental: N/A
Class: GF
Card Mod
1 = 100 North Winds

IFRIT

Level: 8
Elemental: N/A
Class: GF
Card Mod
1 = 3 Elem Atks

SIREN

Level: 8
Elemental: N/A
Class: GF
Card Mod
1 = 3 Status Atks

SACRED

Level: 8
Elemental: N/A
Class: GF
Card Mod
1 = 100 Dino Bones

MINOTAUR

Level: 8
Elemental: N/A
Class: GF
Card Mod
1 = 10 Adamantines

Level 9: GF Cards

CARBUNCLE

Level: 9
Elemental: N/A
Class: GF
Card Mod
1 = 3 Glow Curtains

DIABLOS

Level: 9
Elemental: N/A
Class: GF
Card Mod
1 = 100 Black Holes

LEVIATHAN

Level: 9
Elemental: Water
Class: GF
Card Mod
1 = 3 Doc's Codes

ODIN

Level: 9
Elemental: N/A
Class: GF
Card Mod
1 = 100 Dead Spirits

PANDEMONA

Level: 9
Elemental: Wind
Class: GF
Card Mod
1 = 100 Windmills

CERBERUS

Level: 9
Elemental: N/A
Class: GF
Card Mod
1 = 100 Lightweights

ALEXANDER

Level: 9
Elemental: Holy
Class: GF
Card Mod
1 = 3 Moon Curtains

PHOENIX

Level: 9
Elemental: Fire
Class: Gf
Card Mod
1 = 3 Phoenix Spirits

BAHAMUT

Level: 9
Elemental: N/A
Class: GF
Card Mod
1 = 100 Megalixirs

DOOMTRAIN

Level: 9
Elemental: Poison
Class: GF
Card Mod
1 = 3 Status Guards

EDEN

Level: 9
Elemental: N/A
Class: GF
Card Mod
1 = 3 Monk's Codes

Level 10: Player Cards

WARD

Level: 10
Elemental: N/A
Class: Player
Card Mod
1 = 3 Gaea's Rings

KIROS

Level: 10
Elemental: N/A
Class: Player
Card Mod
1 = 3 Accelerators

LAGUNA

Level: 10
Elemental: N/A
Class: Player
Card Mod
1 = 100 Heroes

SELPHIE

Level: 10
Elemental: N/A
Class: Player
Card Mod
1 = 3 Elem Guards

QUISTIS

Level: 10
Elemental: N/A
Class: Player
Card Mod
1 = 3 Samantha Souls

IRVINE

Level: 10
Elemental: N/A
Class: Player
Card Mod
1 = 3 Rocket Engines

ZELL

Level: 10
Elemental: N/A
Class: Player
Card Mod
1 = 3 Hyper Wrists

RINOA

Level: 10
Elemental: N/A
Class: Player
Card Mod
1 = 3 Magic Armlets

EDEA

Level: 10
Elemental: N/A
Class: Player
Card Mod
1 = 3 Royal Crowns

SEIFER

Level: 10
Elemental: N/A
Class: Player
Card Mod
1 = 3 Diamond Armors

SQUALL

Level: 10
Elemental: N/A
Class: Player
Card Mod
1 = 3 Three Stars

Rare Card Locations

The following is a list of the rare cards in Final Fantasy VIII. This section shows each card's whereabouts and how you can get them all.

Level 5 Card

Name: PuPu

Location: Balamb Area

Condition: Must complete the Alien Encounter Side Quest by giving the Alien 5 Elixirs. If the alien is killed, you can't get the card. (See "Side Quests" for more info.)

Level 8 Cards

Name: Chubby Chocobo

Location: Balamb Garden

Condition: Must take part in the Queen of Cards Quest (see "Side Quests" for more info.) A male student, who's sitting on a bench outside the Library, has this card.

Name: Angelo

Location: Forest Owl's Train/White SeeD Ship

Condition: Must win from Watts of the Forest Owl's resistance group. Can do so in the Forest Owl's Train (Disc One), or later at the White SeeD Ship (Disc Three).

Name: Gilgamesh

Location: Balamb Garden

Condition: Must take part in the CC Group Side Quest. The CC Group's King has this card. (See "Side Quests" section for more info.)

Name: MiniMog

Location: Balamb Garden

Condition: Challenge the under-classman jogging around the Hall.

Name: Chicobo

Location: Chocobo Sanctuary

Condition: Must visit each Chocobo Forest and solve the puzzles. Then go to the Chocobo Sanctuary to receive this card. (See "Side Quests" for more info.)

Name: Quezacotl

Location: Fisherman's Horizon

Condition: Challenge Mayor Dobe in FH. Try to get this card when you first arrive at FH.

Name: Shiva

Location: White SeeD Ship

Condition: Receive from Zone of the Forest Owls resistance group. He's on the White SeeD's Ship (Disc Three). Must have the "Girl Next Door" magazine (found at Timber Maniacs in Timber) in your inventory before Zone will give up this card. You must give Zone the magazine for free.

Name: Ifrit

Location: Fire Cavern

Condition: Defeat the Fire Cavern's Boss, Ifrit.

Name: Siren

Location: Dollet

Condition: Visit the Pub in Dollet, and challenge the Pub's manager on the second floor. Once you defeat him, he'll take you to a back room, where you can challenge him again and win the Siren Card normally.

Name: Sacred

Location: Tomb of the Unknown King

Condition: Defeat the Brothers in the Tomb of the Unknown King.

Name: Minotaur

Location: Tomb of the Unknown King

Condition: Defeat the Brothers in the Tomb of the Unknown King.

Level 9 Cards

Name: Carbuncle

Location: Balamb Garden

Condition: Must take part in the CC Group Side Quest. Heart, a CC Group member, has this card. (See "Side Quests" for more info.)

Name: Diablos

Location: Balamb Garden

Condition: Cid will give you a Magical Lamp before you leave on your first mission. Use the lamp to challenge the GF Diablos. Defeat Diablos to get its card.

Name: Leviathan

Location: Balamb Garden

Condition: Must take part in the CC Group Side Quest. Joker, a CC Group member, has the card. (See "Side Quests" for more info.)

Name: Odin

Location: Centra Ruins

Condition: Take part in the Centra Ruins Side Quest, and defeat the GF Odin. (See "Side Quest" for more info.)

Name: Pandemona

Location: Balamb

Condition: Challenge the Hotel's Owner, who's standing in the street outside the hotel. Must wait until Galbadia's invasion of Balamb has ended.

Name: Cerberus

Location: Galbadia Garden

Condition: While at Galbadia Garden a second time (Disc Two), challenge Cerberus in the central hall. Defeat it to win the card.

Name: Alexander

Location: Lunar Base

Condition: Challenge Piet, the head technician at Lunar Base (Disc Three). Also, you can challenge him later on Disc Three by finding the escape pod's crash site, south of Tears' Point.

Name: Phoenix

Location: Esthar

Condition: Must take part in the Queen of Cards Side Quest. The Presidential Aide inside the Presidential Palace has this card. The aide is in the room you first visit during your initial visit to Esthar. (See "Side Quests" for more info.)

Name: Bahamut

Location: Deep Sea Research Facility

Condition: Locate the Deep Sea Research Center in the southwest corner of the World Map. Go there using the Ragnarok, and challenge the GF Bahamut. Defeat Bahamut to win the card. (See "Side Quests" for more info.)

Name: Doomtrain

Location: Timber

Condition: Must participate in the Queen of Cards Side Quest. The Pub's owner will have this card in his deck once you complete the necessary requirements. (See "Side Quests" for more info.)

Name: Eden

Location: Deep Sea Deposit

Condition: Defeat Bahamut at the Deep Sea Research Center, and go into the facility's lower levels to solve the steam puzzle. You must defeat Ultima Weapon, who carries the GF Eden, to get the card.

Level 10

Name: Ward

Location: Esthar

Condition: Challenge Dr. Odine to a game of cards (Disc Three).

Name: Kiros

Location: Deling City

Condition: Not available until you've completed a portion of the Queen of Cards Sub Quest. A man dressed in black, who stands across the street from the shops in Deling City's shopping district, has this card. (See "Side Quests" for more info.)

Name: Laguna

Location: Lunar Base

Condition: Ellone has this card. Must get this card while on the Lunar Base; if not, you must get it on Disc Four from the Card Queen.

Name: Selphie

Location: Trabia Garden

Condition: Selphie's friend near the gargoyle statue has this card. Challenge her after your first visit to Trabia Garden to get the card.

Name: Quistis

Location: Balamb Garden

Condition: Can win this card from any of the "Trepies" in Balamb Garden. The "Trepies" are: the two girls in the second floor classroom, and the daydreaming guy in the Cafeteria.

Name: Irvine

Location: Fisherman's Horizon

Condition: Must complete the proper portion of the Queen of Cards Side Quest. Flo, Mayor Dobe's wife, has the card. Challenge her in the Mayor's House. (See "Side Quests" for more info.)

Name: Zell

Location: Balamb

Condition: Visit Zell's mother in Balamb with Zell in your party. Challenge Zell's mother to get this card.

Name: Rinoa

Location: Deling City

Condition: Rinoa's Father, General Caraway, has this card, but doesn't use it. To make him use it, intentionally lose your Ifrit Card to him and then win the Rinoa Card from him. You can get the Ifrit Card back from Martine in FH.

Name: Edea

Location: Edea's House

Condition: The evil sorceress carries her own card. Challenge her at her home to get this card (Disc Three).

Name: Seifer

Location: Balamb Garden/Edea's House

Condition: Challenge Cid (Disc One) before your first mission, or on Disc Three at Edea's House.

Name: Squall

Location: Esthar/Ragnarok

Condition: Laguna has Squall's card. You can win it from him at the end of Disc Three (while at Esthar or once everyone is on board the Ragnarok).

SIDE QUESTS AND SECRETS

SHUMI VILLAGE

What Is a Side Quest?

Throughout the game, there are optional events that you can complete to better round out your party and to find useful and rare items. You cannot take part in most of these events until you've reached a certain portion of the game, but once they're available you can complete them at nearly any time you want. In general, though, it's best to take on a Side Quest as soon as possible, since some will have a profound effect on the game. In the walkthrough, you'll be pointed to this section occasionally when a new Side Quest is available. Make sure you read through the Side Quest information and then decide whether or not you want to deviate from the story.

1

Visit the Sculptor's Workshop at the end of the village

2

Speak with the Village Elder

3

Assist the Sculptor in the Workshop

4

Revisit the Village Elder to get your reward

5

Exit the village, and then go to the Workshop and talk to the Elder's Attendant

6

Go to the Elder's house and talk to the Elder

7

Talk to the Moomba outside of the Elder's house

8

Follow the Moomba back to the Workshop and speak with the Elder's Attendant

9

Go to the Elder's house and speak with the Elder

10

Return to the Workshop and speak with the Attendant

11

Step next door to the Artisan's house and speak with the Artisan

12

Go to the Elder's house and talk to the Elder

13

Travel to Fisherman's Horizon and speak to the Grease Monkey

14

Return to Shumi Village and give the Moomba Doll to the Artisan

15

Speak with the Elder to receive the Status Guard

Available When
Disc Two (Once Balamb Garden is mobile)

Difficulty
Easy

Rewards
Fair

Unavailable When
Disc Four

Draw Points
Ultima (Entrance— 5,000 Gil)
Firaga (Sculptor's Workshop)
Blizzaga (Outside Elder's house)

Save Points
Hotel room
Outside Elder's house (Hidden)

Magazine
Timber Maniacs (Artisan's House—on bed)

The Five Stones

During your trip to Shumi Village, you'll be asked to locate five stones. Here's a short list to assist you in your search.

Blue Stone

This one is easy. The Blue Stone is just to the left of the statue. Examine it and you'll only have four more stones to locate.

Wind Stone

To get this one, you must head back toward the elevator. The Wind Stone is just to the left of the Hotel. Inspect the large boulder and Squall will notice a breeze coming from the stone. Only three more to go!

Life Stone

Think vegetation for this one. You'll find the Life Stone in the tree roots to the right of the Elder's house. The Life Stones are what allow so much vegetation to grow on such a barren rock.

Shadow Stone

Return to the surface via the elevator, go down the steps and search to the right in a large shadow that overlaps the shadows cast by the dome overhead. This is where you'll find the ever-elusive Shadow Stone.

Water Stone

This one isn't as easy as you might think. You can check the stone the frog is sitting on in the pond outside the Artisan's Workshop, but that's not it. The real Water Stone is used for washing; you'll find it in the Artisan's house.

Your Reward

All of that work for a simple **Phoenix Pinion**?!? It doesn't sound like much, but the Phoenix Pinion is a summon spell that can be used only once. Used during battle when your party is in dire straits, a Phoenix will come to your rescue. Just make sure you save it until you absolutely need it. Also, once the Phoenix Pinion is used, the **Phoenix Summon** spell will randomly appear throughout the remainder of the game when your party members are knocked out in battle.

You're Not Done Yet!

After obtaining the Phoenix Pinion and leaving the village, return to the Workshop and talk to the Elder's Attendant, who's now been assigned to help with the statue. He doesn't feel like helping, so return to the Elder and ask for more assistance. After speaking with the Elder, go outside and speak with the Moomba sitting on the ground.

Follow the Moomba to the Workshop and observe the conversation between Moomba and the Elder's Attendant. Return and speak with the Elder and he'll mention that he needs another person to help build the statue. Return to the Workshop and speak with the Elder's Attendant, who wants the Artisan to help. Now go to the house next to the Workshop and speak with the Artisan, who doesn't want to help either. Go back to the Elder once more, and you'll be asked to find a way to convince the Artisan.

To do so, you must return to Fisherman's Horizon and speak with the Grease Monkey who lives in the Repair Shop near the Train Station. He'll give you a **Moomba Doll** that you can take back to Shumi Village and give to the Artisan. After presenting the doll to the Artisan, head back to the Elder's house. The Elder will give you a **Status Guard** for all of your help.

WINHILL

The Vase Quest

Visit the large mansion at the end of Winhill. A person inside will ask you to help locate a missing vase. The vase is broken into several pieces that can be found in the following locations:

Inspect the suit of armor inside the mansion.

Visit the house in the middle of town occupied by an old woman. Check the white flowers toward the foreground of the screen to find a piece of the vase.

Try to grab a Chicobo at the Chocobo Crossing. When you pop it into the air, you should get a piece of the vase. If not, keep trying.

Speak with the woman living in Raine's house several times until she mentions the aroma of the flowers downstairs. Go downstairs, look at the table in the lower, right-hand corner of the screen, examine the flowers, and Raine's ghost will appear behind the bar. Speak with the ghost and Raine's cat will replace it. Inspect the cat to find the final piece of the vase.

Take the pieces back to the person in the mansion to receive a **Holy Stone**.

Available When
Disc Two (Once Balamb Garden is mobile)

Difficulty
Easy

Rewards
Fair

Unavailable When
Disc Four

Draw Points
Curaga (Abandoned House, upstairs—hidden)
Drain (near Old Woman's house)
Reflect (near truck)
Dispel (mansion courtyard)

Save Points
Abandoned House (upstairs)

Free Items

You can get two free items by grabbing Chicobos at the Chocobo Crossing. You'll receive a **Phoenix Pinion** and a **Gysahl Green** if you're quick enough. Also, if you grab too many Chicobos, you can lure out a mother Chocobo.

Note

After the mother Chocobo appears you won't be able to catch any more Chicobos.

CENTRA RUINS (ODIN & TONBERRY KING'S QUESTS)

Available When

Disc Two (Once Balamb Garden is mobile)

Difficulty

Hard

Rewards

Great

Unavailable When

N/A

Enemies

Bomb
Armadodo
Red Bat
Forbidden
Buel
Blobra
Tonberry
Odin (Boss)
Tonberry King (Boss)

Draw Points

Drain (Courtyard—Hidden)
Aero (Tower Side)
Pain (Top of Tower—Hidden)

Odin's Quest

Around the Centra Crater, you'll find a large tower where Odin resides. This is known as the Centra Ruins. The tower is full of dangerous creatures and challenging puzzles. Odin will grant his power to anyone who can climb the tower and defeat him in 20 minutes or less. This is no easy task.

Odin is not a normal GF. Unlike all of the other GFs you've acquired throughout your journey, you cannot summon Odin. At the start of any battle, there is a small chance that Odin will appear at the beginning of the battle and destroy your enemies. Odin will *never* appear to help you during a Boss fight.

Preparing for the Tower

As stated earlier, the tower is full of deadly enemies. Some of them you've seen before, while others will be a surprise. The most deadly enemies you'll encounter are **Tonberrys** and **Forbiddens**. Both enemies are capable of one-hit kills, and their normal attacks are equally powerful.

It should be noted, however, that the bigger threat is the Tonberrys. They have a large amount of HP, so it can take you several minutes to defeat one. With a 20-minute time limit, you can't afford these lengthy battles. In fact, it's best if you don't fight any random encounters at all. To do so, you can either run from every battle or you can use Diablos' GF Abilities **Enc-Half** or **Enc-None**. With Enc-Half, you will still have to run from some battles, but considerably less than you would normally. Enc-None enables you to focus on solving the tower's puzzles without the hassle of random encounters.

Climbing the Tower

The first part of the tower is easy. Just follow the various staircases until you reach an altar, which is actually an elevator. When you get off the elevator, you'll find two ladders. The one on the right leads to an **Aero** Draw Point, while the one on the left leads to a room full of machinery. Climb the left ladder, flip the switch inside the room, and then climb back down the ladder.

Climbing the Tower (Cont.)

You'll notice that the altar in front of the elevator is now lit. Upon examining it, a staircase will appear on the right. Follow the stairs to the top. There's a large demon statue with one red eye on the next level. Climb the short ladder on the left, take the eye from the statue, and then climb up the stairs on the right side of the area to the top of the tower.

Go to the left and climb the side of the dome to find a second demon statue with a red eye. Place the left eye in the statue and a code will appear. (You may want to write it down.) Take both eyes out of the demon statue and go downstairs to the first demon statue. After placing both eyes in the demon statue, a place to input the code will appear. Enter the code using the directional button to open a door below. Behind the door you'll find Odin.

GUARDIAN FORCE ALERT!

Odin

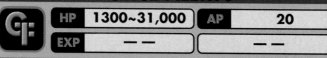

GF	HP	1300~31,000	AP	20	— —
	EXP	— —		— —	

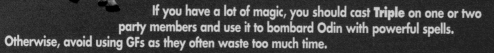

The only tough part about this fight is the time limit. Odin will not attack your party, so you should focus on inflicting as much damage as possible in the amount of time you have remaining. Odin has the spell **Triple**, which you can draw and then use to cast three spells at once. Stock up on this spell if you have time, because it Junctions extremely well. You should also Mug Odin for the **Luck-J Scroll**, which teaches a GF the **Luck Junction** ability.

If you have a lot of magic, you should cast **Triple** on one or two party members and use it to bombard Odin with powerful spells. Otherwise, avoid using GFs as they often waste too much time.

Both magic and GFs also suffer against Odin's strong magical defenses. Cast **Haste** on your party members if you're really running short on time, and just pound on Odin with physical attacks. This Boss has a lot of HPs, but it's not as much as you might expect. After winning the battle, you receive **Odin's Card**, **20 AP**, and Odin will now assist you from time to time during battle.

Tonberry King Quest

On your way out of the Centra Ruins, you may want to take on the Tonberry King, a new GF. Take note, however, that this is NOT an easy task. To prepare, I suggest that you stock up on **Phoenix Downs** and **Hi-Potions**. I also suggest that the character Junctioned with Diablos be at 100% compatibility with the GF. By doing so, you can count on Diablos to arrive quickly when summoned in the battles. If you can't attain 100% compatibility with Diablos, Junction Diablos to the character with the highest compatibility.

Sounds a bit extreme, doesn't it? It's not when you consider your task. You'll find a lot of Tonberrys near the entrance to the Centra Ruins. Your objective is to defeat 18 to 22 Tonberrys, which will lure out the Tonberry King. If you haven't fought Tonberrys before, you should be advised that they're nasty. They have a lot of HP (20,000 on average), and they can kill a character with a single blow. Tonberrys also have a powerful random counterattack known as **Everyone's Grudge**. This attack typically causes over 2,000 points of damage to a single character. To top it all off, you only receive 1 AP and no EXP for defeating a single Tonberry.

To defeat them, I suggest that you equip one character with the **Item command**, and make sure he/she is fully stocked with **Hi-Potions**. You should also Junction another character with **Diablos**, and make sure he/she has full compatibility with the GF. **Demi** is also a very effective spell, as it will reduce a Tonberry's HP by one fourth. During each fight, only have the character equipped with Diablos attack by summoning the GF repeatedly. By doing so, you limit the number of times the Tonberry can counterattack.

This is a race for time against the Tonberry, because once it's in close range to your characters, it will begin using the Chef's Knife. This attack alone causes around 4,000 points of damage. If a Tonberry gets too close, begin unloading on it with all three characters. It helps a great deal to cast Haste on the character with Diablos so that you can summon it as quickly as possible.

After defeating enough Tonberrys, the Tonberry King will appear immediately following your last battle with a Tonberry. You will not exit the last battle. Instead, the Tonberry King will replace the fallen Tonberry, so it's important that everyone be prepared to fight.

GUARDIAN FORCE ALERT!

Tonberry King ⒼⒻ

HP	2500~250,000	AP	20	— —
EXP	— —		Weak vs. Ice/Absorbs Fire	

During the battle with the Tonberry King, Diablos is no longer useful because the Tonyberry King is immune to Diablos' attack. Begin using each party member's best GF, and Boost them all as much as possible. The Tonberry King has A LOT OF HP, so you can expect this battle to take as long as half an hour.

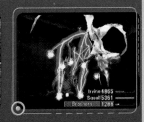

The Tonberry King's attacks are just as powerful as the other Tonberrys, but the Boss is much faster. You can counter this advantage by casting **Haste** on everyone, plus you should also consider using **Protect** to cut down the damage caused to your party.

Fortunately, the Tonberry King has the Full-Life and Curaga spells that you can use to keep your party in the fight. You may want to dedicate one character to healing everyone, but always have another party member ready to take up this role if the dedicated character is knocked out of the fight.

Note

If this battle is too tough at this stage of the game, you may need to try again once your characters are stronger and more compatible with their GFs.

Chocobos in FF8

As with past Final Fantasy games, you can find Chocobos and use them as transportation. This time around, however, you'll only find Chocobos in Chocobo Forests, of which there are seven. A Chocobo Forest looks similar to other forests, but they're dome-shaped. In order to catch a Chocobo, you must solve a puzzle in the forest you're visiting. After solving the puzzle, you can find hidden items that make it so you never need to solve the puzzle again. In the following section, you'll learn how to locate all seven forests and we'll provide the answers for each puzzle.

Available When
Disc Two (Balamb Garden mobile)

Difficulty
Hard

Rewards
Great

Unavailable When
N/A

Your First Visit

Upon first entering a Chocobo Forest, you'll meet an interesting boy appropriately named Chocoboy. He'll give you a **ChocoWhis** and teach you how to use it for a mere 1000 Gil. The ChocoWhis is your tool for locating the baby Chocobos, called **Chicobos** in forests, so I'm afraid there's no way to get around paying the initial 1000 Gil.

The ChocoWhis has two modes: ChocoSonar and ChocoZiner. ChocoSonar is used to sniff out a Chicobos location. The ChocoWhis will emit a soft ping as you search an area and changes to a fast-pitched, louder ping when you're standing on the right spot. After locating such a spot, you must switch the ChocoWhis over to ChocoZiner mode. Blowing the ChocoZiner will cause a Chicobo(s) to drop from above or go into hiding if you're on the right spot. If you're not on the right spot, a Chicobo will steal your ChocoWhis, thus forcing you to buy a new one from the Chocoboy for 700 Gil.

Solving Puzzles

Your goal in every forest is to call out Chicobos in a pattern that leaves only one Chicobo on the ground. This may take some effort in some of the forests. A lone Chicobo makes the parent Chocobo nervous, and causes it to come out of hiding when you approach its baby and examine it.

After solving the puzzle, you can search for hidden items in the ground. By locating them, the Chocobos become your friends and will no longer hide from you when you enter their forest. If you leave a forest without finding the hidden items, you must solve the puzzle again to get another Chocobo to show itself.

About Chocoboy

While you're attempting to solve the puzzles, Chocoboy will be standing by ready to assist you in several ways. He's not the giving type, though, so you'll have to pay him for his services. Here's a rundown of the things he can do:

ChocoWhis Sales	You can't catch a Chocobo without a ChocoWhis. The first one will cost you 1000 Gil. Any replacements will cost 700 Gil.
Cost: 1000 Gil/700 Gil	

Hints	This is the most worthwhile service he provides. Chocoboy tells you the name of the forest you're currently in, and gives you a rather cryptic clue to help you solve the puzzle.
Cost: 100 Gil	

Buy Gysahl Greens	These Greens can be used in battle to summon a "GF-like" Chocobo. The Chocobo GF hits your opponents with a flare attack.
Cost: 600 Gil per Green	

Questions	For a pittance, the Chocoboy will answer questions about the ChocoWhis and about himself. This option won't assist you in catching a Chocobo, but it may prove useful if you're having trouble using your ChocoWhis.
Cost: 10 Gil	

Help Me!	The Chocoboy is willing to catch a Chocobo for you, but at a high cost. Only select this option if you really need a Chocobo and you don't want to deal with the puzzles. You can't find the hidden items using this option, so you'll either have to solve the puzzle later or pay this fee again if you want another Chocobo later on in the game.
Cost: 1200 Gil	

Using This Section

In the following pages, you'll find detailed information to help you catch your very own Chocobo. The maps indicate the locations where you must use the ChocoZiner to catch Chicobos, and where you'll find the hidden items. The corresponding charts indicate what occurs when you use the ChocoZiner at each location. A "O" stands for a Chicobo on the ground at the designated point. An "X" stands for a Chicobo in the air. Dashes indicate that it doesn't matter whether or not a Chicobo is present on the ground or in the air when using the ChocoZiner at a location.

Below the chart, you'll find a step-by-step walkthrough on how to solve the puzzle. Just follow along and you can solve each puzzle without having to put any work into it. Additionally, you'll find all the possible solutions for the accompanying puzzle. Some puzzles only have one solution, but some have as many as three.

"The Roaming Forest"

ITEM

Intermediate Chocobo Forest

Location: *North of Trabia Garden*

Location	Before Catch				After Catch			
	1	2	3	4	1	2	3	4
1	X	X	—	—	O	O	—	—
	O	O	—	—	X	X	X	—
2	X	X	—	—	O	O	—	—
	O	O	—	—	X	X	X	—
3	X	X	X	—	O	O	O	—
	O	O	X	—	X	X	X	—
4	O	O	O	—	O	O	X	—
	—	—	—	X	—	—	—	O
	—	—	—	O	—	—	—	X

Chocoboy's Clue: "Be careful where the Sonar reacts."

This is an easy one. Start off by using the ChocoZiner at spot ① or ② in order to get both Chicobos back into the trees. Then use the ChocoZiner at spot ③, which brings down all three Chicobos in this area. Head to spot ④ and use the ChocoZiner to bring down the last of the four Chicobos. Return to spot ① or ② and use the ChocoZiner one last time to return the three Chicobos at the top back to the trees. Speak with the remaining Chicobo to solve the puzzle. Don't forget to locate the hidden items: **Shell Stone** and **Holy Stone**.

Solution

```
1 ┐
  ├─ 3 → 4 ┬─ 1
2 ┘         └─ 2
```

"The Basics Forest"

ITEM

Easy Chocobo Forest

Location: *At Sorbald Snowfield on Trabia's west coast, south of Shumi Village*

Location	Before Catch					After Catch				
	1	2	3	4	5	1	2	3	4	5
1	X	—	—	—	—	O	O	O	—	—
	O	—	—	—	—	X	X	X	—	—
2	—	X	—	—	—	—	O	O	—	—
	—	O	X	—	—	—	O	O	—	—
	—	O	O	—	—	—	X	X	—	—
	—	—	X	—	—	O	O	O	—	—
	X	—	O	—	—	O	O	X	—	—
	O	—	O	—	—	X	—	X	—	—
4	—	—	—	X	X	—	—	—	O	O
	—	—	—	O	O	—	—	—	X	X
5	—	—	—	X	X	—	—	—	O	O
	—	—	—	O	O	—	—	—	X	X

Chocoboy's Clue: "You only need to blow the whistle twice."

There are a lot of Chicobos in this area, but don't let that confuse you. If you buy a hint from Chocoboy, he'll tell you that you only need to blow the whistle twice in this area. Start by using the ChocoZiner at spot ①. This action drops three Chicobos from above. Follow this by using the ChocoZiner at either spot ② or ③ to narrow the three down to one. Be sure to search for the hidden item **Flare Stone**.

Solution

```
    ┌─ 2
1 ──┤
    └─ 3
```

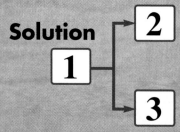

"The Beginner's Forest"

Beginner Chocobo Forest

Location: *Next to Shumi Village on Winter Island*

ITEM

Chocoboy's Clue: "Try to find a spot where only one falls down."

They simply don't get any easier than this. Take the Chocoboy's advice and locate the spot where only one Chicobo will fall when you whistle. Spot ④ is the one you want. Don't miss out on the hidden item **Aura Stone**.

Solution **4**

Location	Before Catch 1	2	3	4	After Catch 1	2	3	4
1	X	X	X	—	O	O	O	—
	O	O	O	—	X	X	X	—
2	X	X	X	—	O	O	O	—
	O	O	O	—	X	X	X	—
3	X	X	X	—	O	O	O	—
	O	O	O	—	X	X	X	—
4	—	—	—	X	—	—	—	O
	—	—	—	O	—	—	—	X

"Forest of Fun"

Challenging Chocobo Forest

Location: *East of Edea's House, in the Lenown Plains on the Centra Continent*

ITEM

Chocoboy's Clue:

"Chocobowling with 4 bottles, 1 ball."

There are several ways to solve this nasty little puzzle. However, if you want to see the Chocobowling, you must end with spot ⑤. Begin with spot ① to bring down three Chicobos. Then use the ChocoZiner at either spot ② or ④ to set the "pins." Follow this by using the ChocoZiner at spots ③ or ⑤, which places the "ball." End by using the ChocoZiner at spot ⑤ and watch the Chicobo's version of a strike. Make sure you get the hidden items **Meteor Stone**, **Flare Stone**, and **Ultima Stone**.

Location	Before Catch 1	2	3	4	5	After Catch 1	2	3	4	5
1	X	—	—	—	—	O	O	O	—	—
	O	—	—	—	—	X	X	O	X	X
2	O	X	—	X	—	X	O	—	X	O
	O	O	—	X	—	O	O	—	O	—
	—	O	O	O	O	X	X	O	X	O
	—	O	—	O	—	X	X	X	X	X
3	—	—	X	—	—	—	—	O	—	O
	—	—	O	—	—	—	—	X	—	X
4	—	O	—	O	—	O	X	—	O	—
	—	O	—	O	—	X	X	—	O	—
5	O	O	O	O	X	O	O	O	O	O
	O	O	O	O	O	X	X	X	X	X
	O	O	O	O	O	O	O	O	O	O
	—	—	—	X	—	—	—	—	X	—

Solution

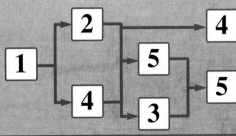

"Forest of Solitude"

Tricky Chocobo Forest

Location: *On the Nectar Peninsula, along the east coast of the Centra continent, south of Fisherman's Horizon*

ITEM

Location	Before Catch	After Catch
	①	①
①	X	O
	O	X

There's only one Chicobo in this area, so it should be easy; unfortunately, it's not. To catch the Chicobo, you must pinpoint the *exact* spot on the map and this spot is MUCH smaller than the points in other forests. Just slowly search the area marked on the map, and find the spot where the ChocoSonar goes nuts. To find the hidden items in this area, you have to ask the Chocoboy to move. Challenge him to a game of cards, and then choose "Forget it, just move." Search the spot directly where he was standing to find a **Protect Stone** and a **Meteor Stone**.

"C-C-Cards? Y-Yeah, let's play!"
Yes
No
► Forget it, just move

Chocoboy's Clue:
"Search carefully where the Sonar reacts."

Solution 1

"The Enclosed Forest"

Expert Chocobo Forest

Location: *On the south side of the Talle Mountains in southern Esthar*

ITEM

Location	\[Before Catch\] 1	2	3	4	5	\[After Catch\] 1	2	3	4	5
①	X	X	X	X	—	O	X	O	X	—
	X	O	O	X	—	O	O	X	X	—
	O	—	—	—	—	X	X	X	X	—
②	X	X	X	X	—	X	O	O	X	—
	O	X	O	X	—	O	O	X	X	—
	O	O	X	X	—	O	X	O	X	—
	—	O	O	—	—	X	X	X	X	—
③	X	—	—	X	—	O	—	—	X	—
	O	—	O	—	—	X	X	X	X	—
	O	O	X	X	—	O	—	—	X	—
④	O	O	O	X	—	O	O	O	O	—
	O	O	O	O	—	O	O	O	X	—

Any others   Chicobo #4 appears and disappears

⑤	O	O	O	X	O	X	X	X	X	O
	—	—	—	X	O	—	—	—	X	X

Any others   All Chicobos disappear

Chocoboy's Clue: "Collect on outer side, then go in."

Once again, you have a whole mess of Chicobos to work with, but with this group you have to do everything just right. Start off by using the ChocoZiner at spot ① to bring down two Chicobos. Then go to spot ② and one of the Chicobos will leave and another will appear. From here on out, just go straight through the order (③, ④ and ⑤) and you'll add a Chicobo each time until only one remains. After that, make sure you get the items **Meteor Stone**, **Holy Stone**, and **Ultima Stone**.

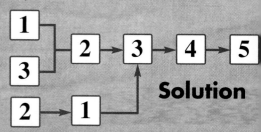

Solution

The Chocobo Sanctuary

There's one last Chocobo Forest in the world. It's in a place so remote that only someone riding a Chocobo can reach it. Nothing much happens there, but Chocobos sometime congregate in this sacred place.

After solving the puzzles and collecting the hidden items in the previous six forests, you can head for the Chocobo Sanctuary. You can actually go there earlier, but the only things there are Chocobos from the forests you've already solved at that point. When all six Chocobos congregate, they'll perform a special dance for you. Speak with the Chicobo afterwards, and it will reward you with the **Chicobo Card**. Speak with it a second time, and it will give you some **Gysahl Greens**, but it will also steal 600 Gil.

Getting to the Chocobo Sanctuary isn't easy, however, it isn't as tough as it seems. Get a Chocobo from the Chocobo Forest north of Trabia Garden. Ride it to the east onto the Heath Peninsula and "examine" the ocean. There's a long strip of shallow water that connects Trabia to Esthar. Follow the shallow water and you'll enter Grandidi Forest. The Chocobo Sanctuary is almost directly to the north. To return to Trabia, simply speak to a Chocobo or speak with Chocoboy, who will find a Chocobo for you to ride back.

Here are a few other things you can do while exploring:

Timber

By revisiting Timber, you'll get the chance to save a girl from an oncoming train near the Dollet Station. Doing so gets you a free night in the Hotel, plus it enables you to pick up a copy of **Timber Maniacs** inside the hotel room.

Available When
Disc Two (Once Balamb Garden is mobile)

Difficulty
Easy to Fair

Rewards
Varies

Unavailable When
Disc Four

Dollet

You can do a couple of things in Dollet. Visit the local Pub and head upstairs to the blackjack tables. You can find a copy of **Timber Maniacs** on one of the tables. If you challenge the manager to a card game and win, he'll allow you to enter the Pub's private room where he'll give you five Geezard Cards, four Red Bat Cards, three Buel Cards, two Anacondaur Cards, and one Cactuar Card. You can also find a copy of **Occult Fan II** hidden in the magazine stacks, as well as a couple of other items and useful tidbits of information. In addition, you can win the **Siren Card** from the manager if you challenge him enough times.

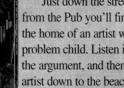

Just down the street from the Pub you'll find the home of an artist with a problem child. Listen in on the argument, and then check out the painting. Follow the artist down to the beach, and speak with him and the girl with him. They'll give you a hint that the bone on the painting is more than it appears. Return to the artist's house and examine the painting again. Recognize the area? It's a section of Dollet. Go there and you'll find a dog. After examining the dog's collar, you'll find a Potion hidden there. You can repeat this two more times to receive a Phoenix Down and a Soft. You don't need to go to the beach each time; instead, just find the dog in the section shown in the painting. You can obtain an **X-Potion**, a **Mega-Potion**, and an **Elixir** if you complete this event during Disc Three.

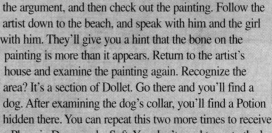

Deling City

Return to Deling City and visit Rinoa's father again. He admits to having **Rinoa's Card**, but says that he rarely uses it. However, if you're willing to relinquish your Ifrit Card, he'll consider putting Rinoa's Card into play. To give him Ifrit, you must put it in your hand and make absolutely sure it's your best card. Intentionally lose the card game and Rinoa's father will take the Ifrit Card. After acknowledging what you've done, Rinoa's father will indeed begin to use Rinoa's Card, so you can now win it from him. To get your Ifrit Card back, you must do a little traveling. Rinoa's father has already lost the Ifrit Card to the one-time headmaster of Galbadia Garden, Martine. You'll find Martine at FH to the right of the Mayor's house. You must challenge him to win back your Ifrit Card.

Are you ready to take on the best of the best? The CC group is a collection of seven card-playing fanatics. Each person has a solid set of cards, and knows how to work the rules in their favor. By defeating each of them, you can collect some rare cards and bulk up your collection of cards for modifying later on if necessary.

To face the entire CC group, you must challenge them one at a time from the lowest-ranking member to the highest-ranking member. The following list covers the order you must follow when challenging them, where you'll find them, and what rare cards each member has (if any).

Available When
Disc Three

Difficulty
Medium

Rewards
Good

Unavailable When
Disc Four

(#1) Jack

Location: In the Balamb Garden Hallway near the Directory.

Tends to enter from the bottom of the screen on either side of the divider. Jack has *no* rare cards.

(#2) Club

Location: In the Balamb Garden Hallway near the entrance to the Cafeteria.

Appears randomly and is often difficult to find. Club has *no* rare cards.

(#3) Diamond

Location: In front of the Directory in the Balamb Garden Hallway.

Diamond is actually a pair of female SeeD cadets. They have *no* rare cards.

(#4) Spade

Location: On the second floor next to the elevator.

Spade is one of two people that normally hangs out in this area. Spade has *no* rare cards.

(#5) Heart

Location: On the bridge.

This is none other than Xu. She has the **Carbuncle Card.**

(#6) Joker

Location: Inside the Training Center.

Joker appears randomly, so he isn't always easy to find. He has the **Leviathan Card** and will upgrade your Battle Meter to include GF information if you defeat him. You can challenge Joker at any time once you have beaten Jack.

(#7) King

Location: Finding King is a bit tougher. Speak with Nida on the bridge and then visit the Infirmary and challenge Dr. Kadowaki to a game. She will suggest that you'll soon find King. Return to your dorm room and take a nap. King will appear while you're resting.

You can win the **Gilgamesh Card** from King.

If the CC group won't challenge you, it's probably because you haven't been playing enough card games at Balamb Garden. You must build up your reputation as a card player by defeating card players at the Garden. Walk around and win about 15 card games, and then attempt this quest again.

Available When
Disc Three (With Ragnarok)

Difficulty
Hard

Rewards
Great

Unavailable When
N/A

Cactuar Island is a small, desert island on the southeast corner of the Esthar continent. You can distinguish it from all of the other islands in the area due to its landscape and a small, green figure that appears randomly here and there in the desert sands. This small, green figure is known as the **Jumbo Cactuar**.

The Jumbo Cactuar is an ancient Cactuar that has grown to immense proportions. If you can defeat it, you'll earn the **Cactuar GF**, but that's no small task. In preparation for this battle, I suggest that you have the **Revive** and **Recover** abilities equipped on two different characters. I also suggest that the characters without the Revive ability be able to cast either **Life** or **Full-Life**. The

Jumbo Cactuar has the ability to eliminate one of your characters with a single attack, so you'll be using Life and Revive a lot. Also, make sure **Leviathan** is Junctioned to a party member (preferably not the person with the Revive ability), because the Jumbo Cactuar has a weakness to Water magic.

Need Some AP?

If you don't have the skills listed above, they're easy enough to get. Cactuar Island is full of—what else—Cactuars. These creatures are difficult to defeat, because they evade attacks really well and tend to escape from battle in a hurry. Keep in mind, though, that you receive 20 AP for each Cactuar you defeat.

Squall's high hit percentage makes it easy for him to eliminate at least one Cactuar in each battle, so winning just 10 battles can earn you 200 AP. Just make sure you avoid the Jumbo Cactuar until you're ready to do battle.

Jumbo Cactuar

HP	6000~60,000	AP	20	--
EXP	--		Weak vs Water	

This battle is all about patience and controlled attacks. The Jumbo Cactuar utilizes a nasty, random counterattack called **10,000 Needles**. This attack causes more than 10,000 points of damage, which can't be reduced by spells like Protect. The rest of the Jumbo Cactuar's attacks are strong, but are nothing to worry about.

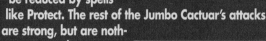

Have one of your characters (preferably the one with the **Revive** ability) serve as a "medic" for the entire fight. Your "medic" will be very busy reviving the other two characters each time they're hit by the 10,000 Needles counterattack. As long as the "medic" never attacks and you constantly use **Recover** or **Cure** spells to keep his/her HP at maximum, you'll never have trouble reviving downed party members.

Of the remaining two attacking characters, focus one on constantly using Water magic or physical attacks. The other should concentrate on repeatedly summoning **Leviathan**. Because the Jumbo Cactuar has a weakness against Water magic, Leviathan can cause around 9999 points of damage with each summon. This will speed up the battle considerably.

After causing substantial damage to the Jumbo Cactuar, you may see a message stating that the Jumbo Cactuar is hesitating. BE VERY CAREFUL AT THIS POINT! This means that the Boss is thinking about running away. Refrain from attacking the Boss, with Leviathan being the exception. You must quickly finish off Jumbo Cactuar with your strongest attacks; if not, you're forced to fight it all over again once it runs. Leviathan's 9999 points of damage is your best bet.

DEEP SEA RESEARCH CENTER

Available When
Disc Three (With Ragnarok)

Difficulty
Very Hard

Rewards
Incredible

Unavailable When
N/A

Enemies
Grendel
Bomb
Tri-Face
Imp
Iron Giant
Behemoth
Ruby Dragon
Bahamut
Ultima Weapon

Draw Points
Triple (Deep Sea Deposit)
Ultima (Deep Sea Deposit)
Dispel (Deep Sea Deposit)
Esuna (Deep Sea Deposit/
Steam Room)

Save Points
Entrance
6th Floor
Bottom Floor (Hidden)

GFs
Eden (Draw from Ultima Weapon)
Bahamut (must defeat)

Where Is It???

Finding the Deep Sea Research Center isn't easy. It doesn't appear on any map, it's very small, and very, very remote. You can locate it using the mobile Balamb Garden, but you won't be able to land anywhere on it. The only way into the Deep Sea Research Center is landing on top of it, so you'll need to have the Ragnarok to get inside.

Bahamut's Quest

Upon entering the facility, you'll notice a blue, glowing core. Your objective is to walk up to the core. Sounds easy, but it isn't. The random encounter rate in this area is astoundingly high and the Enc-Half and Enc-None abilities don't work in here. You may very well get into a fight every couple of steps you take. There's a trick to getting through this room without having to face random encounters. Notice how the core pulses? If you only move while the core isn't glowing, one or two steps tops, you can avoid any random encounters. If you're not having any luck with this, you can try another trick. Make sure you push in the direction you wish to walk as each battle ends. By doing so, you'll ensure that you're walking as the screen fades back in and before the core can glow. You should be able to take three or four steps this way. If you pause for too long, you'll get into a fight as soon as you move even a tiny bit, as the core will have begun to glow again.

At the core, Bahamut will ask you several questions. After each question, you'll be forced to fight a powerful Ruby Dragon and you won't have the opportunity to heal between battles. If you choose the wrong answer, you'll be forced to fight a Ruby Dragon and then be given the same question again until you select the right answer.

The questions and answers are:

Bahamut: "So you wish to challenge me..."

Choose: "It's not our will to fight"

Bahamut: "Begging me for mercy?"

Choose: "Never"

Bahamut: "Damned imbeciles. Why do you wish to fight?"

Choose: Select the third option, which is hidden below "None of your business"

After answering all three questions correctly, you'll be taken into a Boss fight with Bahamut.

Bahamut

GF | HP 10,800~90,000 | AP 40 | Flying Monster
EXP — — | Weak vs. Ice/Absorbs Fire

This battle isn't as tough as you might expect it to be. Start the fight by casting **Blind** on Bahamut if you don't have Blind or Pain Junctioned to a party member's Status-Atk. This will cut down Bahamut's powers considerably, because half of its attacks are physical attacks.

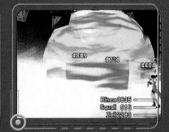

Now all you have to worry about are Bahamut's magic attacks and its ultimate weapon: Mega Flare. Keep everyone's HP high, and use protective spells like **Shell** and **Protect** to cut down on the damage caused by these attacks. When Bahamut uses the Mega Flare, quickly have everyone draw Curaga from the GF so they can heal themselves.

Attack the GF with your best GFs, but avoid Ifrit, Brothers, and Quezacotl. Limit Breaks are great in this fight. Use Aura spells if you have them so that you can easily get every character's Limit Breaks activated.

Under the Sea

After defeating Bahamut, leave the research center by boarding the Ragnarok and then enter the Conference Room. Return to the research center after exiting the Ragnarok and you'll find that the core has been destroyed and there's a passage down to the lower levels. The new area is a strange, rotating structure filled with steam powered airlocks.

Your goal in this section is to work your way down to the bottom floor by using the remaining 20 units of reserve steam power to open the various airlocks. When you reach the bottom, you must have 10 units left in order to start the final control panel.

There are a couple of ways to go about this:

Solution #1 (without Zell)

Floor 1:

> 4 units spent automatically to open the door to Floor 2.
>
> **Total RSP:** 16

Floor 2:

> Spend 2 units to open the door to Floor 3: Sector 2.
>
> **Total RSP:** 14

Floor 3:

"The Steam Room and the left door are linked. 4 RSP will be expended to enter the Steam Room."

"Current stocked Reserve Steam Pressure: 7 As an emergency precaution, would you like to replenish your supply?" Yes No

Use the monitor on the left under the stairs and spend 4 units to open the Steam Room. Inside the Steam Room you can use the Esuna Draw Point and use the station there to recharge 7 Units for a total of 17 Units. Use the second station in the main room to spend 1 Unit, and open the door to Floor 4: Sector 6.

> **Total RSP:** 16

Floor 4:

> Spend 1 unit to open the door to Floor 5: Sector 9.
>
> **Total RSP:** 15

Floor 5:

> Spend 1 unit to open the door to Floor 6.
>
> **Total RSP:** 14

Floor 6:

> Spend 4 units to open the door into the excavation site.
>
> **Total RSP:** 10

Solution #2: (With Zell)

Floor 1:

> 4 units spent automatically to open the door to Floor 2.
>
> **Total RSP:** 16

Floor 2:

> Use 1 unit to open the door to Floor 3: Sector 3.
>
> **Total RSP:** 15

Floor 3:

> Use 1 unit to open the door to Floor 4: Sector 6.
>
> **Total RSP:** 14

Floor 4:

> Use 1 unit to open the door to Floor 5: Sector 9
>
> **Total RSP:** 13

Floor 5:

> Use 1 unit to open the door to Floor 6.
>
> **Total RSP:** 12

Floor 6:

Inspect the machinery to the right of the levers, and Zell will suggest that he can handle the machine. Allow him to do so, and the door will open without spending any steam units.

Zell "Hold up a sec. Let me take care of this machine here. (I don't know if you can...) (Well... Zell's pretty good with machinery)

> **Total RSP:** 12

With either solution, you'll be able to reach the bottom floor with the required 10 RSP. Make your way through the excavation site, and at the bottom you'll find another control panel. Save your game at the hidden Save Point and use the 10 RSP to activate the final control panel. Inside you'll face a very tough Boss: Ultima Weapon.

"Steam pressure 10 needed to continue operation."

Ultima Weapon GF

HP	51,100-160,000	AP	100	— —
EXP	— —		— —	

Ultima Weapon is no pushover. This beast has 1-hit kills and powerful magic spells that attack the entire party simultaneously. You'll have to use every advantage you have in your arsenal to defeat it.

It helps to have the **Revive** ability on one of your characters. Make sure you have at least one character who can cast magic and has the **Triple, Aura, Curaga**, and **Meltdown** spells in his/her inventory. Also, try to set everyone up so that they can revive fallen characters either with magic, abilities, or items. If you can get Squall's Lionheart weapon, it will help out a lot as well.

Start the fight by casting **Haste** on everyone to give yourself a speed advantage. Then follow that up by summoning Doomtrain or casting Meltdown on Ultima Weapon to cut its defenses. Also, make sure you draw the **Eden GF** before you forget. You wouldn't want to miss obtaining the strongest GF in the game!

Cast Triple or use Cerberus so that a magic user can heal everyone at once. Follow this up by casting Aura on everyone if you can. By doing so, you can unload on the Boss with constant Limit Breaks. Keep the pressure up and Ultima Weapon should fall quickly.

Available When

Disc Three (with Ragnarok)

Difficulty

Medium

Rewards

Good

Unavailable When

N/A

Just north of Timber is tranquil Obel Lake. There's a small peninsula in the center of the lake where you can find **hidden options** if you search the edge of the peninsula.

The options are "Throw a rock" or "Try humming." After choosing "Try humming" several times, you'll encounter a strange shadowy creature in the water. Speak with the creature and it will ask you to do it a favor by finding its friend, Mr. Monkey. The only clues the creature of Obel Lake gives you are: 1.) Mr. Monkey may have hopped a train toward Dollet; and 2). Mr. Monkey enjoys hanging out in forests.

Head for Dollet and search the forest to the west of the city. During your search, you should eventually encounter Mr. Monkey. After finding Mr. Monkey, return to Obel Lake and speak with the creature of Obel Lake again. It will tell you several cryptic clues:

- **"Take a break at the railroad bridge."**
- **"At the beach in Balamb, something special washes ashore at times."**
- **"Take some time off at Eldbeak Peninsula."**
- **"You'll find something on an island east of Timber, too."**
- **"There's also something on top of a mountain with a lake and cavern."**
- **"Back in the day, south of here, there used to be a small but beautiful village surrounded by deep forests. Everyone lived a happy life there."**
- **"Mr. Monkey had a rock like this I think..."**

What the creature of Obel Lake is trying to say is that you should visit all of these places to find objects of interest. First, you'll be looking for small rocks in four locations. Here's where you'll find them.

Rock #1: ("Mr. Monkey had a rock like this I think...") You won't get the clue for this one until you've found at least one other rock. Stand at Obel Lake and throw rocks until you get the message reading **"The rock skipped many, many times."** This may take many tries as the message appears at random. Now head for the forest near Dollet to find Mr. Monkey. Throw rocks at Mr. Monkey until he throws a rock back at you with the inscription "U R H A E O."

Rock #2: ("**You'll find something on an island east of Timber, too.**") The small island east of Timber is the one on the north side of the railroad bridge, known as a part of Mandy Beach. Search the ground to find a small rock with the inscription "R E A I D R."

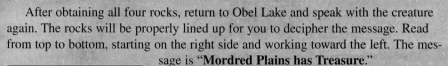

Rock #3: ("**At the beach in Balamb, something special washes ashore at times.**") There are a lot of rocks on the beach just south of Balamb. Keep searching to eventually find the right one. The small rock found here bears the inscription "S T S L R M."

Rock #4: ("**There's also something on top of a mountain with a lake and cavern.**") You MUST have the Ragnarok to find this rock. On top of a mountain called the Monterosa Plateau, northwest of Timber, search the ground and you'll find a bird warming an egg directly above a small cavern with a waterfall in the side of the plateau. Fight off the birds to find a small rock inscribed with the letters "E A S N P D."

After obtaining all four rocks, return to Obel Lake and speak with the creature again. The rocks will be properly lined up for you to decipher the message. Read from top to bottom, starting on the right side and working toward the left. The message is "**Mordred Plains has Treasure.**"

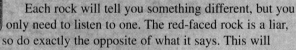

Head for Mordred Plains, which is the large plain north of Esthar, and explore the area while searching the ground. Upon searching, you'll discover four rocks, each with a human face.

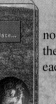

Each rock will tell you something different, but you only need to listen to one. The red-faced rock is a liar, so do exactly the opposite of what it says. This will eventually lead you to the treasure. When you search a spot and the red-faced rock says, "The treasure is not here," you know you've found it. Search a second time to discover a **Three Stars**, which can be used to teach a GF the **Expendx3-1 ability**.

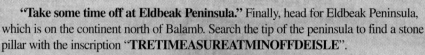

"**Take some time off at Eldbeak Peninsula.**" Finally, head for Eldbeak Peninsula, which is on the continent north of Balamb. Search the tip of the peninsula to find a stone pillar with the inscription "**TRETIMEASUREATMINOFFDEISLE**".

What does it mean? Well, according to the clue, you should "Take some TIME OFF at Eldbeak Peninsula." So eliminate the words TIME and OFF from the message and you get "**TREASUREATMINDEISLE**" or "**Treasure at Minde Isle**." Minde Island is a small island located south of Esthar. Search the island to find a **Luck-J Scroll**.

"**Back in the day, south of here, there used to be a small but beautiful village surrounded by deep forests. Everyone lived a happy life there.**" This is referring to a weird shaped forest east of Edea's House with a sort of round clearing in the middle containing a grassy area. If you land here and go into the grassy part, Squall will mention that there is a lot of rubble around. That is all that you can do regarding this clue.

"**Take a break at the railroad bridge.**" This clue is a hint at the many hidden Draw Points that can be found on railroad bridges.

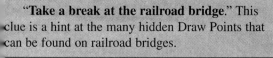

Available When
Disc Three (With Ragnarok)

Difficulty
Medium

Rewards
Good

Unavailable When
N/A

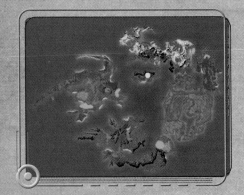

While exploring certain areas, you may have been surprised to encounter a UFO. That's right! Aliens have invaded the world of FFVIII, and it's your job to track them down. You can spot the UFO in the four places shown on this map.

Travel to the highlighted area and walk around until you enter a battle with no enemies. The UFO will appear in the distance, carrying an object, and then it will fly away. You can speed up your search by equipping Diablos' **Enc-None** ability. Although seeing the UFO is considered an encounter, you can still find the UFO with the Enc-None ability equipped, however, you won't have to deal with fighting any monsters.

Encounter #1:
Winhill Bluffs

Cow

Encounter #2:
Mandy Beach, south of Timber

Moa Head Statue

Encounter #3:
Kashkabald Desert, located on an island on the east side of the Centra Ruins

Pyramid

Encounter #4:
Trabia Heath Peninsula, east of Trabia Garden

Strange Symbol

After encountering the UFO in all four locations, pilot the Ragnarok to the plateau just north of Grandidi Forest's Chocobo Forest. After walking around on this plateau, you'll

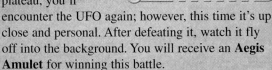

encounter the UFO again; however, this time it's up close and personal. After defeating it, watch it fly off into the background. You will receive an **Aegis Amulet** for winning this battle.

> **NOTE**
> Before moving onward, you should equip one of your characters with the **Item** command. In addition, you should have five Elixirs in your inventory.

Now return to Balamb and explore the area where Balamb Garden was once positioned (Alcauld Plains). Here you'll encounter the alien known as **PuPu**. The alien will ask you for an Elixir. Use an Elixir on the

Alien, and it will continue to ask you for more Elixirs. Give the PuPu a total of five Elixirs and it will give you the **PuPu card**.

You can fight the alien if you want to win an **Accelerator**, however, giving the PuPu Elixirs is the only way to get its one-of-a-kind card.

QUEEN OF CARDS QUEST

At the beginning of the game, you can find the Queen of Cards in Balamb near Balamb Station. She will remain here until you either lose (or win) a rare card (any level eight card or better) to/from her. Once this requirement is fulfilled, speak with her and she'll give you a hint as to her next destination, which can be at one of the following eight places around the world: Balamb, Shumi Village, Dollet, Deling City, Winhill, Esthar, F.H., and Lunar Gate.

Available When
Disc Three (with Ragnarok)

Difficulty
Hard

Rewards
Great

Unavailable When
Disc Four

The Card Queen's quest takes place in the town of Dollet. When speaking with her normally (using the ⊙ button) while in Dollet, you'll notice a fourth option, "About your artist father," that hasn't been available in other cities. When you choose this option, the Card Queen will ask you for a specific card. The first card she requests is the **MiniMog Card**. To advance the quest you must lose the MiniMog Card to her in a card game. This enables her father to create a new card that you can win from someone elsewhere in the world. Cards created by her father are all rare, and aren't available to you unless you take on the Card Queen's quest.

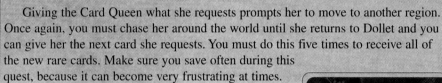

Giving the Card Queen what she requests prompts her to move to another region. Once again, you must chase her around the world until she returns to Dollet and you can give her the next card she requests. You must do this five times to receive all of the new rare cards. Make sure you save often during this quest, because it can become very frustrating at times.

Paired with this text are several tables. Use the tables to determine the Card Queen's movement, destination, and requests. You may need to pause in the middle of this quest in order to hunt down a card or two you may have missed earlier. Just make sure you note the Card Queen's destination so as to avoid searching several locations when you return to complete the quest at a later time.

> **NOTE** *You can retrieve any of the five cards you are required to give to the Card Queen from her little brother in Dollet. He is the child living with the artist one screen down from the Pub. As soon as you give the Card Queen any of the five requested cards, they are immediately transferred to the boy's inventory. Any other cards lost to the Card Queen must be won back from her in normal fashion.*

Card Queen Says...	She's Going To...
Galbadia	The Galbadia Hotel in Deling City
FH	On train tracks in Fisherman's Horizon
Esthar	The Presidential Palace in Esthar
Trabia	The Hotel in Shumi Village
Centra	The Hotel in Winhill
Dollet	The Pub in Dollet
Balamb	Balamb Station in Balamb
Far Away	Lunar Gate's Concourse Area
Present Location	**Will Move to...**
Balamb	Dollet (37.5%), Deling City (62.5%)
Deling City	Balamb (12.5%), Dollet (12.5%), Winhill (12.5%), F.H. (62.5%)
Dollet	Balamb (37.5%), Deling City (62.5%)
Shumi Village	Balamb (25%), Dollet (50%), Lunar Gate (25%)
Winhill	Deling City (37.5%), Dollet (37.5%), F.H. (25%)
F.H.	Dollet (12.5%), Winhill (25%), Esthar (62.5%)
Esthar	Dollet (12.5%), Shumi Village (25%), F.H. (12.5%), Lunar Gate (50%)
Lunar Gate	Random Area (any of the eight; gives no clue to destination)

Balamb

Winhill

Deling City

F.H.

Dollet

Esthar

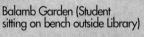

Shumi Village

Lunar Gate

Card Given	Card Created	Where to find New Card	Card Given	Card Created	Where to find New Card
MiniMog	Kiros	Deling City (Man in black across from Junk Shop)	Chicobo	Chubby Chicobo	Balamb Garden (Student sitting on bench outside Library)

Card Given	Card Created	Where to find New Card	Card Given	Card Created	Where to find New Card
Sacred	Irvine	F.H. (Flo, wife of F.H.'s Mayor Dobe)	Alexander	Doomtrain	Timber (Pub's owner, man behind right counter)

Card Given	Card Created	Where to find New Card
Doomtrain	Phoenix	Esthar (Presidental Palace, Presidential Assistant in blue)

SOLOMON RING
GUARDIAN FORCE ALERT!

There are four places you can visit in the area outside of Esthar: Lunatic Pandora Laboratory, Sorceress Memorial, Lunar Gate, and Tears' Point. All four locations are now highlighted on the World Map.

Before you head for Lunar Gate, however, you should take a quick detour and go to Tears' Point. There's a valuable item at Tears' Point known as the **Solomon Ring**. To use it, you'll need 18 items: six **Steel Pipes**, six

Remedy+, and six **Malboro Tentacles**. This item enables you to summon the GF **Doomtrain**.

You can get the necessary items by stealing Steel Pipes from Wendigos, using the Medicine Level Up ability to create Remedy+, and by stealing (or winning) Malboro Tentacles from Malboros. You don't have to fight Doomtrain, and once you summon it, it joins you without putting you through another grueling test.

SECRETS

Gifts from Esthar Shops

Cloud's shop will randomly give you a **Hi-Potion** during the first visit, and an **X-Potion** during your second visit. Johnny's Shop will randomly give you a **Hi-Potion** during the first visit, and a **Mega-Potion** during your second visit. Karen's Shop will randomly give you a **Hi-Potion** during the first visit, and a **Mega-Phoenix** during your second visit. Cheryl's Shop will only randomly give you one item: the **Rosetta Stone**. Visit Cheryl's Shop during the Lunatic Pandora event in Esthar when you are in control of Zell.

Crash Site

If you missed out on the **Alexander Card** in the Lunar Base, you can still win it from Piet. The escape pod crashed in the Abadan Plains, which is south of Tears' Point outside of Esthar's cloak. Land on the island and search the area. You can't see the crash site, but you'll automatically get taken there if you step in the right area. Piet is sitting next to the escape pod cursing his bad luck.

Quick AP and EXP

Toward the end of the game, you may need to do some quick level building. If you're looking for AP there's only one place to go: Cactuar Island. Each Cactaur you defeat is worth a whopping 20 AP. In no time, you can learn skills worth 200 AP.

If you need EXP visit either the Island Closest to Heaven, or the Island Closest to Hell. Both are found on either the far east or west coasts. There you'll find only the toughest enemies in the game. Bring Quistis along and leave her HP in the yellow. Then begin each battle by using her Degenerator Limit Break. You'll quickly amass more experience than you ever thought possible. Also, be on the lookout for a mass of Draw Points on both of these islands. They're all "unseen," but they contain the best spells in the game and they all refill quickly.

Control Panel Secret

You can toy around a bit with the Missile Control Panel at the Galbadian Missile Base. Choose to go to the Equipment inspection screen and you'll see the equipment used by the Galbadian Army. Hold down both the 🔘 and 🔘 buttons and press up or down on the control pad. The scene will switch to either a dancing Galbadian Soldier or Elite Soldier. Pretty strange stuff.

Unlimited Gil

You can make extra Gil with Edea's Letter. Take it to a shop and you can sell it for 125 Gil. It isn't much, but it can help if you're short on cash. Return to Edea's House and speak with Edea again. She'll scold you and then hand over another letter. You can continue to sell her letters and get new ones to your heart's content. Granted this isn't a great money maker, but it's kind of humorous.

The Laguna Effect

Depending on the actions you took while exploring the Excavation Site (a.k.a. Lunatic Pandora's Excavation Site) as Laguna on Disc One, you may be able to locate some useful items and Draw Points when you explore Lunatic Pandora as Squall at the end of Disc Three. The following covers the action taken by Laguna in the past and the result in the present:

As Laguna
Pick up the first Old Key near the Confuse Draw Point.

Later Effect
You can now access an Ultima Draw Point hidden in a doorway past the floor panels.

As Laguna
Remove a lever from the middle floor panel to set a trap for the Esthar Soldiers.

Later Effect
The floor panel is now open and inside is a Silence Draw Point.

As Laguna
Find the gray detonator switch, and press the red switch prior to pushing the blue switch.

Later Effect
The door at the base of the long ladder is now open. Inside you can find a LuvLuvG item.

As Laguna
Find the second Old Key at the first intersection.

Later Effect
Both boulders fall into gaps in the floor, which enables you to get to some of the secrets listed here. It also enables you to reach a copy of Combat King 005.

As Laguna
Move the rock away from a tunnel wall to reveal a Cure Draw Point.

Later Effect
Searching the spot where the Draw Point once was, reveals a hidden Spd-J Scroll.

Finding the Ragnarok on Disc Four

The Ragnarok is still around and full of people from the C.C. Group, provided that you defeated the C.C. Group's King earlier in the game. It's a long trek, but you can win some rare cards that you may have missed throughout your journey from the C.C. Group's members. You can also use the Ragnarok to find the Card Queen, who's hiding somewhere on the World Map.

While the journey to the Ragnarok isn't tough, it is very long and slow. After going through the second portal outside Ultimecia's Castle, you'll arrive in Centra's Serengetti Plains area just a bit north of the Centra Ruins. Check the World Map and you'll see a red dot southeast of your position. The red dot signifies the Ragnarok. To reach it, you need to find transportation across the ocean, and without the Garden, you must rely on Chocobos.

While on foot, head to the northwest and wrap your way around the bay to the Chocobo Forest on the northeast tip of the Centra continent. Get a Chocobo and return the way you came. Ride the Chocobo to the southern border until you spot a beach. Ride across the ocean to the continent below, which will take you very, very close to Edea's House.

From Edea's House, travel to the east along the mountains. However, keep an eye out for a small pass through the middle of the mountain range. On the other side, you'll find the Kashkabald Desert and the **Ragnarok**. There's a fourth portal near the Ragnarok. Upon entering this portal, a new portal will appear in front of Ultimecia's Castle. Now you can travel to this location any time you wish.

Finding the Queen of Cards on Disc Four

After finding the Ragnarok, you can begin your hunt for the Card Queen and explore the world. The Card Queen is hiding in the Abadan Plains, just to the south of Esthar.

You'll find her near the escape pod crash site (the same place where you found Piet on Disc 3). Keep in mind that there's no visible sign of the crash from the World Map. To locate it, you must scour the southern tip of the plains until you enter the area.

BESTIARY

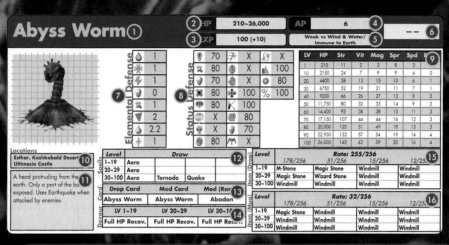

Abyss Worm ①

② HP	210~26,000
③ EXP	100 (+10)
AP ④	6
⑤	Weak vs Wind & Water / Immune to Earth
⑥	--

⑦ Elemental Defense

💧	1
❄	1
⚡	1
💧	0
🍃	1
🌀	2
🌊	2.2
✦	1

⑧ Status Defense

70	⚡ X	🏃	X
80	X		100
70	X	⚙	80
80	100	⚔	100
80	100	⚔	
X	X	⚙	80
X	100	✋	70
80	X	⚙	X

⑨

LV	HP	Str	Vit	Mag	Spr	Spd	E
1	210	11	2	3	8	3	3
10	2150	24	7	9	9	4	0
20	4400	38	13	15	10	6	1
30	6750	52	19	21	11	7	1
40	9200	66	26	27	13	8	2
50	11,750	80	32	33	14	9	2
60	14,400	93	38	38	15	11	3
70	17,150	107	44	44	16	12	3
80	20,000	120	51	49	18	13	3
90	22,950	132	57	54	19	14	4
100	26,000	145	63	59	20	16	4

Locations ⑩
Esthar, Kashkabald Desert, Ultimecia Castle

⑪ A head protruding from the earth. Only a part of the body is exposed. Uses Earthquake when attacked by enemies.

Spells / Draw ⑫

Level	Draw		
1~19	Aero		
20~29	Aero		
30~100	Aero	Tornado	Quake

Devour Card ⑬

Drop Card	Mod Card	Mod (Rare)
Abyss Worm	Abyss Worm	Abadon

⑭

LV 1~19	LV 20~29	LV 30~100
Full HP Recov.	Full HP Recov.	Full HP Recov.

Item (Drop) ⑮

Level	Rate: 255/256			
	178/256	51/256	15/256	12/256
1~19	M-Stone	Magic Stone	Windmill	Windmill
20~29	Magic Stone	Wizard Stone	Windmill	Windmill
30~100	Windmill	Windmill	Windmill	Windmill

Item (Mug) ⑯

Level	Rate: 32/256			
	178/256	51/256	15/256	12/256
1~19	Magic Stone	Windmill	Windmill	Windmill
20~29	Windmill	Windmill	Windmill	Windmill
30~100	Windmill	Windmill	Windmill	Windmill

1.	Name of the enemy
2.	Enemy's HP range, from lowest to highest
3.	Experience Points gained from defeating enemy
4.	Ability Points gained from defeating enemy
5.	Elemental strengths and weaknesses
6.	Enemy type

---

7. Enemy's strengths and weaknesses against all 8 elements.

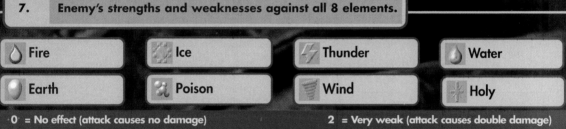

💧 Fire	❄ Ice	⚡ Thunder	💧 Water
🌐 Earth	🐾 Poison	🌀 Wind	✦ Holy

- **0** = No effect (attack causes no damage)
- **1** = Normal (attack causes normal damage)
- **1.5** = Weak (attack causes 50% more damage than normal)
- **2** = Very weak (attack causes double damage)
- **-1** = Absorbs (attack causes no damage; enemy healed by attack)

---

8. Determines if a status attack will have an effect on the enemy.

🕆 Death	🐾 Poison	Petrify	👁 Blind
🗨 Silence	Berserk	💀 Zombie	💤 Sleep
⚡ Haste	🕐 Slow	✋ Stop	Regen
⚔ Reflect	🕆 Slow Death	✋ Slow Petrify	Float
Confuse	Drain	🌟 Blow Away	% Percentage

X = Status attack has no effect on enemy

0~100 % = Indicates the percentage change that the status attack will affect the enemy. Note that this percentage can be altered by the casting character's magic ability or the number of the status effect that is junctioned.

9.   An enemy's vital statistics as they progress throughout the game.

LV (Level) = Enemy's level, which determines the enemy's experience
HP (Hit Points) = Number of Hit Points (health) an enemy possesses
Str (Strength) = Enemy's attack power
Vit (Vitality) = Defense against physical attacks
Mag (Magic) = Determines the power of the spells cast
Spr (Spirit) = Defense against magical attacks
Spd (Speed) = Determines how quickly an enemy will attack
Eva (Evade) = Enemy's ability to evade attacks

10.   Indicates the location at which you can find the enemy.

11.   Brief description of each enemy.

12.   List of spells drawn from an enemy at its various levels.

13.   Cards an enemy will drop after battle (Card) or card received when using the Card Mod ability in battle (Mod Card). Mod Rare indicates a card you may receive on a rare occasion when using the Card Mod ability.

14.   Different effects when using the Devour ability on an enemy during battle. The effects vary depending on the enemy's level.

15.   Item dropped by an enemy after defeating it in battle.

Level	Rate: 255/256			
	178/256	51/256	15/256	12/256
1~19	M-Stone	Magic Stone	Windmill	Windmill
20~29	Magic Stone	Wizard Stone	Windmill	Windmill
30~100	Windmill	Windmill	Windmill	Windmill

For example, the Abyss Worm drops an item 255/256 times you fight it. Each creature has a common item it drops, and additional items it drops at a lesser rate.

16.   Using the Mug ability, this shows the items you can steal from an enemy during battle.

Level	Rate: 32/256			
	178/256	51/256	15/256	12/256
1~19	Magic Stone	Windmill	Windmill	Windmill
20~29	Windmill	Windmill	Windmill	Windmill
30~100	Windmill	Windmill	Windmill	Windmill

The rate indicates the chance of success at mugging an item during battle.

Enemy Bosses are distinguished from regular enemies by the gold bar on the top of its status area

Abadon

HP	510~17,010	AP	40	*Undead Monster*
EXP	— —		Weak vs Fire, Holy & Cure	

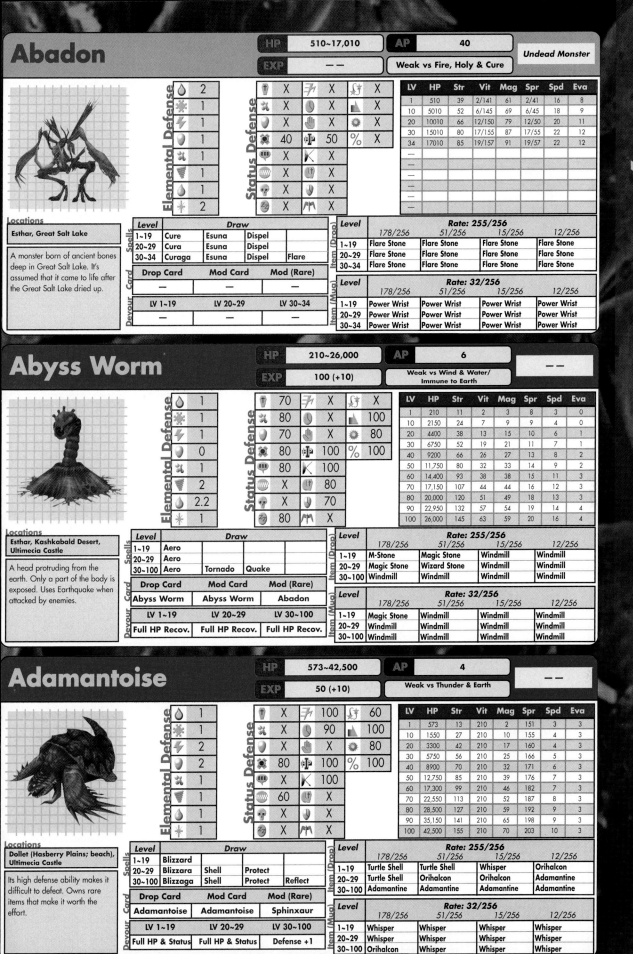

Elemental Defense: 2, 1, 1, 1, 1, 1, 1, 2

Status Defense: X, X, X, 40, X, X, X, X / X, X, X, 50, X, X, X, X / X, X, X, %, K, X, X, X

LV	HP	Str	Vit	Mag	Spr	Spd	Eva
1	510	39	2/141	61	2/41	16	8
10	5010	52	6/145	69	6/45	18	9
20	10010	66	12/150	79	12/50	20	11
30	15010	80	17/155	87	17/55	22	12
34	17010	85	19/157	91	19/57	22	12

Locations

Esthar, Great Salt Lake

A monster born of ancient bones deep in Great Salt Lake. It's assumed that it came to life after the Great Salt Lake dried up.

Spells — Draw

Level		Draw		
1~19	Cure	Esuna	Dispel	
20~29	Cura	Esuna	Dispel	
30~34	Curaga	Esuna	Dispel	Flare

Card

Drop Card	Mod Card	Mod (Rare)
—	—	—

Devour

LV 1~19	LV 20~29	LV 30~34
—	—	—

Item (Drop) — Rate: 255/256

Level	178/256	51/256	15/256	12/256
1~19	Flare Stone	Flare Stone	Flare Stone	Flare Stone
20~29	Flare Stone	Flare Stone	Flare Stone	Flare Stone
30~34	Flare Stone	Flare Stone	Flare Stone	Flare Stone

Item (Mug) — Rate: 32/256

Level	178/256	51/256	15/256	12/256
1~19	Power Wrist	Power Wrist	Power Wrist	Power Wrist
20~29	Power Wrist	Power Wrist	Power Wrist	Power Wrist
30~34	Power Wrist	Power Wrist	Power Wrist	Power Wrist

Abyss Worm

HP	210~26,000	AP	6	— —
EXP	100 (+10)		Weak vs Wind & Water/ Immune to Earth	

Elemental Defense: 1, 1, 1, 0, 1, 2, 2.2, 1

Status Defense: 70, 80, 70, 80, 80, X, X, 80 / X, X, X, 100, X, X, X, X / X, 100, 80, 100, 100, 80, 70, X

LV	HP	Str	Vit	Mag	Spr	Spd	Eva
1	210	11	2	3	8	3	0
10	2150	24	7	9	9	4	0
20	4400	38	13	15	10	6	1
30	6750	52	19	21	11	7	1
40	9200	66	26	27	13	8	2
50	11,750	80	32	33	14	9	2
60	14,400	93	38	38	15	11	3
70	17,150	107	44	44	16	12	3
80	20,000	120	51	49	18	13	3
90	22,950	132	57	54	19	14	4
100	26,000	145	63	59	20	16	4

Locations

Esthar, Kashkabald Desert, Ultimecia Castle

A head protruding from the earth. Only a part of the body is exposed. Uses Earthquake when attacked by enemies.

Spells — Draw

Level		Draw	
1~19	Aero		
20~29	Aero		
30~100	Aero	Tornado	Quake

Card

Drop Card	Mod Card	Mod (Rare)
Abyss Worm	Abyss Worm	Abadon

Devour

LV 1~19	LV 20~29	LV 30~100
Full HP Recov.	Full HP Recov.	Full HP Recov.

Item (Drop) — Rate: 255/256

Level	178/256	51/256	15/256	12/256
1~19	M-Stone	Magic Stone	Windmill	Windmill
20~29	Magic Stone	Wizard Stone	Windmill	Windmill
30~100	Windmill	Windmill	Windmill	Windmill

Item (Mug) — Rate: 32/256

Level	178/256	51/256	15/256	12/256
1~19	Magic Stone	Windmill	Windmill	Windmill
20~29	Windmill	Windmill	Windmill	Windmill
30~100	Windmill	Windmill	Windmill	Windmill

Adamantoise

HP	573~42,500	AP	4	— —
EXP	50 (+10)		Weak vs Thunder & Earth	

Elemental Defense: 1, 1, 2, 2, 1, 1, 1, 1

Status Defense: X, X, X, 80, X, 60, X, X / 100, 90, X, 100, 100, X, X, X / 60, 100, 80, 100, 100, X, X, X

LV	HP	Str	Vit	Mag	Spr	Spd	Eva
1	573	13	210	2	151	3	3
10	1550	27	210	10	155	4	3
20	3300	42	210	17	160	4	3
30	5750	56	210	25	166	5	3
40	8900	70	210	32	171	6	3
50	12,750	85	210	39	176	7	3
60	17,300	99	210	46	182	7	3
70	22,550	113	210	52	187	8	3
80	28,500	127	210	59	192	9	3
90	35,150	141	210	65	198	9	3
100	42,500	155	210	70	203	10	3

Locations

Dollet (Hasberry Plains; beach), Ultimecia Castle

Its high defense ability makes it difficult to defeat. Owns rare items that make it worth the effort.

Spells — Draw

Level		Draw		
1~19	Blizzard			
20~29	Blizzara	Shell	Protect	
30~100	Blizzaga	Shell	Protect	Reflect

Card

Drop Card	Mod Card	Mod (Rare)
Adamantoise	Adamantoise	Sphinxaur

Devour

LV 1~19	LV 20~29	LV 30~100
Full HP & Status	Full HP & Status	Defense +1

Item (Drop) — Rate: 255/256

Level	178/256	51/256	15/256	12/256
1~19	Turtle Shell	Turtle Shell	Whisper	Orihalcon
20~29	Turtle Shell	Orihalcon	Orihalcon	Adamantine
30~100	Adamantine	Adamantine	Adamantine	Adamantine

Item (Mug) — Rate: 32/256

Level	178/256	51/256	15/256	12/256
1~19	Whisper	Whisper	Whisper	Whisper
20~29	Whisper	Whisper	Whisper	Whisper
30~100	Orihalcon	Whisper	Whisper	Whisper

Adel

HP	6000~51,000	AP	— —		— —
EXP	— —		— —		

Elemental Defense

Element	Value
💧	1
❄️	1
⚡	1
🌀	1
🌪️	1.5
💧	1
✳️	-1

Status Defense

🗡️	X	⚡	X	🦊	X
🐍	X	⭕	X	⛰️	X
💧	X	✋	X	☀️	X
☣️	X	✝️	100	%	X
💬	X	🗡️	100		
💀	X	🎩	X		
⚰️	X	🛡️	X		
🌀	X	🎮	X		

LV	HP	Str	Vit	Mag	Spr	Spd	Eva
1	6000	46	32	59	42	35	0
10	15,000	64	47	78	61	40	1
20	25,000	83	65	98	82	44	1
30	35,000	101	82	118	103	49	2
40	45,000	120	100	137	124	53	2
46	51,000	131	110	148	136	56	2
—							
—							
—							

Locations
Lunar Pandora

Esthar's ruler before Laguna and company confined her. Released by Ultimecia, and regaining strength.

Spells

Level	Draw		
1~19	Fire	Thunder	Blizzard
20~29	Fira	Thundara	Blizzara
30~46	Firaga	Thundaga	Blizzaga

Card

Drop Card	Mod Card	Mod (Rare)
—		

LV 1~19	LV 20~29	LV 30~46

Item (Drop)

Level	Rate: 255/256			
	178/256	51/256	15/256	12/256
1~19	—	—	—	—
20~29	—	—	—	—
30~46	—	—	—	—

Item (Mug)

Level	Rate: 32/256			
	178/256	51/256	15/256	12/256
1~19	Samantha Soul	Samantha Soul	Samantha Soul	Samantha Soul
20~29	Samantha Soul	Samantha Soul	Samantha Soul	Samantha Soul
30~46	Samantha Soul	Samantha Soul	Samantha Soul	Samantha Soul

---

Anacondaur

HP	842~24,800	AP	4		— —
EXP	60 (+10)		Weak vs Ice/Strong vs Fire/ Absorbs Poison		

Elemental Defense

Element	Value
💧	0.5
❄️	2
⚡	1
🌀	1
🌪️	-0.5
💧	1
✳️	1

Status Defense

🗡️	50	⚡	40	🦊	40
🐍	X	⭕	40	⛰️	40
💧	40	✋	40	☀️	40
☣️	70	✝️	40	%	100
💬	40	🗡️	40		
💀	40	🎩	40		
⚰️	X	🛡️	60		
🌀	40	🎮	40		

LV	HP	Str	Vit	Mag	Spr	Spd	Eva
1	842	18	10	2	2	10	0
10	1400	30	15	13	9	11	1
20	2400	42	20	26	17	12	1
30	3800	55	25	38	26	13	2
40	5600	67	30	50	34	14	2
50	7800	79	35	62	42	15	3
60	10,400	91	40	75	51	16	3
70	13,400	103	45	86	59	17	4
80	16,800	115	50	98	67	18	4
90	20,660	126	55	110	76	19	5
100	24,800	138	60	122	84	20	6

Locations
Dollet (Hasberry Plateau), Timber, Deep Sea Research Center

A large venomous snake that use squeeze attacks. Use caution when its HP are low; it spits poisonous fluid.

Spells

Level	Draw		
1~19	Fire	Cure	
20~29	Fira	Cura	
30~100	Firaga	Curaga	Bio

Card

Drop Card	Mod Card	Mod (Rare)
Anacondaur	Anacondaur	Mobile Type 8

LV 1~19	LV 20~29	LV 30~100
Damage(small) & Poison	Damage (small) & Poison	Damage (small) & Poison

Item (Drop)

Level	Rate: 255/256			
	178/256	51/256	15/256	12/256
1~19	M-Stone	Venom Fang	Venom Fang	Dragon Skin
20~29	Venom Fang	Venom Fang	Venom Fang	Dragon Skin
30~100	Dragon Skin	Dragon Skin	Dragon Skin	Star Fragment

Item (Mug)

Level	Rate: 32/256			
	178/256	51/256	15/256	12/256
1~19	Venom Fang	Venom Fang	Venom Fang	Venom Fang
20~29	Venom Fang	Venom Fang	Venom Fang	Venom Fang
30~100	Venom Fang	Venom Fang	Venom Fang	Venom Fang

Armadodo

HP	731~18,700	AP	3		— —
EXP	80 (+15)		— —		

Elemental Defense

Element	Value
💧	1
❄️	1
⚡	1
🌀	1
🌪️	1
💧	1
✳️	1

Status Defense

🗡️	70	⚡	100	🦊	X
🐍	80	⭕	90	⛰️	100
💧	70	✋	0	☀️	80
☣️	80	✝️	100	%	100
💬	80	🗡️	100		
💀	60	🎩	80		
⚰️	70	🛡️	70		
🌀	80	🎮	100		

LV	HP	Str	Vit	Mag	Spr	Spd	Eva
1	731	12	120	1	4	4	0
10	1150	23	120	10	5	5	0
20	1900	34	121	18	6	6	1
30	2950	45	122	27	7	7	1
40	4300	56	123	35	9	8	2
50	5950	67	124	43	10	9	2
60	7900	77	125	50	11	10	3
70	10,150	87	125	58	12	11	3
80	12,700	97	126	65	14	12	3
90	15,550	107	127	72	15	13	4
100	18,700	116	128	79	16	14	4

Locations
Tomb of the Unknown King, Ultimecia Castle

Its hard shell is difficult to damage physically. The legs are small compared to the body and it falls easily when attacked with force.

Spells

Level	Draw		
1~19	Protect		
20~29	Protect	Shell	
30~100	Protect	Shell	Quake

Card

Drop Card	Mod Card	Mod (Rare)
Armadodo	Armadodo	Catoblepas

LV 1~19	LV 20~29	LV 30~100
Full HP Recov.	Full HP Recov.	Full HP Recov.

Item (Drop)

Level	Rate: 255/256			
	178/256	51/256	15/256	12/256
1~19	M-Stone	Sharp Spike	Sharp Spike	Sharp Spike
20~29	Magic Stone	Sharp Spike	Sharp Spike	Turtle Shell
30~100	Turtle Shell	Sharp Spike	Sharp Spike	Turtle Shell

Item (Mug)

Level	Rate: 32/256			
	178/256	51/256	15/256	12/256
1~19	Magic Stone	Magic Stone	Magic Stone	Magic Stone
20~29	Magic Stone	Magic Stone	Magic Stone	Magic Stone
30~100	Magic Stone	Magic Stone	Magic Stone	Magic Stone

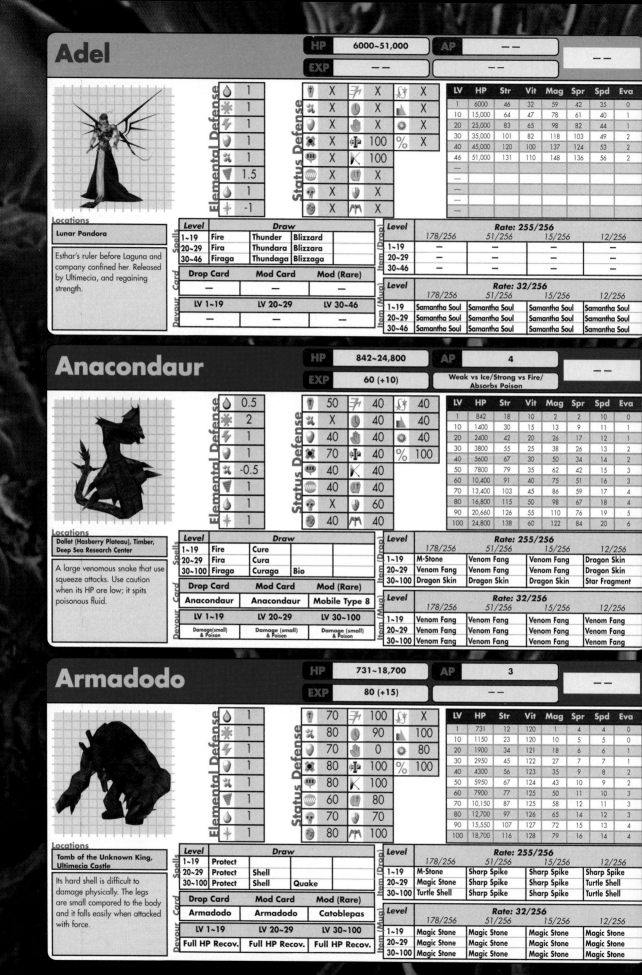

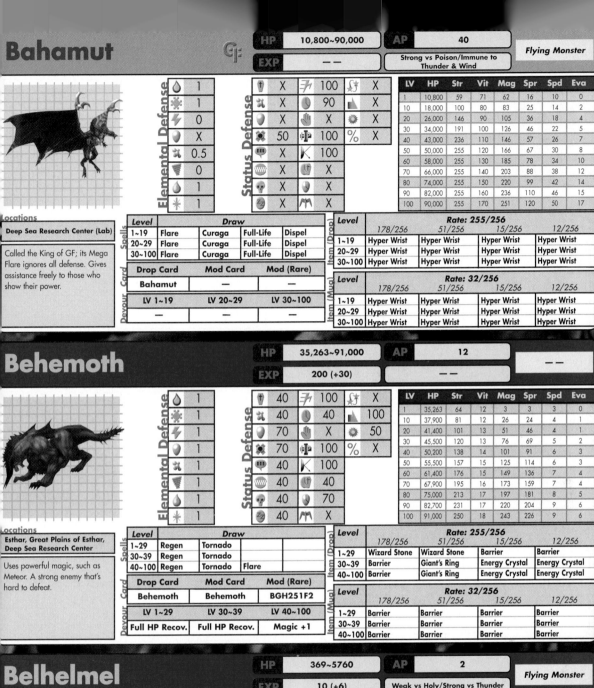

Bahamut

HP	10,800~90,000
AP	40
EXP	— —

Strong vs Poison/Immune to Thunder & Wind — *Flying Monster*

Elemental Defense: 💧1, ❄1, ⚡0, 💧X, 0.5, 0, 1, ❄1

Status Defense: X / 100, X / 90, X / X, 50 / 100, X / X, X / X, X / X, X / X, 100, X, X, 100, X, X, X, X, X

LV	HP	Str	Vit	Mag	Spr	Spd	Eva
1	10,800	59	71	62	16	10	0
10	18,000	100	80	83	25	14	2
20	26,000	146	90	105	36	18	4
30	34,000	191	100	126	46	22	5
40	43,000	236	110	146	57	26	7
50	50,000	255	120	166	67	30	8
60	58,000	255	130	185	78	34	10
70	66,000	255	140	203	88	38	12
80	74,000	255	150	220	99	42	14
90	82,000	255	160	236	110	46	15
100	90,000	255	170	251	120	50	17

Locations: Deep Sea Research Center (Lab)

Called the King of GF; its Mega Flare ignores all defense. Gives assistance freely to those who show their power.

Spells / Draw

Level	Draw			
1~19	Flare	Curaga	Full-Life	Dispel
20~29	Flare	Curaga	Full-Life	Dispel
30~100	Flare	Curaga	Full-Life	Dispel

Card

Drop Card	Mod Card	Mod (Rare)
Bahamut	—	—

Devour

LV 1~19	LV 20~29	LV 30~100
—	—	—

Item (Drop) — Rate: 255/256

Level	178/256	51/256	15/256	12/256
1~19	Hyper Wrist	Hyper Wrist	Hyper Wrist	Hyper Wrist
20~29	Hyper Wrist	Hyper Wrist	Hyper Wrist	Hyper Wrist
30~100	Hyper Wrist	Hyper Wrist	Hyper Wrist	Hyper Wrist

Item (Mug) — Rate: 32/256

Level	178/256	51/256	15/256	12/256
1~19	Hyper Wrist	Hyper Wrist	Hyper Wrist	Hyper Wrist
20~29	Hyper Wrist	Hyper Wrist	Hyper Wrist	Hyper Wrist
30~100	Hyper Wrist	Hyper Wrist	Hyper Wrist	Hyper Wrist

Behemoth

HP	35,263~91,000
AP	12
EXP	200 (+30)

— —

Elemental Defense: 💧1, ❄1, ⚡1, 💧1, 1, 1, 1, ❄1

Status Defense: 40 / 100, 40 / 40, 70 / X, 70 / 100, 40 / 100, 40 / 40, 40 / 70, 40 / X, X, 100, 50, X, X, 40, 100, X

LV	HP	Str	Vit	Mag	Spr	Spd	Eva
1	35,263	64	12	3	3	3	0
10	37,900	81	12	26	24	4	1
20	41,400	101	13	51	46	4	1
30	45,500	120	13	76	69	5	2
40	50,200	138	14	101	91	6	3
50	55,500	157	15	125	114	6	3
60	61,400	176	15	149	136	7	4
70	67,900	195	16	173	159	7	4
80	75,000	213	17	197	181	8	5
90	82,700	231	17	220	204	9	6
100	91,000	250	18	243	226	9	6

Locations: Esthar, Great Plains of Esthar, Deep Sea Research Center

Uses powerful magic, such as Meteor. A strong enemy that's hard to defeat.

Spells / Draw

Level	Draw		
1~29	Regen	Tornado	
30~39	Regen	Tornado	
40~100	Regen	Tornado	Flare

Card

Drop Card	Mod Card	Mod (Rare)
Behemoth	Behemoth	BGH251F2

Devour

LV 1~29	LV 30~39	LV 40~100
Full HP Recov.	Full HP Recov.	Magic +1

Item (Drop) — Rate: 255/256

Level	178/256	51/256	15/256	12/256
1~29	Wizard Stone	Wizard Stone	Barrier	Barrier
30~39	Barrier	Giant's Ring	Energy Crystal	Energy Crystal
40~100	Barrier	Giant's Ring	Energy Crystal	Energy Crystal

Item (Mug) — Rate: 32/256

Level	178/256	51/256	15/256	12/256
1~29	Barrier	Barrier	Barrier	Barrier
30~39	Barrier	Barrier	Barrier	Barrier
40~100	Barrier	Barrier	Barrier	Barrier

Belhelmel

HP	369~5760
AP	2
EXP	10 (+6)

Weak vs Holy/Strong vs Thunder — *Flying Monster*

Elemental Defense: 💧1, ❄1, ⚡0.5, 💧X, 1, 1, 1, ❄2

Status Defense: 70 / X, 80 / 90, 70 / 50, 80 / 100, 80 / 100, X / 80, 70 / 70, X / X, X, 100, 80, 100, 100, 80, 70, X

LV	HP	Str	Vit	Mag	Spr	Spd	Eva
1	369	4	30	5	10	10	0
10	495	14	30	14	11	12	0
20	720	25	30	23	12	13	1
30	1035	36	30	33	13	15	1
40	1440	46	31	42	15	17	2
50	1935	57	31	51	16	18	2
60	2520	67	31	60	17	20	3
70	3195	77	32	69	18	22	3
80	3960	87	32	78	20	23	4
90	4815	97	32	87	21	25	4
100	5760	106	33	95	22	27	5

Locations: Galbadia (Monterosa Plateau), Lollapalooza Canyon, Ultimecia Castle

Has a rotating blade around its face. Its battle tactics change when its face changes.

Spells / Draw

Level	Draw	
1~19	Sleep	Thunder
20~29	Berserk	Thundara
30~100	Confuse	Thundaga

Card

Drop Card	Mod Card	Mod (Rare)
Belhelmel	Belhelmel	Tri-Point

Devour

LV 1~19	LV 20~29	LV 30~100
Damage (small) & Dark	Damage (small) & Dark	Damage (small) & Dark

Item (Drop) — Rate: 255/256

Level	178/256	51/256	15/256	12/256
1~19	M-Stone	Saw Blade	Saw Blade	M-Stone
20~29	Magic Stone	Saw Blade	Saw Blade	Magic Stone
30~100	Wizard Stone	Saw Blade	Saw Blade	Laser Cannon

Item (Mug) — Rate: 32/256

Level	178/256	51/256	15/256	12/256
1~19	Saw Blade	Saw Blade	Saw Blade	Saw Blade
20~29	Saw Blade	Saw Blade	Saw Blade	Saw Blade
30~100	Saw Blade	Saw Blade	Saw Blade	Saw Blade

BGH251F2 (1st round)

HP	4200~8400
EXP	—
AP	20
	Weak vs Thunder Earth & Water/Immune to Poison

Elemental Defense

Element	Value
💧	1
❄	1
⚡	1.5
🌊	1.5
🍂	0
🌀	1
💧	1.5
✶	1

Status Defense

✝ X	🗲 100	X			
☠ X	◐ 90	X			
🛡 X	🖐 X	☀ X			
👁 50	⚔ 100	% X			
▦ X	⚔ 100				
🌀 X	🗡 X				
💀 X	👇 X				
🌀 X	🏹 X				

LV	HP	Str	Vit	Mag	Spr	Spd	Eva
—	4200	40	52	65	130	7	0
10	6000	62	65	82	131	7	1
20	8000	87	80	101	132	7	3
22	8400	91	83	105	132	7	3

Locations: Galbadia Missle Base

Named Iron Clad for its defense capability. The main cannon is more powerful than X-ATMO92's Rail Gun.

Spells — Draw

Level			
1~19	Shell	Protect	Stop
20~22	Shell	Protect	Stop

Drop Card	Mod Card	Mod (Rare)
—	—	—

Devour	
LV 1~19	—
LV 20~22	—

Item (Drop) — Rate: 255/256

Level	178/256	51/256	15/256	12/256
1~19	—	—	—	—
20~22				

Item (Mug) — Rate: 32/256

Level	178/256	51/256	15/256	12/256
1~19	—	—	—	—
20~22				

BGH251F2 (2nd round)

HP	5100~7800
EXP	—
AP	20
	Weak vs Thunder, Water, & Earth/Immune to Poison

Elemental Defense

Element	Value
💧	1
❄	1
⚡	1.5
🌊	1.5
🍂	0
🌀	1
💧	2
✶	1

Status Defense

✝ X	🗲 100	X	
☠ X	◐ 90	X	
🛡 X	🖐 X	☀ X	
👁 50	⚔ 100	% X	
▦ X	⚔ 100		
🌀 X	🗡 X		
💀 X	👇 X		
🌀 X	🏹 X		

LV	HP	Str	Vit	Mag	Spr	Spd	Eva
1	5100	27	52	14	130	20	0
10	6000	47	65	35	131	21	1
20	7000	69	80	57	132	22	3
28	7800	87	93	74	133	23	4

Locations: Fishermans Horizon

Out of control after being destroyed at the Missile Base. Can only fight for a short amount of time.

Spells — Draw

Level			
1~19	Shell	Protect	Stop
20~28	Shell	Protect	Stop

Drop Card	Mod Card	Mod (Rare)
—	—	—

Devour	
LV 1~19	—
LV 20~28	—

Item (Drop) — Rate: 255/256

Level	178/256	51/256	15/256	12/256
1~19	Running Fire	Missile	Missile	Missile
20~28	Running Fire	Missile	Missile	Missile

Item (Mug) — Rate: 32/256

Level	178/256	51/256	15/256	12/256
1~19	Adamantine	Adamantine	Adamantine	Adamantine
20~28	Adamantine	Adamantine	Adamantine	Adamantine

Biggs (1st round)

HP	467~705
EXP	—
AP	4
	—

Elemental Defense

Element	Value
💧	1
❄	1
⚡	1
🌊	1
🍂	1
🌀	1
💧	1
✶	1

Status Defense

✝ X	🗲 X	X	
☠ X	◐ X	X	
🛡 X	🖐 X	☀ X	
👁 X	⚔ X	% 100	
▦ X	🗡 X		
🌀 X	👇 X		
💀 X	👇 X		
🌀 X	🏹 X		

LV	HP	Str	Vit	Mag	Spr	Spd	Eva
1	467	6	31	8	45	6	2
10	705	18	37	17	49	7	3

Locations: Dollet (Comm Tower)

A Galbadian Major. An officer who's not well versed in combat. In charge of activating the Dollet Communication Tower. Forgetful and short-tempered.

Spells — Draw

Level			
1~10	Fire	Thunder	Blizzard	Esuna

Drop Card	Mod Card	Mod (Rare)
—	—	—

Devour	
LV 1~10	

Item (Drop) — Rate: 255/256

Level	178/256	51/256	15/256	12/256
1~10	Elixir	Elixir	Elixir	Elixir

Item (Mug) — Rate: 32/256

Level	178/256	51/256	15/256	12/256
1~10				

Biggs (2nd round)

	HP	1467~2235	AP	10		
	EXP	—		—		— —

Elemental Defense

💧	X
☀	80
⚡	X
💧	80
❄	80
🌀	X
💧	70
✦	X

Status Defense

✝	X	⚡	100
☠	80		90
🛡	X	✋	X
✴	80	⬌	100
❄	80		100
💬	80	⚔	100
💀	X	⚓	X
💧	70		X
⚡	X		100

LV	HP	Str	Vit	Mag	Spr	Spd	Eva
1	1467	6	31	9	45	6	2
10	1705	22	37	24	49	7	3
20	2130	38	44	41	54	7	4
22	2235	41	45	44	55	8	4
—							
—							
—							

Locations

Galbadia D-District Prison

He was a major during the Dollet Communication Tower Operation, but was demoted after the operation failed. Hates SeeD.

Spells

Level	Draw			
1~19	Cure	Haste	Slow	Regen
20~22	Cura	Haste	Slow	Regen

Devour / Card

Drop Card	Mod Card	Mod (Rare)
—	—	—
LV 1~19	LV 20~22	
—	—	

Item (Drop)

Level	Rate: 255/256			
	178/256	51/256	15/256	12/256
1~19	Elixir	Elixir	Elixir	Elixir
20~22	Elixir	Elixir	Elixir	Elixir

Item (Mug)

Level	Rate: 32/256			
	178/256	51/256	15/256	12/256
1~19	Regen Ring	Regen Ring	Regen Ring	Regen Ring
20~22	Regen Ring	Regen Ring	Regen Ring	Regen Ring

Bite Bug

	HP	114~2510	AP	1	
	EXP	15 (+5)		Weak vs Ice & Wind	Flying Monster

Elemental Defense

💧	1
☀	2
⚡	1
💧	X
❄	1
🌀	2
💧	1
✦	1

Status Defense

✝	70	⚡	100
☠	80		90
🛡	70	✋	0
✴	80	⬌	100
❄	80		100
💬	60	⚔	80
💀	70		70
⚡	80		60

LV	HP	Str	Vit	Mag	Spr	Spd	Eva
1	114	2	4	4	2	4	2
10	170	9	4	7	3	5	3
20	270	17	4	13	5	5	4
30	410	24	4	19	7	6	4
40	590	32	4	24	8	6	5
50	810	39	5	30	10	7	6
60	1070	46	5	35	12	7	6
70	1370	53	5	40	13	8	7
80	1710	59	5	44	15	8	8
90	2090	65	5	49	17	9	8
100	2510	72	6	53	18	9	9

Locations

Balamb (Alcauld Plains), Trabia (Bika Snowfield)

A bug monster that flies. Stay calm and attack precisely. It's not a very strong enemy.

Spells

Level	Draw		
1~19	Fire	Scan	
20~29	Fira	Scan	
30~100	Firaga	Scan	

Devour / Card

Drop Card	Mod Card	Mod (Rare)
Bite Bug	Bite Bug	Elnoyle
LV 1~19	LV 20~29	LV 30~100
HP Recovery	HP Recovery	HP Recovery

Item (Drop)

Level	Rate: 255/256			
	178/256	51/256	15/256	12/256
1~19	M-Stone	M-Stone	M-Stone	M-Stone
20~29	M-Stone	Magic Stone	Magic Stone	Magic Stone
30~100	Wizard Stone	Wizard Stone	Wizard Stone	Wizard Stone

Item (Mug)

Level	Rate: 32/256			
	178/256	51/256	15/256	12/256
1~19	M-Stone	M-Stone	M-Stone	M-Stone
20~29	Magic Stone	Magic Stone	Magic Stone	Magic Stone
30~100	Wizard Stone	Wizard Stone	Wizard Stone	Wizard Stone

Blitz

	HP	611~7200	AP	2	
	EXP	20 (+10)		Absorbs Thunder	— —

Elemental Defense

💧	1
☀	1
⚡	-1
💧	1
❄	1
🌀	1
💧	1
✦	1

Status Defense

✝	70	⚡	100
☠	80		90
🛡	70	✋	50
✴	80	⬌	100
❄	X		X
💬	60	⚔	80
💀	70		70
⚡	80		100

LV	HP	Str	Vit	Mag	Spr	Spd	Eva
1	611	9	35	57	25	2	0
10	765	18	35	60	25	4	1
20	1040	29	35	62	26	6	1
30	1425	39	36	65	26	7	2
40	1920	48	36	67	27	9	2
50	2525	58	37	69	28	10	3
60	3240	68	37	71	28	12	3
70	4065	77	37	73	29	14	4
80	5000	86	38	75	30	16	4
90	6045	95	38	76	30	17	5
100	7200	103	39	78	31	19	5

Locations

Galbadia Garden, Centra Plains

Becomes electified when attacked with Thunder. Attacking it while electified causes thunder damage.

Spells

Level	Draw		
1~19	Thunder		
20~29	Thunder	Thundara	
30~100	Thunder	Thundara	Thundaga

Devour / Card

Drop Card	Mod Card	Mod (Rare)
Blitz	Blitz	Propagator
LV 1~19	LV 20~29	LV 30~100
No change	No change	No change

Item (Drop)

Level	Rate: 255/256			
	178/256	51/256	15/256	12/256
1~19	M-Stone	Betrayal Sword	Coral Fragment	Coral Fragment
20~29	Magic Stone	Magic Stone	Betrayal Sword	Betrayal Sword
30~100	Dynamo Stone	Dynamo Stone	Dynamo Stone	Dynamo Stone

Item (Mug)

Level	Rate: 32/256			
	178/256	51/256	15/256	12/256
1~19	Betrayal Sword	Betrayal Sword	Betrayal Sword	Betrayal Sword
20~29	Betrayal Sword	Betrayal Sword	Betrayal Sword	Betrayal Sword
30~100	Betrayal Sword	Betrayal Sword	Betrayal Sword	Power Generator

Blobra

HP	246~3840	AP	3	— —
EXP	40 (+8)		Very Weak vs ???	

Elemental Defense

💧	1
❄	1
⚡	1
🌀	1
☄	1
▼	1
💧	1
✴	1

Status Defense

☠	70	⚡	100	☺	40
☠	80	✋	90	📉	100
🛡	80	✋	50	☀	80
☣	80	⬚	100	%	100
💤	80	🗡	100		
🌀	60	✋	80		
💀	70	✋	70		
🔄	100	👐	X		

LV	HP	Str	Vit	Mag	Spr	Spd	Eva
1	246	8	240	9	170	6	0
10	330	15	240	23	171	6	1
20	480	22	241	38	172	7	2
30	690	29	241	53	173	7	3
40	960	36	242	67	174	7	4
50	1290	43	242	82	175	8	5
60	1680	49	243	96	176	8	6
70	2130	56	243	111	177	9	7
80	2640	62	244	125	178	9	8
90	3210	68	244	139	180	9	9
100	3840	74	245	153	181	10	10

Locations
Tomb of the Unknown King, Balamb Garden (MD Level)

A half-liquid creature resistant to physical attacks. Elemental weaknesses differ with each one that appears.

Spells

Level	Draw			
1~19	Shell			
20~29	Shell	Blind	Berserk	
30~100	Shell	Reflect	Blind	Confuse

Drop Card	Mod Card	Mod (Rare)
Blobra	Blobra	Granaldo

Devour Card

LV 1~19	LV 20~29	LV 30~100
Full HP Recov.	Full HP Recov.	Full HP Recov.

Item (Drop)

Level	Rate: 255/256			
	178/256	51/256	15/256	12/256
1~19	M-Stone	M-Stone	M-Stone	Three Stars
20~29	Magic Stone	Magic Stone	Rune Armlet	Rune Armlet
30~100	Wizard Stone	Wizard Stone	Rune Armlet	Rune Armlet

Item (Mug)

Level	Rate: 32/256			
	178/256	51/256	15/256	12/256
1~19	M-Stone	M-Stone	Rune Armlet	Rune Armlet
20~29	Magic Stone	Magic Stone	Rune Armlet	Rune Armlet
30~100	Wizard Stone	Wizard Stone	Rune Armlet	Rune Armlet

Blood Soul

HP	510~6500	AP	1	Flying Monster/ Undead Monster
EXP	15 (+5)		Very Weak vs Holy/Weak vs Fire/ Strong vs Poison	

Elemental Defense

💧	2
❄	1
⚡	1
🌀	X
☄	0.5
▼	1
💧	1
✴	3

Status Defense

☠	100	⚡	100	☺	60
☠	X	✋	90	📉	100
🛡	X	✋	X	☀	80
☣	X	⬚	30	%	100
💤	X	🗡	X		
🌀	X	✋	80		
💀	X	✋	X		
🔄	80	👐	X		

LV	HP	Str	Vit	Mag	Spr	Spd	Eva
1	510	4	7	10	150	8	0
10	650	10	11	21	153	9	0
20	900	16	17	32	156	11	1
30	1250	23	22	44	160	12	1
40	1700	28	28	55	163	13	2
50	2250	34	34	66	166	14	2
60	2900	39	39	77	170	16	3
70	3650	45	45	88	173	17	3
80	4500	49	51	98	176	18	4
90	5450	54	56	109	180	19	4
100	6500	58	62	119	183	21	5

Locations
Galbadia (Monterosa Plateau), Winhill (Winhill Bluffs)

Floats with gas that fills its body. Looks weak, but its status-changing attacks may prove otherwise.

Spells

Level	Draw			
1~19	Zombie	Float		
20~29	Zombie	Float	Silence	
30~100	Zombie	Float	Silence	Dispel

Drop Card	Mod Card	Mod (Rare)
Blood Soul	Blood Soul	Abadon

Devour Card

LV 1~19	LV 20~29	LV 30~100
Damage (small) & Poison	Damage (small) & Poison	Damage (small) & Poison

Item (Drop)

Level	Rate: 255/256			
	178/256	51/256	15/256	12/256
1~19	M-Stone	Zombie Powder	M-Stone	M-Stone
20~29	Zombie Powder	Zombie Powder	M-Stone	M-Stone
30~100	Zombie Powder	Zombie Powder	Magic Stone	Magic Stone

Item (Mug)

Level	Rate: 32/256			
	178/256	51/256	15/256	12/256
1~19	Zombie Powder	Zombie Powder	Zombie Powder	Zombie Powder
20~29	Zombie Powder	Zombie Powder	Zombie Powder	Zombie Powder
30~100	Zombie Powder	Zombie Powder	Zombie Powder	Zombie Powder

---

Blue Dragon

HP	236~41,000	AP	6	— —
EXP	100 (+20)		Weak vs Ice/Absorbs Poison	

Elemental Defense

💧	1
❄	2
⚡	1
🌀	1
☄	-1
▼	1
💧	1
✴	1

Status Defense

☠	50	⚡	100	☺	60
☠	X	✋	90	📉	X
🛡	60	✋	X	☀	80
☣	70	⬚	100	%	100
💤	70	🗡	100		
🌀	60	✋	70		
💀	60	✋	60		
🔄	X	👐	X		

LV	HP	Str	Vit	Mag	Spr	Spd	Eva
1	236	15	71	27	120	5	0
10	2525	29	76	46	125	8	1
20	5400	45	82	67	130	10	1
30	8625	60	88	87	135	13	2
40	12,200	76	95	108	140	15	3
50	16,125	91	101	128	145	18	3
60	20,400	107	107	148	150	20	5
70	25,025	122	113	167	155	23	5
80	30,000	137	120	187	160	25	5
90	35,325	151	126	206	165	28	6
100	41,000	166	132	225	170	30	6

Locations
Trabia Snowfield

A dragon that walks on 2 legs. Attacks with breath that causes status changes and drops a rare item called Fury Fragment.

Spells

Level	Draw			
1~19	Blind			
20~29	Blind	Drain	Bio	
30~100	Drain	Break	Death	Bio

Drop Card	Mod Card	Mod (Rare)
Blue Dragon	Blue Dragon	Mobile Type 8

Devour Card

LV 1~19	LV 20~29	LV 30~100
Full HP Recov.	Full HP Recov. & Status Recov.	Full HP Recov. & Status Recov.

Item (Drop)

Level	Rate: 255/256			
	178/256	51/256	15/256	12/256
1~19	Dragon Fang	Dragon Fang	Fury Fragment	Fury Fragment
20~29	Dragon Fang	Dragon Fang	Fury Fragment	Fury Fragment
30~100	Dragon Fang	Dragon Fang	Fury Fragment	Fury Fragment

Item (Mug)

Level	Rate: 32/256			
	178/256	51/256	15/256	12/256
1~19	Fury Fragment	Fury Fragment	Fury Fragment	Fury Fragment
20~29	Fury Fragment	Fury Fragment	Fury Fragment	Fury Fragment
30~100	Fury Fragment	Fury Fragment	Fury Fragment	Fury Fragment

Bomb

HP	288~5080	AP	1	**Flying Monster**
EXP	30 (+5)		Weak vs Wind/Absorbs Fire/ Very Weak vs Ice	

Elemental Defense

💧	-1
❄	3
⚡	1
🔥	X
🌀	1
⛰	1.5
💧	1
☠	1
✦	1

Status Defense

✝	X	⚡	100	🌀	0
🦋	80	👊	90	⛰	100
👁	40	✋	50	☀	80
☢	80	⬅	100	%	100
💀	80	🗡	100		
🐛	60	👊	X		
☠	70	🛡	40		
⚡	80	🕷	X		

LV	HP	Str	Vit	Mag	Spr	Spd	Eva
1	288	2	2	1	4	2	0
10	400	11	6	14	13	3	0
20	600	21	12	28	23	5	1
30	880	30	17	42	33	6	1
40	1240	40	23	56	44	7	2
50	1680	49	29	69	54	8	2
60	2200	58	34	82	64	10	3
70	2800	66	40	95	75	11	3
80	3480	75	46	108	85	12	4
90	4240	83	51	120	95	13	4
100	5080	91	57	132	105	15	5

Locations
Fire Cavern, Deep Sea Research Center (Lab, Work Zone)

A monster powered by fire. Usually calm, but still a dangerous monster that becomes gigantic or explodes when attacked.

Spells — Draw

Level	Draw			
1~19	Fire			
20~29	Fire	Fira		
30~100	Fire	Fira	Firaga	Meltdown

Card

Drop Card	Mod Card	Mod (Rare)
Bomb	Bomb	Krysta

Devour Card

LV 1~19	LV 20~29	LV 30~100
Damage (high) & random effect	Damage (high) & random effect	Damage (high) & random effect

Item (Drop) — Rate: 255/256

Level	178/256	51/256	15/256	12/256
1~19	M-Stone	M-Stone	Bomb Fragment	Bomb Fragment
20~29	Bomb Fragment	Bomb Fragment	Magic Stone	Magic Stone
30~100	Bomb Fragment	Bomb Fragment	Bomb Fragment	Bomb Fragment

Item (Mug) — Rate: 32/256

Level	178/256	51/256	15/256	12/256
1~19	Bomb Fragment	Bomb Fragment	Bomb Fragment	Bomb Fragment
20~29	Bomb Fragment	Bomb Fragment	Bomb Fragment	Bomb Fragment
30~100	Bomb Fragment	Bomb Fragment	Bomb Spirit	Bomb Spirit

Buel

HP	43~1840	AP	1	**Flying Monster**
EXP	5 (+1)		Weak vs Wind & Holy	

Elemental Defense

💧	1
❄	1
⚡	1
🔥	X
🌀	1
⛰	2
💧	1
☠	1
✦	2

Status Defense

✝	70	⚡	100	🌀	60
🦋	80	👊	90	⛰	100
👁	70	✋	50	☀	80
☢	80	⬅	100	%	100
💀	80	🗡	100		
🐛	60	👊	80		
☠	70	🛡	70		
⚡	80	🕷	100		

LV	HP	Str	Vit	Mag	Spr	Spd	Eva
1	43	1	1	3	200	10	0
10	85	6	1	24	201	11	0
20	160	10	2	47	202	11	1
30	265	15	2	70	203	12	1
40	400	19	3	93	205	13	1
50	565	24	4	115	206	14	2
60	760	28	4	138	207	14	2
70	985	32	5	160	208	15	3
80	1240	36	6	183	210	16	3
90	1525	39	6	205	211	16	3
100	1840	43	7	227	212	17	4

Locations
Fire Cavern, Centra Ruins, Balamb Garden (MD Level)

Very strong against magic. Any magic attacks are almost completely ineffective. However, very weak against physical attacks.

Spells — Draw

Level	Draw			
1~19	Fire	Thunder	Blizzard	
20~29	Fira	Thundara	Blizzara	
30~100	Firaga	Thundaga	Blizzaga	

Card

Drop Card	Mod Card	Mod (Rare)
Buel	Buel	Krysta

Devour Card

LV 1~19	LV 20~29	LV 30~100
HP Recovery	HP Recovery	HP Recovery

Item (Drop) — Rate: 255/256

Level	178/256	51/256	15/256	12/256
1~19	M-Stone	M-Stone	M-Stone	M-Stone
20~29	Magic Stone	Magic Stone	Magic Stone	Magic Stone
30~100	Wizard Stone	Wizard Stone	Wizard Stone	Wizard Stone

Item (Mug) — Rate: 32/256

Level	178/256	51/256	15/256	12/256
1~19	M-Stone	M-Stone	M-Stone	M-Stone
20~29	Magic Stone	Magic Stone	Magic Stone	Circlet
30~100	Wizard Stone	Wizard Stone	Circlet	Circlet

Cactuar

HP	202~1400	AP	20	– –
EXP	1 (+1)		– –	

Elemental Defense

💧	1
❄	1
⚡	1
🔥	1
🌀	1
⛰	1
💧	2.9
☠	1

Status Defense

✝	X	⚡	100	🌀	X
🦋	80	👊	90	⛰	100
👁	70	✋	50	☀	X
☢	80	⬅	100	%	100
💀	80	🗡	100		
🐛	X	👊	80		
☠	X	🛡	70		
⚡	80	🕷	100		

LV	HP	Str	Vit	Mag	Spr	Spd	Eva
1	202	2	16	5	254	8	100
10	230	5	31	19	254	9	100
20	280	9	49	33	254	11	100
30	350	12	66	47	254	12	100
40	440	15	84	60	254	13	100
50	550	17	101	73	254	14	100
60	680	20	119	86	254	16	100
70	830	22	136	99	254	17	100
80	1000	24	154	111	254	18	100
90	1190	25	171	123	254	19	100
100	1400	27	189	134	254	21	100

Locations
Centra Ruins, Cactuar Island

A speedy cactus of the desert. Damege always amounts to 1,000 with its special skill, 1,000 Needles.

Spells — Draw

Level	Draw			
1~19	Haste			
20~29	Haste			
30~100	Haste			

Card

Drop Card	Mod Card	Mod (Rare)
Cactuar	Cactuar	Gerogero

Devour Card

LV 1~19	LV 20~29	LV 30~100
HP Recovery	Full HP Recov.	Full HP Recov. & Status Recovery

Item (Drop) — Rate: 255/256

Level	178/256	51/256	15/256	12/256
1~19	Cactus Thorn	Cactus Thorn	Cactus Thorn	Lightweight
20~29	Cactus Thorn	Cactus Thorn	Cactus Thorn	Lightweight
30~100	Cactus Thorn	Cactus Thorn	Cactus Thorn	Jet Engine

Item (Mug) — Rate: 32/256

Level	178/256	51/256	15/256	12/256
1~19	Cactus Thorn	Cactus Thorn	Cactus Thorn	Cactus Thorn
20~29	Cactus Thorn	Cactus Thorn	Cactus Thorn	Cactus Thorn
30~100	Cactus Thorn	Cactus Thorn	Cactus Thorn	Cactus Thorn

Caterchipiller

HP	172~7360	AP	2	— —
EXP	28 (+5)		Weak vs Fire & Ice/Strong vs Earth	

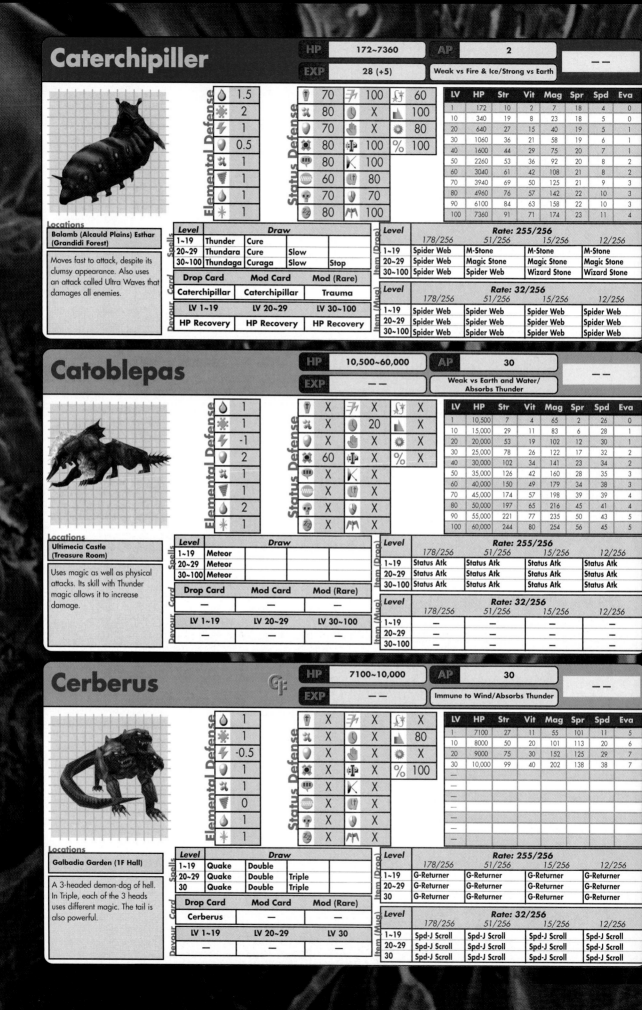

Elemental Defense: 1.5, 2, 1, 0.5, 1, 1, 1, 1

Status Defense: 70 / 100 / 60, 80 / X / 100, 70 / X / 80, 80 / 100 / 100, 80 / 100, 60 / 80, 70 / 70, 80 / 100

LV	HP	Str	Vit	Mag	Spr	Spd	Eva
1	172	10	2	7	18	4	0
10	340	19	8	23	18	5	0
20	640	27	15	40	19	5	1
30	1060	36	21	58	19	6	1
40	1600	44	29	75	20	7	1
50	2260	53	36	92	20	8	2
60	3040	61	42	108	21	8	2
70	3940	69	50	125	21	9	3
80	4960	76	57	142	22	10	3
90	6100	84	63	158	22	10	3
100	7360	91	71	174	23	11	4

Locations
Balamb (Alcauld Plains) Esthar (Grandidi Forest)

Moves fast to attack, despite its clumsy appearance. Also uses an attack called Ultra Waves that damages all enemies.

Spells — Draw

Level				
1~19	Thunder	Cure		
20~29	Thundara	Cure	Slow	
30~100	Thundaga	Curaga	Slow	Stop

Drop Card	Mod Card	Mod (Rare)
Caterchipillar	Caterchipillar	Trauma

Devour Card

LV 1~19	LV 20~29	LV 30~100
HP Recovery	HP Recovery	HP Recovery

Item (Drop) — Rate: 255/256

Level	178/256	51/256	15/256	12/256
1~19	Spider Web	M-Stone	M-Stone	M-Stone
20~29	Spider Web	Magic Stone	Magic Stone	Magic Stone
30~100	Spider Web	Spider Web	Wizard Stone	Wizard Stone

Item (Mug) — Rate: 32/256

Level	178/256	51/256	15/256	12/256
1~19	Spider Web	Spider Web	Spider Web	Spider Web
20~29	Spider Web	Spider Web	Spider Web	Spider Web
30~100	Spider Web	Spider Web	Spider Web	Spider Web

Catoblepas

HP	10,500~60,000	AP	30	— —
EXP	— —		Weak vs Earth and Water/Absorbs Thunder	

Elemental Defense: 1, 1, -1, 2, 1, 1, 2, 1

Status Defense: X, X / 20, X, X / 60, X, X, X, X

LV	HP	Str	Vit	Mag	Spr	Spd	Eva
1	10,500	7	4	65	2	26	0
10	15,000	29	11	83	6	28	1
20	20,000	53	19	102	12	30	1
30	25,000	78	26	122	17	32	2
40	30,000	102	34	141	23	34	2
50	35,000	126	42	160	28	35	3
60	40,000	150	49	179	34	38	3
70	45,000	174	57	198	39	39	4
80	50,000	197	65	216	45	41	4
90	55,000	221	77	235	50	43	5
100	60,000	244	80	254	56	45	5

Locations
Ultimecia Castle (Treasure Room)

Uses magic as well as physical attacks. Its skill with Thunder magic allows it to increase damage.

Spells — Draw

Level	
1~19	Meteor
20~29	Meteor
30~100	Meteor

Drop Card	Mod Card	Mod (Rare)
—	—	—

Devour Card

LV 1~19	LV 20~29	LV 30~100
—	—	—

Item (Drop) — Rate: 255/256

Level	178/256	51/256	15/256	12/256
1~19	Status Atk	Status Atk	Status Atk	Status Atk
20~29	Status Atk	Status Atk	Status Atk	Status Atk
30~100	Status Atk	Status Atk	Status Atk	Status Atk

Item (Mug) — Rate: 32/256

Level	178/256	51/256	15/256	12/256
1~19	—	—	—	—
20~29	—	—	—	—
30~100	—	—	—	—

Cerberus (GF)

HP	7100~10,000	AP	30	— —
EXP	— —		Immune to Wind/Absorbs Thunder	

Elemental Defense: 1, 1, -0.5, 1, 1, 0, 1, 1

Status Defense: X, X / 80, X, X / 100, X, X, X, X

LV	HP	Str	Vit	Mag	Spr	Spd	Eva
1	7100	27	11	55	101	11	5
10	8000	50	20	101	113	20	6
20	9000	75	30	152	125	29	7
30	10,000	99	40	202	138	38	7

Locations
Galbadia Garden (1F Hall)

A 3-headed demon-dog of hell. In Triple, each of the 3 heads uses different magic. The tail is also powerful.

Spells — Draw

Level			
1~19	Quake	Double	
20~29	Quake	Double	Triple
30	Quake	Double	Triple

Drop Card	Mod Card	Mod (Rare)
Cerberus	—	—

Devour Card

LV 1~19	LV 20~29	LV 30
—	—	—

Item (Drop) — Rate: 255/256

Level	178/256	51/256	15/256	12/256
1~19	G-Returner	G-Returner	G-Returner	G-Returner
20~29	G-Returner	G-Returner	G-Returner	G-Returner
30	G-Returner	G-Returner	G-Returner	G-Returner

Item (Mug) — Rate: 32/256

Level	178/256	51/256	15/256	12/256
1~19	Spd-J Scroll	Spd-J Scroll	Spd-J Scroll	Spd-J Scroll
20~29	Spd-J Scroll	Spd-J Scroll	Spd-J Scroll	Spd-J Scroll
30	Spd-J Scroll	Spd-J Scroll	Spd-J Scroll	Spd-J Scroll

Chimera

HP	352~60,000	AP	10
EXP	150 (+20)		

Weak vs Holy/Immune to Poison/Absorbs Thunder, Wind, & Water

Elemental Defense

Icon	Value
💧	1
❄	1
⚡	-1
💧	1
🌀	0
🌪	-1
💧	-1
✦	1.5

Status Defense

Icon	Value	Icon	Value	Icon	Value
🗡	X	⚡	100	✴	X
☠	X	🕐	50	⛰	50
🛡	X	✋	X	☀	70
☣	80	⚔	100	%	100
💬	X	🗝	100		
☠	X	👊	X		
💀	X	🛡	X		
💤	X	🕸	X		

LV	HP	Str	Vit	Mag	Spr	Spd	Eva
1	352	21	41	27	89	5	2
10	3750	38	49	46	97	7	3
20	8000	55	59	68	106	9	3
30	12,750	73	67	90	115	11	4
40	18,000	90	77	111	125	13	4
50	23,750	107	86	133	134	15	5
60	30,000	124	95	154	143	17	6
70	36,750	141	104	175	152	19	6
80	44,000	158	114	197	161	21	7
90	51,750	174	122	217	170	23	8
100	60,000	190	132	238	180	25	8

Locations
Esthar (Kashkabald Desert)
Ultimecia Castle

A monster with 4 heads that use magic, physical attacks, status changes, and their original skill, Aqua Breath.

Spells / Draw

Level	Draw			
1~19	Water	Thunder	Esuna	
20~29	Water	Bio	Thundara	Esuna
30~100	Water	Bio	Thundaga	Esuna

Card

Drop Card	Mod Card	Mod (Rare)
Chimera	Chimera	Hexadragon

Devour

LV 1~19	LV 20~29	LV 30~100
Full HP Recov. & Status Recov.	Full HP Recov. & Status Recov.	Full HP Recov. & Status Recov.

Item (Drop) — Rate: 255/256

Level	178/256	51/256	15/256	12/256
1~19	Water Crystal	Water Crystal	Red Fang	Red Fang
20~29	Water Cystal	Red Fang	Star Fragment	Star Fragment
30~100	Water Crystal	Red Fang	Regen Ring	Star Fragment

Item (Mug) — Rate: 32/256

Level	178/256	51/256	15/256	12/256
1~19	Red Fang	Red Fang	Red Fang	Red Fang
20~29	Red Fang	Red Fang	Red Fang	Red Fang
30~100	Red Fang	Red Fang	Red Fang	Red Fang

Cockatrice

HP	1007~5200	AP	2
EXP	40 (+10)		

Weak vs. Wind/Immune to Thunder & Poison

Elemental Defense

Icon	Value
💧	1
❄	1
⚡	0
💧	1
🌀	0
🌪	2.5
💧	1
✦	1

Status Defense

Icon	Value	Icon	Value	Icon	Value
🗡	60	⚡	100	✴	70
☠	X	🕐	90	⛰	100
🛡	X	✋	50	☀	80
☣	80	⚔	100	%	100
💬	80	🗝	100		
☠	60	👊	10		
💀	70	🛡	X		
💤	80	🕸	100		

LV	HP	Str	Vit	Mag	Spr	Spd	Eva
1	1007	9	9	14	91	12	2
10	1105	18	15	32	97	14	4
20	1280	28	22	52	105	15	6
30	1525	37	29	71	111	17	7
40	1840	46	36	90	119	19	9
50	2225	55	43	108	126	20	10
60	2680	64	50	127	133	22	12
70	3205	72	57	145	140	24	14
80	3800	64	64	163	148	25	16
90	4465	88	71	180	154	27	17
100	5200	96	78	198	162	29	19

Locations
Timber (Roshfall Forest), Obel Lake, Esthar (Grandidi Forest)

Petrifies enemies with its stare. Uses thunder by flapping its wings. Uses Electrocute when fully grown.

Spells / Draw

Level	Draw	
1~19	Thunder	
20~29	Thundara	Break
30~100	Thundaga	Break

Card

Drop Card	Mod Card	Mod (Rare)
Cockatrice	Cockatrice	Oilboyle

Devour

LV 1~19	LV 20~29	LV 30~100
Stone	Stone	Full HP Recov.

Item (Drop) — Rate: 255/256

Level	178/256	51/256	15/256	12/256
1~19	Coral Fragment	Cockatrice Pinion	Cockatrice Pinion	Cockatrice Pinion
20~29	Cockatrice Pinion	Coral Fragment	Dynamo Stone	Dynamo Stone
30~100	Cockatrice Pinion	Dynamo Stone	Cockatrice Pinion	Dynamo Stone

Item (Mug) — Rate: 32/256

Level	178/256	51/256	15/256	12/256
1~19	Cockatrice Pinion	Cockatrice Pinion	Cockatrice Pinion	Cockatrice Pinion
20~29	Cockatrice Pinion	Cockatrice Pinion	Cockatrice Pinion	Cockatrice Pinion
30~100	Cockatrice Pinion	Cockatrice Pinion	Cockatrice Pinion	Cockatrice Pinion

---

Command Leader

HP	806~4400	AP	2
EXP	30 (+5)		

Weak vs Poison

Elemental Defense

Icon	Value
💧	1
❄	1
⚡	1
💧	1
🌀	1.5
🌪	1
💧	1
✦	1

Status Defense

Icon	Value	Icon	Value	Icon	Value
🗡	X	⚡	100	✴	X
☠	X	🕐	90	⛰	100
🛡	X	✋	X	☀	X
☣	80	⚔	100	%	100
💬	100	🗝	100		
☠	X	👊	X		
💀	X	🛡	X		
💤	80	🕸	100		

LV	HP	Str	Vit	Mag	Spr	Spd	Eva
1	806	6	31	9	45	6	2
10	890	22	37	24	49	7	3
20	1040	38	44	41	54	7	4
30	1250	54	51	57	60	8	5
40	1520	70	58	74	65	9	5
50	1850	86	65	90	70	10	6
60	2240	102	72	106	76	10	7
70	2690	118	79	122	81	11	8
80	3200	133	86	138	86	12	9
90	3770	148	93	154	92	12	10
100	4400	163	100	170	97	13	10

Locations
Galbadia Missle Base

Galbadia Missile Base security leader. Stronger than regular Galbadian soldiers.

Spells / Draw

Level	Draw			
1~19	Thunder	Confuse	Slow	Reflect
20~29	Thundara	Confuse	Slow	Reflect
30~100	Thundaga	Confuse	Slow	Reflect

Card

Drop Card	Mod Card	Mod (Rare)
—		

Devour

LV 1~19	LV 20~29	LV 30~100
—	—	—

Item (Drop) — Rate: 255/256

Level	178/256	51/256	15/256	12/256
1~19	Potion	Phoenix Down	Shotgun Ammo	Cottage
20~29	Potion	Phoenix Down	Hi-Potion	Cottage
30~100	Potion	Hi-Potion	Cottage	Cottage

Item (Mug) — Rate: 32/256

Level	178/256	51/256	15/256	12/256
1~19	Tent	Tent	Cottage	Cottage
20~29	Tent	Tent	Cottage	Cottage
30~100	Tent	Tent	Cottage	Cottage

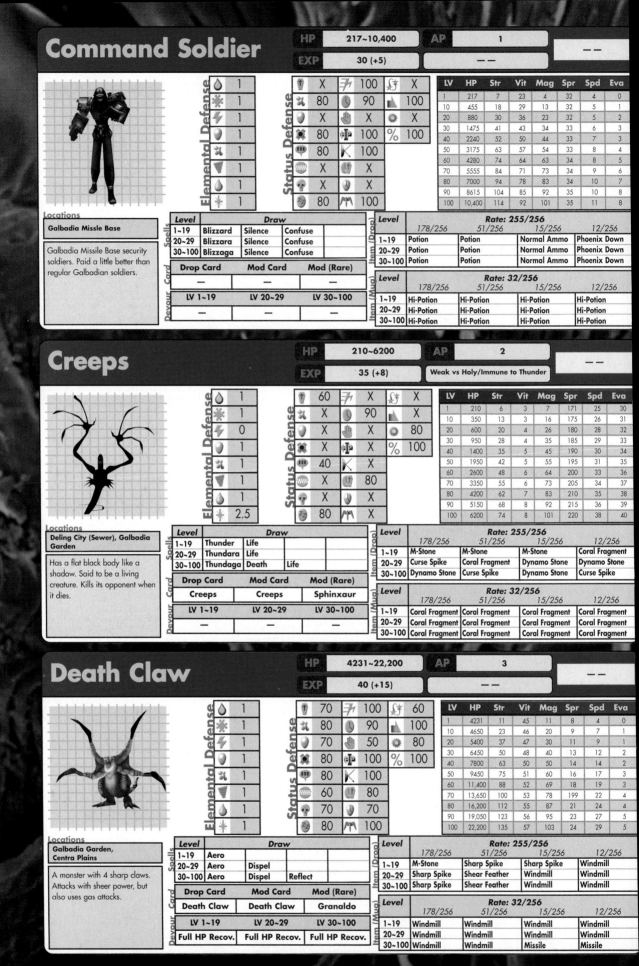

Command Soldier

HP	217~10,400
EXP	30 (+5)
AP	1

Elemental Defense

💧	1
❄	1
⚡	1
🌀	1
☄	1
🌪	1
💧	1
✦	1

Status Defense

☠	X	⚡	100		X
	80	🕐	90		100
	X	✋	X	☀	X
	80		100	%	100
	80		100		
	X		X		
	X		X		
	80		100		

LV	HP	Str	Vit	Mag	Spr	Spd	Eva
1	217	7	23	4	32	4	0
10	455	18	29	13	32	5	1
20	880	30	36	23	32	5	2
30	1475	41	43	34	33	6	3
40	2240	52	50	44	33	7	3
50	3175	63	57	54	33	8	4
60	4280	74	64	63	34	9	5
70	5555	84	71	73	34	9	6
80	7000	94	78	83	34	10	7
90	8615	104	85	92	35	10	8
100	10,400	114	92	101	35	11	8

Locations

Galbadia Missle Base

Galbadia Missile Base security soldiers. Paid a little better than regular Galbadian soldiers.

Spells

Level	Draw		
1~19	Blizzard	Silence	Confuse
20~29	Blizzara	Silence	Confuse
30~100	Blizzaga	Silence	Confuse

Card

Drop Card	Mod Card	Mod (Rare)
—		
LV 1~19	LV 20~29	LV 30~100
—	—	—

Item (Drop)

Level	Rate: 255/256			
	178/256	51/256	15/256	12/256
1~19	Potion	Potion	Normal Ammo	Phoenix Down
20~29	Potion	Potion	Normal Ammo	Phoenix Down
30~100	Potion	Potion	Normal Ammo	Phoenix Down

Item (Mug)

Level	Rate: 32/256			
	178/256	51/256	15/256	12/256
1~19	Hi-Potion	Hi-Potion	Hi-Potion	Hi-Potion
20~29	Hi-Potion	Hi-Potion	Hi-Potion	Hi-Potion
30~100	Hi-Potion	Hi-Potion	Hi-Potion	Hi-Potion

Creeps

HP	210~6200
EXP	35 (+8)
AP	2

Weak vs Holy/Immune to Thunder

Elemental Defense

💧	1
❄	1
⚡	0
🌀	1
☄	1
🌪	1
💧	1
✦	2.5

Status Defense

☠	60	⚡	X		X
	X	🕐	90		X
	X	✋	X	☀	80
	X		X	%	100
	40		X		
	X		80		
	X		X		
	80		X		

LV	HP	Str	Vit	Mag	Spr	Spd	Eva
1	210	6	3	7	171	25	30
10	350	13	3	16	175	26	31
20	600	20	4	26	180	28	32
30	950	28	4	35	185	29	33
40	1400	35	5	45	190	30	34
50	1950	42	5	55	195	31	35
60	2600	48	6	64	200	33	36
70	3350	55	6	73	205	34	37
80	4200	62	7	83	210	35	38
90	5150	68	8	92	215	36	39
100	6200	74	8	101	220	38	40

Locations

Deling City (Sewer), Galbadia Garden

Has a flat black body like a shadow. Said to be a living creature. Kills its opponent when it dies.

Spells

Level	Draw		
1~19	Thunder	Life	
20~29	Thundara	Life	
30~100	Thundaga	Death	Life

Card

Drop Card	Mod Card	Mod (Rare)
Creeps	Creeps	Sphinxaur
LV 1~19	LV 20~29	LV 30~100
—	—	—

Item (Drop)

Level	Rate: 255/256			
	178/256	51/256	15/256	12/256
1~19	M-Stone	M-Stone	M-Stone	Coral Fragment
20~29	Curse Spike	Coral Fragment	Dynamo Stone	Dynamo Stone
30~100	Dynamo Stone	Curse Spike	Dynamo Stone	Curse Spike

Item (Mug)

Level	Rate: 32/256			
	178/256	51/256	15/256	12/256
1~19	Coral Fragment	Coral Fragment	Coral Fragment	Coral Fragment
20~29	Coral Fragment	Coral Fragment	Coral Fragment	Coral Fragment
30~100	Coral Fragment	Coral Fragment	Coral Fragment	Coral Fragment

Death Claw

HP	4231~22,200
EXP	40 (+15)
AP	3

Elemental Defense

💧	1
❄	1
⚡	1
🌀	1
☄	1
🌪	1
💧	1
✦	1

Status Defense

☠	70	⚡	100		60
	80	🕐	90		100
	70	✋	50	☀	80
	80		100	%	100
	80		100		
	60		80		
	70		70		
	80		100		

LV	HP	Str	Vit	Mag	Spr	Spd	Eva
1	4231	11	45	11	8	4	0
10	4650	23	46	20	9	7	1
20	5400	37	47	30	11	9	1
30	6450	50	48	40	13	12	2
40	7800	63	50	50	14	14	2
50	9450	75	51	60	16	17	3
60	11,400	88	52	69	18	19	3
70	13,650	100	53	78	199	22	4
80	16,200	112	55	87	21	24	4
90	19,050	123	56	95	23	27	5
100	22,200	135	57	103	24	29	5

Locations

Galbadia Garden, Centra Plains

A monster with 4 sharp claws. Attacks with sheer power, but also uses gas attacks.

Spells

Level	Draw		
1~19	Aero		
20~29	Aero	Dispel	
30~100	Aero	Dispel	Reflect

Card

Drop Card	Mod Card	Mod (Rare)
Death Claw	Death Claw	Granaldo
LV 1~19	LV 20~29	LV 30~100
Full HP Recov.	Full HP Recov.	Full HP Recov.

Item (Drop)

Level	Rate: 255/256			
	178/256	51/256	15/256	12/256
1~19	M-Stone	Sharp Spike	Sharp Spike	Windmill
20~29	Sharp Spike	Shear Feather	Windmill	Windmill
30~100	Sharp Spike	Shear Feather	Windmill	Windmill

Item (Mug)

Level	Rate: 32/256			
	178/256	51/256	15/256	12/256
1~19	Windmill	Windmill	Windmill	Windmill
20~29	Windmill	Windmill	Windmill	Windmill
30~100	Windmill	Windmill	Missile	Missile

Diablos GF

HP	1600~80,800		AP	20
EXP	––		Weak vs Wind	

Flying Monster

Elemental Defense
💧	1
❄	1
⚡	1
💧	X
☣	1
🌀	1.5
💧	1
✹	1

Status Defense
💡	X	⚡	100	🌀	X
☠	X	🕐	90	▲	50
🛡	X	✋	X	☀	X
☠	50	⚔	100	%	100
💬	X	🗡	100		
☠	X	⚕	X		
💀	X	✋	X		
💤	X	👁	X		

LV	HP	Str	Vit	Mag	Spr	Spd	Eva
1	1600	17	51	5	77	15	0
10	8800	57	56	28	90	20	1
20	16,800	102	62	52	105	25	2
30	24,800	146	68	76	120	30	2
40	32,800	190	75	100	135	34	4
50	40,800	234	81	122	150	39	4
60	48,800	255	87	144	165	44	5
70	56,800	255	93	166	180	48	6
80	64,800	255	100	187	195	53	7
90	72,800	255	106	207	210	58	8
100	80,800	255	112	226	225	62	8

Locations
Appears after using the Item Magical Lamp

A mysterious GF living in another dimension. Uses gravity attack to take away all HP from enemies with one hit.

Spells
Level	Draw			
1~19	Cure	Demi		
20~29	Cura	Demi		
30~100	Curaga	Demi	Holy	Holy

Card
Drop Card	Mod Card	Mod (Rare)
Diablos	—	—

Devour
LV 1~19	LV 20~29	LV 30~100
—	—	—

Item (Drop)
Level	Rate: 255/256			
	178/256	51/256	15/256	12/256
1~19	G-Returner	G-Returner	G-Returner	G-Returner
20~29	G-Returner	G-Returner	G-Returner	G-Returner
30~100	Hero	Hero	Hero	Hero

Item (Mug)
Level	Rate: 32/256			
	178/256	51/256	15/256	12/256
1~19	—	—	—	—
20~29	—	—	—	—
30~100	—	—	—	—

Droma

HP	1010~3128		AP	––
EXP	––		Weak vs Wind	

Flying Monster

Elemental Defense
💧	1
❄	1
⚡	1
💧	X
☣	1
🌀	2
💧	1
✹	1

Status Defense
💡	X	⚡	X	🌀	X
☠	X	🕐	90	▲	100
🛡	X	✋	X	☀	X
☠	X	⚔	100	%	X
💬	X	🗡	X		
☠	X	⚕	X		
💀	X	✋	X		
💤	X	👁	X		

LV	HP	Str	Vit	Mag	Spr	Spd	Eva
1	1010	12	8	12	5	50	10
10	1150	24	8	30	5	51	13
20	1400	37	8	50	5	51	15
30	1750	49	8	70	5	52	18
40	2200	62	8	89	5	52	20
50	2750	74	8	109	5	53	23
56	3128	82	8	121	5	53	24
—							
—							
—							

Locations
Ultimecia Castle (Art Gallery)

Born from Trauma, a small support machine. Despite its small size, uses Pulse Cannon just like Trauma.

Spells
Level	Draw		
1~19	Esuna	Dispel	
20~29	Esuna	Dispel	
30~56	Esuna	Dispel	

Card
Drop Card	Mod Card	Mod (Rare)
—	—	—

Devour
LV 1~19	LV 20~29	LV 30~56
—	—	—

Item (Drop)
Level	Rate: 255/256			
	178/256	51/256	15/256	12/256
1~19	—	—	—	—
20~29	—	—	—	—
30~56	—	—	—	—

Item (Mug)
Level	Rate: 32/256			
	178/256	51/256	15/256	12/256
1~19	Meteor Stone	Meteor Stone	Meteor Stone	Meteor Stone
20~29	Meteor Stone	Meteor Stone	Meteor Stone	Meteor Stone
30~56	Meteor Stone	Meteor Stone	Meteor Stone	Meteor Stone

Edea (1st round)

HP	1300~7000		AP	20
EXP	––		––	

Elemental Defense
💧	1
❄	1
⚡	1
💧	1
☣	1
🌀	1
💧	1
✹	1

Status Defense
💡	X	⚡	100	🌀	X
☠	X	🕐	X	▲	X
🛡	X	✋	X	☀	X
☠	X	⚔	100	%	X
💬	X	🗡	X		
☠	X	⚕	X		
💀	X	✋	X		
💤	X	👁	X		

LV	HP	Str	Vit	Mag	Spr	Spd	Eva
1	1300	3	16	45	76	6	1
10	4000	11	25	50	84	15	2
20	7000	19	35	55	94	24	2

Locations
Deling City (Gateway)

A powerful sorceress and ruler of Galbadia. Her sorceress powers may be the most powerful in the world.

Spells
Level	Draw			
1~19	Cura	Dispel	Life	Double
20	Cura	Dispel	Life	Double

Card
Drop Card	Mod Card	Mod (Rare)
—	—	

Devour
LV 1~19	LV 20
—	

Item (Drop)
Level	Rate: 255/256			
	178/256	51/256	15/256	12/256
1~19	—	—	—	—
20	—	—	—	—

Item (Mug)
Level	Rate: 32/256			
	178/256	51/256	15/256	12/256
1~19	Elixir	Elixir	Elixir	Elixir
20	Elixir	Elixir	Elixir	Elixir

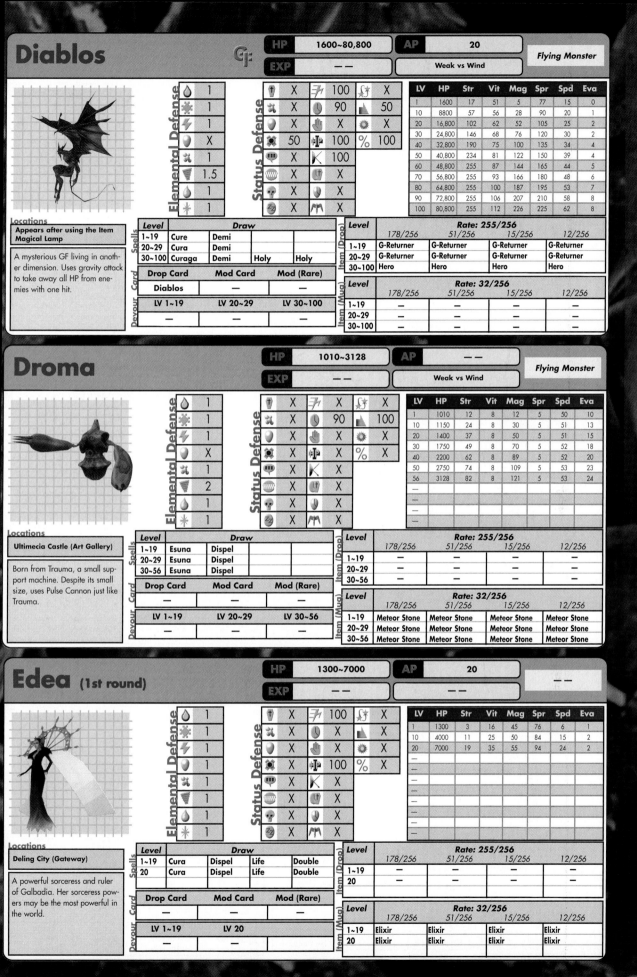

Edea (2nd round)

HP	500~16,000
AP	50
EXP	— —
	— —
	— —

Elemental Defense
Element	Value
💧	1
❄	1
⚡	1
💧	1
🔥	1
▽	1
💧	1
❄	1

Status Defense
☨ X	🗲 100	🌀 X	
🐍 X	✋ 90	🔺 100	
🥚 X	✋ X	☀ X	
☢ 80	⬚ 100	% 100	
▦ X	🗡 100		
▽ X	✋ X		
💀 X	✋ X		
⟐ 80	🙌 X		

LV	HP	Str	Vit	Mag	Spr	Spd	Eva
1	500	8	41	64	151	20	0
10	5000	8	48	80	157	21	3
20	10,000	10	56	98	165	23	5
30	15,000	13	65	115	172	24	8
32	16,000	13	66	118	174	24	8
—							
—							
—							
—							
—							

Locations
Galbadia Garden (Auditorium)

A sorceress bent on conquering the world. Hired Galbadia Garden forces to destroy SeeD, which stands in her way.

Spells — Draw
Level		Draw		
1~19	Blizzard	Demi	Esuna	Alexander
20~29	Blizzara	Demi	Esuna	Alexander
30~32	Blizzaga	Demi	Esuna	Alexander

Card
Drop Card	Mod Card	Mod (Rare)
—	—	—

Devour
LV 1~19	LV 20~29	LV 30~32

Item (Drop) — Rate: 255/256
Level	178/256	51/256	15/256	12/256
1~19	Force Armlet	Force Armlet	Force Armlet	Force Armlet
20~29	Force Armlet	Force Armlet	Force Armlet	Force Armlet
30~32	Force Armlet	Force Armlet	Force Armlet	Force Armlet

Item (Mug) — Rate: 32/256
Level	178/256	51/256	15/256	12/256
1~19	Royal Crown	Royal Crown	Royal Crown	Royal Crown
20~29	Royal Crown	Royal Crown	Royal Crown	Royal Crown
30~32	Royal Crown	Royal Crown	Royal Crown	Royal Crown

Elastoid

HP	531~18,500
AP	3
EXP	80 (+20)
	Weak vs Thunder/ Immune to Poison
	Flying Monster

Elemental Defense
Element	Value
💧	1
❄	1
⚡	1.5
💧	X
🔥	0
▽	1
💧	1
❄	1

Status Defense
☨ X	🗲 100	🌀 X	
🐍 X	✋ 90	🔺 X	
🥚 X	✋ 50	☀ 80	
☢ X	⬚ X	% 100	
▦ X	🗡 100		
▽ X	✋ X		
💀 X	✋ X		
⟐ X	🙌 X		

LV	HP	Str	Vit	Mag	Spr	Spd	Eva
1	531	9	130	10	120	3	4
10	950	22	130	26	121	5	5
20	1700	36	130	44	122	7	6
30	2750	50	130	62	123	8	7
40	4100	63	130	79	125	10	7
50	5750	77	130	97	126	11	8
60	7700	90	130	114	127	13	9
70	9950	103	130	131	128	15	10
80	12,500	116	130	149	130	17	11
90	15,350	128	130	166	131	18	12
100	18,500	141	131	182	132	20	12

Locations
Centra Ruins (Excavation Site; w/Laguna), Lunatic Pandora Laboratory (w/Laguna)

Anti-personnel weapon made in Esthar. Floats with an anti-gravity engine. Attacks with its 4 pliable metallic legs.

Spells — Draw
Level		Draw	
1~19	Dispel		
20~29	Dispel	Stop	
30~100	Dispel	Stop	Meltdown

Card
Drop Card	Mod Card	Mod (Rare)
Elastoid	Elastoid	Ultimate Weapon

Devour
LV 1~19	LV 20~29	LV 30~100
No change	No change	Damage (small) & Poison

Item (Drop) — Rate: 255/256
Level	178/256	51/256	15/256	12/256
1~19	M-Stone	M-Stone	M-Stone	M-Stone
20~29	Magic Stone	Magic Stone	Magic Stone	Laser Cannon
30~100	Wizard Stone	Wizard Stone	Laser Cannon	Laser Cannon

Item (Mug) — Rate: 32/256
Level	178/256	51/256	15/256	12/256
1~19	Dynamo Stone	Dynamo Stone	Dynamo Stone	Dynamo Stone
20~29	Dynamo Stone	Dynamo Stone	Dynamo Stone	Dynamo Stone
30~100	Laser Cannon	Laser Cannon	Laser Cannon	Laser Cannon

Elite Soldier

HP	148~4940
AP	2
EXP	30 (+5)
	Weak vs Poison
	— —

Elemental Defense
Element	Value
💧	1
❄	1
⚡	1
💧	1
🔥	1.5
▽	1
💧	1
❄	1

Status Defense
☨ 60	🗲 35	🌀 20	
🐍 60	✋ 35	🔺 35	
🥚 70	✋ 35	☀ 80	
☢ 80	⬚ 35	% 100	
▦ 35	🗡 35		
▽ 35	✋ 35		
💀 35	✋ 70		
⟐ 35	🙌 35		

LV	HP	Str	Vit	Mag	Spr	Spd	Eva
1	148	3	36	6	38	6	2
10	260	15	37	17	38	7	3
20	460	28	38	29	38	8	4
30	740	41	39	42	38	9	5
40	1100	54	41	54	39	9	5
50	1540	67	42	66	39	10	6
60	2060	79	43	77	39	11	7
70	2660	91	44	89	40	12	8
80	3340	103	46	101	40	13	9
90	4100	115	47	112	40	14	10
100	4940	127	48	123	41	14	10

Locations
Dollet, Galbadia D-District Prison

An officer acting together with Galbadian soldiers. Defeat him first, before he uses recovery magic on the other soldiers.

Spells — Draw
Level		Draw		
1~19	Fire	Thunder	Blizzard	Scan
20~29	Fira	Thundara	Blizzara	Scan
30~100	Firaga	Thundaga	Blizzaga	Dispell

Card
Drop Card	Mod Card	Mod (Rare)
—	—	—

Devour
LV 1~19	LV 20~29	LV 30~100
HP Recovery	HP Recovery	HP Recover

Item (Drop) — Rate: 255/256
Level	178/256	51/256	15/256	12/256
1~19	Potion	Phoenix Down	Shotgun Ammo	Cottage
20~29	Potion	Phoenix Down	Hi-Potion	Cottage
30~100	Potion	Hi-Potion	Cottage	Cottage

Item (Mug) — Rate: 32/256
Level	178/256	51/256	15/256	12/256
1~19	Tent	Tent	Cottage	Cottage
20~29	Tent	Cottage	Cottage	Cottage
30~100	Cottage	Cottage	Cottage	Cottage

Elnoyle

HP	30,968~159,000	AP	18	
EXP	220 (+20)		Weak vs Wind	*Flying Monster*

Elemental Defense

💧	1
❄	1
⚡	1
🌀	X
🔥	1
🌪	2
💧	1
❄	1

Status Defense

🗡	20	⚡	100	👁	X
☠	30	💊	50	🔺	X
🛡	1	✋	X	☀	20
👁	20	🔱	70	%	X
💬	X	🔑	100		
〰	X			🌀	20
☠	20	👊	1		
💤	20	🎮	X		

LV	HP	Str	Vit	Mag	Spr	Spd	Eva
1	30,968	64	11	64	81	10	0
10	39,975	82	17	81	90	11	0
20	50,600	101	25	101	100	11	1
30	61,875	120	32	120	110	12	1
40	73,800	139	39	138	120	13	1
50	86,375	158	47	157	130	13	1
60	99,600	177	54	176	140	14	2
70	113,475	196	61	195	150	14	2
80	128,000	214	69	213	160	15	2
90	143,175	233	76	231	170	16	3
100	159,000	251	83	250	180	16	3

Locations

Esthar, Ultimecia Castle

A powerful monster. Uses magic, but also uses Tail Needle, which causes heavy Flying Monster

Spells

Level	Draw			
1~29	Pain	Double		
30~39	Pain	Double		
40~100	Pain	Double		

Devour / Card

Drop Card	Mod Card	Mod (Rare)
Elnoyle	Elnoyle	Catoblepas
LV 1~29	LV 30~39	LV 40~100

Item (Drop)

Level	Rate: 255/256			
	178/256	51/256	15/256	12/256
1~29	Wizard Stone	Wizard Stone	Moon Stone	Moon Stone
30~39	Wizard Stone	Moon Stone	Energy Crystal	Energy Crystal
40~100	Energy Crystal	Energy Crystal	Energy Crystal	Energy Crystal

Item (Mug)

Level	Rate: 32/256			
	178/256	51/256	15/256	12/256
1~29	Moon Stone	Moon Stone	Moon Stone	Moon Stone
30~39	Moon Stone	Moon Stone	Moon Stone	Moon Stone
40~100	Moon Stone	Moon Stone	Moon Stone	Moon Stone

Elvoret

HP	1563~3523	AP	10	
EXP	— —		Immune to Poison/ Strong Def vs Magic (high Spirit)	*Flying Monster*

Elemental Defense

💧	1
❄	1
⚡	1
🌀	X
❄	0
🌪	1
💧	1
❄	1

Status Defense

🗡	X	⚡	100	👁	X
☠	X	💊	90	🔺	100
🛡	X	✋	X	☀	X
👁	60	🔱	100	%	100
💬	X	🔑	100		
〰	X			🌀	X
☠	X	👊	X		
💤	X	🎮	X		

LV	HP	Str	Vit	Mag	Spr	Spd	Eva
1	1563	17	2	10	127	8	0
10	3300	27	4	27	130	10	1
11	3523	28	4	28	130	10	1
-							
-							
-							
-							
-							
-							
-							

Locations

Dollet (Comm Tower)

A monster that lives in the abandoned Dollet Communication Tower. No one knows where it came from.

Spells

Level	Draw			
1~11	Thunder	Cure	Double	Siren

Devour / Card

Drop Card	Mod Card	Mod (Rare)
—		
LV 1~11		
—		

Item (Drop)

Level	Rate: 255/256			
	178/256	51/256	15/256	12/256
1~11	G-Returner	G-Returner	G-Returner	G-Returner

Item (Mug)

Level	Rate: 32/256			
	178/256	51/256	15/256	12/256
1~11	—	—	—	—

Esthar Soldier (Human)

HP	98~4890	AP	1	
EXP	20 (+3)		Weak vs Poison	— —

Elemental Defense

💧	1
❄	1
⚡	1
🌀	X
❄	2
🌪	1
💧	1
❄	1

Status Defense

🗡	70	⚡	100	👁	60
☠	80	💊	90	🔺	100
🛡	70	✋	50	☀	80
👁	80	🔱	100	%	100
💬	80	🔑	100		
〰	60			🌀	80
☠	70	👊	70		
💤	80	🎮	100		

LV	HP	Str	Vit	Mag	Spr	Spd	Eva
1	98	3	2	1	5	5	0
10	210	13	2	8	6	7	1
20	410	22	3	16	7	9	3
30	690	32	3	24	8	10	4
40	1050	41	4	31	10	12	5
50	1490	50	5	39	11	13	6
60	2010	59	5	46	12	15	8
70	2610	68	6	54	13	17	9
80	3290	77	7	61	15	19	10
90	4050	85	7	68	16	20	11
100	4890	93	8	75	17	22	13

Locations

Centra Ruins (Excavation Site; w/Laguna), Lunatic Pandora Laboratory (w/Laguna)

Esthar soldier who uses both gun and sword. Shotgun attack can cause major damage. Not a strong enemy.

Spells

Level	Draw			
1~19	Fire	Thunder	Blizzard	Cure
20~29	Fira	Thundara	Blizzara	Cura
30~100	Firaga	Thundaga	Blizzaga	Curaga

Devour / Card

Drop Card	Mod Card	Mod (Rare)
—		
LV 1~19	LV 20~29	LV 30~100
HP Recovery	HP Recovery	HP Recovery

Item (Drop)

Level	Rate: 255/256			
	178/256	51/256	15/256	12/256
1~19	Potion	Potion	Phoenix Down	Phoenix Down
20~29	Potion	Potion	Phoenix Down	Phoenix Down
30~100	Potion	Hi-Potion	Phoenix Down	Phoenix Down

Item (Mug)

Level	Rate: 32/256			
	178/256	51/256	15/256	12/256
1~19	Potion	Potion	Potion	Potion
20~29	Potion	Potion	Potion	Potion
30~100	Hi-Potion	Hi-Potion	Hi-Potion	Hi-Potion

Esthar Soldier (Cyborg)

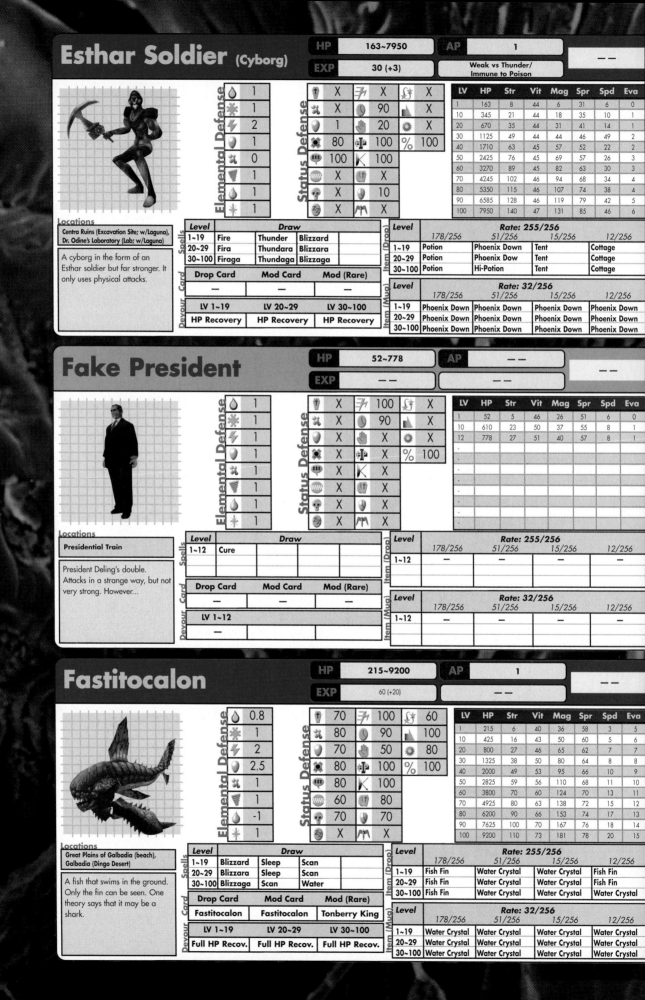

HP	163~7950	AP 1
EXP	30 (+3)	Weak vs Thunder/Immune to Poison

Elemental Defense: 1, 1, 2, 1, 0, 1, 1, 1

Status Defense: X, X; X, 90; 1, 20; 80, 100, %100; 100, 100; X, X; X, 10; X, X

LV	HP	Str	Vit	Mag	Spr	Spd	Eva
1	163	8	44	6	31	6	0
10	345	21	44	18	35	10	1
20	670	35	44	31	41	14	1
30	1125	49	44	44	46	49	2
40	1710	63	45	57	52	22	2
50	2425	76	45	69	57	26	3
60	3270	89	45	82	63	30	3
70	4245	102	46	94	68	34	4
80	5350	115	46	107	74	38	4
90	6585	128	46	119	79	42	5
100	7950	140	47	131	85	46	6

Locations: Centra Ruins (Excavation Site; w/Laguna), Dr. Odine's Laboratory (Lab; w/Laguna)

A cyborg in the form of an Esthar soldier but far stronger. It only uses physical attacks.

Spells — Draw

Level	Draw		
1~19	Fire	Thunder	Blizzard
20~29	Fira	Thundara	Blizzara
30~100	Firaga	Thundaga	Blizzaga

Card

Drop Card	Mod Card	Mod (Rare)
—	—	—

Devour

LV 1~19	LV 20~29	LV 30~100
HP Recovery	HP Recovery	HP Recovery

Item (Drop) — Rate: 255/256

Level	178/256	51/256	15/256	12/256
1~19	Potion	Phoenix Down	Tent	Cottage
20~29	Potion	Phoenix Dow	Tent	Cottage
30~100	Potion	Hi-Potion	Tent	Cottage

Item (Mug) — Rate: 32/256

Level	178/256	51/256	15/256	12/256
1~19	Phoenix Down	Phoenix Down	Phoenix Down	Phoenix Down
20~29	Phoenix Down	Phoenix Down	Phoenix Down	Phoenix Down
30~100	Phoenix Down	Phoenix Down	Phoenix Down	Phoenix Down

Fake President

HP	52~778	AP — —
EXP	— —	— —

Elemental Defense: 1, 1, 1, 1, (—), (—), (—), 1

Status Defense: X, 100; X, 90; X, X; X, X, %100; X, X; X, X; X, X; X, X

LV	HP	Str	Vit	Mag	Spr	Spd	Eva
1	52	5	46	26	51	6	0
10	610	23	50	37	55	8	1
12	778	27	51	40	57	8	1

Locations: Presidential Train

President Deling's double. Attacks in a strange way, but not very strong. However…

Spells — Draw

Level	Draw		
1~12	Cure		

Card

Drop Card	Mod Card	Mod (Rare)
—	—	—

Devour

LV 1~12
—

Item (Drop) — Rate: 255/256

Level	178/256	51/256	15/256	12/256
1~12	—	—	—	—

Item (Mug) — Rate: 32/256

Level	178/256	51/256	15/256	12/256
1~12	—	—	—	—

Fastitocalon

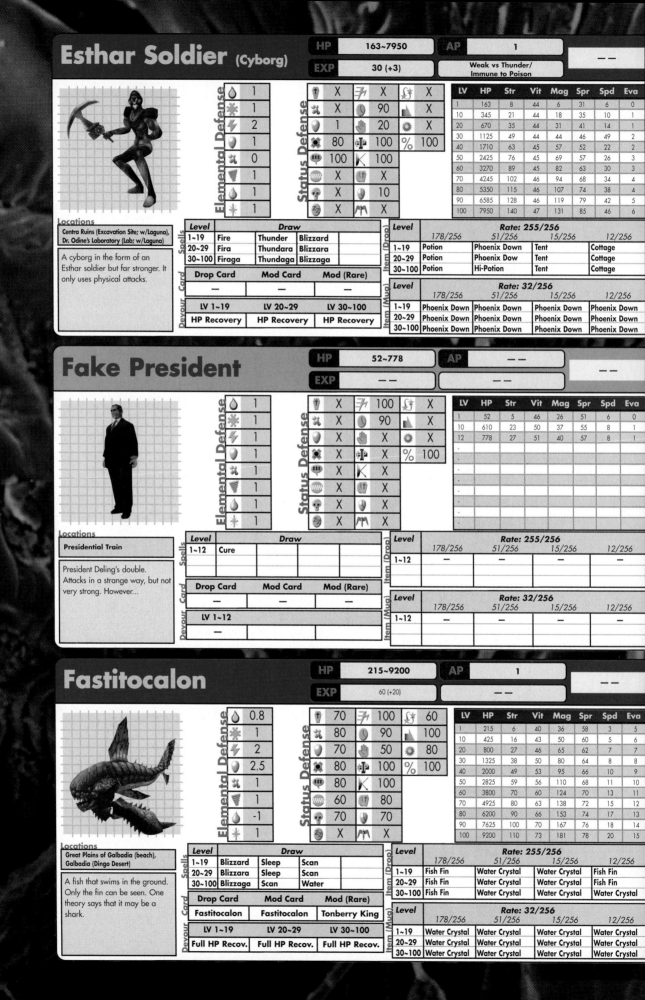

HP	215~9200	AP 1
EXP	60 (+20)	— —

Elemental Defense: 0.8, 1, 2, 2.5, 1, 1, -1, 1

Status Defense: 70, 100, 60; 80, 90, 100; 70, 50, 80; 80, 100, %100; 80, 100; 60, 80; 70, 70; X, X

LV	HP	Str	Vit	Mag	Spr	Spd	Eva
1	215	6	40	36	58	3	5
10	425	16	43	50	60	5	6
20	800	27	46	65	62	7	7
30	1325	38	50	80	64	8	8
40	2000	49	53	95	66	10	9
50	2825	59	56	110	68	11	10
60	3800	70	60	124	70	13	11
70	4925	80	63	138	72	15	12
80	6200	90	66	153	74	17	13
90	7625	100	70	167	76	18	14
100	9200	110	73	181	78	20	15

Locations: Great Plains of Galbadia (beach), Galbadia (Dingo Desert)

A fish that swims in the ground. Only the fin can be seen. One theory says that it may be a shark.

Spells — Draw

Level	Draw		
1~19	Blizzard	Sleep	Scan
20~29	Blizzara	Sleep	Scan
30~100	Blizzaga	Scan	Water

Card

Drop Card	Mod Card	Mod (Rare)
Fastitocalon	Fastitocalon	Tonberry King

Devour

LV 1~19	LV 20~29	LV 30~100
Full HP Recov.	Full HP Recov.	Full HP Recov.

Item (Drop) — Rate: 255/256

Level	178/256	51/256	15/256	12/256
1~19	Fish Fin	Water Crystal	Water Crystal	Fish Fin
20~29	Fish Fin	Water Crystal	Water Crystal	Fish Fin
30~100	Fish Fin	Water Crystal	Water Crystal	Water Crystal

Item (Mug) — Rate: 32/256

Level	178/256	51/256	15/256	12/256
1~19	Water Crystal	Water Crystal	Water Crystal	Water Crystal
20~29	Water Crystal	Water Crystal	Water Crystal	Water Crystal
30~100	Water Crystal	Water Crystal	Water Crystal	Water Crystal

Fastitocalon-F

	HP	215~9200	AP	3	
	EXP	15 (+5)		— —	— —

Elemental Defense

💧	0.8
❄	1
⚡	2
🌪	2.5
🔥	1
〰	1
💧	-1
✳	1

Status Defense

✝	70	⚡	100	🌀	60
♨	80	●	90	⛰	100
🛡	70	✋	50	☀	80
✴	80	⬛	100	%	100
🕸	80	🗡	100		
〰	60	👆	80		
☠	70	🔺	70		
💤	X	🎮	X		

LV	HP	Str	Vit	Mag	Spr	Spd	Eva
1	215	6	40	36	58	3	5
10	425	16	43	50	60	5	6
20	800	27	46	65	62	7	7
30	1325	38	50	80	64	8	8
40	2000	49	53	95	66	10	9
50	2825	59	56	110	68	11	10
60	3800	70	60	124	70	13	11
70	4925	80	63	138	72	15	12
80	6200	90	66	153	74	17	13
90	7625	100	70	167	76	18	14
100	9200	110	73	181	78	20	15

Locations
Galbadia (Near Beaches)

A fish that swims in the ground. Only the fin can be seen. One theory says that it may be a shark.

Spells / Draw

Level	Draw			
1~19	Blizzard	Sleep	Scan	
20~29	Blizzara	Sleep	Scan	
30~100	Blizzaga	Scan	Water	

Card

Drop Card	Mod Card	Mod (Rare)
Fastitocalon-F	Fastitocalon-F	—

Devour

LV 1~19	LV 20~29	LV 30~100
HP Recovery	HP Recovery	HP Recovery

Item (Drop)

Level	Rate: 255/256			
	178/256	51/256	15/256	12/256
1~19	Fish Fin	Fish Fin	Fish Fin	Fish Fin
20~29	Fish Fin	Fish Fin	Water Crystal	Water Crystal
30~100	Fish Fin	Fish Fin	Water Crystal	Water Crystal

Item (Mug)

Level	Rate: 32/256			
	178/256	51/256	15/256	12/256
1~19	Fish Fin	Fish Fin	Fish Fin	Fish Fin
20~29	Fish Fin	Fish Fin	Fish Fin	Fish Fin
30~100	Fish Fin	Fish Fin	Fish Fin	Fish Fin

Forbidden

	HP	221~22,100	AP	4	
	EXP	85 (+15)		Very weak vs Holy/Weak vs Fire/ Immune to Poison	**Undead Monster**

Elemental Defense

💧	2
❄	1
⚡	1
🌪	1
🔥	0
〰	1
💧	1
✳	1

Status Defense

✝	100	⚡	100	🌀	X
♨	X	●	90	⛰	X
🛡	X	✋	20	☀	80
✴	X	⬛	X	%	100
🕸	X	🗡	100		
〰	X	👆	X		
☠	X	🔺	X		
💤	70	🎮	X		

LV	HP	Str	Vit	Mag	Spr	Spd	Eva
1	221	14	25	1	200	11	2
10	1400	28	26	14	201	15	4
20	2900	43	27	28	202	20	6
30	4600	59	28	41	203	25	7
40	6500	74	30	54	205	30	9
50	8600	89	31	68	206	35	10
60	10,900	104	32	81	207	40	12
70	13,400	119	33	94	208	45	14
80	16,100	134	35	107	210	50	16
90	19,000	149	36	120	211	55	17
100	22,100	163	37	133	212	60	19

Locations
Tomb of the Unknown King, Esthar (Grandidi Forest)

Undead soldier. Not afraid of death. Its death blow kills enemies with one hit.

Spells / Draw

Level	Draw			
1~19	Zombie			
20~29	Zombie	Blind	Stop	
30~100	Zombie	Blind	Stop	Death

Card

Drop Card	Mod Card	Mod (Rare)
Forbidden	Forbidden	Red Giant

Devour

LV 1~19	LV 20~29	LV 30~100
Damage (small) & Zombie	Damage (small) & Zombie	Damage (small) & Zombie

Item (Drop)

Level	Rate: 255/256			
	178/256	51/256	15/256	12/256
1~19	Betrayal Sword	Dead Spirit	Zombie Powder	Zombie Powder
20~29	Dead Spirit	Zombie Powder	Curse Spike	Curse Spike
30~100	Curse Spike	Zombie Powder	Curse Spike	Force Amulet

Item (Mug)

Level	Rate: 32/256			
	178/256	51/256	15/256	12/256
1~19	Dead Spirit	Dead Spirit	Dead Spirit	Dead Spirit
20~29	Dead Spirit	Dead Spirit	Dead Spirit	Dead Spirit
30~100	Dead Spirit	Dead Spirit	Dead Spirit	Dead Spirit

Fujin (1st round)

	HP	300~8700	AP	10	
	EXP	— —		Weak vs Poison/Absorbs Wind	— —

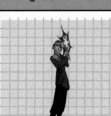

Elemental Defense

💧	1
❄	1
⚡	1
🌪	1
🔥	1.5
〰	-1
💧	1
✳	1

Status Defense

✝	X	⚡	100	🌀	X
♨	X	●	60	⛰	40
🛡	X	✋	X	☀	X
✴	60	⬛	100	%	100
🕸	X	🗡	100		
〰	X	👆	X		
☠	X	🔺	X		
💤	60	🎮			

LV	HP	Str	Vit	Mag	Spr	Spd	Eva
1	300	23	6	8	121	15	10
10	3000	39	10	27	128	18	11
20	6000	57	15	48	136	20	12
29	8700	72	20	67	144	22	13
—							
—							
—							
—							
—							

Locations
Balamb Town Square, Balamb Hotel

Looking for Ellone under Seifer's command. Uses wind magic through the help of another being with wind power. Also attacks with Pinwheel

Spells / Draw

Level	Draw			
1~19	Aero	Cura	Life	Pandemona
20~29	Aero	Cura	Life	Pandemona

Card

Drop Card	Mod Card	Mod (Rare)
—	—	—

Devour

LV 1~19	LV 20~29
—	—

Item (Drop)

Level	Rate: 255/256			
	178/256	51/256	15/256	12/256
1~19	Megalixir	Megalixir	Megalixir	Megalixir
20~29	Megalixir	Megalixir	Megalixir	Megalixir

Item (Mug)

Level	Rate: 32/256			
	178/256	51/256	15/256	12/256
1~19	Megalixir	Megalixir	Hero	Hero
20~29	Megalixir	Megalixir	Hero	Hero

Fujin (2nd round)

HP	5300~18,200	AP	8
EXP	— —		Weak vs Poison/Absorbs Wind

Elemental Defense

💧	1
❄️	1
⚡	1
🌀	1
🔥	1.5
🌪️	-1
💧	1
✳️	1

Status Defense

✝	X	⚡	100	✨	X
☠	X	🕐	40	⛰	70
🛡	X	✋	X	☀	X
💀	40	✚	100	%	100
💀	X	🗡	10		
	X	👊	X		
	X	✋	X		
	50	〽	X		

LV	HP	Str	Vit	Mag	Spr	Spd	Eva
1	5300	24	31	8	121	30	10
10	8000	43	37	27	128	33	11
20	11,000	63	44	48	136	35	12
30	14,000	83	50	69	145	38	14
40	17,000	103	58	90	153	40	14
44	18,200	110	61	99	156	41	15
—							
—							
—							

Locations

Lunatic Pandora

Assisting Seifer inside Lunatic Pandora. Uses support magic, as well as attack magic.

Spells

Level	Draw			
1~19	Aero	Cure	Life	
20~29	Aero	Cura	Life	
30~44	Aero	Curaga	Full-Life	Tornado

Card

Drop Card	Mod Card	Mod (Rare)
—	—	—

Devour

LV 1~19	LV 20~29	LV 30~44
—	—	—

Item (Drop) — Rate: 255/256

Level	178/256	51/256	15/256	12/256
1~19	Megalixir	Megalixir	Megalixir	Megalixir
20~29	Megalixir	Megalixir	Megalixir	Megalixir
30~44	Megalixir	Megalixir	Megalixir	Megalixir

Item (Mug) — Rate: 32/256

Level	178/256	51/256	15/256	12/256
1~19	Megalixir	Megalixir	Megalixir	Megalixir
20~29	Megalixir	Megalixir	Megalixir	Megalixir
30~44	Megalixir	Megalixir	Megalixir	Megalixir

Funguar

HP	303~2100	AP	1
EXP	20 (+3)		— —

Elemental Defense

💧	1
❄️	1
⚡	1
🌀	1
🌪️	1
💧	1
✳️	1

Status Defense

✝	100	⚡	100	✨	60
☠	80	🕐	90	⛰	100
🛡	70	✋	50	☀	80
💀	X	✚	100	%	100
💀	X	🗡	100		
	X	👊	80		
	70	✋	70		
	X	〽	X		

LV	HP	Str	Vit	Mag	Spr	Spd	Eva
1	303	5	2	1	2	2	0
10	345	11	6	8	6	3	0
20	420	18	12	16	12	3	1
30	525	24	17	24	17	4	1
40	660	30	23	31	23	5	2
50	825	36	28	38	28	5	2
60	1020	42	34	45	34	6	3
70	1245	47	39	52	39	6	3
80	1500	52	45	59	45	7	3
90	1785	57	50	66	50	8	4
100	2100	62	56	72	56	8	4

Locations

Timber Forest (w/Laguna), Dollet (Hasberry Plains)

A giant walking mushroom. Uses status change attacks with damage attacks. Use caution when fighting this monster.

Spells

Level	Draw			
1~19	Sleep	Scan		
20~29	Sleep	Scan	Silence	
30~100	Sleep	Scan	Silence	Confuse

Card

Drop Card	Mod Card	Mod (Rare)
Funguar	Funguar	Biggs, Wedge

Devour

LV 1~19	LV 20~29	LV 30~100
Damage (small) & Dark	Damage (small) & Poison	Damage (medium) & Poison

Item (Drop) — Rate: 255/256

Level	178/256	51/256	15/256	12/256
1~19	M-Stone	M-Stone	Sleep Powder	Sleep Powder
20~29	Magic Stone	Magic Stone	Sleep Powder	Sleep Powder
30~100	Wizard Stone	Sleep Powder	Sleep Powder	Sleep Powder

Item (Mug) — Rate: 32/256

Level	178/256	51/256	15/256	12/256
1~19	Sleep Powder	Sleep Powder	Sleep Powder	Sleep Powder
20~29	Sleep Powder	Sleep Powder	Sleep Powder	Sleep Powder
30~100	Sleep Powder	Sleep Powder	Sleep Powder	Sleep Powder

Galbadian Soldier

HP	45~3040	AP	1
EXP	20 (+3)		Weak vs Poison

Elemental Defense

💧	1
❄️	1
⚡	1
🌀	1
🌪️	2
💧	1
✳️	1

Status Defense

✝	70	⚡	100	✨	60
☠	80	🕐	90	⛰	100
🛡	70	✋	50	☀	80
💀	80	✚	100	%	100
💀	80	🗡	100		
	60	👊	80		
	70	✋	70		
	80	〽	100		

LV	HP	Str	Vit	Mag	Spr	Spd	Eva
1	45	3	1	1	2	4	0
10	115	11	2	8	3	5	1
20	240	18	3	16	4	5	2
30	415	26	4	24	5	6	3
40	640	33	6	31	7	7	3
50	915	40	7	39	8	8	4
60	1240	47	8	46	9	8	5
70	1615	54	9	54	10	9	6
80	2040	61	11	61	12	10	7
90	2515	67	12	68	13	10	8
100	3040	73	13	75	14	11	8

Locations

Dollet, Galbadia Missle Base

Galbadian Soldier that uses magic with a sword. Strong enough, but nowhere near as strong as any SeeD member.

Spells

Level	Draw			
1~19	Fire	Thunder	Blizzard	Cure
20~29	Fira	Thundara	Blizzara	Cura
30~100	Firaga	Thundaga	Blizzaga	Curaga

Card

Drop Card	Mod Card	Mod (Rare)
—	—	—

Devour

LV 1~19	LV 20~29	LV 30~100
HP Recov.	HP Recov.	HP Recov.

Item (Drop) — Rate: 255/256

Level	178/256	51/256	15/256	12/256
1~19	Potion	Potion	Normal Ammo	Phoenix Down
20~29	Potion	Potion	Phoenix Down	Phoenix Down
30~100	Potion	Potion	Phoenix Down	Phoenix Down

Item (Mug) — Rate: 32/256

Level	178/256	51/256	15/256	12/256
1~19	Potion	Potion	Phoenix Down	Phoenix Down
20~29	Potion	Phoenix Down	Hi-Potion	Hi-Potion
30~100	Hi-Potion	Phoenix Down	Phoenix Down	Phoenix Down

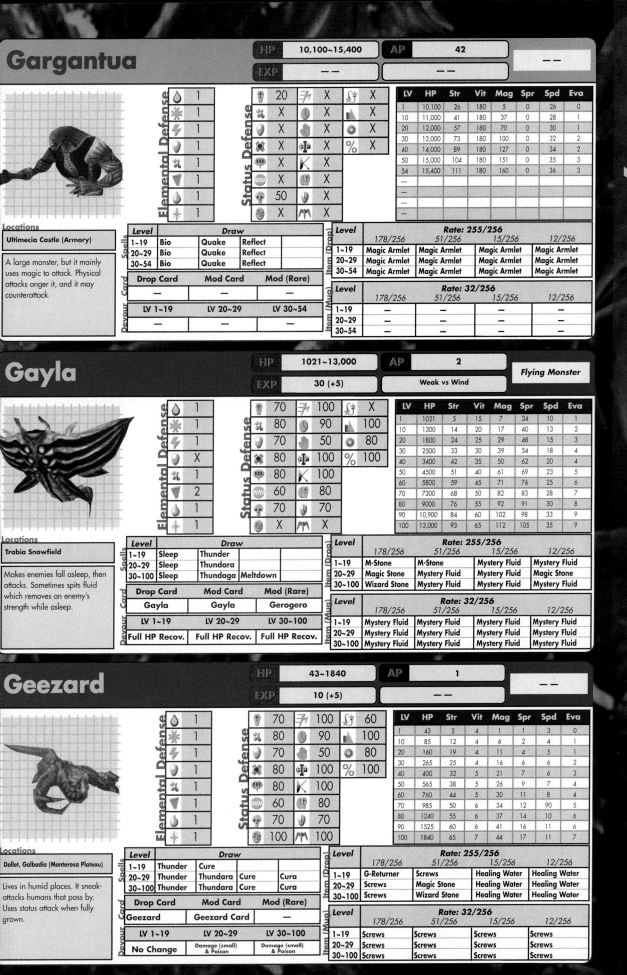

Gargantua

	HP	10,100~15,400	AP	42		--
	EXP	--		--		

Elemental Defense: 1, 1, 1, 1, 1, 1, 1, 1

Status Defense: 20, X / X, X / X, X / X, X / X, X / X, X / 50, X / X, X

LV	HP	Str	Vit	Mag	Spr	Spd	Eva
1	10,100	26	180	5	0	26	0
10	11,000	41	180	37	0	28	1
20	12,000	57	180	70	0	30	1
30	13,000	73	180	100	0	32	2
40	14,000	89	180	127	0	34	2
50	15,000	104	180	151	0	35	3
54	15,400	111	180	160	0	36	3

Locations: Ultimecia Castle (Armory)

A large monster, but it mainly uses magic to attack. Physical attacks anger it, and it may counterattack.

Spells / Draw

Level		Draw	
1~19	Bio	Quake	Reflect
20~29	Bio	Quake	Reflect
30~54	Bio	Quake	Reflect

Card

Drop Card	Mod Card	Mod (Rare)
—	—	—

Devour Card

LV 1~19	LV 20~29	LV 30~54
—	—	—

Item (Drop) — Rate: 255/256

Level	178/256	51/256	15/256	12/256
1~19	Magic Armlet	Magic Armlet	Magic Armlet	Magic Armlet
20~29	Magic Armlet	Magic Armlet	Magic Armlet	Magic Armlet
30~54	Magic Armlet	Magic Armlet	Magic Armlet	Magic Armlet

Item (Mug) — Rate: 32/256

Level	178/256	51/256	15/256	12/256
1~19	—	—	—	—
20~29	—	—	—	—
30~54	—	—	—	—

Gayla

	HP	1021~13,000	AP	2		**Flying Monster**
	EXP	30 (+5)		Weak vs Wind		

Elemental Defense: 1, 1, 1, X, 1, 2, 1, 1

Status Defense: 70, 100 / 80, 90 / 70, 50 / 80, 100 / 80, 100 / 60, 80 / 70, 70 / X, X

LV	HP	Str	Vit	Mag	Spr	Spd	Eva
1	1021	5	15	7	34	10	1
10	1300	14	20	17	40	13	2
20	1800	24	25	29	48	15	3
30	2500	33	30	39	54	18	4
40	3400	42	35	50	62	20	4
50	4500	51	40	61	69	23	5
60	5800	59	45	71	76	25	6
70	7300	68	50	82	83	28	7
80	9000	76	55	92	91	30	8
90	10,900	84	60	102	98	33	8
100	13,000	93	65	112	105	35	9

Locations: Trabia Snowfield

Makes enemies fall asleep, then attacks. Sometimes spits fluid which removes an enemy's strength while asleep.

Spells / Draw

Level		Draw	
1~19	Sleep	Thunder	
20~29	Sleep	Thundara	
30~100	Sleep	Thundaga	Meltdown

Card

Drop Card	Mod Card	Mod (Rare)
Gayla	Gayla	Gerogero

Devour Card

LV 1~19	LV 20~29	LV 30~100
Full HP Recov.	Full HP Recov.	Full HP Recov.

Item (Drop) — Rate: 255/256

Level	178/256	51/256	15/256	12/256
1~19	M-Stone	M-Stone	Mystery Fluid	Mystery Fluid
20~29	Magic Stone	Mystery Fluid	Mystery Fluid	Magic Stone
30~100	Wizard Stone	Mystery Fluid	Mystery Fluid	Mystery Fluid

Item (Mug) — Rate: 32/256

Level	178/256	51/256	15/256	12/256
1~19	Mystery Fluid	Mystery Fluid	Mystery Fluid	Mystery Fluid
20~29	Mystery Fluid	Mystery Fluid	Mystery Fluid	Mystery Fluid
30~100	Mystery Fluid	Mystery Fluid	Mystery Fluid	Mystery Fluid

---

Geezard

	HP	43~1840	AP	1		--
	EXP	10 (+5)		--		

Elemental Defense: 1, 1, 1, 1, 1, 1, 1, 1

Status Defense: 70, 100 / 80, 90 / 70, 50 / 80, 100 / 80, 100 / 60, 80 / 70, 70 / 100, 100 — 60, 100, 80, 80

LV	HP	Str	Vit	Mag	Spr	Spd	Eva
1	43	5	4	1	1	3	0
10	85	12	4	6	2	4	1
20	160	19	4	11	4	5	1
30	265	25	4	16	6	6	2
40	400	32	5	21	7	6	3
50	565	38	5	26	9	7	4
60	760	44	5	30	11	8	4
70	985	50	6	34	12	90	5
80	1240	55	6	37	14	10	6
90	1525	60	6	41	16	11	6
100	1840	65	7	44	17	11	7

Locations: Dollet, Galbadia (Monterosa Plateau)

Lives in humid places. It sneak-attacks humans that pass by. Uses status attack when fully grown.

Spells / Draw

Level		Draw		
1~19	Thunder	Cure		
20~29	Thunder	Thundara	Cure	Cura
30~100	Thunder	Thundara	Cure	Cura

Card

Drop Card	Mod Card	Mod (Rare)
Geezard	Geezard Card	—

Devour Card

LV 1~19	LV 20~29	LV 30~100
No Change	Damage (small) & Poison	Damage (small) & Poison

Item (Drop) — Rate: 255/256

Level	178/256	51/256	15/256	12/256
1~19	G-Returner	Screws	Healing Water	Healing Water
20~29	Screws	Magic Stone	Healing Water	Healing Water
30~100	Screws	Wizard Stone	Healing Water	Healing Water

Item (Mug) — Rate: 32/256

Level	178/256	51/256	15/256	12/256
1~19	Screws	Screws	Screws	Screws
20~29	Screws	Screws	Screws	Screws
30~100	Screws	Screws	Screws	Screws

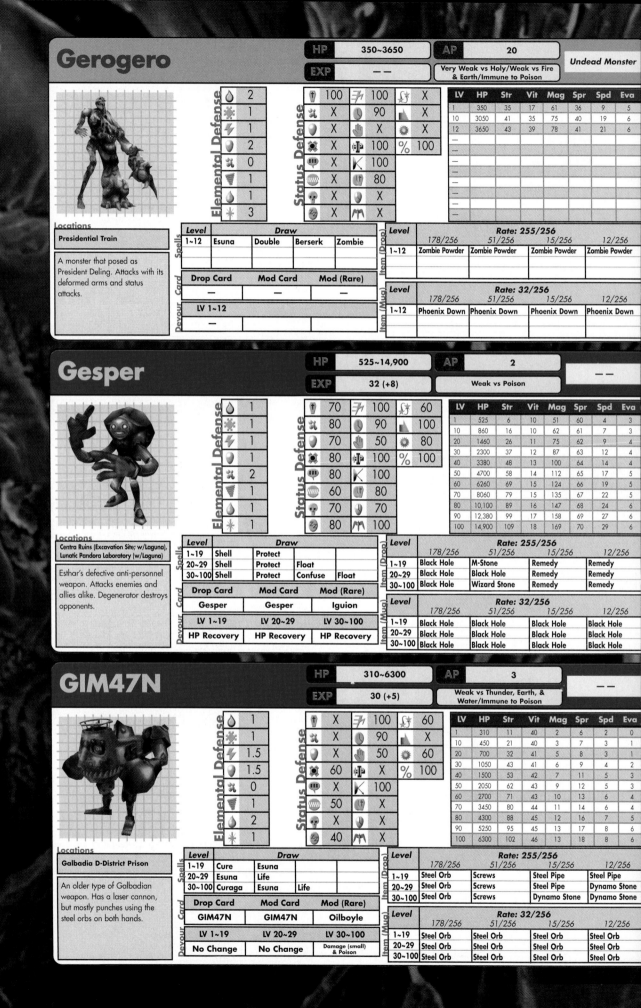

Gerogero

HP	350~3650	AP 20
EXP	— —	Very Weak vs Holy/Weak vs Fire & Earth/Immune to Poison

Undead Monster

Elemental Defense

🔥	2
❄	1
⚡	1
💧	2
🌪	0
🍃	1
💧	1
✴	3

Status Defense

🗡	100	⚡	100	✴	X
🐍	X	☠	90		X
🛡	X	✋	X	☀	X
💀	X	⬧	100	%	100
🌀	X	🗡	100		
💧	X	⏱	80		
💀	X	👁	X		
⚡	X	🔇	X		

LV	HP	Str	Vit	Mag	Spr	Spd	Eva
1	350	35	17	61	36	9	5
10	3050	41	35	75	40	19	6
12	3650	43	39	78	41	21	6
—							
—							
—							
—							
—							

Locations

Presidential Train

A monster that posed as President Deling. Attacks with its deformed arms and status attacks.

Spells

Level	Draw			
1~12	Esuna	Double	Berserk	Zombie

Card

Drop Card	Mod Card	Mod (Rare)
—	—	—

LV 1~12
—

Item (Drop)

Level	Rate: 255/256			
	178/256	51/256	15/256	12/256
1~12	Zombie Powder	Zombie Powder	Zombie Powder	Zombie Powder

Item (Mug)

Level	Rate: 32/256			
	178/256	51/256	15/256	12/256
1~12	Phoenix Down	Phoenix Down	Phoenix Down	Phoenix Down

Gesper

HP	525~14,900	AP 2
EXP	32 (+8)	Weak vs Poison

— —

Elemental Defense

🔥	1
❄	1
⚡	1
💧	1
🌪	2
🍃	1
💧	1
✴	1

Status Defense

🗡	70	⚡	100	✴	60
🐍	80	☠	90		100
🛡	70	✋	50	☀	80
💀	80	⬧	100	%	100
🌀	80	🗡	100		
💧	60	⏱	80		
💀	70	👁	70		
⚡	80	🔇	100		

LV	HP	Str	Vit	Mag	Spr	Spd	Eva
1	525	6	10	51	60	4	3
10	860	16	10	62	61	7	3
20	1460	26	11	75	62	9	4
30	2300	37	12	87	63	12	4
40	3380	48	13	100	64	14	4
50	4700	58	14	112	65	17	5
60	6260	69	15	124	66	19	5
70	8060	79	15	135	67	22	5
80	10,100	89	16	147	68	24	6
90	12,380	99	17	158	69	27	6
100	14,900	109	18	169	70	29	6

Locations

Centra Ruins (Excavation Site; w/Laguna), Lunatic Pandora Laboratory (w/Laguna)

Esthar's defective anti-personnel weapon. Attacks enemies and allies alike. Degenerator destroys opponents.

Spells

Level	Draw			
1~19	Shell	Protect		
20~29	Shell	Protect	Float	
30~100	Shell	Protect	Confuse	Float

Card

Drop Card	Mod Card	Mod (Rare)
Gesper	Gesper	Iguion

LV 1~19	LV 20~29	LV 30~100
HP Recovery	HP Recovery	HP Recovery

Item (Drop)

Level	Rate: 255/256			
	178/256	51/256	15/256	12/256
1~19	Black Hole	M-Stone	Remedy	Remedy
20~29	Black Hole	Black Hole	Remedy	Remedy
30~100	Black Hole	Wizard Stone	Remedy	Remedy

Item (Mug)

Level	Rate: 32/256			
	178/256	51/256	15/256	12/256
1~19	Black Hole	Black Hole	Black Hole	Black Hole
20~29	Black Hole	Black Hole	Black Hole	Black Hole
30~100	Black Hole	Black Hole	Black Hole	Black Hole

GIM47N

HP	310~6300	AP 3
EXP	30 (+5)	Weak vs Thunder, Earth, & Water/Immune to Poison

— —

Elemental Defense

🔥	1
❄	1
⚡	1.5
💧	1.5
🌪	0
🍃	1
💧	2
✴	1

Status Defense

🗡	X	⚡	100	✴	60
🐍	X	☠	90		X
🛡	X	✋	50	☀	60
💀	60	⬧	X	%	100
🌀	X	🗡	100		
💧	50	⏱	X		
💀	X	👁	X		
⚡	40	🔇	X		

LV	HP	Str	Vit	Mag	Spr	Spd	Eva
1	310	11	40	2	6	2	0
10	450	21	40	3	7	3	1
20	700	32	41	5	8	3	1
30	1050	43	41	6	9	4	2
40	1500	53	42	7	11	5	3
50	2050	62	43	9	12	5	3
60	2700	71	43	10	13	6	4
70	3450	80	44	11	14	6	4
80	4300	88	45	12	16	7	5
90	5250	95	45	13	17	8	6
100	6300	102	46	13	18	8	6

Locations

Galbadia D-District Prison

An older type of Galbadian weapon. Has a laser cannon, but mostly punches using the steel orbs on both hands.

Spells

Level	Draw		
1~19	Cure	Esuna	
20~29	Esuna	Life	
30~100	Curaga	Esuna	Life

Card

Drop Card	Mod Card	Mod (Rare)
GIM47N	GIM47N	Oilboyle

LV 1~19	LV 20~29	LV 30~100
No Change	No Change	Damage (small) & Poison

Item (Drop)

Level	Rate: 255/256			
	178/256	51/256	15/256	12/256
1~19	Steel Orb	Screws	Steel Pipe	Steel Pipe
20~29	Steel Orb	Screws	Steel Pipe	Dynamo Stone
30~100	Steel Orb	Screws	Dynamo Stone	Dynamo Stone

Item (Mug)

Level	Rate: 32/256			
	178/256	51/256	15/256	12/256
1~19	Steel Orb	Steel Orb	Steel Orb	Steel Orb
20~29	Steel Orb	Steel Orb	Steel Orb	Steel Orb
30~100	Steel Orb	Steel Orb	Steel Orb	Steel Orb

GIM52A

HP	1431~19,400	AP	3			
EXP	30 (+8)		Weak vs Thunder, Earth, & Water/Immune to Poison			— —

Elemental Defense

💧	1
❄️	1
⚡	1.5
🌀	1.5
🌪️	0
🍃	1
💧	1.5
✴️	1

Status Defense

✝️	X	⚡	100	🌀	X
☠️	X	●	90	⛰️	X
🛡️	X	✋	50	☀️	80
☣️	X	✚	X	%	100
💊	X	K	X		
🌪️	X	✋	X		
☠️	X	✋	X		
🥚	X	🎮	X		

LV	HP	Str	Vit	Mag	Spr	Spd	Eva
1	1431	13	3	5	120	5	0
10	1850	26	12	15	121	6	1
20	2600	39	22	26	122	8	1
30	3650	53	32	37	123	9	2
40	5000	66	43	47	125	10	2
50	6650	79	53	57	126	11	3
60	8600	91	63	67	127	13	3
70	10,850	104	73	77	128	14	4
80	13,400	116	84	86	130	15	4
90	16,250	128	94	95	131	16	5
100	19,400	140	104	104	132	18	5

Locations: Galbadia D-District Prison, Lunatic Pandora

A machine made by Galbadia to support soldiers. Attacks with magic and missiles. The most advanced models used.

Spells

Level	Draw			
1~19	Haste	Slow		
20~29	Haste	Slow	Dispel	
30~100	Haste	Slow	Esuna	Dispel

Card

Drop Card	Mod Card	Mod (Rare)
—	—	—

Devour

LV 1~19	LV 20~29	LV 30~100
No Change	No Change	Damage (small) & Poison

Item (Drop)

Level	Rate: 255/256			
	178/256	51/256	15/256	12/256
1~19	Screw	Missile	Windmill	Fuel
20~29	Screw	Missile	Windmill	Fuel
30~100	Missile	Fuel	Windmill	Fuel

Item (Mug)

Level	Rate: 32/256			
	178/256	51/256	15/256	12/256
1~19	Missile	Missile	Missile	Missile
20~29	Missile	Missile	Missile	Missile
30~100	Missile	Missile	Missile	Missile

Glacial Eye

HP	205~3200	AP	1			
EXP	15 (+5)		Weak vs Fire/Immune to Ice			Flying Monster

Elemental Defense

💧	1.5
❄️	0
⚡	1
🌀	X
🌪️	1
🍃	1
💧	1
✴️	1

Status Defense

✝️	X	⚡	100	🌀	60
☠️	80	●	90	⛰️	100
🛡️	70	✋	50	☀️	80
☣️	80	✚	100	%	100
💊	30	K	100		
🌪️	50	✋	80		
☠️	70	✋	70		
🥚	100	🎮	100		

LV	HP	Str	Vit	Mag	Spr	Spd	Eva
1	205	3	12	5	100	10	0
10	275	9	15	12	100	10	0
20	400	15	18	20	101	11	1
30	575	21	22	28	101	11	1
40	800	26	25	36	102	12	1
50	1075	31	28	43	103	12	2
60	1400	35	32	51	103	13	2
70	1775	39	35	58	104	13	3
80	2200	42	38	65	105	13	3
90	2675	45	42	72	105	14	3
100	3200	47	45	79	106	14	3

Locations: Balamb (Alcauld Plains), Esthar City

A floating monster that uses Ice magic. When running low on HP, uses Vampire to suck HP from opponents.

Spells

Level	Draw		
1~19	Blizzard	Cure	Scan
20~29	Blizzara	Cure	Scan
30~100	Blizzaga	Curaga	Scan

Card

Drop Card	Mod Card	Mod (Rare)
Glacial Eye	Glacial Eye	Jumbo Cactuar

Devour

LV 1~19	LV 20~29	LV 30~100
HP Recovery	HP Recovery	HP Recovery

Item (Drop)

Level	Rate: 255/256			
	178/256	51/256	15/256	12/256
1~19	M-Stone	M-Stone	Vampire Fang	Arctic Wind
20~29	Vampire Fang	North Wind	Arctic Wind	Arctic Wind
30~100	Vampire Fang	North Wind	North Wind	North Wind

Item (Mug)

Level	Rate: 32/256			
	178/256	51/256	15/256	12/256
1~19	Vampire Fang	Arctic Wind	Arctic Wind	Arctic Wind
20~29	Vampire Fang	North Wind	North Wind	North Wind
30~100	Vampire Fang	North Wind	North Wind	North Wind

Granaldo

HP	1314~9700	AP	5			
EXP	40 (+10)		Weak vs Wind			Flying Monster

Elemental Defense

💧	1
❄️	1
⚡	1
🌀	X
🌪️	1
🍃	2
💧	X
✴️	1

Status Defense

✝️	10	⚡	100	🌀	X
☠️	40	●	90	⛰️	100
🛡️	X	✋	10	☀️	80
☣️	X	✚	100	%	100
💊	X	K	100		
🌪️	X	✋	40		
☠️	X	✋	X		
🥚	40	🎮	X		

LV	HP	Str	Vit	Mag	Spr	Spd	Eva
1	1314	2	3	2	3	10	0
10	1510	14	26	20	22	11	2
20	1860	26	51	40	43	13	3
30	2350	39	76	64	60	14	5
40	2980	51	101	79	86	15	7
50	3750	63	126	98	107	16	8
60	4660	74	151	117	128	18	10
70	5710	86	176	135	149	19	12
80	6900	97	201	153	171	20	13
90	8230	108	226	170	192	21	15
100	9700	118	251	188	213	23	17

Locations: Balamb Garden Training Center, Ultimecia Castle

A large, insect-type monster that is a survivor of some ancient race. Uses its large spikes and tail to attack.

Spells

Level	Draw			
1~19	Sleep	Blind	Shell	
20~29	Sleep	Blind	Shell	
30~100	Sleep	Confuse	Shell	Pain

Card

Drop Card	Mod Card	Mod (Rare)
—	—	—

Devour

LV 1~19	LV 20~29	LV 30~100
—	—	—

Item (Drop)

Level	Rate: 255/256			
	178/256	51/256	15/256	12/256
1~19	Wizard Stone	Wizard Stone	Wizard Stone	Wizard Stone
20~29	Wizard Stone	Wizard Stone	Wizard Stone	Wizard Stone
30~100	Wizard Stone	Wizard Stone	Wizard Stone	Wizard Stone

Item (Mug)

Level	Rate: 32/256			
	178/256	51/256	15/256	12/256
1~19	Wizard Stone	Wizard Stone	Wizard Stone	Wizard Stone
20~29	Wizard Stone	Wizard Stone	Wizard Stone	Wizard Stone
30~100	Wizard Stone	Wizard Stone	Wizard Stone	Wizard Stone

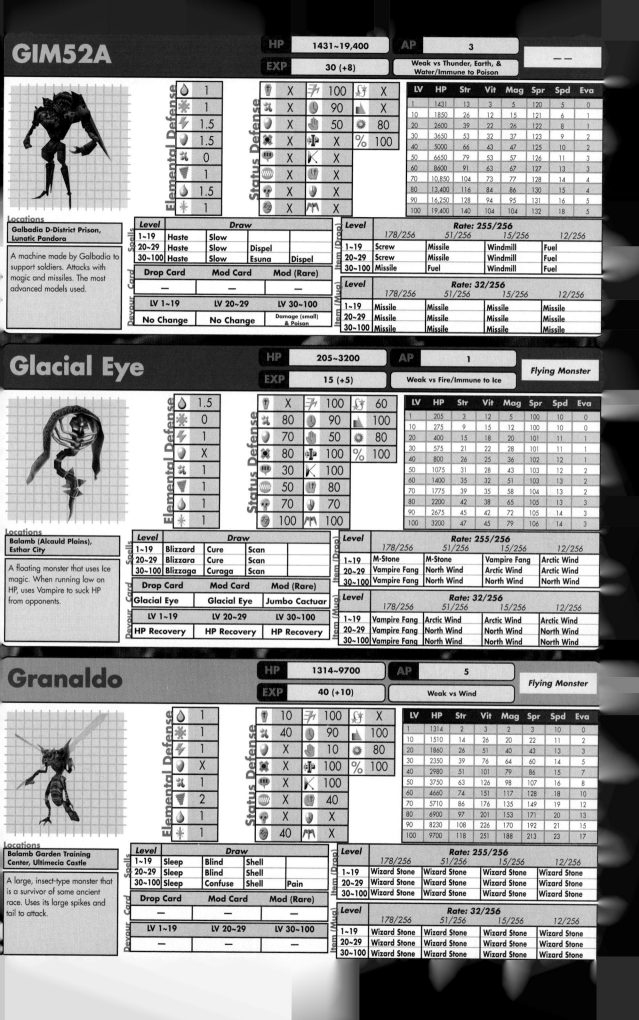

Grand Mantis

HP	5213~13,000	AP	4	— —
EXP	80 (+20)	Weak vs Ice & Thunder/ Strong vs Water		

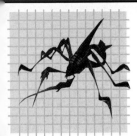

Elemental Defense

(water)	1
(ice)	2
(thunder)	2
(earth)	1
(wind)	1
(tornado)	1
(water)	0.5
(holy)	1

Status Defense

70	100		60
80	90		100
70	50		80
X	100		100
80	100		
60	80		
70	70		
80	100		

LV	HP	Str	Vit	Mag	Spr	Spd	Eva
1	5213	8	150	2	2	3	0
10	5395	18	152	3	6	4	0
20	5720	28	155	5	12	5	1
30	6135	37	157	6	17	6	1
40	6760	47	160	7	23	7	1
50	7475	56	162	9	28	8	2
60	8320	65	165	10	34	9	2
70	9295	73	167	11	39	10	3
80	10,400	81	170	12	45	11	3
90	11,635	89	172	13	50	12	3
100	13,000	97	175	13	56	13	4

Locations

Deling City (Sewer), Centra Ruins

Used to live in water, but now lives above ground. Skewers enemies with its large claw and causes major damage.

Spells

Level	Draw		
1~19	Water	Esuna	
20~29	Water	Esuna	
30~100	Water	Esuna	Life

Drop Card	Mod Card	Mod (Rare)
Grand Mantis	Grand Mantis	BGH251F2

Devour Card

LV 1~19	LV 20~29	LV 30~100
Full HP Recov.	Full HP Recov.	Full HP Recov.

Item (Drop)

Level	Rate: 255/256			
	178/256	51/256	15/256	12/256
1~19	Sharp Spike	Sharp Spike	Curse Spike	Water Crystal
20~29	Sharp Spike	Sharp Spike	Curse Spike	Water Crystal
30~100	Sharp Spike	Water Crystal	Water Crystal	Water Crystal

Item (Mug)

Level	Rate: 32/256			
	178/256	51/256	15/256	12/256
1~19	Sharp Spike	Sharp Spike	Sharp Spike	Sharp Spike
20~29	Sharp Spike	Sharp Spike	Sharp Spike	Sharp Spike
30~100	Sharp Spike	Sharp Spike	Sharp Spike	Sharp Spike

Grat

HP	209~5600	AP	2	— —
EXP	38 (+10)	Weak vs Fire & Ice		

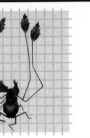

Elemental Defense

(water)	1.3
(ice)	1.3
(thunder)	1
(earth)	1
(wind)	1
(tornado)	1
(water)	1
(holy)	1

Status Defense

X	X		70
50	X		X
40	X		X
X	X		100
X	X		
X	X		
X	50		
70	X		

LV	HP	Str	Vit	Mag	Spr	Spd	Eva
1	209	3	3	2	8	8	0
10	335	14	3	12	9	9	0
20	560	26	4	24	10	10	1
30	875	38	4	35	11	11	1
40	1280	50	5	46	12	11	1
50	1775	61	6	57	13	12	2
60	2360	73	6	68	14	13	3
70	3035	84	7	78	15	14	3
80	3800	96	7	89	16	15	4
90	4655	107	8	99	17	16	4
100	5600	118	9	110	18	16	4

Locations

Balamb Garden Training Center, Balamb Garden

Its body is mostly a digestive bag. Digests enemies by catching them in its vine. Uses a gas attack that causes Sleep.

Spells

Level	Draw		
1~19	Sleep	Silence	
20~29	Sleep	Silence	Berserk
30~100	Sleep	Silence	Berserk

Drop Card	Mod Card	Mod (Rare)
Grat	Grat	Shumi Tribe

Devour Card

LV 1~19	LV 20~29	LV 30~100
Damage (small) & Poison	Damage (small) & Poison	Damage (small) & Poison

Item (Drop)

Level	Rate: 255/256			
	178/256	51/256	15/256	12/256
1~19	Sleep Powder	Silence Powder	Poison Powder	Poison Powder
20~29	Sleep Powder	Silence Powder	Poison Powder	Poison Powder
30~100	Sleep Powder	Silence Powder	Poison Powder	Poison Powder

Item (Mug)

Level	Rate: 32/256			
	178/256	51/256	15/256	12/256
1~19	Silence Powder	Silence Powder	Silence Powder	Silence Powder
20~29	Silence Powder	Silence Powder	Silence Powder	Silence Powder
30~100	Silence Powder	Silence Powder	Silence Powder	Silence Powder

Grendel

HP	2131~30,000	AP	6	— —
EXP	80 (+15)	Weak vs Earth, Wind, & Holy		

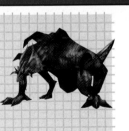

Elemental Defense

(water)	1
(ice)	1
(thunder)	1
(earth)	1.5
(wind)	1
(tornado)	1.5
(water)	1
(holy)	1.5

Status Defense

30	100		60
X	90		100
20	50		80
80	100		100
80	100		
60	5		
10	20		
80	100		

LV	HP	Str	Vit	Mag	Spr	Spd	Eva
1	2131	22	51	52	121	10	2
10	3450	41	58	70	127	11	3
20	5200	62	66	89	135	12	3
30	7250	83	73	109	141	13	4
40	9600	103	81	128	149	14	5
50	12,250	124	89	147	156	15	6
60	15,200	145	96	165	163	16	6
70	18,450	165	104	184	170	17	7
80	22,000	185	112	202	178	18	8
90	25,850	206	119	220	185	19	8
100	30,000	226	127	238	192	20	8

Locations

Timber (Roshfall Forest), Deep Sea Research Center (Work Zone)

A smaller type of dragon, sometimes appears in groups of 2. May be more dangerous than other dragons.

Spells

Level	Draw		
1~19	Fire	Blizzard	Double
20~29	Fira	Blizzara	Double
30~100	Firaga	Blizzaga	Double

Drop Card	Mod Card	Mod (Rare)
Grendel	Grendel	Tiamat

Devour Card

LV 1~19	LV 20~29	LV 30~100
Full HP Recov.	Full HP Recov.	Full HP Recov.

Item (Drop)

Level	Rate: 255/256			
	178/256	51/256	15/256	12/256
1~19	Dragon Fang	Dragon Fang	Dragon Skin	Dragon Fang
20~29	Dragon Fin	Dragon Fang	Fury Fragment	Fury Fragment
30~100	Dragon Fin	Dragon Fin	Fury Fragment	Fury Fragment

Item (Mug)

Level	Rate: 32/256			
	178/256	51/256	15/256	12/256
1~19	Dragon Fin	Dragon Fin	Dragon Fin	Dragon Fin
20~29	Dragon Fin	Dragon Fin	Dragon Fin	Dragon Fin
30~100	Dragon Fin	Dragon Fin	Power Wrist	Power Wrist

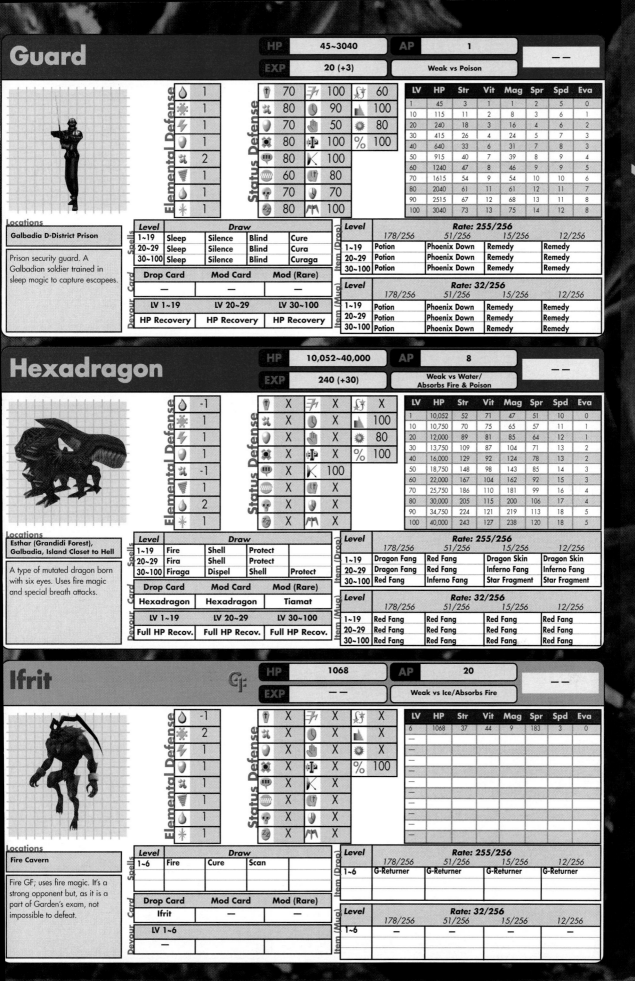

Guard

HP	45~3040	AP	1	— —
EXP	20 (+3)		Weak vs Poison	

Elemental Defense

💧	1				
❄	1				
⚡	1				
🌀	1				
🔥	2				
🌪	1				
💧	1				
✴	1				

Status Defense

⚰	70	⚔	100	👁	60
🗡	80	⭕	90	⛰	100
🥚	70	✋	50	☀	80
🥚	80	✚	100	%	100
💀	80	⚔	100		
💀	60	👊	80		
☠	70	⭕	70		
💤	80	🙌	100		

LV	HP	Str	Vit	Mag	Spr	Spd	Eva
1	45	3	1	1	2	5	0
10	115	11	2	8	3	6	1
20	240	18	3	16	4	6	1
30	415	26	4	24	5	7	2
40	640	33	6	31	7	8	3
50	915	40	7	39	8	9	4
60	1240	47	8	46	9	9	5
70	1615	54	9	54	10	10	6
80	2040	61	11	61	12	11	7
90	2515	67	12	68	13	11	8
100	3040	73	13	75	14	12	8

Locations

Galbadia D-District Prison

Prison security guard. A Galbadian soldier trained in sleep magic to capture escapees.

Spells

Level	Draw			
1~19	Sleep	Silence	Blind	Cure
20~29	Sleep	Silence	Blind	Cura
30~100	Sleep	Silence	Blind	Curaga

Card

Drop Card	Mod Card	Mod (Rare)
—	—	—

Devour

LV 1~19	LV 20~29	LV 30~100
HP Recovery	HP Recovery	HP Recovery

Item (Drop)

Level	Rate: 255/256			
	178/256	51/256	15/256	12/256
1~19	Potion	Phoenix Down	Remedy	Remedy
20~29	Potion	Phoenix Down	Remedy	Remedy
30~100	Potion	Phoenix Down	Remedy	Remedy

Item (Mug)

Level	Rate: 32/256			
	178/256	51/256	15/256	12/256
1~19	Potion	Phoenix Down	Remedy	Remedy
20~29	Potion	Phoenix Down	Remedy	Remedy
30~100	Potion	Phoenix Down	Remedy	Remedy

Hexadragon

HP	10,052~40,000	AP	8	— —
EXP	240 (+30)		Weak vs Water/ Absorbs Fire & Poison	

Elemental Defense

💧	-1
❄	1
⚡	1
🥚	1
🔥	-1
🌪	1
💧	2
✴	1

Status Defense

⚰	X	⚔	X	👁	X
🗡	X	⭕	X	⛰	100
🥚	X	✋	X	☀	80
🥚	X	✚	X	%	100
💀	X	⚔	100		
💀	X	👊	X		
☠	X	⭕	X		
💤	X	🙌	X		

LV	HP	Str	Vit	Mag	Spr	Spd	Eva
1	10,052	52	71	47	51	10	0
10	10,750	70	75	65	57	11	1
20	12,000	89	81	85	64	12	1
30	13,750	109	87	104	71	13	2
40	16,000	129	92	124	78	13	2
50	18,750	148	98	143	85	14	3
60	22,000	167	104	162	92	15	3
70	25,750	186	110	181	99	16	4
80	30,000	205	115	200	106	17	4
90	34,750	224	121	219	113	18	5
100	40,000	243	127	238	120	18	5

Locations

Esthar (Grandidi Forest), Galbadia, Island Closet to Hell

A type of mutated dragon born with six eyes. Uses fire magic and special breath attacks.

Spells

Level	Draw			
1~19	Fire	Shell	Protect	
20~29	Fira	Shell	Protect	
30~100	Firaga	Dispel	Shell	Protect

Card

Drop Card	Mod Card	Mod (Rare)
Hexadragon	Hexadragon	Tiamat

Devour

LV 1~19	LV 20~29	LV 30~100
Full HP Recov.	Full HP Recov.	Full HP Recov.

Item (Drop)

Level	Rate: 255/256			
	178/256	51/256	15/256	12/256
1~19	Dragon Fang	Red Fang	Dragon Skin	Dragon Skin
20~29	Dragon Fang	Red Fang	Inferno Fang	Inferno Fang
30~100	Red Fang	Inferno Fang	Star Fragment	Star Fragment

Item (Mug)

Level	Rate: 32/256			
	178/256	51/256	15/256	12/256
1~19	Red Fang	Red Fang	Red Fang	Red Fang
20~29	Red Fang	Red Fang	Red Fang	Red Fang
30~100	Red Fang	Red Fang	Red Fang	Red Fang

Ifrit

GF

HP	1068	AP	20	— —
EXP	— —		Weak vs Ice/Absorbs Fire	

Elemental Defense

💧	-1
❄	2
⚡	1
🥚	1
🔥	1
🌪	1
💧	1
✴	1

Status Defense

⚰	X	⚔	X	👁	X
🗡	X	⭕	X	⛰	X
🥚	X	✋	X	☀	X
🥚	X	✚	X	%	100
💀	X	⚔	X		
💀	X	👊	X		
☠	X	⭕	X		
💤	X	🙌	X		

LV	HP	Str	Vit	Mag	Spr	Spd	Eva
6	1068	37	44	9	183	3	0
—							
—							
—							
—							
—							
—							
—							
—							
—							
—							

Locations

Fire Cavern

Fire GF; uses fire magic. It's a strong opponent but, as it is a part of Garden's exam, not impossible to defeat.

Spells

Level	Draw		
1~6	Fire	Cure	Scan

Card

Drop Card	Mod Card	Mod (Rare)
Ifrit	—	—

Devour

LV 1~6		
—		

Item (Drop)

Level	Rate: 255/256			
	178/256	51/256	15/256	12/256
1~6	G-Returner	G-Returner	G-Returner	G-Returner

Item (Mug)

Level	Rate: 32/256			
	178/256	51/256	15/256	12/256
1~6	—	—	—	—

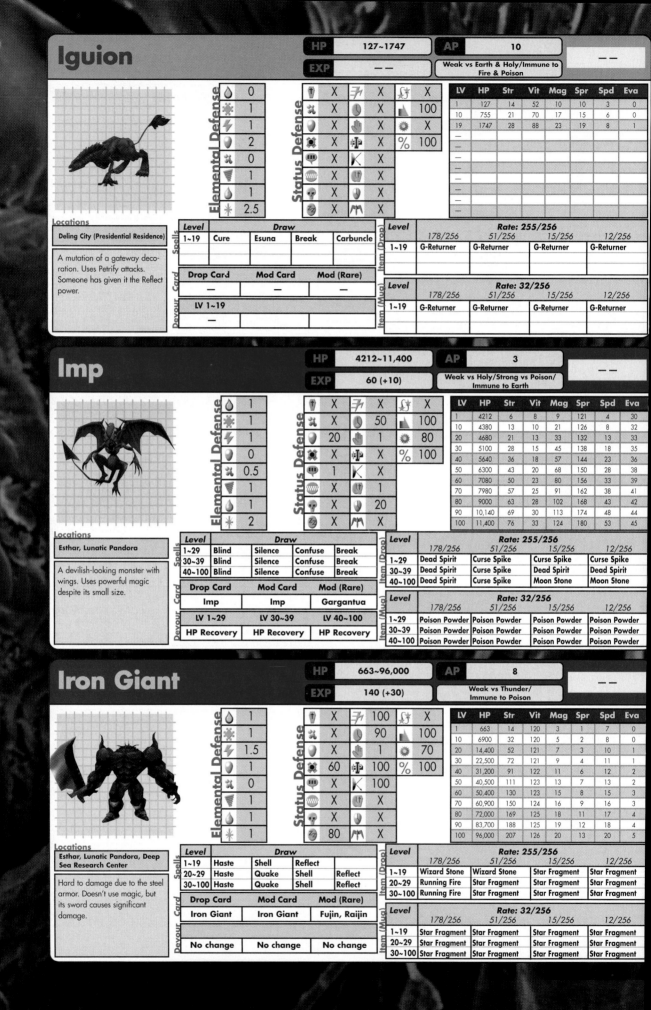

Iguion

	HP	127~1747		AP	10		--
	EXP	--		Weak vs Earth & Holy/Immune to Fire & Poison			

Elemental Defense

💧	0
❄	1
⚡	1
🌀	2
🍃	0
🌊	1
💧	1
✦	2.5

Status Defense

⚰	X	🗡	X	🌀	X
☠	X	⏱	X	▲	100
🛡	X	✋	X	☀	X
🕷	X	🔱	X	%	100
💀	X	🗡	X		
🔻	X	✋	X		
💀	X	✋	X		
💤	X	🕸	X		

LV	HP	Str	Vit	Mag	Spr	Spd	Eva
1	127	14	52	10	10	3	0
10	755	21	70	17	15	6	0
19	1747	28	88	23	19	8	1
—							
—							
—							
—							

Locations
Deling City (Presidential Residence)

A mutation of a gateway decoration. Uses Petrify attacks. Someone has given it the Reflect power.

Spells

Level	Draw			
1~19	Cure	Esuna	Break	Carbuncle

Devour / Card

Drop Card	Mod Card	Mod (Rare)
—	—	—
LV 1~19		

Item (Drop)

Level	Rate: 255/256			
	178/256	51/256	15/256	12/256
1~19	G-Returner	G-Returner	G-Returner	G-Returner

Item (Mug)

Level	Rate: 32/256			
	178/256	51/256	15/256	12/256
1~19	G-Returner	G-Returner	G-Returner	G-Returner

Imp

	HP	4212~11,400		AP	3		--
	EXP	60 (+10)		Weak vs Holy/Strong vs Poison/Immune to Earth			

Elemental Defense

💧	1
❄	1
⚡	1
🌀	0
🍃	0.5
🌊	1
💧	1
✦	2

Status Defense

⚰	X	🗡	X	🌀	X
☠	X	⏱	50	▲	100
🛡	20	✋	1	☀	80
🕷	X	🔱	X	%	100
💀	1	🗡	X		
🔻	X	✋	1		
💀	X	✋	20		
💤	X	🕸	X		

LV	HP	Str	Vit	Mag	Spr	Spd	Eva
1	4212	6	8	9	121	4	30
10	4380	13	10	21	126	8	32
20	4680	21	13	33	132	13	33
30	5100	28	15	45	138	18	35
40	5640	36	18	57	144	23	36
50	6300	43	20	68	150	28	38
60	7080	50	23	80	156	33	39
70	7980	57	25	91	162	38	41
80	9000	63	28	102	168	43	42
90	10,140	69	30	113	174	48	44
100	11,400	76	33	124	180	53	45

Locations
Esthar, Lunatic Pandora

A devilish-looking monster with wings. Uses powerful magic despite its small size.

Spells

Level	Draw			
1~29	Blind	Silence	Confuse	Break
30~39	Blind	Silence	Confuse	Break
40~100	Blind	Silence	Confuse	Break

Devour / Card

Drop Card	Mod Card	Mod (Rare)
Imp	Imp	Gargantua
LV 1~29	LV 30~39	LV 40~100
HP Recovery	HP Recovery	HP Recovery

Item (Drop)

Level	Rate: 255/256			
	178/256	51/256	15/256	12/256
1~29	Dead Spirit	Curse Spike	Curse Spike	Curse Spike
30~39	Dead Spirit	Curse Spike	Dead Spirit	Dead Spirit
40~100	Dead Spirit	Curse Spike	Moon Stone	Moon Stone

Item (Mug)

Level	Rate: 32/256			
	178/256	51/256	15/256	12/256
1~29	Poison Powder	Poison Powder	Poison Powder	Poison Powder
30~39	Poison Powder	Poison Powder	Poison Powder	Poison Powder
40~100	Poison Powder	Poison Powder	Poison Powder	Poison Powder

---

Iron Giant

	HP	663~96,000		AP	8		--
	EXP	140 (+30)		Weak vs Thunder/Immune to Poison			

Elemental Defense

💧	1
❄	1
⚡	1.5
🌀	1
🍃	0
🌊	1
💧	1
✦	1

Status Defense

⚰	X	🗡	100	🌀	X
☠	X	⏱	90	▲	100
🛡	X	✋	1	☀	70
🕷	60	🔱	100	%	100
💀	X	🗡	100		
🔻	X	✋	X		
💀	X	✋	X		
💤	80	🕸	X		

LV	HP	Str	Vit	Mag	Spr	Spd	Eva
1	663	14	120	3	1	7	0
10	6900	32	120	5	2	8	0
20	14,400	52	121	7	3	10	1
30	22,500	72	121	9	4	11	1
40	31,200	91	122	11	6	12	2
50	40,500	111	123	13	7	13	2
60	50,400	130	123	15	8	15	3
70	60,900	150	124	16	9	16	3
80	72,000	169	125	18	11	17	4
90	83,700	188	125	19	12	18	4
100	96,000	207	126	20	13	20	5

Locations
Esthar, Lunatic Pandora, Deep Sea Research Center

Hard to damage due to the steel armor. Doesn't use magic, but its sword causes significant damage.

Spells

Level	Draw			
1~19	Haste	Shell	Reflect	
20~29	Haste	Quake	Shell	Reflect
30~100	Haste	Quake	Shell	Reflect

Devour / Card

Drop Card	Mod Card	Mod (Rare)
Iron Giant	Iron Giant	Fujin, Raijin
No change	No change	No change

Item (Drop)

Level	Rate: 255/256			
	178/256	51/256	15/256	12/256
1~19	Wizard Stone	Wizard Stone	Star Fragment	Star Fragment
20~29	Running Fire	Star Fragment	Star Fragment	Star Fragment
30~100	Running Fire	Star Fragment	Star Fragment	Star Fragment

Item (Mug)

Level	Rate: 32/256			
	178/256	51/256	15/256	12/256
1~19	Star Fragment	Star Fragment	Star Fragment	Star Fragment
20~29	Star Fragment	Star Fragment	Star Fragment	Star Fragment
30~100	Star Fragment	Star Fragment	Star Fragment	Star Fragment

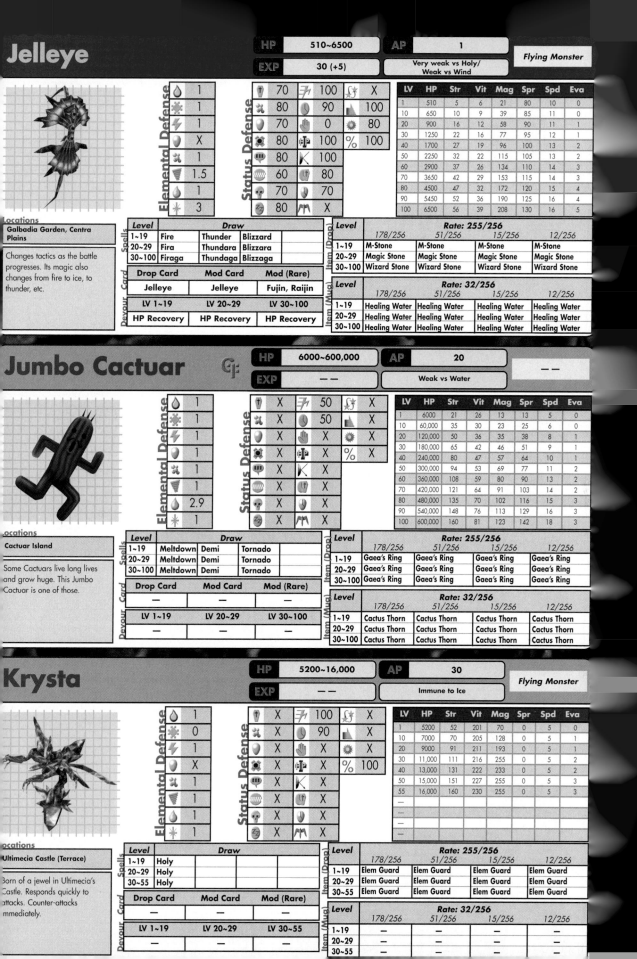

Jelleye

HP	510~6500	AP	1
EXP	30 (+5)		Very weak vs Holy / Weak vs Wind

Flying Monster

Elemental Defense: 1, 1, 1, X, 1, 1.5, 1, 3

Status Defense: 70, 80, 70, 80, 80, 60, 70, 80 / 100, 90, 0, 100, 100, 80, 70, X / X, 100, 80, 100, 100

LV	HP	Str	Vit	Mag	Spr	Spd	Eva
1	510	5	6	21	80	10	0
10	650	10	9	39	85	11	0
20	900	16	12	58	90	11	1
30	1250	22	16	77	95	12	1
40	1700	27	19	96	100	13	2
50	2250	32	22	115	105	13	2
60	2900	37	26	134	110	14	3
70	3650	42	29	153	115	14	3
80	4500	47	32	172	120	15	4
90	5450	51	36	190	125	16	4
100	6500	56	39	208	130	16	5

Locations: Galbadia Garden, Centra Plains

Changes tactics as the battle progresses. Its magic also changes from fire to ice, to thunder, etc.

Spells — Draw

Level			
1~19	Fire	Thunder	Blizzard
20~29	Fira	Thundara	Blizzara
30~100	Firaga	Thundaga	Blizzaga

Card

Drop Card	Mod Card	Mod (Rare)
Jelleye	Jelleye	Fujin, Raijin

Devour

LV 1~19	LV 20~29	LV 30~100
HP Recovery	HP Recovery	HP Recovery

Item (Drop) — Rate: 255/256

Level	178/256	51/256	15/256	12/256
1~19	M-Stone	M-Stone	M-Stone	M-Stone
20~29	Magic Stone	Magic Stone	Magic Stone	Magic Stone
30~100	Wizard Stone	Wizard Stone	Wizard Stone	Wizard Stone

Item (Mug) — Rate: 32/256

Level	178/256	51/256	15/256	12/256
1~19	Healing Water	Healing Water	Healing Water	Healing Water
20~29	Healing Water	Healing Water	Healing Water	Healing Water
30~100	Healing Water	Healing Water	Healing Water	Healing Water

---

Jumbo Cactuar

HP	6000~600,000	AP	20
EXP	— —		Weak vs Water

Elemental Defense: 1, 1, 1, 1, 1, 1, 2.9, 1

Status Defense: X (all) / 50, 50, X, X, X, X, X, X / X (all)

LV	HP	Str	Vit	Mag	Spr	Spd	Eva
1	6000	21	26	13	13	5	0
10	60,000	35	30	23	25	6	0
20	120,000	50	36	35	38	8	1
30	180,000	65	42	46	51	9	1
40	240,000	80	47	57	64	10	1
50	300,000	94	53	69	77	11	2
60	360,000	108	59	80	90	13	2
70	420,000	121	64	91	103	14	2
80	480,000	135	70	102	116	15	3
90	540,000	148	76	113	129	16	3
100	600,000	160	81	123	142	18	3

Locations: Cactuar Island

Some Cactuars live long lives and grow huge. This Jumbo Cactuar is one of those.

Spells — Draw

Level			
1~19	Meltdown	Demi	Tornado
20~29	Meltdown	Demi	Tornado
30~100	Meltdown	Demi	Tornado

Card

Drop Card	Mod Card	Mod (Rare)
—	—	—

Devour

LV 1~19	LV 20~29	LV 30~100
—	—	—

Item (Drop) — Rate: 255/256

Level	178/256	51/256	15/256	12/256
1~19	Gaea's Ring	Gaea's Ring	Gaea's Ring	Gaea's Ring
20~29	Gaea's Ring	Gaea's Ring	Gaea's Ring	Gaea's Ring
30~100	Gaea's Ring	Gaea's Ring	Gaea's Ring	Gaea's Ring

Item (Mug) — Rate: 32/256

Level	178/256	51/256	15/256	12/256
1~19	Cactus Thorn	Cactus Thorn	Cactus Thorn	Cactus Thorn
20~29	Cactus Thorn	Cactus Thorn	Cactus Thorn	Cactus Thorn
30~100	Cactus Thorn	Cactus Thorn	Cactus Thorn	Cactus Thorn

Krysta

HP	5200~16,000	AP	30
EXP	— —		Immune to Ice

Flying Monster

Elemental Defense: 1, 0, 1, X, 1, 1, 1, 1

Status Defense: X (all) / 100, 90, X, X, X, X, X, X / X, X, X, 100

LV	HP	Str	Vit	Mag	Spr	Spd	Eva
1	5200	52	201	70	0	5	0
10	7000	70	205	128	0	5	1
20	9000	91	211	193	0	5	1
30	11,000	111	216	255	0	5	2
40	13,000	131	222	233	0	5	2
50	15,000	151	227	255	0	5	3
55	16,000	160	230	255	0	5	3

Locations: Ultimecia Castle (Terrace)

Born of a jewel in Ultimecia's Castle. Responds quickly to attacks. Counter-attacks immediately.

Spells — Draw

Level			
1~19	Holy		
20~29	Holy		
30~55	Holy		

Card

Drop Card	Mod Card	Mod (Rare)
—	—	—

Devour

LV 1~19	LV 20~29	LV 30~55

Item (Drop) — Rate: 255/256

Level	178/256	51/256	15/256	12/256
1~19	Elem Guard	Elem Guard	Elem Guard	Elem Guard
20~29	Elem Guard	Elem Guard	Elem Guard	Elem Guard
30~55	Elem Guard	Elem Guard	Elem Guard	Elem Guard

Item (Mug) — Rate: 32/256

Level	178/256	51/256	15/256	12/256
1~19	—	—	—	—
20~29	—	—	—	—
30~55	—	—	—	—

Lefty

HP	1821~13,800	AP	3
EXP	40 (+10)	**Weak vs Holy**	— —

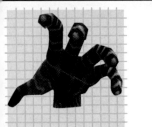

Elemental Defense: 1 / 1 / 1 / 1 / 1 / 1 / 1 / 2

Status Defense:

X		X		X	
80		X		100	
X		X		X	
80		100		100	
80		100			
X		X			
X		X			
X		X			

LV	HP	Str	Vit	Mag	Spr	Spd	Eva
1	1821	1	1	33	180	2	0
10	2100	6	1	52	181	3	1
20	2600	11	2	72	182	4	1
30	3300	16	3	93	184	5	2
40	4200	20	4	113	185	6	2
50	5300	25	5	134	187	7	3
60	6600	29	6	154	188	8	3
70	8100	33	7	174	190	9	4
80	9800	37	8	194	191	10	4
90	11,700	40	9	214	192	11	5
100	13,800	44	10	234	194	12	5

Locations
Timber (Shenand Hill), Great Salt Lake

A large left hand protruding from the earth. At higher levels, sometimes cures party members with status abnormalities.

Spells — Draw

Level	Draw			
1~19	Blind	Drain		
20~29	Blind	Drain	Slow	
30~100	Bio	Demi	Quake	Regen

Devour Card

Drop Card	Mod Card	Mod (Rare)
Vsyage	—	—

LV 1~19	LV 20~29	LV 30~100
—		

Item (Drop)

Level	Rate: 255/256			
	178/256	51/256	15/256	12/256
1~19	M-Stone	M-Stone	Life Ring	Life Ring
20~29	Life Ring	Magic Stone	Magic Stone	Regen Ring
30~100	Life Ring	Wizard Stone	Regen Ring	Regen Ring

Item (Mug)

Level	Rate: 32/256			
	178/256	51/256	15/256	12/256
1~19	Life Ring	Life Ring	Life Ring	Life Ring
20~29	Life Ring	Life Ring	Life Ring	Life Ring
30~100	Life Ring	Life Ring	Life Ring	Life Ring

Malboro

HP	1410~146,000	AP	12
EXP	220 (+40)	**Weak vs Fire & Ice/Immune to Earth/Absorbs Poison**	— —

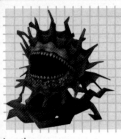

Elemental Defense: 2 / 1.5 / 1 / 0 / -1 / 1 / 1 / 1

Status Defense:

X		X		X	
X		X		100	
X		X		80	
X		X		100	
X		100			
X		X			
X		X			
X		X			

LV	HP	Str	Vit	Mag	Spr	Spd	Eva
1	1410	26	10	4	8	4	0
10	14,150	39	11	27	9	6	1
20	28,400	53	12	52	10	7	1
30	42,750	67	13	78	11	8	2
40	57,200	80	15	102	13	10	2
50	71,750	94	16	127	14	11	3
60	86,400	107	17	152	15	12	3
70	101,150	120	18	177	16	14	4
80	116,000	133	20	202	18	15	4
90	130,950	145	21	226	19	16	5
100	146,000	158	22	251	20	18	6

Locations
Great Plains of Esthar, Grandidi Forest

Uses Bad Breath, which causes all status abnormalities. Be ready with status defenses before fighting.

Spells — Draw

Level	Draw		
1~19	Bio		
20~29	Bio	Demi	
30~100	Bio	Demi	Quake

Devour Card

Drop Card	Mod Card	Mod (Rare)
Malboro	Malboro	Tonberry King

LV 1~19	LV 20~29	LV 30~100
Damage (large) & random effect	Damage (large) & random effect	Spirit +1

Item (Drop)

Level	Rate: 255/256			
	178/256	51/256	15/256	12/256
1~19	Malboro Tentacle	Curse Spike	Curse Spike	Curse Spike
20~29	Malboro Tentacle	Curse Spike	Curse Spike	Curse Spike
30~100	Malboro Tentacle	Curse Spike	Hypno Crown	Hypno Crown

Item (Mug)

Level	Rate: 32/256			
	178/256	51/256	15/256	12/256
1~19	Malboro Tentacle	Malboro Tentacle	Malboro Tentacle	Malboro Tentacle
20~29	Malboro Tentacle	Malboro Tentacle	Malboro Tentacle	Malboro Tentacle
30~100	Malboro Tentacle	Malboro Tentacle	Malboro Tentacle	Malboro Tentacle

---

Mesmerize

HP	460~6450	AP	2
EXP	15 (+4)		— —

Elemental Defense: 1 / 1 / 1 / 1 / 1 / 1 / 1 / 1

Status Defense:

70		100		60	
80		90		100	
70		X		80	
80		100		100	
X		100			
X		80			
70		70			
X		X			

LV	HP	Str	Vit	Mag	Spr	Spd	Eva
1	400	5	11	6	26	12	0
10	600	13	16	15	33	16	1
20	850	20	22	25	41	20	1
30	1200	28	28	35	50	24	2
40	1650	36	34	45	58	27	3
50	2200	43	40	55	66	31	4
60	2850	50	46	64	75	35	4
70	3600	58	52	74	83	39	5
80	4450	65	58	83	91	42	6
90	5400	72	64	92	100	46	6
100	6450	78	70	101	108	50	7

Locations
Trabia (Bika Snowfield)

Has a large blade for a horn. This blade has a healing effect when used as an item or to make magic.

Spells — Draw

Level	Draw			
1~19	Cure	Esuna		
20~29	Cura	Esuna	Life	
30~100	Curaga	Esuna	Dispel	Life

Devour Card

Drop Card	Mod Card	Mod (Rare)
Mesmerize	Mesmerize	Propagator

LV 1~19	LV 20~29	LV 30~100
Full HP Recov.	Full HP Recov. & Status Recov.	Full HP Recov. & Status Recov.

Item (Drop)

Level	Rate: 255/256			
	178/256	51/256	15/256	12/256
1~19	Life Ring	Mesmerize Blade	Healing Water	Healing Water
20~29	Life Ring	Mesmerize Blade	Healing Mail	Healing Mail
30~100	Mezmerize Blade	Life Ring	Regen Ring	Healing Mail

Item (Mug)

Level	Rate: 32/256			
	178/256	51/256	15/256	12/256
1~19	Mezmerize Blade	Mesmerize Blade	Mesmerize Blade	Mesmerize Blade
20~29	Mezmerize Blade	Mesmerize Blade	Mesmerize Blade	Mesmerize Blade
30~100	Mezmerize Blade	Mesmerize Blade	Mesmerize Blade	Mesmerize Blade

Minotaur

HP	578~27,218
AP	20
EXP	— —

Weak vs Wind & Poison/ Absorbs Earth

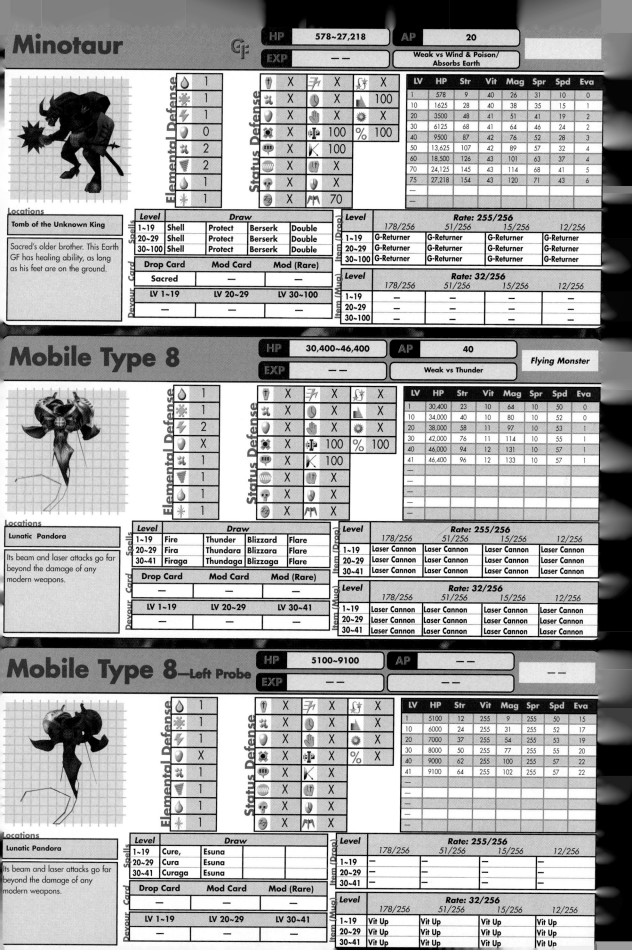

Elemental Defense: 1, 1, 1, 0, 2, 2, 1, 1

Status Defense: X, X, X, X, X, X, X, X (various), 100, 100, 100, 100, 70

LV	HP	Str	Vit	Mag	Spr	Spd	Eva
1	578	9	40	26	31	10	0
10	1625	28	40	38	35	15	1
20	3500	48	41	51	41	19	2
30	6125	68	41	64	46	24	2
40	9500	87	42	76	52	28	3
50	13,625	107	42	89	57	32	4
60	18,500	126	43	101	63	37	4
70	24,125	145	43	114	68	41	5
75	27,218	154	43	120	71	43	6
—							

Locations

Tomb of the Unknown King

Sacred's older brother. This Earth GF has healing ability, as long as his feet are on the ground.

Spells — Draw

Level	Draw			
1~19	Shell	Protect	Berserk	Double
20~29	Shell	Protect	Berserk	Double
30~100	Shell	Protect	Berserk	Double

Card

Drop Card	Mod Card	Mod (Rare)
Sacred	—	—

Devour Card

LV 1~19	LV 20~29	LV 30~100
—	—	—

Item (Drop) Rate: 255/256

Level	178/256	51/256	15/256	12/256
1~19	G-Returner	G-Returner	G-Returner	G-Returner
20~29	G-Returner	G-Returner	G-Returner	G-Returner
30~100	G-Returner	G-Returner	G-Returner	G-Returner

Item (Mug) Rate: 32/256

Level	178/256	51/256	15/256	12/256
1~19	—	—	—	—
20~29	—	—	—	—
30~100	—	—	—	—

Mobile Type 8

HP	30,400~46,400
AP	40
EXP	— —

Weak vs Thunder

Flying Monster

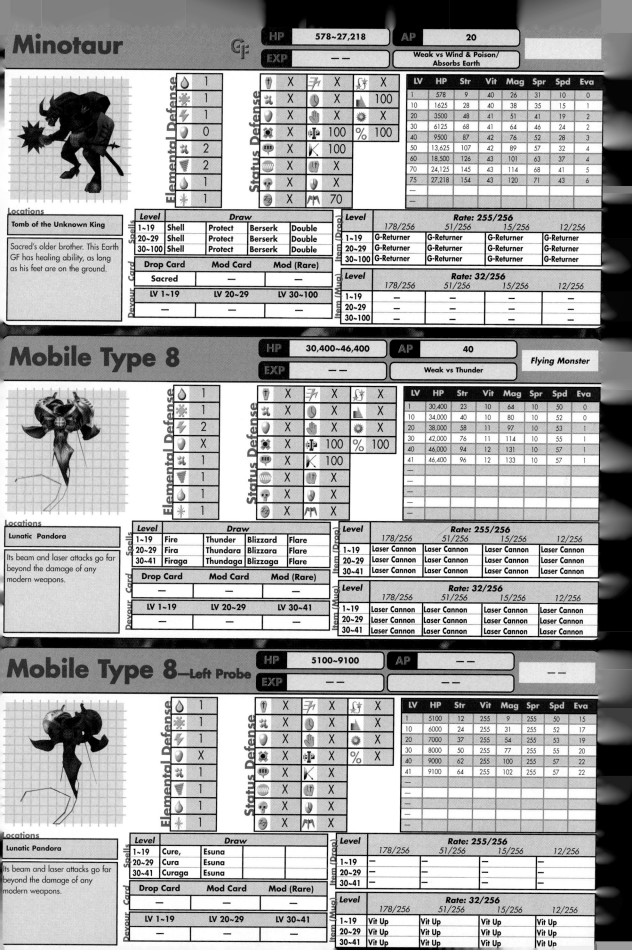

Elemental Defense: 1, 1, 2, X, 1, 1, 1, 1

Status Defense: X … 100, 100

LV	HP	Str	Vit	Mag	Spr	Spd	Eva
1	30,400	23	10	64	10	50	0
10	34,000	40	10	80	10	52	0
20	38,000	58	11	97	10	53	1
30	42,000	76	11	114	10	55	1
40	46,000	94	12	131	10	57	1
41	46,400	96	12	133	10	57	1

Locations

Lunatic Pandora

Its beam and laser attacks go far beyond the damage of any modern weapons.

Spells — Draw

Level	Draw			
1~19	Fire	Thunder	Blizzard	Flare
20~29	Fira	Thundara	Blizzara	Flare
30~41	Firaga	Thundaga	Blizzaga	Flare

Card

Drop Card	Mod Card	Mod (Rare)
—	—	—

Devour Card

LV 1~19	LV 20~29	LV 30~41
—	—	—

Item (Drop) Rate: 255/256

Level	178/256	51/256	15/256	12/256
1~19	Laser Cannon	Laser Cannon	Laser Cannon	Laser Cannon
20~29	Laser Cannon	Laser Cannon	Laser Cannon	Laser Cannon
30~41	Laser Cannon	Laser Cannon	Laser Cannon	Laser Cannon

Item (Mug) Rate: 32/256

Level	178/256	51/256	15/256	12/256
1~19	Laser Cannon	Laser Cannon	Laser Cannon	Laser Cannon
20~29	Laser Cannon	Laser Cannon	Laser Cannon	Laser Cannon
30~41	Laser Cannon	Laser Cannon	Laser Cannon	Laser Cannon

Mobile Type 8—Left Probe

HP	5100~9100
AP	— —
EXP	— —

— —

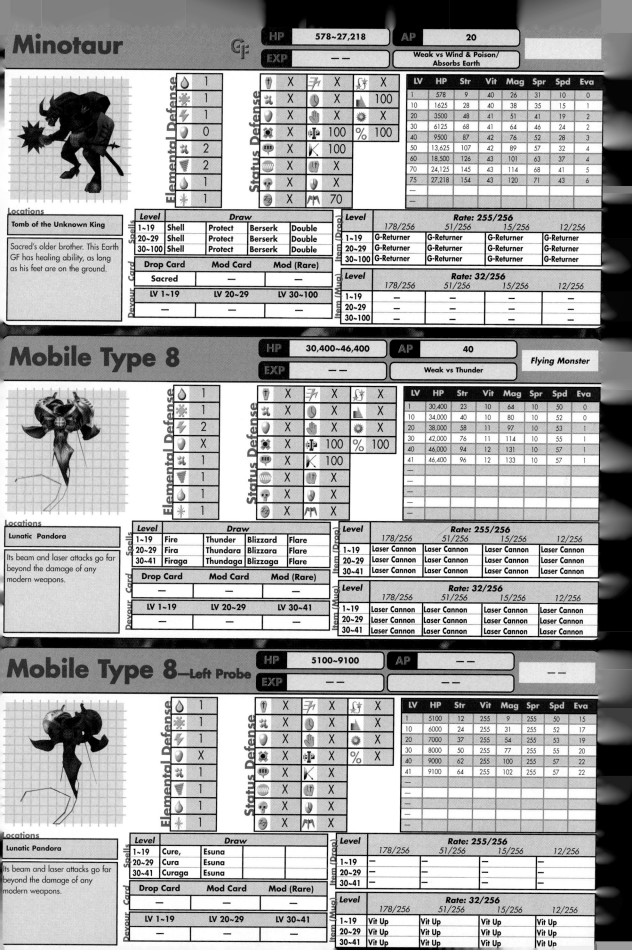

Elemental Defense: 1, 1, 1, X, 1, 1, 1, 1

Status Defense: X (all)

LV	HP	Str	Vit	Mag	Spr	Spd	Eva
1	5100	12	255	9	255	50	15
10	6000	24	255	31	255	52	17
20	7000	37	255	54	255	53	19
30	8000	50	255	77	255	55	20
40	9000	62	255	100	255	57	22
41	9100	64	255	102	255	57	22

Locations

Lunatic Pandora

Its beam and laser attacks go far beyond the damage of any modern weapons.

Spells — Draw

Level	Draw	
1~19	Cure,	Esuna
20~29	Cura	Esuna
30~41	Curaga	Esuna

Card

Drop Card	Mod Card	Mod (Rare)
—	—	—

Devour Card

LV 1~19	LV 20~29	LV 30~41
—	—	—

Item (Drop) Rate: 255/256

Level	178/256	51/256	15/256	12/256
1~19	—	—	—	—
20~29	—	—	—	—
30~41	—	—	—	—

Item (Mug) Rate: 32/256

Level	178/256	51/256	15/256	12/256
1~19	Vit Up	Vit Up	Vit Up	Vit Up
20~29	Vit Up	Vit Up	Vit Up	Vit Up
30~41	Vit Up	Vit Up	Vit Up	Vit Up

Mobile Type 8—Right Probe

	HP	5100~9100	AP	— —	— —
	EXP	— —		— —	

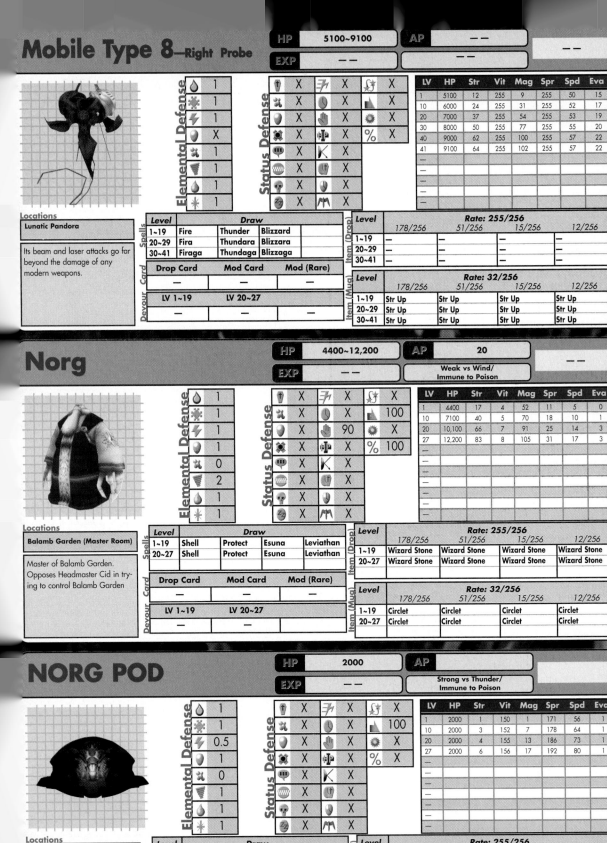

Elemental Defense: 1, 1, 1, X, 1, 1, 1, 1

Status Defense: X, X, X, X, X, X, X, X, X, X, X, X, X, X, X, X (% X)

LV	HP	Str	Vit	Mag	Spr	Spd	Eva
1	5100	12	255	9	255	50	15
10	6000	24	255	31	255	52	17
20	7000	37	255	54	255	53	19
30	8000	50	255	77	255	55	20
40	9000	62	255	100	255	57	22
41	9100	64	255	102	255	57	22
—							
—							
—							
—							

Locations: Lunatic Pandora

Its beam and laser attacks go far beyond the damage of any modern weapons.

Spells — Draw

Level		Draw	
1~19	Fire	Thunder	Blizzard
20~29	Fira	Thundara	Blizzara
30~41	Firaga	Thundaga	Blizzaga

Card

Drop Card	Mod Card	Mod (Rare)
—	—	—

Devour

LV 1~19	LV 20~27
—	—

Item (Drop)

Level	Rate: 255/256			
	178/256	51/256	15/256	12/256
1~19	—	—	—	—
20~29	—	—	—	—
30~41	—	—	—	—

Item (Mug)

Level	Rate: 32/256			
	178/256	51/256	15/256	12/256
1~19	Str Up	Str Up	Str Up	Str Up
20~29	Str Up	Str Up	Str Up	Str Up
30~41	Str Up	Str Up	Str Up	Str Up

Norg

	HP	4400~12,200	AP	20	— —
	EXP	— —		Weak vs Wind/Immune to Poison	

Elemental Defense: 1, 1, 1, 1, 0, 2, 1, 1

Status Defense: X, X, X, 100, X, X, 90, X, X, X, X, 100, X, X, X, X

LV	HP	Str	Vit	Mag	Spr	Spd	Eva
1	4400	17	4	52	11	5	0
10	7100	40	5	70	18	10	1
20	10,100	66	7	91	25	14	3
27	12,200	83	8	105	31	17	3
—							
—							
—							
—							

Locations: Balamb Garden (Master Room)

Master of Balamb Garden. Opposes Headmaster Cid in trying to control Balamb Garden

Spells — Draw

Level		Draw		
1~19	Shell	Protect	Esuna	Leviathan
20~27	Shell	Protect	Esuna	Leviathan

Card

Drop Card	Mod Card	Mod (Rare)
—	—	—

Devour

LV 1~19	LV 20~27
—	—

Item (Drop)

Level	Rate: 255/256			
	178/256	51/256	15/256	12/256
1~19	Wizard Stone	Wizard Stone	Wizard Stone	Wizard Stone
20~27	Wizard Stone	Wizard Stone	Wizard Stone	Wizard Stone

Item (Mug)

Level	Rate: 32/256			
	178/256	51/256	15/256	12/256
1~19	Circlet	Circlet	Circlet	Circlet
20~27	Circlet	Circlet	Circlet	Circlet

NORG POD

	HP	2000	AP		
	EXP	— —		Strong vs Thunder/Immune to Poison	

Elemental Defense: 1, 1, 0.5, 1, 0, 1, 1, 1

Status Defense: X, X, X, 100, X, X, X, X, X, X, X, X, X, X, X, X (% X)

LV	HP	Str	Vit	Mag	Spr	Spd	Eva
1	2000	1	150	1	171	56	1
10	2000	3	152	7	178	64	1
20	2000	4	155	13	186	73	1
27	2000	6	156	17	192	80	1
—							
—							
—							
—							

Locations: Balamb Garden (Master Room)

A defense shelter protecting Master NORG. The shelter must be destroyed in order to attack NORG, who is inside the shelter.

Spells — Draw

Level	Draw
1~19	Cure
20~27	Cura

Card

Drop Card	Mod Card	Mod (Rare)
—	—	—

Devour

LV 1~19	LV 20~27
—	—

Item (Drop)

Level	Rate: 255/256			
	178/256	51/256	15/256	12/256
1~19	—	—	—	—
20~27	—	—	—	—

Item (Mug)

Level	Rate: 32/256			
	178/256	51/256	15/256	12/256
1~19	—			
20~27	—			

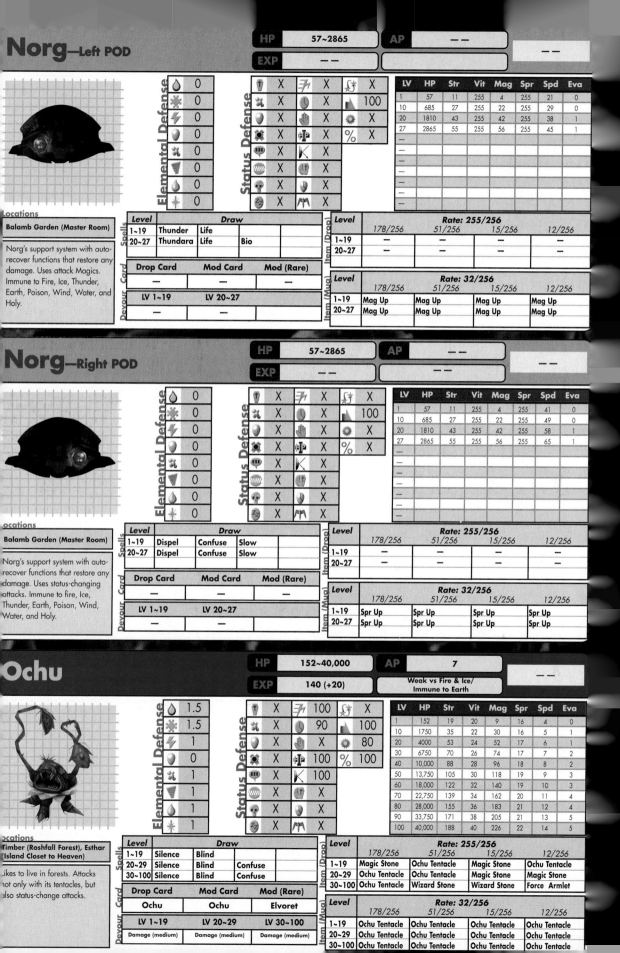

Norg—Left POD

HP	57~2865	AP	——	——
EXP	——		——	

Elemental Defense: 0, 0, 0, 0, 0, 0, 0, 0

Status Defense: X, X, X; X, X, 100; X, X, X; X, X, %X; X, X; X, X; X, X; X, X

LV	HP	Str	Vit	Mag	Spr	Spd	Eva
1	57	11	255	4	255	21	0
10	685	27	255	22	255	29	0
20	1810	43	255	42	255	38	1
27	2865	55	255	56	255	45	1

Locations
Balamb Garden (Master Room)

Norg's support system with auto-recover functions that restore any damage. Uses attack Magics. Immune to Fire, Ice, Thunder, Earth, Poison, Wind, Water, and Holy.

Spells — Draw

Level		Draw	
1~19	Thunder	Life	
20~27	Thundara	Life	Bio

Drop Card	Mod Card	Mod (Rare)
—	—	—

Devour Card

LV 1~19	LV 20~27
—	—

Level	Rate: 255/256			
	178/256	51/256	15/256	12/256
1~19	—	—	—	—
20~27	—	—	—	—

Level	Rate: 32/256			
	178/256	51/256	15/256	12/256
1~19	Mag Up	Mag Up	Mag Up	Mag Up
20~27	Mag Up	Mag Up	Mag Up	Mag Up

Norg—Right POD

HP	57~2865	AP	——	——
EXP	——		——	

Elemental Defense: 0, 0, 0, 0, 0, 0, 0, 0

Status Defense: X, X, X; X, X, 100; X, X, X; X, X, %X; X, X; X, X; X, X; X, X

LV	HP	Str	Vit	Mag	Spr	Spd	Eva
1	57	11	255	4	255	41	0
10	685	27	255	22	255	49	0
20	1810	43	255	42	255	58	1
27	2865	55	255	56	255	65	1

Locations
Balamb Garden (Master Room)

Norg's support system with auto-recover functions that restore any damage. Uses status-changing attacks. Immune to fire, Ice, Thunder, Earth, Poison, Wind, Water, and Holy.

Spells — Draw

Level		Draw	
1~19	Dispel	Confuse	Slow
20~27	Dispel	Confuse	Slow

Drop Card	Mod Card	Mod (Rare)
—	—	—

Devour Card

LV 1~19	LV 20~27
—	—

Level	Rate: 255/256			
	178/256	51/256	15/256	12/256
1~19	—	—	—	—
20~27	—	—	—	—

Level	Rate: 32/256			
	178/256	51/256	15/256	12/256
1~19	Spr Up	Spr Up	Spr Up	Spr Up
20~27	Spr Up	Spr Up	Spr Up	Spr Up

Ochu

HP	152~40,000	AP	7	——
EXP	140 (+20)		Weak vs Fire & Ice / Immune to Earth	

Elemental Defense: 1.5, 1.5, 1, 0, 1, 1, 1, 1

Status Defense: X, 100, X; X, 90, 100; X, X, 80; X, 100, 100; X, 100; X, X; X, X; X, X

LV	HP	Str	Vit	Mag	Spr	Spd	Eva
1	152	19	20	9	16	4	0
10	1750	35	22	30	16	5	1
20	4000	53	24	52	17	6	1
30	6750	70	26	74	17	7	2
40	10,000	88	28	96	18	8	2
50	13,750	105	30	118	19	9	3
60	18,000	122	32	140	19	10	3
70	22,750	139	34	162	20	11	4
80	28,000	155	36	183	21	12	4
90	33,750	171	38	205	21	13	5
100	40,000	188	40	226	22	14	5

Locations
Timber (Roshfall Forest), Esthar (Island Closet to Heaven)

Likes to live in forests. Attacks not only with its tentacles, but also status-change attacks.

Spells — Draw

Level		Draw	
1~19	Silence	Blind	
20~29	Silence	Blind	Confuse
30~100	Silence	Blind	Confuse

Drop Card	Mod Card	Mod (Rare)
Ochu	Ochu	Elvoret

Devour Card

LV 1~19	LV 20~29	LV 30~100
Damage (medium)	Damage (medium)	Damage (medium)

Level	Rate: 255/256			
	178/256	51/256	15/256	12/256
1~19	Magic Stone	Ochu Tentacle	Magic Stone	Ochu Tentacle
20~29	Ochu Tentacle	Ochu Tentacle	Magic Stone	Magic Stone
30~100	Ochu Tentacle	Wizard Stone	Wizard Stone	Force Armlet

Level	Rate: 32/256			
	178/256	51/256	15/256	12/256
1~19	Ochu Tentacle	Ochu Tentacle	Ochu Tentacle	Ochu Tentacle
20~29	Ochu Tentacle	Ochu Tentacle	Ochu Tentacle	Ochu Tentacle
30~100	Ochu Tentacle	Ochu Tentacle	Ochu Tentacle	Ochu Tentacle

Odin

HP	1300~31,000	AP	20	— —
EXP	— —		— —	

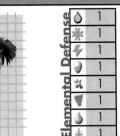

Elemental Defense: 1, 1, 1, 1, 1, 1, 1, 1

Status Defense: all X

LV	HP	Str	Vit	Mag	Spr	Spd	Eva
1	1300	4	121	26	151	1	0
10	4000	18	130	45	158	6	2
20	7000	33	140	64	166	10	4
30	10,000	47	150	84	174	15	6
40	13,000	61	159	103	182	19	8
50	16,000	75	169	122	191	23	10
60	19,000	89	179	140	198	28	12
70	22,000	103	189	159	207	32	14
80	25,000	117	199	177	215	36	16
90	28,000	130	209	195	223	41	18
100	31,000	143	218	212	231	45	20

Locations
Centra Ruins

A legendary GF that sleeps in a dungeon. Zantetsuken cuts anything that stands in its way.

Spells (Draw)

Level	Draw			
1~19	Stop	Death	Double	Triple
20~29	Stop	Death	Double	Triple
30~100	Stop	Death	Double	Triple

Card

Drop Card	Mod Card	Mod (Rare)
Odin	—	—

Devour

LV 1~19	LV 20~29	LV 30~100
—	—	—

Item (Drop) — Rate: 255/256

Level	178/256	51/256	15/256	12/256
1~19	G-Mega-Potion	G-Mega-Potion	G-Mega-Potion	G-Mega-Potion
20~29	G-Mega-Potion	G-Mega-Potion	G-Mega-Potion	G-Mega-Potion
30~100	G-Mega-Potion	G-Mega-Potion	G-Mega-Potion	G-Mega-Potion

Item (Mug) — Rate: 32/256

Level	178/256	51/256	15/256	12/256
1~19	Luck-J Scroll	Luck-J Scroll	Luck-J Scroll	Luck-J Scroll
20~29	Luck-J Scroll	Luck-J Scroll	Luck-J Scroll	Luck-J Scroll
30~100	Luck-J Scroll	Luck-J Scroll	Luck-J Scroll	Luck-J Scroll

---

Oilboyle

HP	2136~15,630	AP	10	— —
EXP	40 (+10)		Weak vs Fire/Immune to Water	

Elemental Defense: 2, 1, 1, 1, 1, 1, 0, 1

Status Defense (visible values): 50, 90, 100; 80; 100, 100; 80, 100; 80

LV	HP	Str	Vit	Mag	Spr	Spd	Eva
1	2136	37	47	26	76	6	0
10	3120	55	60	38	80	6	1
20	4720	75	76	51	86	6	1
30	5480	95	91	64	91	6	2
40	6750	115	107	76	97	6	3
50	8080	135	122	89	102	6	4
60	9470	155	138	101	108	6	4
70	10,920	174	153	113	113	6	5
80	12,430	194	169	125	119	6	6
90	14,000	213	184	137	124	6	6
100	15,630	232	200	149	130	6	7

Locations
Balamb Garden (MD Level), Ultimecia Castle

This creature lives underground. Its slimy body is full of oil. Attacks by spitting oil.

Spells (Draw)

Level	Draw			
1~19	Esuna	Blind	Cure	Confuse
20~29	Esuna	Blind	Cura	Confuse
30~100	Esuna	Curaga	Confuse	Dispel

Card

Drop Card	Mod Card	Mod (Rare)
—	—	—

Devour

LV 1~19	LV 20~29	LV 30~100
—	—	—

Item (Drop) — Rate: 255/256

Level	178/256	51/256	15/256	12/256
1~19	Wizard Stone	Wizard Stone	Wizard Stone	Wizard Stone
20~29	Wizard Stone	Wizard Stone	Wizard Stone	Wizard Stone
30~100	Wizard Stone	Wizard Stone	Orihalcon	Orihalcon

Item (Mug) — Rate: 32/256

Level	178/256	51/256	15/256	12/256
1~19	Fuel	Fuel	Fuel	Fuel
20~29	Fuel	Fuel	Fuel	Fuel
30~100	Fuel	Fuel	Orihalcon	Orihalcon

Omega Weapon

HP	111,105~1,161,000	AP	250	— —
EXP	— —		— —	

Elemental Defense: -1, -1, -1, -1, -1, -1, -1, -1

Status Defense: all X

LV	HP	Str	Vit	Mag	Spr	Spd	Eva
1	111,105	67	61	70	121	61	0
10	202,500	113	65	128	125	61	1
20	305,500	163	70	193	131	61	1
30	408,500	213	76	255	136	61	2
40	513,000	255	81	255	142	61	2
50	618,500	255	86	255	147	61	3
60	725,500	255	92	255	153	61	4
70	832,500	255	97	255	158	61	4
80	941,000	255	102	255	164	61	5
90	1,050,500	255	108	255	169	61	5
100	1,161,000	255	113	255	175	61	6

Locations
Ultimecia Castle (Chapel)

Stronger than Ultima Weapon, Omega Weapon is the strongest monster. It is bad luck to run into this monster.

Spells (Draw)

Level	Draw			
1~19	Flare	Holy	Meteor	Ultima
20~29	Flare	Holy	Meteor	Ultima
30~100	Flare	Holy	Meteor	Ultima

Card

Drop Card	Mod Card	Mod (Rare)
—	—	—

Devour

LV 1~19	LV 20~29	LV 30~100
—	—	—

Item (Drop) — Rate: 255/256

Level	178/256	51/256	15/256	12/256
1~19	Three Stars	Three Stars	Three Stars	Three Stars
20~29	Three Stars	Three Stars	Three Stars	Three Stars
30~100	Three Stars	Three Stars	Three Stars	Three Stars

Item (Mug) — Rate: 32/256

Level	178/256	51/256	15/256	12/256
1~19	—	—	—	—
20~29	—	—	—	—
30~100	—	—	—	—

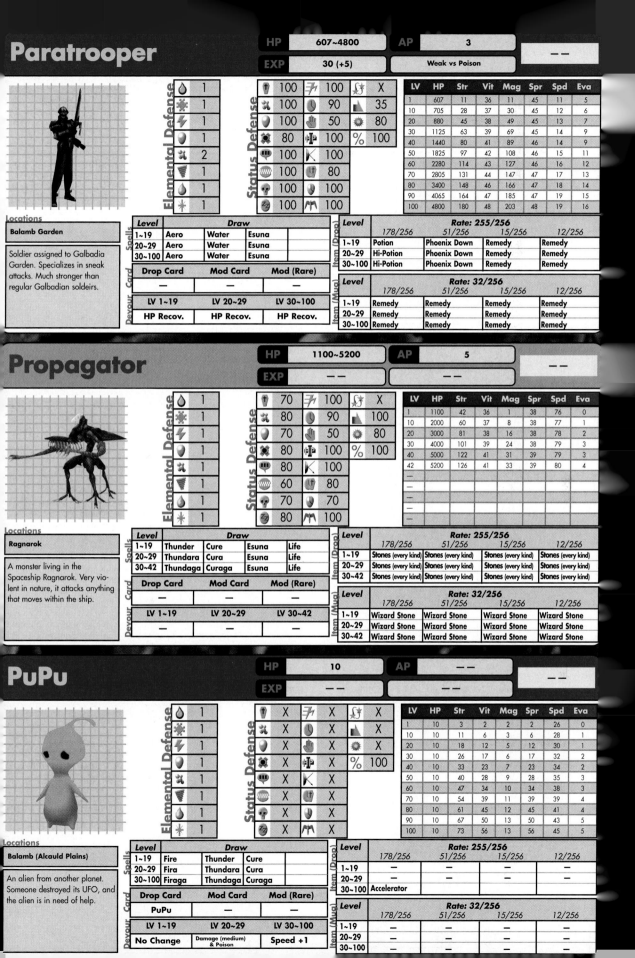

Paratrooper

HP	607~4800	AP	3	—
EXP	30 (+5)	Weak vs Poison		

Elemental Defense: 1, 1, 1, 1, 2, 1, 1, 1

Status Defense: 100, 100, X | 100, 90, 35 | 100, 50, 80 | 80, 100, 100 | 100, 100 | 100, 80 | 100, 100 | 100, 100

LV	HP	Str	Vit	Mag	Spr	Spd	Eva
1	607	11	36	11	45	11	5
10	705	28	37	30	45	12	6
20	880	45	38	49	45	13	7
30	1125	63	39	69	45	14	9
40	1440	80	41	89	46	14	9
50	1825	97	42	108	46	15	11
60	2280	114	43	127	46	16	12
70	2805	131	44	147	47	17	13
80	3400	148	46	166	47	18	14
90	4065	164	47	185	47	19	15
100	4800	180	48	203	48	19	16

Spells — Draw

Level		Draw	
1~19	Aero	Water	Esuna
20~29	Aero	Water	Esuna
30~100	Aero	Water	Esuna

Drop Card	Mod Card	Mod (Rare)
—	—	—

Devour Card

LV 1~19	LV 20~29	LV 30~100
HP Recov.	HP Recov.	HP Recov.

Item (Drop)

Level	Rate: 255/256			
	178/256	51/256	15/256	12/256
1~19	Potion	Phoenix Down	Remedy	Remedy
20~29	Hi-Potion	Phoenix Down	Remedy	Remedy
30~100	Hi-Potion	Phoenix Down	Remedy	Remedy

Item (Mug)

Level	Rate: 32/256			
	178/256	51/256	15/256	12/256
1~19	Remedy	Remedy	Remedy	Remedy
20~29	Remedy	Remedy	Remedy	Remedy
30~100	Remedy	Remedy	Remedy	Remedy

Locations

Balamb Garden

Soldier assigned to Galbadia Garden. Specializes in sneak attacks. Much stronger than regular Galbadian soldeirs.

Propagator

HP	1100~5200	AP	5	—
EXP	—	—		

Elemental Defense: 1, 1, 1, 1, 1, 1, 1, 1

Status Defense: 70, 100, X | 80, 90, 100 | 70, 50, 80 | 80, 100, 100 | 80, 100 | 60, 80 | 70, 70 | 80, 100

LV	HP	Str	Vit	Mag	Spr	Spd	Eva
1	1100	42	36	1	38	76	0
10	2000	60	37	8	38	77	1
20	3000	81	38	16	38	78	2
30	4000	101	39	24	38	79	3
40	5000	122	41	31	39	79	3
42	5200	126	41	33	39	80	4

Spells — Draw

Level		Draw		
1~19	Thunder	Cure	Esuna	Life
20~29	Thundara	Cura	Esuna	Life
30~42	Thundaga	Curaga	Esuna	Life

Drop Card	Mod Card	Mod (Rare)
—	—	—

Devour Card

LV 1~19	LV 20~29	LV 30~42
—	—	—

Item (Drop)

Level	Rate: 255/256			
	178/256	51/256	15/256	12/256
1~19	Stones (every kind)	Stones (every kind)	Stones (every kind)	Stones (every kind)
20~29	Stones (every kind)	Stones (every kind)	Stones (every kind)	Stones (every kind)
30~42	Stones (every kind)	Stones (every kind)	Stones (every kind)	Stones (every kind)

Item (Mug)

Level	Rate: 32/256			
	178/256	51/256	15/256	12/256
1~19	Wizard Stone	Wizard Stone	Wizard Stone	Wizard Stone
20~29	Wizard Stone	Wizard Stone	Wizard Stone	Wizard Stone
30~42	Wizard Stone	Wizard Stone	Wizard Stone	Wizard Stone

Locations

Ragnarok

A monster living in the Spaceship Ragnarok. Very violent in nature, it attacks anything that moves within the ship.

PuPu

HP	10	AP	—	—
EXP	—	—		

Elemental Defense: 1, 1, 1, 1, 1, 1, 1, 1

Status Defense: X, X, X | X, X, X | X, X, X | X, X, 100 | X, X | X, X | X, X | X, X

LV	HP	Str	Vit	Mag	Spr	Spd	Eva
1	10	3	2	2	2	26	0
10	10	11	6	3	6	28	1
20	10	18	12	5	12	30	1
30	10	26	17	6	17	32	2
40	10	33	23	7	23	34	2
50	10	40	28	9	28	35	3
60	10	47	34	10	34	38	3
70	10	54	39	11	39	39	4
80	10	61	45	12	45	41	4
90	10	67	50	13	50	43	5
100	10	73	56	13	56	45	5

Spells — Draw

Level		Draw	
1~19	Fire	Thunder	Cure
20~29	Fira	Thundara	Cura
30~100	Firaga	Thundaga	Curaga

Drop Card	Mod Card	Mod (Rare)
PuPu	—	—

Devour Card

LV 1~19	LV 20~29	LV 30~100
No Change	Damage (medium) & Poison	Speed +1

Item (Drop)

Level	Rate: 255/256			
	178/256	51/256	15/256	12/256
1~19	—	—	—	—
20~29	—	—	—	—
30~100	Accelerator			

Item (Mug)

Level	Rate: 32/256			
	178/256	51/256	15/256	12/256
1~19	—			
20~29	—			
30~100	—			

Locations

Balamb (Alcauld Plains)

An alien from another planet. Someone destroyed its UFO, and the alien is in need of help.

Raijin (1st round)

HP	400~11,600	AP	10
EXP	— —		

Weak vs Poiso—bsorbs Thunder

Elemental Defense: 1, 1, -1, 1, 1.5, 1, 1, 1

Status Defense: X, 100, X / X, 60, 40 / X, X, X / 60, 100, 100 / 20, 100 / X, X / X, X / 60, X

LV	HP	Str	Vit	Mag	Spr	Spd	Eva
1	400	32	42	3	1	10	2
10	4000	50	57	13	3	12	3
20	8000	70	75	24	6	13	3
29	11,600	88	91	34	8	15	3

Locations: Balamb Town Square, Balamb Hotel

Looking for Ellone with Fujin. Good at physical attacks. Tries to act cool around other people.

Spells / Draw

Level	Draw			
1~19	Thunder	Thundara	Shell	Protect
20~29	Thunder	Thundara	Shell	Protect

Card

Drop Card	Mod Card	Mod (Rare)
—	—	—

Devour

LV 1~19	LV 20~29
—	

Item (Drop) — Rate: 255/256

Level	178/256	51/256	15/256	12/256
1~19	Str Up	Str Up	Str Up	Str Up
20~29	Str Up	Str Up	Str Up	Str Up

Item (Mug) — Rate: 32/256

Level	178/256	51/256	15/256	12/256
1~19	Str Up	Str Up	Str Up	Str Up
20~29	Str Up	Str Up	Str Up	Str Up

Raijin (2nd round)

HP	5400~22,600	AP	12
EXP	— —		

Weak vs Poison/ Absorbs Lightning

Elemental Defense: 1, 1, -1, 1, 1.5, 1, 1, 1

Status Defense: X, 100, X / X, 40, 70 / X, X, X / 40, 100, 100 / X, 10 / X, X / X, X / 50, X

LV	HP	Str	Vit	Mag	Spr	Spd	Eva
1	5400	32	52	3	1	30	2
10	9000	53	69	13	3	32	3
20	13,000	75	88	24	6	33	3
30	17,000	98	106	36	8	35	4
40	21,000	120	125	47	11	37	4
44	22,600	129	132	51	12	37	4

Locations: Lunatic Pandora

Works with Fujin and Seifer. Still relies on his strength, but can now use support magic as well.

Spells / Draw

Level	Draw			
1~19	Thunder	Protect	Shell	
20~29	Thunder	Thundara	Shell	Protect
30~44	Thundara	Thundaga	Shell	Protect

Card

Drop Card	Mod Card	Mod (Rare)
—	—	—

Devour

LV 1~19	LV 20~29	LV 30~44
—		

Item (Drop) — Rate: 255/256

Level	178/256	51/256	15/256	12/256
1~19	Str Up	Str Up	Str Up	Str Up
20~29	Str Up	Str Up	Str Up	Str Up
30~44	Str Up	Str Up	Str Up	Str Up

Item (Mug) — Rate: 32/256

Level	178/256	51/256	15/256	12/256
1~19	Power Wrist	Power Wrist	Power Wrist	Power Wrist
20~29	Power Wrist	Power Wrist	Power Wrist	Power Wrist
30~44	Power Wrist	Power Wrist	Power Wrist	Power Wrist

Raldo

HP	111~6700	AP	3
EXP	40 (+10)		— —

Elemental Defense: 1, 1, 1, 1, 1, 1, 1, 1

Status Defense: 20, 100, X / 40, 90, 100 / X, 10, 80 / 60, 100, 100 / X, 100 / X, 40 / X, X / X, X

LV	HP	Str	Vit	Mag	Spr	Spd	Eva
1	111	2	32	2	57	30	0
10	265	8	54	22	74	32	0
20	540	16	78	43	94	33	1
30	925	23	102	65	113	35	1
40	1420	30	125	86	132	37	1
50	2025	37	149	107	151	38	2
60	2740	44	173	128	171	40	2
70	3565	51	197	149	190	42	2
80	4500	58	220	170	209	43	3
90	5545	65	244	191	228	45	3
100	6700	72	268	212	248	47	3

Locations: Balamb Garden (Training Center), Ultimecia Castle

May look slow due to its stone-like body, but it is actually quite fast. May appear in numbers.

Spells / Draw

Level	Draw		
1~19	Fire	Thunder	Protect
20~29	Fira	Thundara	Protect
30~100	Firaga	Thundaga	Protect

Card

Drop Card	Mod Card	Mod (Rare)
—	—	—

Devour

LV 1~19	LV 20~29	LV 30~100
—		

Item (Drop) — Rate: 255/256

Level	178/256	51/256	15/256	12/256
1~19	Wizard Stone	Wizard Stone	Wizard Stone	Wizard Stone
20~29	Wizard Stone	Wizard Stone	Wizard Stone	Wizard Stone
30~100	Wizard Stone	Wizard Stone	Wizard Stone	Wizard Stone

Item (Mug) — Rate: 32/256

Level	178/256	51/256	15/256	12/256
1~19	Wizard Stone	Wizard Stone	Wizard Stone	Wizard Stone
20~29	Wizard Stone	Wizard Stone	Wizard Stone	Wizard Stone
30~100	Wizard Stone	Wizard Stone	Wizard Stone	Wizard Stone

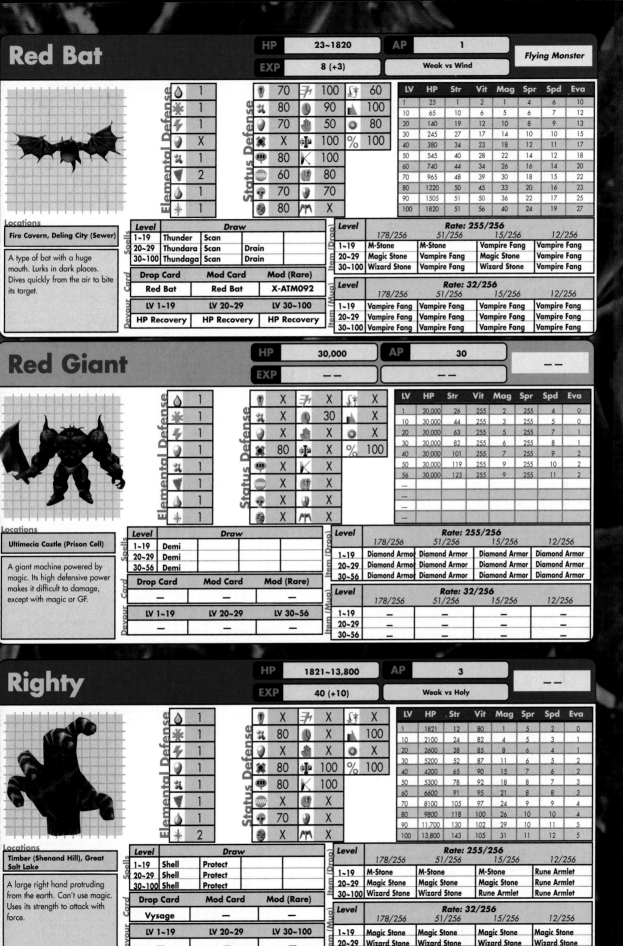

Red Bat

HP	23~1820	AP	1	Flying Monster
EXP	8 (+3)		Weak vs Wind	

LV	HP	Str	Vit	Mag	Spr	Spd	Eva
1	23	1	2	1	4	6	10
10	65	10	6	5	6	7	12
20	140	19	12	10	8	9	13
30	245	27	17	14	10	10	15
40	380	34	23	18	12	11	17
50	545	40	28	22	14	12	18
60	740	44	34	26	16	14	20
70	965	48	39	30	18	15	22
80	1220	50	45	33	20	16	23
90	1505	51	50	36	22	17	25
100	1820	51	56	40	24	19	27

Locations

Fire Cavern, Deling City (Sewer)

A type of bat with a huge mouth. Lurks in dark places. Dives quickly from the air to bite its target.

Spells (Draw)

Level	Draw			
1~19	Thunder	Scan		
20~29	Thundara	Scan	Drain	
30~100	Thundaga	Scan	Drain	

Drop Card	Mod Card	Mod (Rare)
Red Bat	Red Bat	X-ATM092

LV 1~19	LV 20~29	LV 30~100
HP Recovery	HP Recovery	HP Recovery

Item (Drop)

Level	Rate: 255/256			
	178/256	51/256	15/256	12/256
1~19	M-Stone	M-Stone	Vampire Fang	Vampire Fang
20~29	Magic Stone	Vampire Fang	Magic Stone	Vampire Fang
30~100	Wizard Stone	Vampire Fang	Wizard Stone	Vampire Fang

Item (Mug)

Level	Rate: 32/256			
	178/256	51/256	15/256	12/256
1~19	Vampire Fang	Vampire Fang	Vampire Fang	Vampire Fang
20~29	Vampire Fang	Vampire Fang	Vampire Fang	Vampire Fang
30~100	Vampire Fang	Vampire Fang	Vampire Fang	Vampire Fang

Red Giant

HP	30,000	AP	30	— —
EXP	— —		— —	

LV	HP	Str	Vit	Mag	Spr	Spd	Eva
1	30,000	26	255	2	255	4	0
10	30,000	44	255	3	255	5	0
20	30,000	63	255	5	255	7	1
30	30,000	82	255	6	255	8	1
40	30,000	101	255	7	255	9	2
50	30,000	119	255	9	255	10	2
56	30,000	123	255	9	255	11	2
—							
—							
—							

Locations

Ultimecia Castle (Prison Cell)

A giant machine powered by magic. Its high defensive power makes it difficult to damage, except with magic or GF.

Level	Draw			
1~19	Demi			
20~29	Demi			
30~56	Demi			

Drop Card	Mod Card	Mod (Rare)
—	—	—

LV 1~19	LV 20~29	LV 30~56
—	—	—

Item (Drop)

Level	Rate: 255/256			
	178/256	51/256	15/256	12/256
1~19	Diamond Armor	Diamond Armor	Diamond Armor	Diamond Armor
20~29	Diamond Armor	Diamond Armor	Diamond Armor	Diamond Armor
30~56	Diamond Armor	Diamond Armor	Diamond Armor	Diamond Armor

Item (Mug)

Level	Rate: 32/256			
	178/256	51/256	15/256	12/256
1~19	—	—	—	—
20~29	—	—	—	—
30~56	—	—	—	—

Righty

HP	1821~13,800	AP	3	— —
EXP	40 (+10)		Weak vs Holy	

LV	HP	Str	Vit	Mag	Spr	Spd	Eva
1	1821	12	80	1	5	2	0
10	2100	24	82	4	5	3	1
20	2600	38	85	8	6	4	1
30	5200	52	87	11	6	5	2
40	4200	65	90	15	7	6	2
50	5300	78	92	18	8	7	3
60	6600	91	95	21	8	8	4
70	8100	105	97	24	9	9	4
80	9800	118	100	26	10	10	4
90	11,700	130	102	29	10	11	5
100	13,800	143	105	31	11	12	5

Locations

Timber (Shenand Hill), Great Salt Lake

A large right hand protruding from the earth. Can't use magic. Uses its strength to attack with force.

Level	Draw			
1~19	Shell	Protect		
20~29	Shell	Protect		
30~100	Shell	Protect		

Drop Card	Mod Card	Mod (Rare)
Vysage	—	—

LV 1~19	LV 20~29	LV 30~100
—	—	—

Item (Drop)

Level	Rate: 255/256			
	178/256	51/256	15/256	12/256
1~19	M-Stone	M-Stone	M-Stone	Rune Armlet
20~29	Magic Stone	Magic Stone	Magic Stone	Rune Armlet
30~100	Wizard Stone	Wizard Stone	Rune Armlet	Rune Armlet

Item (Mug)

Level	Rate: 32/256			
	178/256	51/256	15/256	12/256
1~19	Magic Stone	Magic Stone	Magic Stone	Magic Stone
20~29	Wizard Stone	Wizard Stone	Wizard Stone	Wizard Stone
30~100	Rune Armlet	Rune Armlet	Rune Armlet	Rune Armlet

Rinoa

HP	6021~9036	AP	— —
EXP	— —		— —

— —

Elemental Defense

💧	1
❄	1
⚡	1
🌀	1
🔥	1
🌊	1
💧	1
✳	1

Status Defense

💡	X	⚡	X	⭐	X
☠	80	⏱	X	⛰	100
🥚	X	✋	X	☀	X
😵	80	💉	100	%	X
💀	80	🗡	100		
〰	X	🔼	80		
💀	X	✋	X		
💤	X	🤲	X		

LV	HP	Str	Vit	Mag	Spr	Spd	Eva
1	6021	4	1	65	1	20	0
10	6300	7	1	83	2	20	1
20	6800	10	1	102	3	20	1
30	7500	13	1	122	4	20	2
40	8400	15	1	141	6	20	2
46	9036	17	1	152	6	20	2
—							
—							
—							
—							

Locations

Lunatic Pandora

Rinoa being Junctioned by Adel. Immobile, because Adel is absorbing her powers. Can be released by defeating Adel.

Spells

Level	Draw		
1~19	Esuna	Dispel	Regen
20~29	Esuna	Dispel	Regen
30~46	Esuna	Dispel	Regen

Card

Drop Card	Mod Card	Mod (Rare)
—	—	—

Devour

LV 1~19	LV 20~29	LV 30~46
Full HP Recovery	Full HP Recovery	Max HP + 10

Item (Drop)

Level	Rate: 255/256			
	178/256	51/256	15/256	12/256
1~19	—	—	—	—
20~29	—	—	—	—
30~46	—	—	—	—

Item (Mug)

Level	Rate: 32/256			
	178/256	51/256	15/256	12/256
1~19	Megalixir	Megalixir	Megalixir	Megalixir
20~29	Megalixir	Megalixir	Megalixir	Megalixir
30~46	Megalixir	Megalixir	Megalixir	Megalixir

Ruby Dragon

HP	668~89,100	AP	14
EXP	210 (+40)		Weak vs Ice & Holy/ Absorbs Fire & Wind

— —

Elemental Defense

💧	-1
❄	1.5
⚡	1
🌀	1
🔥	1
🌊	-1
💧	1
✳	1.5

Status Defense

💡	X	⚡	X	⭐	X
☠	X	⏱	50	⛰	100
🥚	20	✋	X	☀	80
😵	X	💉	X	%	100
💀	X	🗡	100		
〰	X	🔼	X		
💀	X	✋	40		
💤	20	🤲	X		

LV	HP	Str	Vit	Mag	Spr	Spd	Eva
1	668	27	81	65	151	2	0
10	6075	48	90	81	157	3	1
20	12,700	71	100	100	164	5	1
30	19,975	93	110	117	171	6	2
40	27,900	116	120	135	178	7	3
50	36,475	138	130	153	186	8	3
60	45,700	161	140	170	192	10	4
70	55,575	183	150	188	200	11	4
80	66,100	206	160	205	207	12	5
90	77,275	228	170	222	214	13	6
100	89,100	250	180	240	221	15	6

Locations

Trabia Canyon, Deep Sea Reasearch Center (Lab)

Strong and smart dragon. If enemies are using Reflect, it casts Reflect on itself to mirror the attack.

Spells

Level	Draw		
1~34	Aero	Fira		
35~44	Aero	Firaga	Demi	
45~100	Firaga	Reflect	Flare	Meteor

Card

Drop Card	Mod Card	Mod (Rare)
—	—	—

Devour

LV 1~34	LV 35~44	LV 45~100
Full HP Recovery	Full HP Recovery	Max HP + 10

Item (Drop)

Level	Rate: 255/256			
	178/256	51/256	15/256	12/256
1~34	Inferno Fang	Inferno Fang	Fury Fragment	Fury Fragment
35~44	Inferno Fang	Fury Fragment	Star Fragment	Energy Crystal
45~100	Fury Fragment	Energy Crystal	Fury Fragment	Fury Fragment

Item (Mug)

Level	Rate: 32/256			
	178/256	51/256	15/256	12/256
1~34	Inferno Fang	Inferno Fang	Inferno Fang	Inferno Fang
35~44	Inferno Fang	Inferno Fang	Inferno Fang	Inferno Fang
45~100	Inferno Fang	Inferno Fang	Inferno Fang	Inferno Fang

Sacred

HP	855~36,375	AP	20
EXP	— —		Weak vs Poison & Wind/ Immune to Earth

— —

Elemental Defense

💧	1
❄	1
⚡	1
🥚	-1
🔥	2
🌊	2
💧	1
✳	1

Status Defense

💡	X	⚡	X	⭐	X
☠	X	⏱	X	⛰	100
🥚	X	✋	X	☀	X
😵	X	💉	100	%	100
💀	X	🗡	100		
〰	X	🔼	X		
💀	X	✋	X		
💤	X	🤲	50		

LV	HP	Str	Vit	Mag	Spr	Spd	Eva
1	855	12	60	36	31	10	0
10	2250	35	61	48	40	15	1
20	4750	60	62	61	51	19	2
30	8250	85	63	74	61	24	2
40	12,750	110	65	86	72	28	4
50	18,250	134	66	99	82	32	4
60	24,750	158	67	111	93	37	5
70	32,250	182	68	124	103	41	6
75	36,375	194	69	130	108	43	6
—							

Locations

Tomb of the Unknown King

Earth GF in Tomb of the Unknown King. Recovers by power of the earth. Attacks with large steel orb.

Spells

Level	Draw			
1~19	Shell	Protect	Berserk	Life
20~29	Shell	Protect	Berserk	Life
30~75	Shell	Protect	Berserk	Life

Card

Drop Card	Mod Card	Mod (Rare)
—	—	—

Devour

LV 1~19	LV 20~29	LV 30~75
—	—	—

Item (Drop)

Level	Rate: 255/256			
	178/256	51/256	15/256	12/256
1~19	G-Hi-Potion	G-Hi-Potion	G-Hi-Potion	G-Hi-Potion
20~29	G-Hi-Potion	G-Hi-Potion	G-Hi-Potion	G-Hi-Potion
30~75	G-Hi-Potion	G-Hi-Potion	G-Hi-Potion	G-Hi-Potion

Item (Mug)

Level	Rate: 32/256			
	178/256	51/256	15/256	12/256
1~19	—	—	—	—
20~29	—	—	—	—
30~75	—	—	—	—

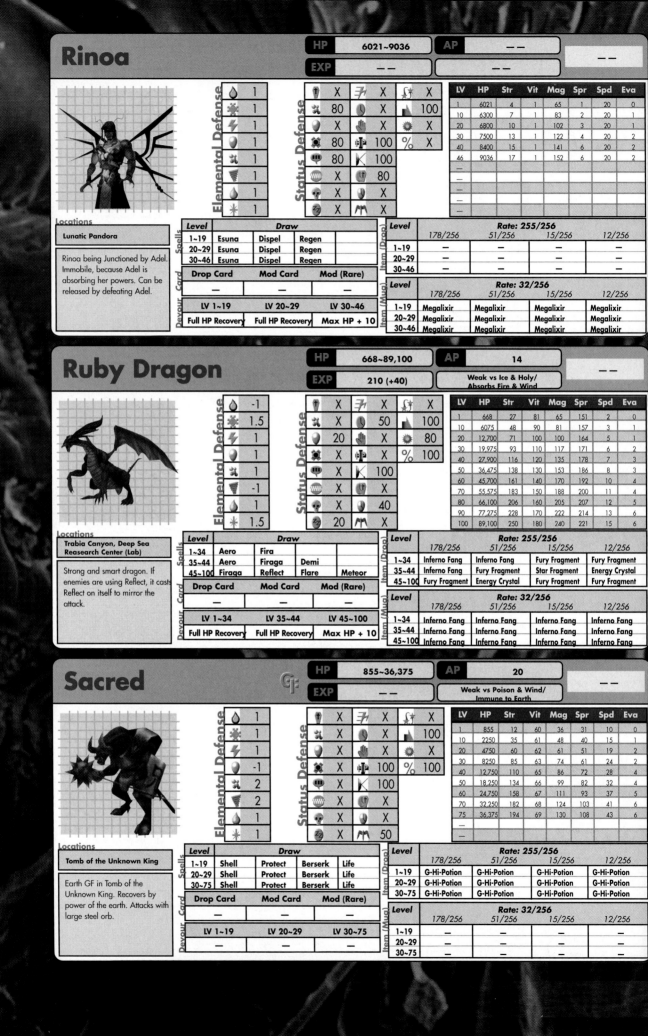

SAM08G

HP	747~27,700	AP	4	
EXP	30 (+5)	Weak vs Thunder & Poison		— —

Elemental Defense: 1, 1, 1.3, 1, 2, 1, 1, 1

Status Defense: X, 80, 70, 80, 30, X, X, X | 100, 90, 50, X, 100, 60, X, X | X, X, 80, 100, X, X, X, X

LV	HP	Str	Vit	Mag	Spr	Spd	Eva
1	747	9	25	8	15	8	0
10	1375	23	27	14	15	9	1
20	2500	37	30	20	15	9	1
30	4075	51	32	26	16	10	2
40	6100	64	35	32	16	10	3
50	8575	77	37	37	17	11	4
60	11,500	89	40	42	17	11	4
70	14,875	101	42	47	17	12	5
80	18,700	112	45	52	18	12	6
90	22,975	123	47	57	18	13	6
100	27,700	133	50	61	19	13	7

Locations

Galbadia Missile Base

A living weapon made by Galbadia. Carries a 155mm cannon on both shoulders and a 60mm Vulcan body is a weapon.

Spells

Level	Draw			
1~19	Shell			
20~29	Shell	Protect		
30~100	Shell	Protect	Reflect	Life

Card

Drop Card	Mod Card	Mod (Rare)
SAM08G	SAM08G	X-ATM092

Devour

LV 1~19	LV 20~29	LV 30~100
Full HP Recov.	Full HP Recov.	Full HP Recov.

Item (Drop) — Rate: 255/256

Level	178/256	51/256	15/256	12/256
1~19	M-Stone	Running Fire	Dragon Fin	Dragon Fang
20~29	Dragon Fin	Running Fire	Dragon Fang	Dragon Fang
30~100	Dragon Fin	Running Fire	Dragon Fang	Dragon Fang

Item (Mug) — Rate: 32/256

Level	178/256	51/256	15/256	12/256
1~19	Running Fire	Running Fire	Running Fire	Running Fire
20~29	Running Fire	Running Fire	Running Fire	Running Fire
30~100	Running Fire	Running Fire	Running Fire	Running Fire

Seifer (1st round)

HP	176~1150	AP	— —	
EXP	— —	Weak vs Poison		— —

Elemental Defense: 1, 1, 1, 1, 1.5, 1, 1, 1

Status Defense: X, X, X, X, X, X, X, 20 | 100, 90, X, 100, X, 100, X, X | X, 100, X, 100, 100, X, X, X

LV	HP	Str	Vit	Mag	Spr	Spd	Eva
1	176	18	82	14	121	5	2
10	525	23	97	35	129	8	3
20	1150	28	114	57	139	10	4
—							
—							
—							
—							
—							
—							

Locations

Deling City (Gateway)

After leaving the Garden, he decided to become a Sorceress Knight under Edea. Uses fire magic in conjunction with sword attacks.

Spells

Level	Draw		
1~19	Fire	Cure	Life
20	Fira	Cura	Life

Card

Drop Card	Mod Card	Mod (Rare)
—	—	—

Devour

LV 1~19	LV 20
—	—

Item (Drop) — Rate: 255/256

Level	178/256	51/256	15/256	12/256
1~19	—	—	—	—
20	—	—	—	—

Item (Mug) — Rate: 32/256

Level	178/256	51/256	15/256	12/256
1~19	Elixir	Elixir	Elixir	Elixir
20	Elixir	Elixir	Elixir	Elixir

Seifer (2nd round)

HP	1300~10,300	AP	20	
EXP	— —	Weak vs Poison		— —

Elemental Defense: 1, 1, 1, 1, 1.5, 1, 1, 1

Status Defense: X, X, X, 80, 80, X, X, 70 | X, X, X, 100, 100, 100, X, X | X, 100, X, 100, 100, X, X, X

LV	HP	Str	Vit	Mag	Spr	Spd	Eva
1	1300	31	14	27	136	31	2
10	4000	48	32	46	145	39	3
20	7000	66	52	67	154	48	4
30	10,000	84	72	88	164	57	4
31	10,300	85	74	90	165	58	4
—							
—							
—							

Locations

Galbadia Garden (Master Room)

Attacks with Edea to destroy SeeD. His sword skills have been refined, and he has gained more skills.

Spells

Level	Draw			
1~19	Fire	Thunder	Dispel	Haste
20~29	Fira	Thundara	Dispel	Haste
30~31	Firaga	Thundaga	Dispel	Haste

Card

Drop Card	Mod Card	Mod (Rare)
—	—	—

Devour

LV 1~19	LV 20~29	LV 30~31
—	—	—

Item (Drop) — Rate: 255/256

Level	178/256	51/256	15/256	12/256
1~19	Mega-Potion	Mega-Potion	Mega-Potion	Mega-Potion
20~29	Mega-Potion	Mega-Potion	Mega-Potion	Mega-Potion
30~31	Mega-Potion	Mega-Potion	Mega-Potion	Mega-Potion

Item (Mug) — Rate: 32/256

Level	178/256	51/256	15/256	12/256
1~19	Mega Phoenix	Mega Phoenix	Mega Phoenix	Mega Phoenix
20~29	Mega Phoenix	Mega Phoenix	Mega Phoenix	Mega Phoenix
30~31	Mega Phoenix	Mega Phoenix	Mega Phoenix	Mega Phoenix

Seifer (3rd round)

HP	1200~7400	AP — —
EXP	— —	Weak vs Poison

Elemental Defense

💧	1
❄	1
⚡	1
🌀	1
🔥	1.5
💧	1
💧	1
❄	1

Status Defense

†	X	⚡	100	⭐	X
☠	X	●	90	▲	100
🛡	X	✋	X	☀	X
💀	X	💠	100	%	100
💧	X	🗡	100		
🌀	X	🎩	X		
💀	X	✋	X		
💤	20	🤲	X		

LV	HP	Str	Vit	Mag	Spr	Spd	Eva
1	1200	16	81	27	131	9	4
10	3000	34	90	47	139	18	5
20	5000	52	101	68	148	28	6
30	7000	70	111	90	158	37	8
32	7400	73	113	94	159	39	8
—							
—							
—							
—							
—							

Locations

Galbadia Garden (Master Room)

Defeated once, and still trying to fight to save his pride. HP is lower due to the defeat, but skills are higher.

Spells – Draw

Level		Draw		
1~19	Fire	Thunder	Dispel	Haste
20~29	Fira	Thundara	Dispel	Haste
30~32	Firaga	Thundaga	Dispel	Haste

Drop Card	Mod Card	Mod (Rare)
—	—	—

Devour Card

LV 1~19	LV 20~29	LV 30~32
—	—	—

Item (Drop)

Level	Rate: 255/256			
	178/256	51/256	15/256	12/256
1~19	Hero	Hero	Holy War	Holy War
20~29	Hero	Hero	Holy War	Holy War
30~32	Hero	Hero	Holy War	Holy War

Item (Mug)

Level	Rate: 32/256			
	178/256	51/256	15/256	12/256
1~19	Hero	Hero	Holy War	Holy War
20~29	Hero	Hero	Holy War	Holy War
30~32	Hero	Hero	Holy War	Holy War

Seifer (4th round)

HP	3700~34,500	AP 40
EXP	— —	Weak vs Poison

Elemental Defense

💧	1
❄	1
⚡	1
🌀	1
🔥	1.5
💧	1
💧	1
❄	1

Status Defense

†	X	⚡	X	⭐	X
☠	X	●	X	▲	100
🛡	X	✋	X	☀	X
💀	X	💠	X	%	X
💧	X	🗡	X		
🌀	X	🎩	X		
💀	X	✋	X		
💤	X	🤲	X		

LV	HP	Str	Vit	Mag	Spr	Spd	Eva
1	3700	38	101	9	121	46	0
10	1000	56	105	52	125	48	1
20	17000	76	111	94	131	50	1
30	24,000	96	116	132	136	152	2
40	31,000	115	122	164	142	54	2
45	34,500	124	125	179	145	55	2
—							
—							
—							

Locations

Lunatic Pandora

To retain his pride as Sorceress' Knight, he is determined to win. His skills are even more deadly.

Spells – Draw

Level		Draw		
1~19	Fire	Thunder	Blizzard	
20~29	Fira	Thundara	Blizzara	
30~45	Firaga	Thundaga	Blizzaga	Aura

Drop Card	Mod Card	Mod (Rare)
—	—	—

Devour Card

LV 1~19	LV 20~29	LV 30~45
—	—	—

Item (Drop)

Level	Rate: 255/256			
	178/256	51/256	15/256	12/256
1~19	Hero	Hero	Holy War	Holy War
20~29	Hero	Hero	Holy War	Holy War
30~45	Hero	Hero	Holy War	Holy War

Item (Mug)

Level	Rate: 32/256			
	178/256	51/256	15/256	12/256
1~19	Hero	Hero	Holy War	Holy War
20~29	Hero	Hero	Holy War	Holy War
30~45	Hero	Hero	Holy War	Holy War

Slapper

HP	44~8430	AP 3
EXP	40 (+10)	— —

Elemental Defense

💧	1
❄	1
⚡	1
🌀	1
🔥	1
💧	1
💧	1
❄	1

Status Defense

†	70	⚡	100	⭐	60
☠	80	●	90	▲	100
🛡	70	✋	50	☀	80
💀	80	💠	100	%	100
💧	80	🗡	100		
🌀	60	🎩	80		
💀	70	✋	70		
💤	80	🤲	100		

LV	HP	Str	Vit	Mag	Spr	Spd	Eva
1	44	8	36	7	40	20	20
10	240	21	37	20	40	22	21
20	590	34	38	33	40	24	22
30	1080	47	39	47	40	26	24
40	1710	60	40	60	41	28	24
50	2480	72	42	73	41	30	26
60	3390	85	43	86	41	32	27
70	4440	97	44	99	42	34	28
80	5630	109	46	112	42	36	29
90	6960	121	47	125	42	38	30
100	8430	133	48	137	43	40	31

Locations

Galbadia Garden (Gymnasium)

A member of Galbadia Garden's demi-human ice-hockey club. Attacks with speed and team work.

Spells – Draw

Level		Draw		
1~19	Blizzard			
20~29	Blizzard	Blizzara		
30~100	Blizzard	Blizzara	Blizzaga	Water

Drop Card	Mod Card	Mod (Rare)
—	—	—

Devour Card

LV 1~19	LV 20~29	LV 30~100
—	—	—

Item (Drop)

Level	Rate: 255/256			
	178/256	51/256	15/256	12/256
1~19	Hi-Potion	Hi-Potion	Hi-Potion	Hi-Potion
20~29	Hi-Potion	Hi-Potion	Hi-Potion	Hi-Potion
30~100	Hi-Potion	Hi-Potion	Hi-Potion	Hi-Potion

Item (Mug)

Level	Rate: 32/256			
	178/256	51/256	15/256	12/256
1~19	Hi-Potion	Hi-Potion	Hi-Potion	Hi-Potion
20~29	Hi-Potion	Hi-Potion	Hi-Potion	Hi-Potion
30~100	Hi-Potion	Hi-Potion	Hi-Potion	Hi-Potion

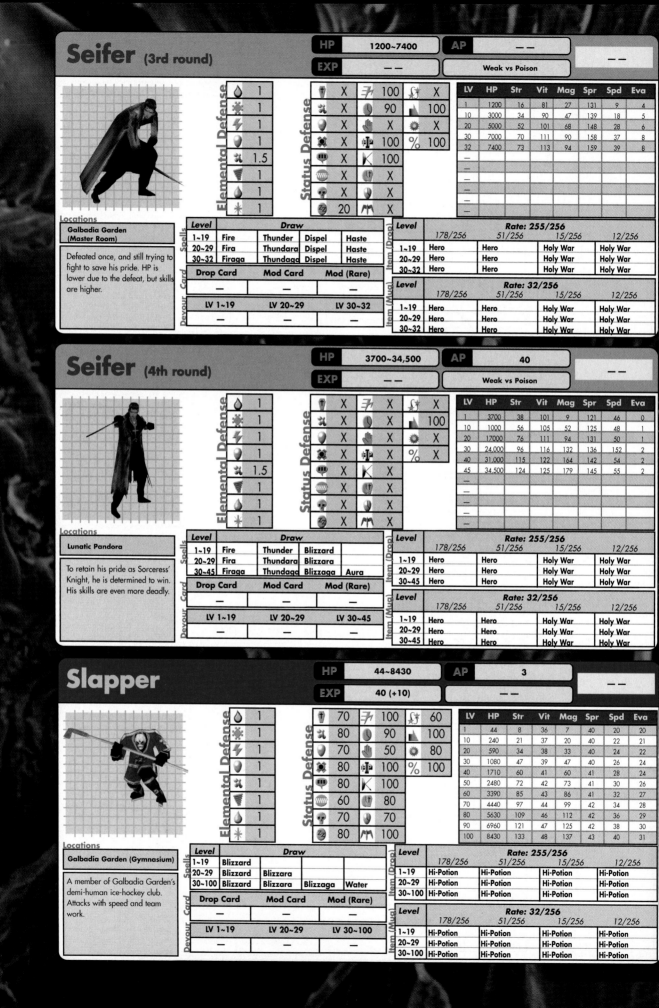

Snow Lion

HP	1063~136,000	AP	8	
EXP	150 (+20)		Weak vs Fire, Earth & Wind/Absorbs Ice	--

Elemental Defense

💧	2.5		
❄	-1		
⚡	1		
💨	1.5		
🌿	1		
🌊	1.5		
💧	1		
✴	1		

Status Defense

💀	1	⚡	100	🌀	60
🐛	X	⬤	90	🏔	100
🥚	1	✋	X	☀	80
✴	80	🔜	100	%	100
💀	80	🗡	100		
🔻	60	⬤	10		
☠	X	⬤	10		
💤	80	〰	X		

LV	HP	Str	Vit	Mag	Spr	Spd	Eva
1	1063	16	25	1	8	10	0
10	10,900	31	28	13	9	11	0
20	22,400	46	31	27	11	13	1
30	34,500	62	35	40	13	14	1
40	47,200	77	38	53	14	15	2
50	60,500	92	41	66	16	16	2
60	74,400	107	45	79	18	18	3
70	88,900	122	48	92	19	19	3
80	104,000	136	51	104	21	20	3
90	119,700	150	55	116	23	21	4
100	136,000	164	58	128	24	23	4

Locations

Trabia (Bika) Snowfield

A large monster living in the norhern snow fields. Takes time to defeat because of its high HP. Uses Ice Breath when angry.

Spells / Draw

Level	Draw			
1~19	Blizzard	Berserk		
20~29	Blizzard	Blizzara	Berserk	
30~100	Blizzard	Blizzara	Blizzaga	Berserk

Card

Drop Card	Mod Card	Mod (Rare)
Snow Lion	Snow Lion	Wedge, Biggs

Devour

LV 1~19	LV 20~29	LV 30~100
Full HP Recov.	Full HP Recov.	Full HP Recov.

Item (Drop)

Level	Rate: 255/256			
	178/256	51/256	15/256	12/256
1~19	North Wind	North Wind	Healing Mail	Healing Mail
20~29	North Wind	North Wind	Healing Mail	Healing Mail
30~100	North Wind	North Wind	Silver Mail	Silver Mail

Item (Mug)

Level	Rate: 32/256			
	178/256	51/256	15/256	12/256
1~19	Healing Mail	Healing Mail	Healing Mail	Healing Mail
20~29	Healing Mail	Healing Mail	Healing Mail	Healing Mail
30~100	Healing Mail	Healing Mail	Healing Mail	Healing Mail

Sorceress (A)

HP	3390	AP	--	
EXP	--		--	--

Elemental Defense

💧	1
❄	1
⚡	1
💨	1
🌿	1
🌊	1
💧	1
✴	1

Status Defense

💀	80	⚡	100	🌀	X
🐛	80	⬤	100	🏔	100
🥚	X	✋	X	☀	X
✴	80	🔜	100	%	100
💀	40	🗡	100		
🔻	X	⬤	80		
☠	70	⬤	X		
💤	80	〰	X		

LV	HP	Str	Vit	Mag	Spr	Spd	Eva
45	3390	73	10	202	1	50	2
—							

Locations

Commencement Room

Sorceress from beyond time who appeared due to Time Compression. Uses magic, but it is not very powerful.

Spells / Draw

Level	Draw		
45	Firaga	Thundaga	Blizzaga

Card

Drop Card	Mod Card	Mod (Rare)
—	—	—

Devour

LV 45
—

Item (Drop)

Level	Rate: 255/256			
	178/256	51/256	15/256	12/256
45	Flare Stone	Holy Stone	Meteor Stone	Ultima Stone

Item (Mug)

Level	Rate: 32/256			
	178/256	51/256	15/256	12/256
45	Meteor Stone	Ultima Stone	Ultima Stone	Ultima Stone

Sorceress (B)

HP	4496	AP	--	
EXP	--		--	--

Elemental Defense

💧	1
❄	1
⚡	1
💨	1
🌿	1
🌊	1
💧	1
✴	1

Status Defense

💀	80	⚡	100	🌀	X
🐛	80	⬤	X	🏔	100
🥚	X	✋	X	☀	X
✴	80	🔜	100	%	100
💀	40	🗡	100		
🔻	X	⬤	80		
☠	70	⬤	X		
💤	80	〰	X		

LV	HP	Str	Vit	Mag	Spr	Spd	Eva
45	4496	98	10	176	1	40	2
—							

Locations

Commencement Room

Sorceress from beyond time who appeared due to Time Compression. Uses magic, but it is not very powerful.

Spells / Draw

Level	Draw	
45	Haste	Double

Card

Drop Card	Mod Card	Mod (Rare)
—	—	—

Devour

LV 45
—

Item (Drop)

Level	Rate: 255/256			
	178/256	51/256	15/256	12/256
45	Flare Stone	Holy Stone	Meteor Stone	Ultima Stone

Item (Mug)

Level	Rate: 32/256			
	178/256	51/256	15/256	12/256
45	Meteor Stone	Ultima Stone	Ultima Stone	Ultima Stone

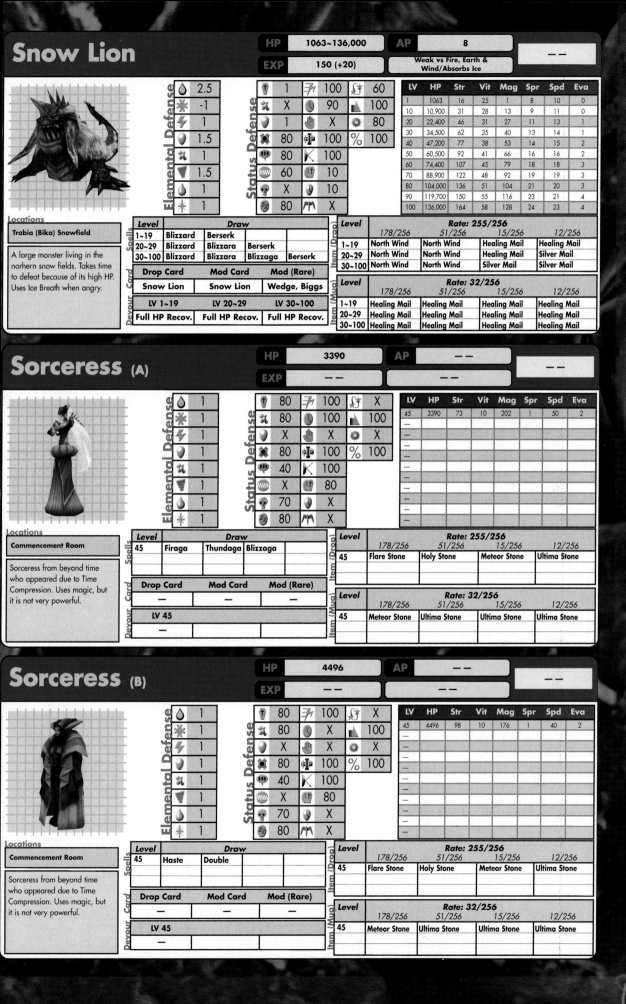

Sorceress (C)

HP	32,500	AP	55	
EXP	——		——	——

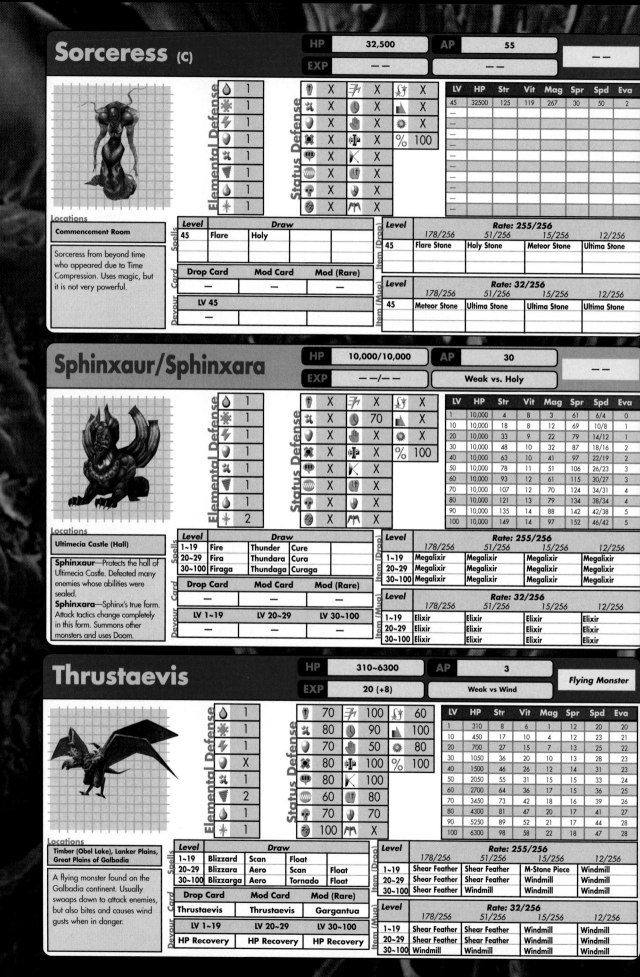

Elemental Defense: 1, 1, 1, 1, 1, 1, 1, 1

Status Defense: X, X, X, X, X, X, X, X, X, X, X, X, X, X, X, X, X; % 100

LV	HP	Str	Vit	Mag	Spr	Spd	Eva
45	32500	125	119	267	30	50	2

Locations
Commencement Room

Sorceress from beyond time who appeared due to Time Compression. Uses magic, but it is not very powerful.

Spells / Draw

Level	Draw		
45	Flare	Holy	

Card

Drop Card	Mod Card	Mod (Rare)
—	—	—

Devour

LV 45

Item (Drop) — Rate: 255/256

Level	178/256	51/256	15/256	12/256
45	Flare Stone	Holy Stone	Meteor Stone	Ultima Stone

Item (Mug) — Rate: 32/256

Level	178/256	51/256	15/256	12/256
45	Meteor Stone	Ultima Stone	Ultima Stone	Ultima Stone

Sphinxaur/Sphinxara

HP	10,000/10,000	AP	30	
EXP	——/——		Weak vs. Holy	——

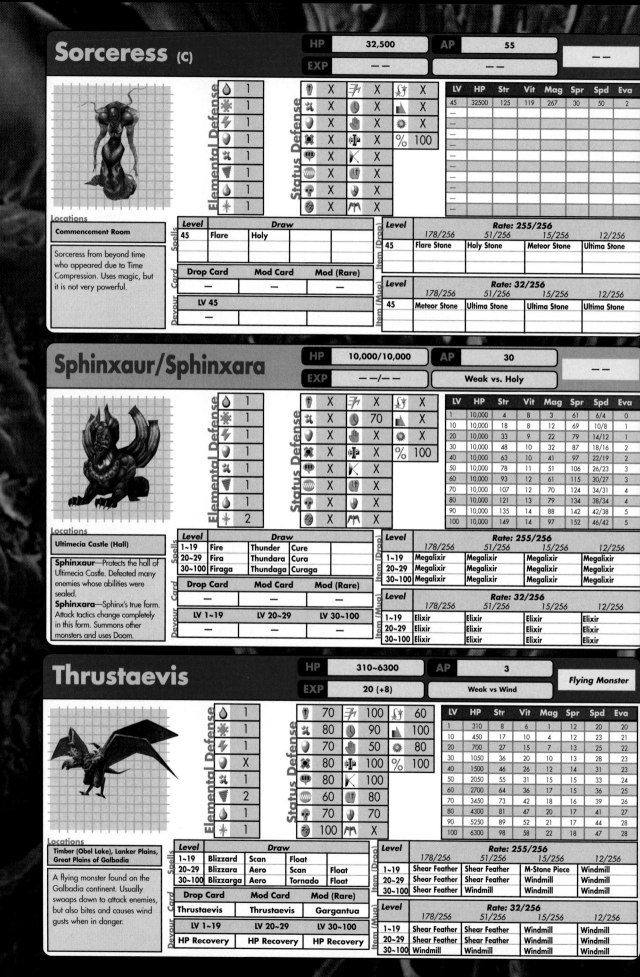

Elemental Defense: 1, 1, 1, 1, 1, 1, 1, 2

Status Defense: X, X, X; X, 70, X; X, X, X; X, X, X; X; X; X; X; X; X; % 100

LV	HP	Str	Vit	Mag	Spr	Spd	Eva
1	10,000	4	8	3	61	6/4	0
10	10,000	18	8	12	69	10/8	1
20	10,000	33	9	22	79	14/12	1
30	10,000	48	10	32	87	18/16	2
40	10,000	63	10	41	97	22/19	2
50	10,000	78	11	51	106	26/23	3
60	10,000	93	12	61	115	30/27	3
70	10,000	107	12	70	124	34/31	4
80	10,000	121	13	79	134	38/34	4
90	10,000	135	14	88	142	42/38	5
100	10,000	149	14	97	152	46/42	5

Locations
Ultimecia Castle (Hall)

Sphinxaur—Protects the hall of Ultimecia Castle. Defeated many enemies whose abilities were sealed.
Sphinxara—Sphinx's true form. Attack tactics change completely in this form. Summons other monsters and uses Doom.

Spells / Draw

Level	Draw		
1~19	Fire	Thunder	Cure
20~29	Fira	Thundara	Cura
30~100	Firaga	Thundaga	Curaga

Card

Drop Card	Mod Card	Mod (Rare)
—	—	—

Devour

LV 1~19	LV 20~29	LV 30~100
—	—	—

Item (Drop) — Rate: 255/256

Level	178/256	51/256	15/256	12/256
1~19	Megalixir	Megalixir	Megalixir	Megalixir
20~29	Megalixir	Megalixir	Megalixir	Megalixir
30~100	Megalixir	Megalixir	Megalixir	Megalixir

Item (Mug) — Rate: 32/256

Level	178/256	51/256	15/256	12/256
1~19	Elixir	Elixir	Elixir	Elixir
20~29	Elixir	Elixir	Elixir	Elixir
30~100	Elixir	Elixir	Elixir	Elixir

Thrustaevis

HP	310~6300	AP	3	
EXP	20 (+8)		Weak vs Wind	Flying Monster

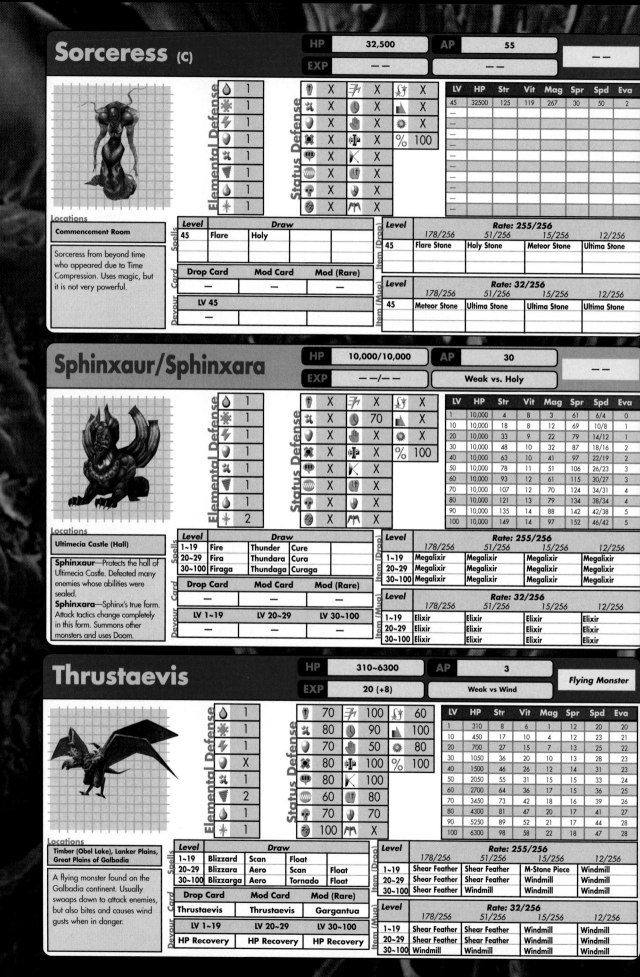

Elemental Defense: 1, 1, 1, X, 1, 2, 1, 1

Status Defense: 70, 100, 60; 80, 90, 100; 70, 50, 80; 80, 100, % 100; 80, 100; 60, 80; 70, 70; 100, X

LV	HP	Str	Vit	Mag	Spr	Spd	Eva
1	310	8	6	1	12	20	20
10	450	17	10	4	12	23	21
20	700	27	15	7	13	25	22
30	1050	36	20	10	13	28	23
40	1500	46	26	12	14	31	23
50	2050	55	31	15	15	33	24
60	2700	64	36	17	15	36	25
70	3450	73	42	18	16	39	26
80	4300	81	47	20	17	41	27
90	5250	89	52	21	17	44	28
100	6300	98	58	22	18	47	28

Locations
Timber (Obel Lake), Lanker Plains, Great Plains of Galbadia

A flying monster found on the Galbadia continent. Usually swoops down to attack enemies, but also bites and causes wind gusts when in danger.

Spells / Draw

Level	Draw			
1~19	Blizzard	Scan	Float	
20~29	Blizzara	Aero	Scan	Float
30~100	Blizzarga	Aero	Tornado	Float

Card

Drop Card	Mod Card	Mod (Rare)
Thrustaevis	Thrustaevis	Gargantua

Devour

LV 1~19	LV 20~29	LV 30~100
HP Recovery	HP Recovery	HP Recovery

Item (Drop) — Rate: 255/256

Level	178/256	51/256	15/256	12/256
1~19	Shear Feather	Shear Feather	M-Stone Piece	Windmill
20~29	Shear Feather	Shear Feather	Windmill	Windmill
30~100	Shear Feather	Windmill	Windmill	Windmill

Item (Mug) — Rate: 32/256

Level	178/256	51/256	15/256	12/256
1~19	Shear Feather	Shear Feather	Windmill	Windmill
20~29	Shear Feather	Shear Feather	Windmill	Windmill
30~100	Windmill	Windmill	Windmill	Windmill

Tiamat

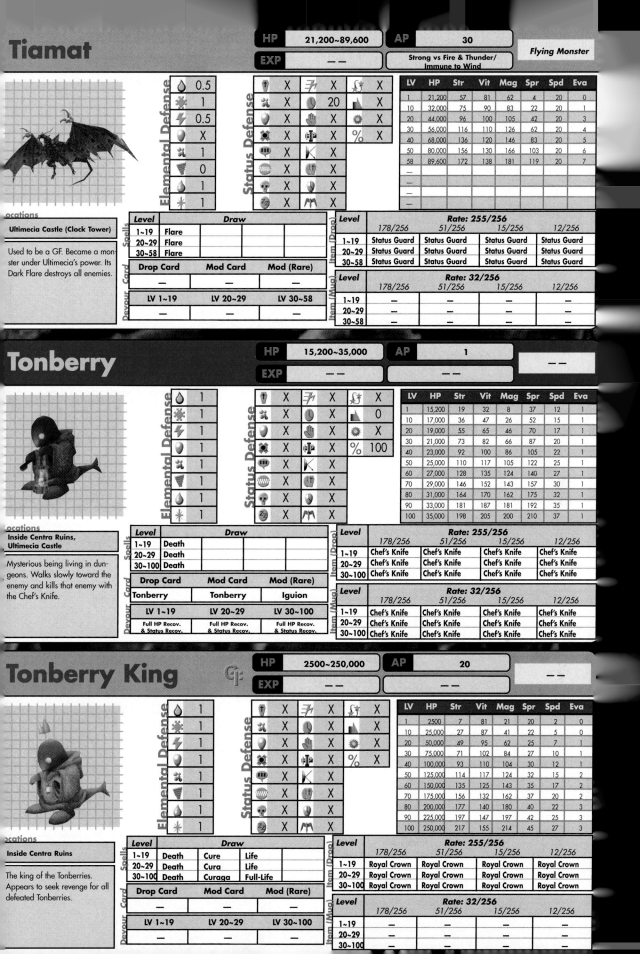

HP	21,200~89,600
AP	30
EXP	——
	Strong vs Fire & Thunder/ Immune to Wind
	Flying Monster

Elemental Defense: 0.5 / 1 / 0.5 / X / 1 / 0 / 1

Status Defense: X / X / X / X / X / X / X / X — 20 — X

LV	HP	Str	Vit	Mag	Spr	Spd	Eva
1	21,200	57	81	62	4	20	0
10	32,000	75	90	83	22	20	1
20	44,000	96	100	105	42	20	3
30	56,000	116	110	126	62	20	4
40	68,000	136	120	146	83	20	5
50	80,000	156	130	166	103	20	6
58	89,600	172	138	181	119	20	7

Locations

Ultimecia Castle (Clock Tower)

Used to be a GF. Became a monster under Ultimecia's power. Its Dark Flare destroys all enemies.

Draw

Level	Draw
1~19	Flare
20~29	Flare
30~58	Flare

Drop Card / Mod Card / Mod (Rare): — / — / —

Devour Card: LV 1~19 — / LV 20~29 — / LV 30~58 —

Item (Drop) — Rate: 255/256

Level	178/256	51/256	15/256	12/256
1~19	Status Guard	Status Guard	Status Guard	Status Guard
20~29	Status Guard	Status Guard	Status Guard	Status Guard
30~58	Status Guard	Status Guard	Status Guard	Status Guard

Item (Mug) — Rate: 32/256

Level	178/256	51/256	15/256	12/256
1~19	—	—	—	—
20~29	—	—	—	—
30~58	—	—	—	—

Tonberry

HP	15,200~35,000
AP	1
EXP	——
	——
	——

Elemental Defense: 1 / 1 / 1 / 1 / 1 / 1 / 1 / 1

Status Defense: X / X / X / X / X / X / X / X — 0 — X — 100

LV	HP	Str	Vit	Mag	Spr	Spd	Eva
1	15,200	19	32	8	37	12	1
10	17,000	36	47	26	52	15	1
20	19,000	55	65	46	70	17	1
30	21,000	73	82	66	87	20	1
40	23,000	92	100	86	105	22	1
50	25,000	110	117	105	122	25	1
60	27,000	128	135	124	140	27	1
70	29,000	146	152	143	157	30	1
80	31,000	164	170	162	175	32	1
90	33,000	181	181	181	192	35	1
100	35,000	198	205	200	210	37	1

Locations

Inside Centra Ruins, Ultimecia Castle

Mysterious being living in dungeons. Walks slowly toward the enemy and kills that enemy with the Chef's Knife.

Draw

Level	Draw
1~19	Death
20~29	Death
30~100	Death

Drop Card / Mod Card / Mod (Rare): Tonberry / Tonberry / Iguion

Devour Card:

LV 1~19	LV 20~29	LV 30~100
Full HP Recov. & Status Recov.	Full HP Recov. & Status Recov.	Full HP Recov. & Status Recov.

Item (Drop) — Rate: 255/256

Level	178/256	51/256	15/256	12/256
1~19	Chef's Knife	Chef's Knife	Chef's Knife	Chef's Knife
20~29	Chef's Knife	Chef's Knife	Chef's Knife	Chef's Knife
30~100	Chef's Knife	Chef's Knife	Chef's Knife	Chef's Knife

Item (Mug) — Rate: 32/256

Level	178/256	51/256	15/256	12/256
1~19	Chef's Knife	Chef's Knife	Chef's Knife	Chef's Knife
20~29	Chef's Knife	Chef's Knife	Chef's Knife	Chef's Knife
30~100	Chef's Knife	Chef's Knife	Chef's Knife	Chef's Knife

Tonberry King GF

HP	2500~250,000
AP	20
EXP	——
	——
	——

Elemental Defense: 1 / 1 / 1 / 1 / 1 / 1 / 1 / 1

Status Defense: X / X / X / X / X / X / X / X

LV	HP	Str	Vit	Mag	Spr	Spd	Eva
1	2500	7	81	21	20	2	0
10	25,000	27	87	41	22	5	0
20	50,000	49	95	62	25	7	1
30	75,000	71	102	84	27	10	1
40	100,000	93	110	104	30	12	1
50	125,000	114	117	124	32	15	2
60	150,000	135	125	143	35	17	2
70	175,000	156	132	162	37	20	2
80	200,000	177	140	180	40	22	3
90	225,000	197	147	197	42	25	3
100	250,000	217	155	214	45	27	3

Locations

Inside Centra Ruins

The king of the Tonberries. Appears to seek revenge for all defeated Tonberries.

Draw

Level	Draw		
1~19	Death	Cure	Life
20~29	Death	Cura	Life
30~100	Death	Curaga	Full-Life

Drop Card / Mod Card / Mod (Rare): — / — / —

Devour Card: LV 1~19 — / LV 20~29 — / LV 30~100 —

Item (Drop) — Rate: 255/256

Level	178/256	51/256	15/256	12/256
1~19	Royal Crown	Royal Crown	Royal Crown	Royal Crown
20~29	Royal Crown	Royal Crown	Royal Crown	Royal Crown
30~100	Royal Crown	Royal Crown	Royal Crown	Royal Crown

Item (Mug) — Rate: 32/256

Level	178/256	51/256	15/256	12/256
1~19	—	—	—	—
20~29	—	—	—	—
30~100	—	—	—	—

Torama

HP	231~38,000
AP	4
EXP	100 (+10)
	——

Elemental Defense: 1, 1, 1, 1, 1, 1, 1, 1

Status Defense: X, X, 20, 30, X, X, 20, 80 / 100, 90, 1, 100, 100, 20, 20, X / X, 100, 80, 100

LV	HP	Str	Vit	Mag	Spr	Spd	Eva
1	231	11	39	64	111	10	10
10	2450	20	44	80	115	11	13
20	5520	30	50	97	121	13	15
30	8250	40	56	114	127	14	18
40	11,600	50	63	131	133	15	20
50	15,250	60	69	149	139	16	23
60	19,200	69	75	166	145	18	25
70	23,450	79	81	183	150	19	28
80	28,000	88	88	199	156	20	30
90	32,850	96	94	216	162	21	33
100	38,000	105	100	233	168	23	35

Locations: Esthar City, Lunatic Pandora

Uses multiple magic attacks while sitting down. Even more powerful when it stands up to use its blaster attacks.

Spells (Draw)

Level	Draw		
1~19	Death	Demi	Life
20~29	Death	Demi	
30~100	Death	Demi	Life

Card

Drop Card	Mod Card	Mod (Rare)
Torama	Torama	Tri-Point

Devour

LV 1~19	LV 20~29	LV 30~100
Full HP Recov.	Full HP Reco. & Status Recov.	Full HP Recov. & Status Recov.

Item (Drop) — Rate: 255/256

Level	178/256	51/256	15/256	12/256
1~19	Wizard Stone	Wizard Stone	Life Ring	Life Ring
20~29	Regen Ring	Regen Ring	Moon Stone	Moon Stone
30~100	Regen Ring	Moon Stone	Regen Ring	Moon Stone

Item (Mug) — Rate: 32/256

Level	178/256	51/256	15/256	12/256
1~19	Regen Ring	Regen Ring	Regen Ring	Regen Ring
20~29	Regen Ring	Regen Ring	Regen Ring	Regen Ring
30~100	Regen Ring	Regen Ring	Regen Ring	Regen Ring

T-Rexaur

HP	10,363~76,000
AP	10
EXP	160 (+10)
	Weak vs Ice/Strong vs Poison

Elemental Defense: 1, 2.5, 1, 1, 0.5, , , 1

Status Defense: 30, 80, 40, 80, 80, 60, 70, 50 / 100, 90, 20, 100, 100, 10, 50, 70 / 100, 80, 100, 40

LV	HP	Str	Vit	Mag	Spr	Spd	Eva
1	10,363	17	6	1	35	3	0
10	13,900	38	7	5	35	4	1
20	18,400	61	8	8	35	5	1
30	23,500	83	9	12	36	6	2
40	29,200	106	11	14	36	7	2
50	35,500	128	12	17	37	8	3
60	42,400	151	13	19	37	9	3
70	49,900	173	14	20	37	10	4
80	58,000	195	16	21	38	11	4
90	66,700	217	17	22	38	12	5
100	76,000	239	18	22	39	13	5

Locations: Balamb (Alcauld Plains), Balamb Garden Training Center

Alive since the beginning of time, its power and HP are very high. It's better to run if you encounter one.

Spells (Draw)

Level	Draw		
1~19	Fire	Thunder	
20~29	Fira	Thundara	
30~100	Firaga	Thundaga	Quake

Card

Drop Card	Mod Card	Mod (Rare)
T-Rexaur	T-Rexaur	Shumi Tribe

Devour

LV 1~19	LV 20~29	LV 30~100
HP Recovery	HP Recovery	Strength +1

Item (Drop) — Rate: 255/256

Level	178/256	51/256	15/256	12/256
1~19	Dino Bone	M-Stone	Magic Stone	Dino Bone
20~29	Dino Bone	Dragon Fang	Dino Bone	Dino Bone
30~100	Dino Bone	Star Fragment	Dino Bone	Star Fragment

Item (Mug) — Rate: 32/256

Level	178/256	51/256	15/256	12/256
1~19	Dino Bone	Dino Bone	Dino Bone	Dino Bone
20~29	Dino Bone	Dino Bone	Dino Bone	Dino Bone
30~100				

Trauma

HP	5555~34,114
AP	30
EXP	——
	Weak vs Wind
	Flying Monster

Elemental Defense: 1, 1, 1, X, 1, 2, 1, 1

Status Defense: X, X, X, X, X, X, X, X / X, 90, X, X, X, X, X, X / X, X, 90, 100

LV	HP	Str	Vit	Mag	Spr	Spd	Eva
1	5555	2	180	12	36	36	3
10	10,125	40	180	35	36	36	3
20	15,250	60	180	60	36	36	3
30	20,425	80	180	85	36	36	3
40	25,650	99	180	110	36	36	3
50	30,925	119	180	134	36	36	3
55	34,114	130	180	149	36	36	3
—							
—							
—							

Locations: Ultimecia Castle (Art Gallery)

Ultimecia gave partial life to this weapon of the future. Pulse Cannon destroys any enemies in its way.

Spells (Draw)

Level	Draw
1~19	Meltdown
20~29	Meltdown
30~55	Meltdown

Card

Drop Card	Mod Card	Mod (Rare)
—		

Devour

LV 1~19	LV 20~29	LV 30~55
—	—	—

Item (Drop) — Rate: 255/256

Level	178/256	51/256	15/256	12/256
1~19	Elem Atk	Elem Atk	Elem Atk	Elem Atk
20~29	Elem Atk	Elem Atk	Elem Atk	Elem Atk
30~55	Elem Atk	Elem Atk	Elem Atk	Elem Atk

Item (Mug) — Rate: 32/256

Level	178/256	51/256	15/256	12/256
1~19	—	—	—	—
20~29	—	—	—	—
30~55	—	—	—	—

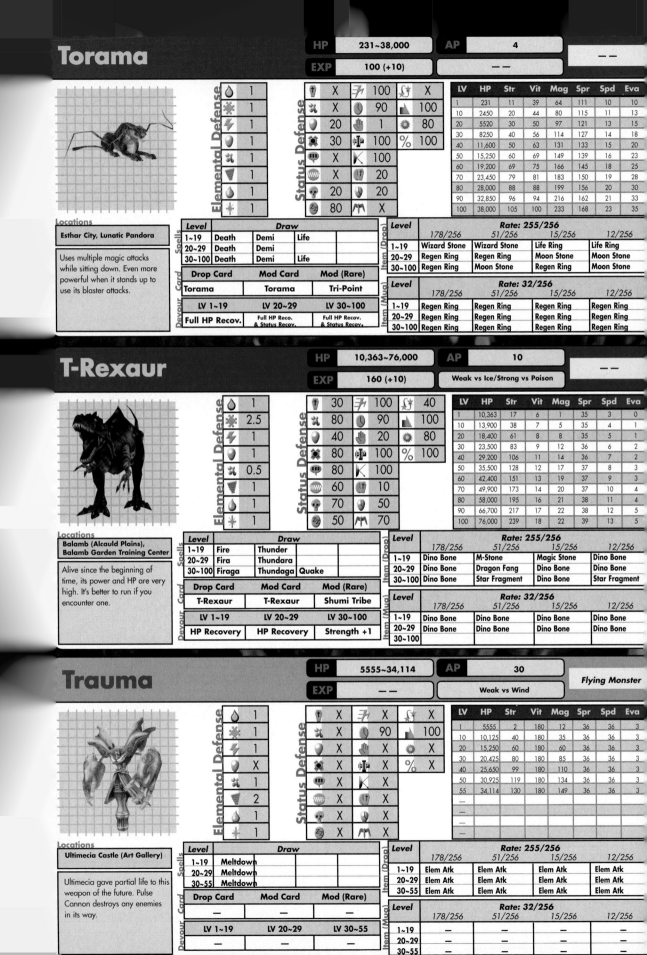

Tri-Face

HP	6027~21,600	AP 8
EXP	130 (+40)	— —

Weak vs Fire/Absorbs Poison/ Very Weak vs Holy

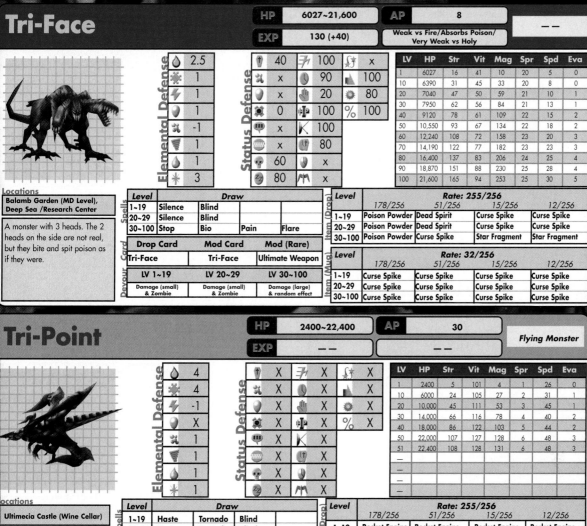

Elemental Defense

💧	2.5
❄	1
⚡	1
🌪	1
☄	-1
🔻	1
💧	1
✴	3

Status Defense

💡 40	⚡ 100		x
☠ x	🥚 90		100
🥚 x	✋ 20	☀	80
☣ 0	🌵 100	%	100
💠 x	🗡 100		
🔩 x	🛡 80		
☮ 60	✋ x		
🎮 80	🕸 x		

Locations
Balamb Garden (MD Level), Deep Sea /Research Center

A monster with 3 heads. The 2 heads on the side are not real, but they bite and spit poison as if they were.

LV	HP	Str	Vit	Mag	Spr	Spd	Eva
1	6027	16	41	10	20	5	0
10	6390	31	45	33	20	8	0
20	7040	47	50	59	21	10	1
30	7950	62	56	84	21	13	1
40	9120	78	61	109	22	15	2
50	10,550	93	67	134	22	18	2
60	12,240	108	72	158	23	20	3
70	14,190	122	77	182	23	23	3
80	16,400	137	83	206	24	25	4
90	18,870	151	88	230	25	28	4
100	21,600	165	94	253	25	30	5

Spells

Level	Draw			
1~19	Silence	Blind		
20~29	Silence	Blind		
30~100	Stop	Bio	Pain	Flare

Drop Card	Mod Card	Mod (Rare)
Tri-Face	Tri-Face	Ultimate Weapon

Devour Card

LV 1~19	LV 20~29	LV 30~100
Damage (small) & Zombie	Damage (small) & Zombie	Damage (large) & random effect

Item (Drop)

Level	Rate: 255/256			
	178/256	51/256	15/256	12/256
1~19	Poison Powder	Dead Spirit	Curse Spike	Curse Spike
20~29	Poison Powder	Dead Spirit	Curse Spike	Curse Spike
30~100	Poison Powder	Curse Spike	Star Fragment	Star Fragment

Item (Mug)

Level	Rate: 32/256			
	178/256	51/256	15/256	12/256
1~19	Curse Spike	Curse Spike	Curse Spike	Curse Spike
20~29	Curse Spike	Curse Spike	Curse Spike	Curse Spike
30~100	Curse Spike	Curse Spike	Curse Spike	Curse Spike

Tri-Point

HP	2400~22,400	AP 30
EXP	— —	— —

Flying Monster

Elemental Defense

💧	4
❄	4
⚡	-1
🌪	X
☄	1
🔻	1
💧	1
✴	1

Status Defense

💡 X	⚡ X		X
☠ X	🥚 X		X
🥚 X	✋ X	☀	X
☣ X	🌵 X	%	X
💠 X	🗡 X		
🔩 X	🛡 X		
☮ X	✋ X		
🎮 X	🕸 X		

Locations
Ultimecia Castle (Wine Cellar)

A living weapon Ultimecia made out of a dragon. Fire or ice are its weak points, but they change when attacked.

LV	HP	Str	Vit	Mag	Spr	Spd	Eva
1	2400	5	101	4	1	26	0
10	6000	24	105	27	2	31	1
20	10,000	45	111	53	3	45	1
30	14,000	66	116	78	4	40	2
40	18,000	86	122	103	5	44	2
50	22,000	107	127	128	6	48	3
51	22,400	108	128	131	6	48	3
—							
—							
—							

Spells

Level	Draw		
1~19	Haste	Tornado	Blind
20~29	Haste	Tornado	Blind
30~51	Haste	Tornado	Blind

Drop Card	Mod Card	Mod (Rare)
—	—	—

Devour Card

LV 1~19	LV 20~29	LV 30~51

Item (Drop)

Level	Rate: 255/256			
	178/256	51/256	15/256	12/256
1~19	Rocket Engine	Rocket Engine	Rocket Engine	Rocket Engine
20~29	Rocket Engine	Rocket Engine	Rocket Engine	Rocket Engine
30~51	Rocket Engine	Rocket Engine	Rocket Engine	Rocket Engine

Item (Mug)

Level	Rate: 32/256			
	178/256	51/256	15/256	12/256
1~19	—	—	—	—
20~29	—	—	—	—
30~51	—	—	—	—

Turtapod

HP	1205~4200	AP 2
EXP	50 (+10)	— —

Elemental Defense

💧	1
❄	1
⚡	1
🌪	1
☄	1
🔻	1
💧	1
✴	1

Status Defense

💡 70	⚡ 100		60
☠ 80	🥚 90		100
🥚 70	✋ 50	☀	80
☣ 80	🌵 100	%	100
💠 80	🗡 100		
🔩 60	🛡 80		
☮ 70	✋ 70		
🎮 80	🕸 100		

Locations
Esthar, Lunatic Pandora

Attacks with magic and sharp claws. When attacked it may change to defense mode in order to protect itself from damage.

LV	HP	Str	Vit	Mag	Spr	Spd	Eva
1	1205	9	110	5	8	10	0
10	1275	18	112	9	9	11	0
20	1400	28	115	12	10	11	1
30	1575	37	117	16	11	12	1
40	1800	46	120	19	13	13	1
50	2075	55	122	23	14	13	1
60	2400	63	125	26	15	14	2
70	2775	71	127	29	16	14	2
80	3200	78	130	31	18	15	2
90	3675	86	132	34	19	16	3
100	4200	93	135	36	20	16	3

Spells

Level	Draw		
1~29	Cure	Esuna	Dispel
30~39	Cura	Esuna	Dispel
40~100	Cura	Esuna	Dispel

Drop Card	Mod Card	Mod (Rare)
Turtapod	Turtapod Card	Trauma

Devour Card

LV 1~29	LV 30~39	LV 40~100
Full HP Recov.	Full HP Recov.	Full HP Recov.

Item (Drop)

Level	Rate: 255/256			
	178/256	51/256	15/256	12/256
1~29	Wizard Stone	Wizard Stone	Life Ring	Life Ring
30~39	Life Ring	Healing Mail	Regen Ring	Regen Ring
40~100	Life Ring	Healing Mail	Regen Ring	Regen Ring

Item (Mug)

Level	Rate: 32/256			
	178/256	51/256	15/256	12/256
1~29	Wizard Stone	Wizard Stone	Wizard Stone	Wizard Stone
30~39	Wizard Stone	Wizard Stone	Wizard Stone	Wizard Stone
40~100	Wizard Stone	Wizard Stone	Wizard Stone	Wizard Stone

UFO

HP	121~12,100	AP	– –
EXP	– –		– –

Elemental Defense: 💧1 ❄1 ⚡1 🌀1 ☠1 🌪1 💧1 ✴1

Status Defense:

✝ X	⚡ X	⭐ X			
🦂 X	● X	▲ X			
🛡 X	✋ X	☀ X			
💀 X	✚ X	% 100			
🔵 X	🗡 X				
💀 X	🎩 X				
☠ X	🛡 X				
💤 X	🎭 X				

LV	HP	Str	Vit	Mag	Spr	Spd	Eva
1	121	3	2	2	2	26	0
10	400	11	6	3	6	28	1
20	900	18	12	5	12	30	1
30	1600	26	17	6	17	32	2
40	2500	33	23	7	23	34	2
50	3600	40	28	9	28	35	3
60	4900	47	34	10	34	38	3
70	6400	54	39	11	39	39	4
80	8100	61	45	12	45	41	4
90	10,000	67	50	13	50	43	5
100	12,100	73	56	13	56	45	5

Locations

Grandidi Forest (mountain side)

Unidentified flying object from outer spae.

Spells / Draw

Level	Draw			
1~19	Demi			
20~29	Demi			
30~100	Demi			

Drop Card	Mod Card	Mod (Rare)
—	—	—

LV 1~19	LV 20~29	LV 30~100
—		

Item (Drop) — Rate: 255/256

Level	178/256	51/256	15/256	12/256
1~19	Aegis Amulet	Aegis Amulet	Aegis Amulet	Aegis Amulet
20~29	Aegis Amulet	Aegis Amulet	Aegis Amulet	Aegis Amulet
30~100	Aegis Amulet	Aegis Amulet	Aegis Amulet	Aegis Amulet

Item (Mug) — Rate: 32/256

Level	178/256	51/256	15/256	12/256
1~19	—	—	—	—
20~29	—	—	—	—
30~100	—	—	—	—

Ultima Weapon

HP	51,100~160,000	AP	100
EXP	– –		– –

Elemental Defense: 💧1 ❄1 ⚡1 🌀1 ☠1 🌪1 💧1 ✴1

Status Defense:

✝ X	⚡ X	⭐ X			
🦂 X	● X	▲ X			
🛡 X	✋ X	☀ X			
💀 X	✚ X	% X			
🔵 X	🗡 X				
💀 X	🎩 X				
☠ X	🛡 X				
💤 X	🎭 X				

LV	HP	Str	Vit	Mag	Spr	Spd	Eva
1	51,100	40	12	8	127	27	0
10	61,000	62	28	27	130	38	1
20	72,000	87	45	48	133	50	1
30	83,000	110	64	69	137	62	2
40	94,000	133	81	90	140	74	2
50	105,000	155	99	111	143	85	3
60	116,000	177	117	132	147	98	3
70	127,000	197	135	152	150	109	4
80	138,000	217	152	173	153	121	4
90	149,000	236	171	1'93	157	133	5
100	160,000	254	188	213	160	145	5

Locations

Deep Sea Deposit

The strongest ultimate monster. It's said to be impossible to defeat.

Spells / Draw

Level	Draw			
1~19	Regen	Dispel	Ultima	Eden
20~29	Regen	Dispel	Ultima	Eden
30~100	Regen	Dispel	Ultima	Eden

Drop Card	Mod Card	Mod (Rare)
Eden	—	—

LV 1~19	LV 20~29	LV 30~100
—		

Item (Drop) — Rate: 255/256

Level	178/256	51/256	15/256	12/256
1~19	Ultima Stone	Ultima Stone	Ultima Stone	Ultima Stone
20~29	Ultima Stone	Ultima Stone	Ultima Stone	Ultima Stone
30~100	Ultima Stone	Ultima Stone	Ultima Stone	Ultima Stone

Item (Mug) — Rate: 32/256

Level	178/256	51/256	15/256	12/256
1~19	Three Stars	Three Stars	Three Stars	Three Stars
20~29	Three Stars	Three Stars	Three Stars	Three Stars
30~100	Three Stars	Three Stars	Three Stars	Three Stars

Vysage

HP	3031~21,000	AP	6
EXP	100 (+15)		Weak vs Holy

Elemental Defense: 💧1 ❄1 ⚡1 🌀1 ☠1 🌪1 💧1 ✴1.5

Status Defense:

✝ X	⚡ X	⭐ X			
🦂 80	● X	▲ 100			
🛡 X	✋ X	☀ X			
💀 80	✚ 100	% 100			
🔵 80	🗡 100				
💀 X	🎩 X				
☠ 70	🛡 X				
💤 X	🎭 X				

LV	HP	Str	Vit	Mag	Spr	Spd	Eva
1	3031	12	18	14	15	5	0
10	3450	23	20	23	20	6	1
20	4200	35	22	33	25	7	1
30	5250	46	24	43	30	8	2
40	6600	57	26	53	35	8	3
50	8250	68	28	62	40	9	3
60	10,200	79	30	72	45	10	4
70	12,450	89	32	81	50	11	4
80	15,000	99	34	91	55	12	5
90	17,850	109	36	100	60	13	6
100	21,000	119	38	109	65	13	6

Locations

Timber (Shenand Hill), Great Salt Lake

A monster shaped like a face. Uses support magic and special attacks when attacking with Righty and Lefty together.

Spells / Draw

Level	Draw		
1~19	Esuna	Haste	
20~29	Esuna	Haste	
30~100	Esuna	Haste	Bio

Drop Card	Mod Card	Mod (Rare)
Vysage	—	—

LV 1~19	LV 20~29	LV 30~100
—	—	—

Item (Drop) — Rate: 255/256

Level	178/256	51/256	15/256	12/256
1~19	M-Stone	Lightweight	M-Stone	M-Stone
20~29	Magic Stone	Lightweight	Magic Stone	Magic Stone
30~100	Wizard Stone	Lightweight	Lightweight	Lightweight

Item (Mug) — Rate: 32/256

Level	178/256	51/256	15/256	12/256
1~19	Lightweight	Lightweight	Lightweight	Lightweight
20~29	Lightweight	Lightweight	Lightweight	Lightweight
30~100	Lightweight	Lightweight	Lightweight	Lightweight

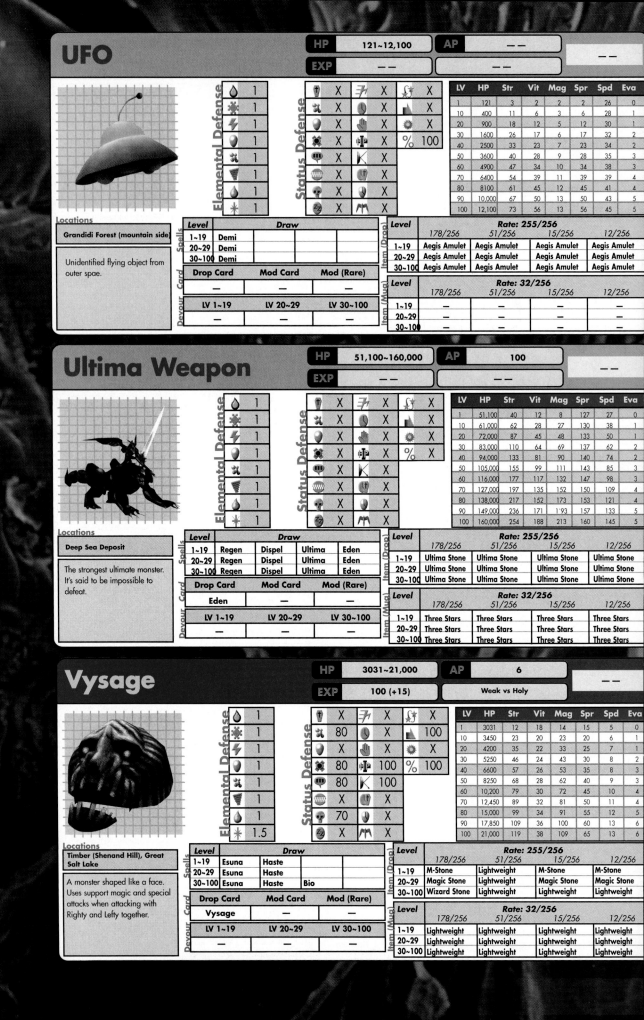

Wedge (1st round)

HP	416~640	AP	4	— —
EXP	— —		Immune to Poison	

Elemental Defense

💧	1
❄	1
⚡	1
🌑	1
🌀	1
🌪	1
💧	1
✦	1

Status Defense

✝	X	⚡	X	👣	X
😷	X	✋	X	▨	X
🎈	X	☀	X		
☠	X	🛡	X	%	100
😵	X	🗡	X		
💀	X	👣	X		
☠	X	💀	X		
🔵	X	👣	X		

LV	HP	Str	Vit	Mag	Spr	Spd	Eva
1	416	7	23	3	33	5	1
10	640	14	29	11	37	6	2
—							

Locations

Dollet (Comm Tower)

A Galbadian soldier assigned to the Dollet Communication Tower. Always picked on by his superior, Major Biggs.

Spells / Draw

Level	Draw			
1~10	Fire	Thunder	Blizzard	Cure

Card

Drop Card	Mod Card	Mod (Rare)
—	—	—

Devour

LV 1~10		

Item (Drop)

Level	Rate: 255/256			
	178/256	51/256	15/256	12/256
1~10	Cottage	Cottage	Cottage	Cottage

Item (Mug)

Level	Rate: 32/256			
	178/256	51/256	15/256	12/256
1~10	—	—	—	—

Wedge (2nd round)

HP	1416~2139	AP	— —	— —
EXP	— —		Immune to Poison	

Elemental Defense

💧	1
❄	1
⚡	1
🌑	1
🌀	1
🌪	1
💧	1
✦	1

Status Defense

✝	X	⚡	100	👣	60
😷	80	✋	90	▨	100
🎈	X	✋	X	☀	X
☠	80	🛡	100	%	100
😵	80	🗡	100		
💀	X	👣	X		
☠	70	👣	X		
🔵	X	👣	100		

LV	HP	Str	Vit	Mag	Spr	Spd	Eva
1	1416	7	23	4	33	5	1
10	1640	18	29	14	37	6	2
20	2040	30	36	26	42	6	2
22	2139	32	37	28	43	7	3

Locations

Galbadia D-District Prison

Demoted along with Biggs for his part in the failure of the Dollet Communication Tower Operation. Unfortunately, still works under Biggs.

Spells / Draw

Level	Draw			
1~19	Fire	Shell	Protect	Reflect
20~22	Fira	Shell	Protect	Reflect

Card

Drop Card	Mod Card	Mod (Rare)
—	—	—

Devour

LV 1~19	LV 20~22
—	—

Item (Drop)

Level	Rate: 255/256			
	178/256	51/256	15/256	12/256
1~19	Remedy	Remedy	Remedy	Remedy
20~22	Remedy	Remedy	Remedy	Remedy

Item (Mug)

Level	Rate: 32/256			
	178/256	51/256	15/256	12/256
1~19	Strength Love	Strength Love	Strength Love	Strength Love
20~22	Strength Love	Strength Love	Strength Love	Strength Love

---

Wendigo

HP	1026~16,000	AP	2	— —
EXP	30 (+5)		— —	

Elemental Defense

💧	1
❄	1
⚡	1
🌑	1
🌀	1
🌪	1
💧	1
✦	1

Status Defense

✝	70	⚡	100	👣	60
😷	80	✋	90	▨	100
🎈	70	✋	50	☀	80
☠	80	🛡	100	%	100
😵	80	🗡	100		
💀	60	👣	80		
☠	70	👣	70		
🔵	80	👣	100		

LV	HP	Str	Vit	Mag	Spr	Spd	Eva
1	1026	7	3	3	4	12	1
10	1375	20	7	6	5	15	1
20	2000	33	13	9	6	17	2
30	2875	46	19	12	7	20	2
40	4000	59	25	15	9	22	3
50	5375	71	31	17	10	25	3
60	7000	83	37	20	11	27	4
70	8875	94	43	22	12	30	4
80	11,000	105	49	25	14	32	4
90	13,375	115	55	27	15	35	5
100	16,000	124	61	29	16	37	5

Locations

Timber (Roshfall Forest), Galbadia Missle Base

A strong monster, but not good at using magic. Uses powerful physical attacks relying on its strength instead.

Spells / Draw

Level	Draw	
1~19	Berserk	
20~29	Berserk	Protect
30~100	Berserk	Protect

Card

Drop Card	Mod Card	Mod (Rare)
Wendigo	Wendigo	Jumbo Cactuar

Devour

LV 1~19	LV 20~29	LV 30~100
HP Recovery	HP Recovery	HP Recovery

Item (Drop)

Level	Rate: 255/256			
	178/256	51/256	15/256	12/256
1~19	Steel Orb	Steel Pipe	Steel Pipe	Steel Orb
20~29	Steel Orb	Steel Pipe	Strength Love	Steel Orb
30~100	Steel Orb	Strength Love	Black Hole	Black Hole

Item (Mug)

Level	Rate: 32/256			
	178/256	51/256	15/256	12/256
1~19	Steel Pipe	Steel Pipe	Steel Pipe	Steel Pipe
20~29	Steel Pipe	Steel Pipe	Steel Pipe	Strength Love
30~100	Strength Love	Steel Pipe	Steel Pipe	Steel Pipe

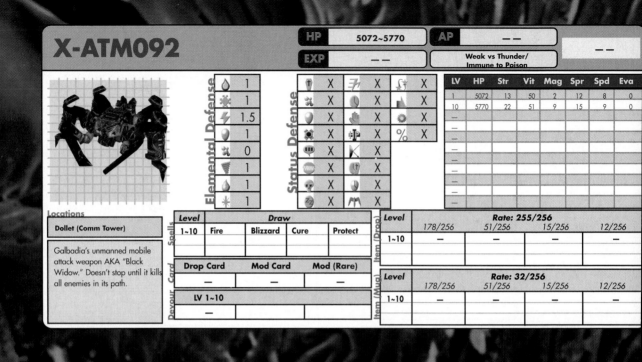

X-ATM092

HP	5072~5770	AP	– –
EXP	– –	Weak vs Thunder/Immune to Poison	

Elemental Defense

💧	1
❄	1
⚡	1.5
💧	1
🌀	0
🔻	1
💧	1
✳	1

Status Defense

All: X

LV	HP	Str	Vit	Mag	Spr	Spd	Eva
1	5072	13	50	2	12	8	0
10	5770	22	51	9	15	9	0
–							
–							
–							
–							
–							
–							

Locations

Dollet (Comm Tower)

Galbadia's unmanned mobile attack weapon AKA "Black Widow." Doesn't stop until it kills all enemies in its path.

Spells

Draw

Level	Fire	Blizzard	Cure	Protect
1~10	Fire	Blizzard	Cure	Protect

Card

Drop Card	Mod Card	Mod (Rare)
–	–	–

Devour

LV 1~10
–

Item (Drop)

Level	Rate: 255/256			
	178/256	51/256	15/256	12/256
1~10	–	–	–	–

Item (Mug)

Level	Rate: 32/256			
	178/256	51/256	15/256	12/256
1~10	–	–	–	–

BALAMB GARDEN

To G

To A

To H

WEAPON'S MONTHLY MAGAZINE
(April Issue)

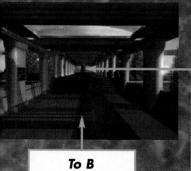

To B

SAVE POINT

SAVE POINT

BALAMB GARDEN (Cont.)

To A

To B

To C

Elevator

To D

To E

To G

To H

SAVE POINT

To C

RECEPTION

CURE DRAW POINT

WORLD MAP

ESUNA DRAW POINT

To E

OCCULT FAN I

3rd Floor Elevator

SAVE POINT

BLIZZARD DRAW POINT

B-16

To D

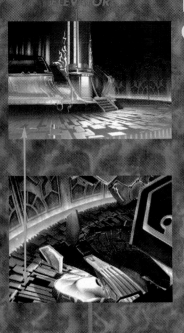

ELEVATOR

BALAMB GARDEN (Cont.)

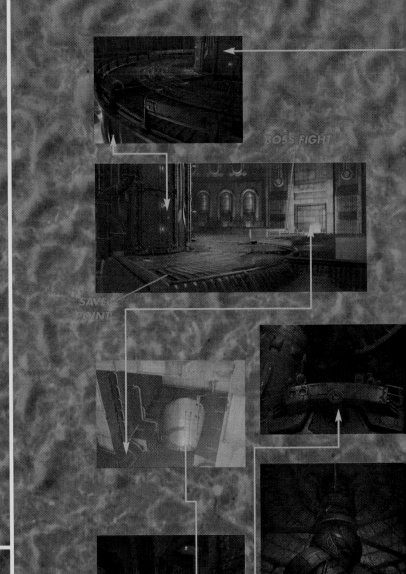

BOSS FIGHT

SAVE POINT

BIO DRAW POINT

Study Panel

2nd Floor Elevator

BALAMB GARDEN (Cont.)

FULL-LIFE DRAW POINT

BALAMB

TIMBER MANIAC
MAGAZINE

WORLD
MAP

ITEM SHOP

CAR RENTAL

JUNK SHOP

SAVE POINT

THUNDER
DRAW POINT

TIMBER MANIACS
MAGAZINE

SAVE POINT

INN

CURE DRAW
POINT

FIRE CAVERN

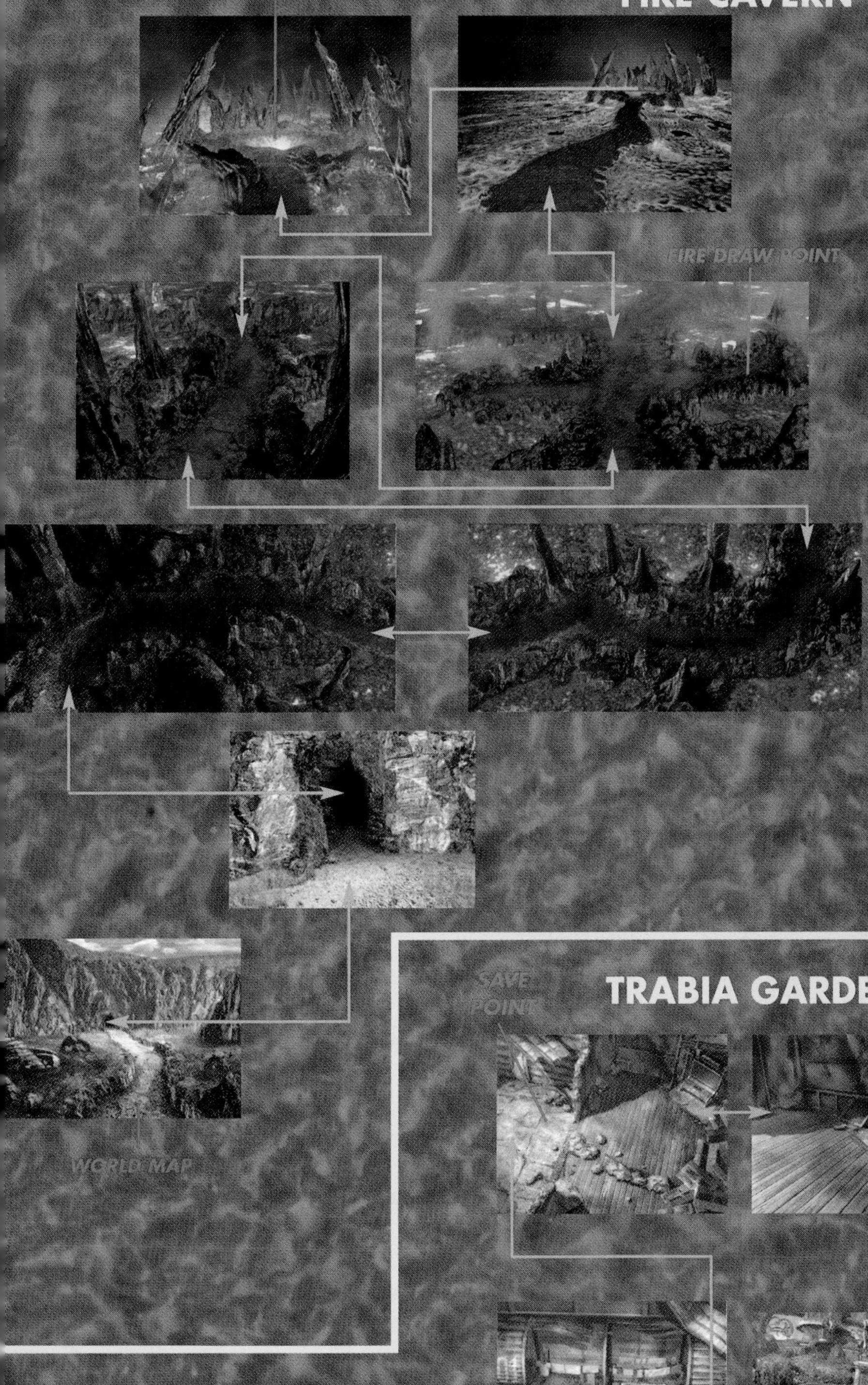
BOSS FIGHT
FIRE DRAW POINT
WORLD MAP

TRABIA GARDEN

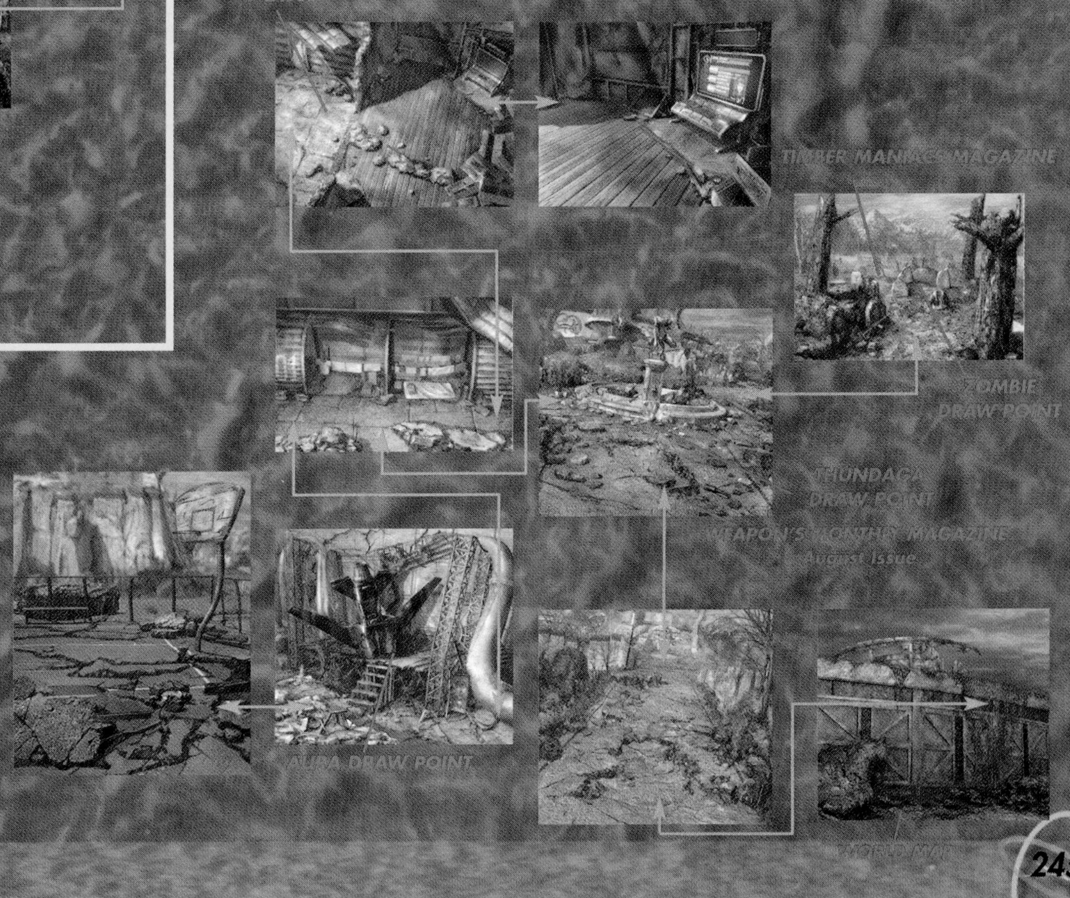
SAVE POINT
TIMBER MANIACS MAGAZINE
ZOMBIE DRAW POINT
THUNDAGA DRAW POINT
WEAPONS MONTHLY MAGAZINE
August Issue
AURA DRAW POINT
WORLD MAP

D-DISTRICT PRISON

B   A

SAVE POINT (6th Floor)

SAVE POINT (HIDDEN)

Floor #	Room A	Room B
1	Combat King 001	Save Point (Hidden)
2	Str Up	Pet Nametag
3	Pet House	N/A
4	N/A	Tent
5	Card Player	N/A
6	N/A	N/A
7	N/A	N/A
8	N/A	Man From Garden (Item Shop)
9	Berserk Draw Point	N/A
10	Card Player	Save Point
11	Thundaga Draw Point	Card Player
12	N/A	N/A

DOLLET

OCCULT FAN II MAGAZINE

SAVE POINT

TIMBER MANIACS MAGAZINE

ITEM/JUNK SHOP

BOSS FIGHT

To A

TIMBER MANIACS MAGAZINE

SAVE POINT

SAVE POINT

DRAW POINT

BLIND DRAW POINT

SAVE POINT

SAVE POINT

WORLD MAP

CAR RENTAL

To A

FISHERMAN'S HORIZON

TO BALAMB
GARDEN

FULL-LIFE DRAW POINT
(HIDDEN)

OCCULT FAN III

ULTIMA
DRAW POINT
(Hidden)

TOMB OF THE
UNKNOWN
KING

BOSS FIGHT

SAVE POINT
(HIDDEN)

FLOAT DRAW POINT

SAVE POINT
(HIDDEN)

LEVER

LEVER

CURA DRAW POINT (HIDDEN)

BOSS FIGHT

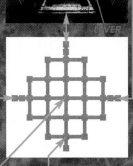

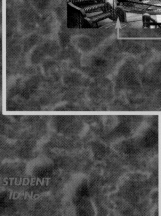

STUDENT
ID No.

SAVE
POINT

PROTECT DRAW POINT

TIMBER MANIACS MAGAZINE

SAVE
POINT

REGEN
DRAW
POINT

TIMBER MANIACS MAGAZINE

HASTE
DRAW
POINT

NEWS
MONITOR

BOSS FIGHT

INN/ITEM SHOP

JUNK SHOP   SHELL DRAW
POINT

GALBADIA GARDEN

SHELL DRAW POINT

To C

To A

HASTE DRAW POINT

BOSS FIGHT

SAVE POINT

KEY 3

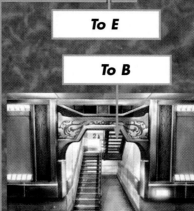

To E

To B

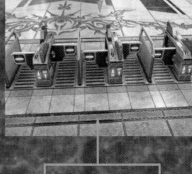

WORLD MAP

SAVE POINT

To E

AURA DRAW POINT (hidden)

PROTECT DRAW POINT

To C

To D

SAVE POINT

BOSS FIGHT

To A

To D

DOUBLE DRAW POINT (Hidden)

To B

KEY

Start

SAVE POINT

SAVE POINT

**To Sewers
"Entrance A"**

To A

To D

To F

WORLD
MAP

CAR
RENTAL

To E

DELING CITY (Cont.)

To B

To C

GATE
SWITCH

To Sewers
"Entrance B"

THUNDAR
DRAW
POINT

SAVE POINT

To A

TIMBER
MANIACS
MAGAZINE

To C

INN

To F

GALBADIA HOTEL

ITEM SHOP

To D

JUNK SHOP

To E

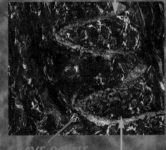

HATCH

**To Sewers
"Entance C"**

SAVE POINT

TRABIA CANYON

WORLD MAP

WATER DRAW POINT

GALBADIA FOREST

SAVE POINT

WORLD MAP

CURE DRAW POINT

WORLD MAP

Area Maps

255

DELLING CITY SEWERS

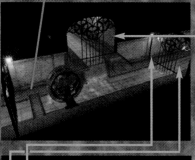

ESUNA DRAW
POINT

To Deling City
"Entrance B"

SAVE POINT

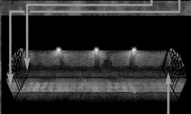

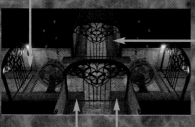

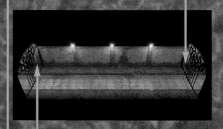

To Deling City
"Entrance C"

ZOMBIE DRAW POINT

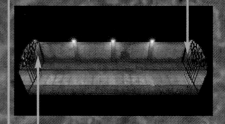

BIO DRAW
POINT

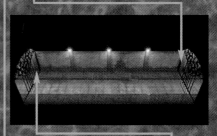

To Deling City
"Entrance A"

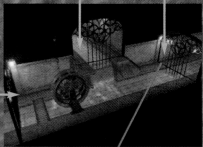

WEAPONS MONTHLY MAGAZINE
MAY ISSUE

TEARS' POINT

REFLECT DRAW POINT

SOLOMON RING

EDEA's HOUSE (Past)

LIFE DRAW POINT

WORLD MAP

EDEA's HOUSE (Present)

CURAGA DRAW POINT

TIMBER MANIACS MAGAZINE

WORLD MAP

257

TIMBER

SOUVENIR SHOP

PET SHOP

TIMBER MANIACS MAGAZINE

"GIRL NEXT DOOR" MAGAZINE

BLIZZAGA DRAW POINT

SCAN DRAW POINT

SAVE POINT

To A

To A

ITEM SHOP

CURE DRAW
POINT

OWL'S TEARS

500 GIL

SAVE
POINT

SAVE POINT

TIMBER
MANIACS

JUNK SHOP   INN

INFORMATION

WORLD MAP

TIMBER
MANIACS
MAGAZINE

259

ESTHAR

OCCULT FAN IV MAGAZINE

COMBAT
KING
005

BLIZZARD DRAW POINT

CONTACT
POINT # 2

SAVE
POINT

CONTACT POINT # 1

CURAGA
DRAW
POINT

Dr. Odine's
Laboratory

QUAKE DRAW
POINT

WORLD MAP

Rent-A-Car

BOSS FIGHT

ESTHAR
ENTRANCE

THUNDAGA
DRAW POINT

SAVE POINT

METEOR
DRAW POINT
(HIDDEN)

GREAT SALT LAKE

Start

Cont. Esthar

CONTACT POINT #3

ESTHAR ENTRANCE

OPS

SHOPS

From Great Salt Lake

TORNADO
DRAW POINT
(Hidden)

Dr. ODINE'S LABORATORY

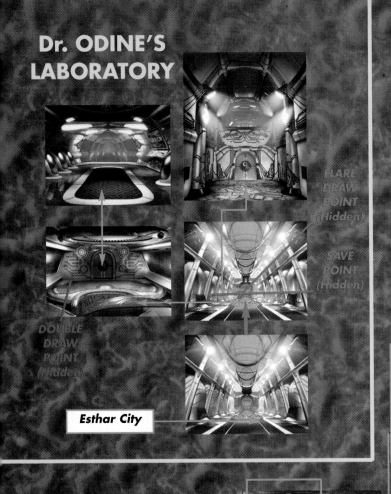

FLARE
DRAW
POINT
(Hidden)

SAVE
POINT
(Hidden)

DOUBLE
DRAW
POINT
(Hidden)

Esthar City

GALBADIAN MISSILE BASE

SAVE POINT

MISSILE CONTROL PANEL

FULL-LIFE DRAW POINT

SWITCH

SELF-DESTRUCT

BLIND DRAW POINT

BLIZZARD DRAW POINT

SAVE POINT

WORLD MAP

WINHILL

CURAGA DRAW POINT
(Hidden)

DRAIN
DRAW
POINT

WORLD
MAP

SAVE POINT

VASE PIECE

REFLECT
DRAW
POINT
(Hidden)

VASE PIECE

VASE PIECE

VASE PIECE

VASE PIECE

INN

ITEM
SHOP

WORLD
MAP

263

RAGNAROK

LIFE DRAW POINT

SAVE POINT

FULL LIFE DRAW POINT

CURA DRAW POINT

SAVE POINT

LUNAR GATE

WORLD MAP

WHITE SeeD SHIP

HOLY DRAW POINT

LUNATIC PANDORA LABORATORY

DEATH DRAW POINT

SAVE POINT

TIMBER MANIACS MAGAZINE

SAVE POINT (Hidden)

WEAPON'S MONTHLY MAGAZINE 1st Issue

MELT-
DOWN
DRAW
POINT

SAVE POINT

SPACE SUIT

SAVE POINT

START

METEOR
DRAW POINT

LUNATIC PANDORA

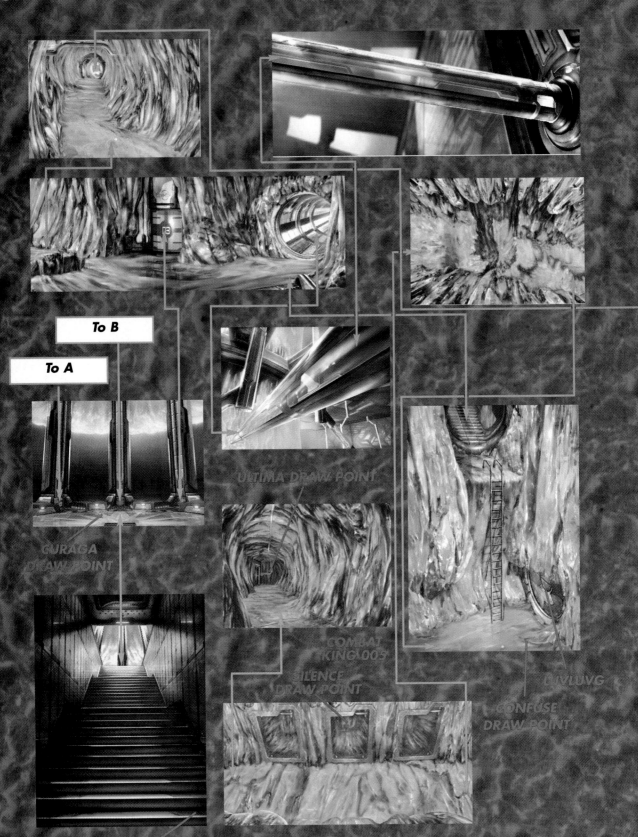

To B

To A

ULTIMA DRAW POINT

CURAGA
DRAW POINT

COMBAT
KING 005
SILENCE
DRAW POINT

L.V LUVG

CONFUSE
DRAW POINT

METEOR
DRAW POINT

SAVE POINT

BOSS FIGHT

To B

To A

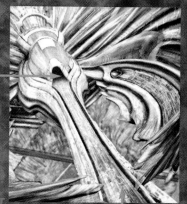

Spd-J
SCROLL

SAVE POINT

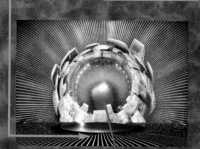

BOSS FIGHT

LUNATIC PANDORA (Past)

SAVE POINT

CURE
DRAW
POINT

OLD KEY

BOSS FIGHT

LOOSE LEVER

CONFUSE
DRAW POINT

DETONATOR
SWITCH

SLEEP DRAW POINT

Start

OLD KEY

SORCERESS MEMORIAL

STOP DRAW POINT

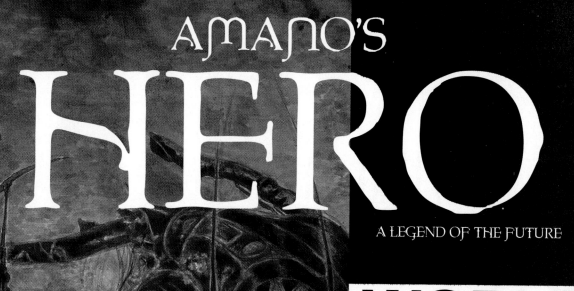

AMANO'S
HERO

A LEGEND OF THE FUTURE

WORLD
PREMIERE
EXHIBITION

OCTOBER 6 THRU
OCTOBER 31,

ANGEL ORENSANZ FOUNDATION
172 NORFOLK STREET, NEW YORK CITY

212-625-3367

www.amanosworld.com

SANDMAN

Featuring artwork from *THE SAND-MAN: The Dream Hunters*, the New SANDMAN Graphic Novel by Neil Gaiman and Yoshitaka Amano coming in October from Vertigo/DC

FINAL FANTASY

Concept Illustrator for the FINAL FANTASY® series Featuring FINAL FANTASY Anthology by SquareSoft.

Try Frosted Cheerios Today!

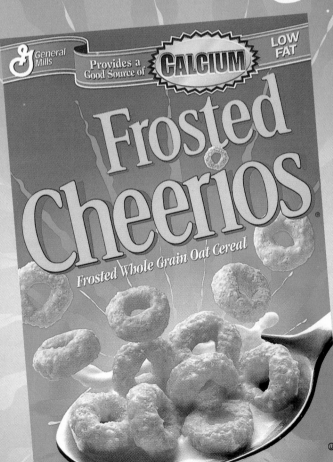

Nothing enhances your playing time like an awesome set of controls.

Lately, we've been busy with a little fantasy of our own. As in one surprising new release called the ECHO.
Cool features include a center-mounted instrument panel, a zippy engine and one amazing storage format.
Which goes to show a little creative thinking can push you to a whole new level.

Introducing the new ECHO.

CHANGING. EVERY DAY.